THE POETICS OF SLUMBERLAND

The publisher gratefully acknowledges the generous support of the Eric Papenfuse and Catherine Lawrence Endowment Fund in Film and Media Studies of the University of California Press Foundation.

The publisher also gratefully acknowledges the generous contribution to this book provided by Stanford University.

THE POETICS
OF SLUMBERLAND

Animated Spirits and the Animating Spirit

———

Scott Bukatman

UNIVERSITY OF CALIFORNIA PRESS

Berkeley   Los Angeles   London

A slightly different version of the first half of Chapter 1 appeared in
Animation: An Interdisciplinary Journal, edited by Suzanne Buchan;
portions of Chapter 4 appeared in somewhat different form in *Enfant
Terrible! Jerry Lewis in American Film,* edited by Murray Pomerance (NYU
Press, 2002), and *Beyond the Finite: The Sublime in Art and Science,* edited
by Roald Hoffmann and Iain Boyd Whyte (Oxford University Press, 2011);
Chapter 5 is a substantial revision of an essay that originally appeared in
Vincente Minnelli: The Art of Entertainment, edited by Joe McElhaney
(Wayne State University Press, 2009); and portions of Chapter 6 appeared
in an essay originally published in *The Contemporary Comic Book
Superhero,* edited by Angela Ndalianis (Routledge, 2009).

University of California Press, one of the most distinguished university
presses in the United States, enriches lives around the world by advancing
scholarship in the humanities, social sciences, and natural sciences. Its
activities are supported by the UC Press Foundation and by philanthropic
contributions from individuals and institutions. For more information,
visit www.ucpress.edu.

University of California Press
Berkeley and Los Angeles, California

University of California Press, Ltd.
London, England

Library of Congress Cataloging-in-Publication Data

Bukatman, Scott, 1957–.
 The poetics of Slumberland : animated spirits and the animating spirit /
Scott Bukatman.
  p. cm.
 Includes bibliographical references and index.
 ISBN 978-0-520-26571-4 (cloth : alk. paper)
 ISBN 978-0-520-26572-1 (pbk. : alk. paper)
  1. Fantastic, The, in art.   2. Fantasy in motion pictures.   3. Comic
books, strips, etc.—History and criticism.   4. Animated films—History
and criticism.   I. Title.
 NX650.F36B85   2011
 700'.415—dc23   2011033308

Manufactured in the United States of America

20 19 18 17 16 15 14 13 12
10 9 8 7 6 5 4 3 2 1

The paper used in this publication meets the minimum requirements
of ANSI/NISO Z39.48-1992 (R 1997) *(Permanence of Paper).*

For Beth

Someone to crowd you with love,
Someone to force you to care,
Someone to make you come through,
Who'll always be there,
As frightened as you
Of being alive

STEPHEN SONDHEIM

THERE was a time when meadow, grove, and stream,
  The earth, and every common sight,
    To me did seem
   Apparell'd in celestial light,
The glory and the freshness of a dream.

—WILLIAM WORDSWORTH

The struggle for subjectivity presents itself, therefore, as
the right to difference, variation and metamorphosis.

—GILLES DELEUZE

CONTENTS

Plates follow page 142

ILLUSTRATIONS

FIGURES

COLOR PLATES *(following page 142)*

APPRECIATIONS

This book was a long time coming, and many people have helped it along, either by reading various versions and iterations, or just by keeping me semi-sane and quasi-content.

I begin by thanking my research budget at Stanford University for buying me every comic book I could ever want, which made this book possible. Alex Nemerov's work has been an inspiration to me—I aspire to be a more cheerful version of the author of *Icons of Grief*—and I'm grateful for his very enthusiastic response to my book proposal. Lela Graybill helped make huge sections of this volume more coherent and smarter, and I'll always be in her debt. Greg Smith and Beth Kessler gave the manuscript heroic eleventh-hour reads that were so, so helpful, and Dana Polan's readings (of both early and late versions) went a long way toward helping me figure out just what the heck this book was about.

Mary Francis has been a supportive and very encouraging editor; her faith in this project (and its need for pictures!) was continually invigorating. Ulrich Merkl generously allowed me the use of his digitally restored *Rarebit Fiend* examples that he used in his own astonishing volume on McCay's great comic strip. And Sianne Ngai graciously allowed me to run with one of her central concepts (though I hope she'll forgive me for what I've done to it). Heather Warren-Crow provided early inspiration and dialogue (and told me my book title "was off the hook," which I appreciated). The librarians at Ohio State University's Billy Ireland Cartoon Library and Museum gave generously of their time during my visit in the summer of 2006 and allowed me to paw numerous examples of McCay's original art (the trip also yielded a *great* Dylan concert). Thierry Smolderen proved a valuable and friendly resource on more than one occasion, and Paul Slade and Joseph Timmons came to my rescue online and provided me with some badly needed comics scans. I appreciated Corey Creekmur's enthusiasm for the book, and his suggestions also helped make it a better one.

Students and colleagues have helped this along in ways large and small, and I thank the students in my Vincente Minnelli class, as well as my graduate student seminar, Animation and the Animated Film. The "Disobedient Machines" chapter took shape through my teaching oodles of freshmen in Stanford's Introduction to the Humanities program, and my co-conspirator, Henry Lowood has broadened my thinking and helped me work through some of the issues—teaching with him stands as one of the signal pleasures of my life at Stanford. This book is filled with figures from art history and the history of art, and I thank my colleagues in the Department of Art and Art History for sharing their methods (and their madness). I've also been fortunate to hire two film studies faculty at Stanford, Jean Ma and Pavle Levi, both of whom have become good friends (I recommend this as a hiring strategy) and who provide an all-important feeling of community. Emerging superstar Fred Turner has been a great booster, continually making me feel as though I have something to say that might actually be worth saying.

I was honored to be the keynote speaker for Yale University's very first graduate student film studies symposium, "The Politics of Superhero Films," and I thank the organizers, Jeremi Szaniawski and Victor Fan, and some *very* good-natured participants who didn't mind hearing about Why I Hate Superhero Films. Bob Rehak, Chris Cagle, and the other participants in the Philadelphia Cinema and Media Seminar provided some very welcome dialogue. Ditto the participants at Berkeley's PARA*SITE New Media Symposium, where I shared keynote honors with Anne Friedberg.

Three colleagues in the world of comics scholarship should be singled out for their work on Winsor McCay. John Canemaker's biography is an impeccably written, extremely informative work that has been indispensible; Ulrich Merkl's exhaustively cross-referenced cataloging of *Dream of the Rarebit Fiend* in his self-published volume was an extraordinary resource; and Peter Maresca's re-presentation of *Little Nemo in Slumberland* at its original printed size in two gargantuan volumes helped redefine my engagement of this already canonical strip. Without their labors my own would have been far more strenuous.

Special thanks must go out to Vivian Sobchack and Dana Polan, who have been there and been there for me, as intellectuals, professionals, and friends. Ditto Tom Gunning. And Anne Friedberg was a wonderful part of my life on the West Coast. I miss her, and the dinners out with Anne and her wonderful partner, Howard Rodman, very much. And my father passed away, but happily not before I realized just how much of his taste in music and movies I'd inherited from him. Joe McElhaney and Steve Barnes are still with us, thank goodness, and as ever, I thank them for everything they've taught me and given me. Alan Labb has been my sanity for many years (which is odd, because he's kind of nuts), from Albuquerque days until now. My brother Kevin has been with me through many, many downs and (now) ups, and I thank him for his heart, his humor, and his helpfulness. Pavle and Jelena Levi, with Luka and Eva, have enhanced my life in all ways.

I think this is a very happy book, and its good spirits owe much to the presence of my wife, the brilliant and beautiful Beth Kessler. And with Beth came her most remarkable and welcoming family, so to Bob and Sue, and Carolyn and Al, and Bob (the younger), and Bill, thank you for being *my* family. And with Beth also came her awesome cat, Pablo, who did me the favor of getting along with my cats, archy and Cleo; they're family, too. I am happy to have them all, but something that I try to remember every day is just how lucky I am that Beth has chosen to share her life with me. Sometimes she even feels the same.

INTRODUCTION

The Lively, the Playful, and the Animated

The phenomenology of perception itself must stand aside for the phenomenology of the creative imagination.

—GASTON BACHELARD, *THE POETICS OF REVERIE*

Winsor McCay's comic strip *Little Nemo in Slumberland* ran from 1905 to 1914 as a full-page fantasia of brilliant colors and enchanting metamorphoses.[1] The strip's protagonist, the boy Nemo, leaves the mundane world of reality to sojourn in a land of wonderful dreams, but McCay's innovative spatiotemporal manipulations also remake the world of the reader, who makes an analogous voyage—albeit a motionless one: drawn into the world of the comics page, with its wondrous transformations and morphing spaces (see, e.g., Plate 1). For the purposes of this book Slumberland is more than just a marvelous world for Nemo and its other citizens; it is an aesthetic space primarily defined through the artist's innovations, an animated space that opens out to embrace the imaginative sensibility of a reader who is never farther than an arm's length from this other realm, a space of play and plasmatic possibility in which the stable site of reading or viewing yields to an onslaught of imaginative fantasy; and it is an impermanent space. A comic like *Little Nemo* served as a brief interlude from the world presented in the *World* (or the *Tribune,* or the *Times*). And Slumberland itself was a land of dreams, a place from which Nemo would waken at the end of each episode, at the bottom of each page. An important aspect of the poetics of Slumberland, then, is that it's temporary. You wake up. Slumberland, as a licensed site of the plasmatic and the animated, can never replace the nonplasmatic world—but it works well as a fleeting refuge from the stolidity of the real.

Gaston Bachelard's *The Poetics of Space* is a most effective guidebook to the Slumberland that I have just described. Bachelard reminds us that for a child, perceptions remain new, and experience still has a freshness that makes each day (and each dream) a kind of adventure. "Through this permanent childhood," he writes, "we maintain the poetry of the past," and through the figure of its child-dreamer and through the

1

audacity of its aesthetics, *Little Nemo* returns us to the newness of the world.[2] The spatiotemporal *illogics*—Bachelard's word—of the objects to be explored create spaces for the projected fantasy of the viewer or the reader, the artist or the dreamer.

Readers might be surprised at the dearth of psychoanalytic theory brought to bear upon this "dream work," but I would argue that *Little Nemo in Slumberland* is a reverie, a daydream, staged as a dream. Nemo's dreams are our daydreams, and Bachelard tells us that psychoanalysis is less suitable to the analysis of daydreams than the nocturnal variety—its symbologies are too fixed, its modalities too determined. Bachelard prefers to emphasize what he calls a "phenomenology of the daydream" that will "untangle the complex of memory and imagination."[3] He will further propose that "the phenomenology of perception itself must stand aside for the phenomenology of the creative imagination."[4] The daydream commingles reverie and memory to produce the *illogics* that allow us to escape the rigors of structured time and established habits of mind. This seems an appropriate model to bring to Slumberland, with its brief respite from the logical strictures of the waking life. It's not that Freud is unwelcome here; it's more that I think I know the story he would tell and choose to tell a different one.[5]

Dreams, the world of children, and artistic creation are privileged sites of playful disobediences, misbehaviors, and even malfunctions (tellingly, they are frequently grouped together).[6] Here the movement of bodies and animation of images generates what Gilles Deleuze once referred to as the *movement of world*: a shift away from the paralysis of reality, toward an oneiric realm of motion and possibility.[7] Comics and animated cartoons are filled with tales of playful disobedience in otherworldly realms and, at the same time, themselves constitute fields of playful disobedience. They offer up little utopias of disorder, provisional sites of temporary resistance.

The Poetics of Slumberland will explore works that follow the example of *Little Nemo in Slumberland,* concentrating primarily on the worlds made possible in comics and cartoons but also in film musicals, comedies, and even melodramas, genres in which the physics and conditions of everyday life are transposed into a new register (and sometimes simply revoked).[8] Comics and cartoons, though, are the archetypes—media that, nearly from their inception, set about overturning established orders and hierarchies, frequently pausing to meditate on their own possibilities. These emergent media of the late nineteenth century and early twentieth don't emerge suddenly or from whole cloth—there are plenty of antecedents for both (for comics, in the serial paintings of William Hogarth or the picture stories of Rodolphe Töpffer; for cartoons, in such optical toys as the thaumatrope or phenakistoscope—as well as comics). But they take off as mass media forms in the early twentieth century or the very last years of the nineteenth: Richard Outcault's *Hogan's Alley* first appears in a newspaper in 1895, the same year as the first public projection of motion pictures.

Comic strips and cartoons were closely related.[9] Both were hand-drawn and featured continuing characters. Some early cartoon features were imports from the comics page.[10] They occupied similarly marginal positions in relation to the culture at large, where they served as minor *divertissements*, but they were also marginal in relation to other media: the comics page was part of the larger agglomeration of the newspaper; cartoons were short subjects that would precede a feature film. Slapstick humor was a mainstay of both media, although comics developed as a storytelling form far more quickly than cartoons (in this important regard the longer history of comics as a storytelling medium, well-established in the nineteenth century, plays a part). They were frequently, though by no means always, oriented toward (or associated with) children; in any case they were not to be taken seriously. And they tapped into an animist fascination with anthropomorphic animals and objects, as well as with plasmatic exaggerations and distortions of the body.

A common cartoon plot involves the toys in a toyshop coming to life—or books in a bookshop, or china figurines . . . you get the idea. And this always happens at night—usually at midnight. This makes sense, if we need it to make sense: the store is closed, so the vivified toys won't frighten the customers—but it's also appropriate because night is the time of dreaming, and this is a child's dream of a toyshop. Night is fundamental to the poetics of Slumberland—it's the time when Nemo journeys there from the safety of his bed. Night is also the time for reading in bed, perhaps with a flashlight or book light making a small pool of illumination that encompasses the book and the reader and nothing more. Reading is never more private, or more intimate, than at night. And for many, night is the time of creation. In Steven Millhauser's fictionalized story of Winsor McCay, night is when the artist makes the thousands of drawings for his cartoons (*his* cartoons—they are made for his pleasure).[11] It's when he pours his dreams onto paper. All kinds of things are possible at night—nights are filled with animistic energy, and plasmatic powers are at their height.

REGULATION AND RESISTANCE

Comics and cartoons are vital, energetic media, and while neither is American by birth, America quickly made them its own. They act out a tension between regulation and resistance that Jackson Lears has argued was a fundament of fin de siècle American culture.

America has always been dedicated to energy and vitality—this was, after all, the *new* world, one that operated in contradistinction to European restrictiveness, feyness, or decadence. America was marked, at least ostensibly, by a fluidity of social hierarchies—not for America were the rigid caste systems of older aristocratic or monarchical cultures. Wealth was the ticket to success, and, in theory anyway, anyone could accumulate wealth. A lowly immigrant could found an empire (in Hollywood, say), and one could become a self-made man. These are clichés of

Americanness, but these clichés were also the operating myths of the American experience.

Americans were pulled in two directions in the early part of the twentieth century. The workplace was an increasingly regulated environment, replete with mechanized assembly lines, scientific management, punch-clocks, and maxims of efficiency. But workers had more leisure time than ever before—the workweek was shorter, wages were higher, and a wealth of new entertainments like amusement parks celebrated and fostered these new freedoms. "Two visions grew in tandem: the self set free from all bonds, Promethean, triumphant, even airborne; and the self enchained in prisons that were sometimes more humane, but also more capacious and enduring than any before imagined. For every boundless self there was an iron cage in waiting."[12] Of course, mass entertainments were regulated in their own ways, and Lears finds the new forms of entertainment—the vaudeville shows, the films— a bit domesticating, revealing in their own ways, the "limits on liberation."[13]

Around this time there arise two mass media that speak strongly to this dialectic: the newspaper comic and the animated film. Both media exemplify, and in fact perform, the tension between Lears's "liberation and limitation"—in fact, they play out an even stronger dialectic of *regulation* and *resistance to regulation*. As we will see, the comic strip turns the logic of the chronophotograph—a tool of scientific management—on its head, while cartoons, fully a product of the factory system's division of labor, continually present characters who refuse to perform their assigned tasks, who aspire to more than the automatism of their programmed actions. Both media present an array of scamps and rapscallions who are either champing at the bit of authority or blissfully unaware of its expectations. These are unruly media at their core.

In the early twentieth century the United States was not only an energetic nation; it was a nation that *worshipped* energy, as cults of vitalism revealed themselves in philosophy and psychology, as well as in the popular arts. Lears, whose major works center on such atavistic or antimodern pockets within modern culture, points to popular culture's obsession with releasing energy from such new sources as the body or the psyche.[14] "Americans yearned to reconnect with some pulsating primal vitality," he writes. "Never before had life-worship acquired such a wide following. Never before had so many people thought that reality was throbbing with vitality, pulsating with excitement, and always just out of reach."[15]

Small wonder, given this vitalist context, that a new medium, the cinema, was such a hit. As much as it was a medium of movement, it was also a medium of *life*, and, to a great degree, movement and life were manifestations of the same force. If in France the medium was the *cinématographe* (the movement-writer), in America it was the Biograph or, more tellingly, the *Vitascope*.

Whatever its name, the new medium was fundamentally bound up with vitalism, staging and restaging what William Nestrick has called a "bringing to life."[16]

The earliest film projections would begin with a projected still image that would abruptly begin to move, and (unless you were Maxim Gorky) to live. Noël Burch has written of the "Frankensteinian" dream that underlay the medium, and Michelle Bloom has written of a "Pygmalionesque imagination" that found its fruition in film.[17] The medium itself speaks to that fascination, or at least it did in its earliest days, and when that novelty had passed, narratives of beings or objects coming to life carried that fascination forward. And, from the very beginnings of cinema, there was the animated film.

Early trick films presented objects moving of their own volition, as in the Edison company's McCay-inspired *Dream of the Rarebit Fiend* (1906), or depicted paintings and statues coming to life. Edison produced an adaptation of *Frankenstein* in 1905, and Méliès had already filmed a version of the Pygmalion myth in 1898 (Gaby Wood has remarked that if there was any justice, *Pygmalion* would have been the first narrative film).[18] In 1908 Emile Cohl produced his *Fantasmagorie*, animating drawings in a stream of metamorphoses, and in 1911 Winsor McCay produced a two-minute animation of his *Little Nemo* characters, introduced by a narrative that showed the audience the production of the thousands of images required to pull off the feat.

Just as the trick films marveled at their own capacity to bring images to life, so did these early cartoons meditate on their own magical properties. In a film like *An Artist's Dream* (1900) the "living images" step through the frame and into the room where their creator sleeps, while in the early McCay films, the camera brings us *into* the animated world—with *Little Nemo* (1911) through a dolly into close-up, with *Gertie the Dinosaur* (1914) via a cut. But in all cases a boundary is violated; a passage between worlds takes place. In McCay's stage act he would command Gertie from his position before the screen, and he coaxes her out of her cave to greet her audience—here the implication is that she moves *out,* into the space of the theater, but the act concluded with a now-animated McCay riding off on Gertie's back. As with Nemo's journey to Slumberland, the borders between worlds are porous— "bringing to life" also brings a movement between worlds—as profoundly metamorphic a phenomenon as any exercise in physical reshaping.

Animated drawings provided something that the stop-motion objects and trick effects did not: *character.* Not only did an image move, but the animated figures seemed to possess personalities—they were not simply *lively* but *living.* My students still let out a sympathetic moan when McCay scolds Gertie, making her cry (Figure 1). And the first cartoons to provide what would come to be called "character animation" were American. It would be difficult to empathize with the stick figures or animated microbes that populated the cartoons of Emile Cohl, but Nemo, Gertie, Felix, and their like were easy to love (when they got voices, with the advent of synchronized sound, it became even easier).

A common trope of early cartoons was the interplay of animator and animated.

FIGURE 1. Winsor McCay makes Gertie cry. *Gertie the Dinosaur,* 1914.

The Out of the Inkwell cartoons, for example, all opened with Max Fleischer creating the character of Ko-Ko the Clown—either drawing him or simply pouring him out of the titular inkwell. And one of the hallmarks of that early byplay was a certain adversarial relationship. Ko-Ko might refuse to perform as directed, or he might show some reluctance to return to the inkwell at cartoon's end. As I have mentioned, these characters do not simply have life; they have a life of their own, and this rebelliousness can be read as a further sign of vitality. These characters are marked by a youthful, exuberant energy that cannot—and should not—be easily contained. They are not mere automata, products of an enervating assembly line—despite the paradoxical fact that this is *precisely* what they are.[19] They are, then, disobedient machines.

The tension between creator and creation is not solely the haven of the animated film, for their dialectical relation plays out both narratively and performatively in live-action films. We will see this when we turn to an examination of the relation between Henry Higgins and Eliza Doolittle in *My Fair Lady* and of Vincent van Gogh's struggle to produce meaningful images in Vincente Minnelli's *Lust for Life*.

Lust for Life turns Van Gogh into an American action painter—a function of the casting of Kirk Douglas, on the one hand, and the timing of the film's appearance, on the other. Van Gogh's vitalism pervades the film, which was released in the post-war period, when America was "stealing" modern art from a presumably exhausted Europe (America was itself something of a disobedient machine).[20] The American creators that enter this book boldly go toward the world, engaging with it and re-making it in their terms. When, in the middle of the film, Vincent opens the shutters and sees the wonders of Arles, he turns outward toward the world; he doesn't shutter himself in as would a Seurat. But the creators also find, perhaps paradoxically, that their acts of making can exceed their own authorial control. Hence, the rebellious figures that escape the control of the animator's hand, or, in the case of Van Gogh, the paintings that have survived their maker.[21]

LIVELY IMAGES, PLAYFUL IMAGES

The comics section in the American newspaper was a haven of liveliness and play-fulness, and examining the relation between comics and newspapers can help demonstrate the nature and structure of its gentle improprieties. Gaston Bachelard has written that "the demands of our *reality function* require that we adapt to reality, that we constitute ourselves as a reality and that we manufacture works which are realities." But he also points to a "normal, useful *irreality function* which keeps the human psyche on the fringe of all the brutality of a hostile and foreign non-self."[22] This is a useful dialectic to keep in mind when thinking about the place of comics in the newspaper. Newspapers, after all, were intended to be a conduit for information, a "fourth estate" that would inform readers, map the connections of an increasingly complex world, and, ideally, build better citizens. It was an operation firmly aligned with Bachelard's "reality function," as demonstrated in its appearance: the orderly columns of text, the allocation of the world into hierarchical sections (International, National, Local).

But by the late nineteenth century the newspaper had become something else, too, something more or less than the above would suggest, depending on whom you asked. In urban America, burgeoning immigrant populations with diverse languages and levels of literacy had become an increasingly attractive demographic, and circulation wars led to both a greater emphasis on nonnews features and a turn toward more sensationalist news coverage.[23] The irreality function pervaded the newspaper, especially on Sunday. Advertisements and color supplements provided visual pleasure, or at least a respite from the blocks of text that covered the rest of the page. Stories were illustrated with drawings or photographs to invite the eye. Images "distracted" more than informed.[24] They are, in a way, the reveries of the newspaper. All work and no play makes for a dull paper, and newspapers contained a range of entertainments that spoke to Bachelard's irreality function—with comics perhaps the most unreal and ludic of all.[25]

What did the comics bring to the newspaper? A handsome compilation of Sunday supplement pages from the *New York World,* edited by Nicholson Baker and Margaret Brentano, implicitly argues against the uniqueness of the comics, treating them as one more colorful feature amidst a bevy of them.[26] The comics were far from the only feature to utilize the new color rotary presses, and nearly every page of the supplements splashed bold, florid titles across the page, with sumptuous illustrations that provided a welcome respite from the tightly packed type of the news sections. There was also a sense of continual plenitude and surprise—anything might happen with the turn of a page: fact, fiction, fantasy, fashion, fun.[27] Seen in this light, the newspaper, especially on Sunday, was a repository of realities and irrealities that commingled in genuine, albeit largely regulated, ways.

But the comics *do* stand apart, owing in part to their stability and in part to their prankishness. The comics featured a returning cast of characters: at various times you could expect Maggie and Jiggs, Nemo, Hans and Fritz, Pat Ryan and the Dragon Lady, Prince Valiant, Little Orphan Annie, Mark Trail, and their various retinues. Each strip would be formatted similarly from week to week: a full page for Valiant, a smaller space for *Bringing Up Father.* Some featured filler strips atop or below the main strip, and these also appeared with reassuring stability. In the "anything goes" world of the color supplements, comics provided continuity. There might be some tonal variation—a Sunday Annie might feature a standalone gag or an episode from the larger ongoing serial featured during the week—but Annie would be there, and Sandy ("Arf!"), and perhaps even "Daddy" Warbucks. Recurring characters began to appear as early as 1892, embarking on their endless cycle of gags and misadventures (and, later in the evolution of the comics, adventures and melodramas). Characters in early comics seemed to exist either to create mischief or to have mischief visited upon them.

One of the earliest comics in the newspaper was also among the most exemplary: Richard Outcault's *Hogan's Alley* was a glorious cartoon feature that began in the *New York World* and, after migrating to the *New York Journal,* appeared as *McFadden's Row of Flats.*[28] *Hogan's Alley* gave the world perhaps its first comics "star," the Yellow Kid, a.k.a. Mickey Dugan. *Hogan's Alley* was a wild comics page, a visual cacophony that each week would track some event in the lives of the Alley's young denizens. It began as a half-page offering, a single panel work featuring some dozen children from the poorer part of town (before the Hogan's Alley name, the neighborhood depicted often went by the name of Shantytown [Plate 2]). Each of the kids would be involved in some activity, with neighbors looking on in amusement or horror. In the first color episode, "At the Circus in Hogan's Alley," the kids are, variously, juggling, miming, jumping through hoops, beating drums, or performing feats of acrobatic derring-do, more or less successfully. Later episodes have them holding an ersatz cup race on Reilly's pond, golfing, having a dog show, and the like, generally imitating their "betters" with charm and energy, if not finesse. Signs posted about the scene provide additional opportunities for humor, accentuated by dialect and creative misspellings ("De Event Will Be De Grate HOBOKEN HANDIKAP"). It's all a lot of attractively rendered fun.

It becomes something more in late May 1896, when the *Hogan's Alley* gang goes to Coney Island (Plate 3). Now the feature occupies the full page, sharing duties with some prose pieces, to be sure, but now the image spills upward (if you'll forgive the oxymoron): balloons soar above the action, carving out a space between the columns of prose, and under the type are silhouettes, in pale blue, of falling children and climbing monkeys. *Hogan's Alley* is no longer contained and will no longer be quite as genteel. Now the strip will contain multitudes—dozens of figures, each with its own character, jostle to attract the reader's eye. It resembles nothing so much as an entire vaudeville program deployed all at once upon the stage: there are animal acts, aerialists, dialect humor, and parodies of current events competing for attention.

The raucous goings-on around the Fourth of July are sensational and, in any other context, rather terrifying: roman candles and firecrackers detonate with reckless abandon, some tied to puppy dog's tails (Plate 4). A couple of the kids sport some serious looking bandages, and three tiers of onlookers are crammed onto the fire escape—in fact, they're not onlookers but victims: it seems that one flat at the rear of an upper floor has caught fire. A ladder provides little hope of escape, as bodies are piling up at the bottom. A woman flees with her featherbed, a small child swaddled within. One woman is caught in mid-descent by a roman candle striking her rear end. Way atop the action, on a high roof, a small goat—a recurring figure—can be glimpsed: "Just tell em that you saw me," he says, enigmatically. The whole thing is nuts, and I mean that in a good way.

Unlike the other features in the newspaper, in *Hogan's Alley* synchrony is privileged over diachrony—it lacks even the sequentiality of the comics that followed in its wake. The single image does not demand any particular "order" to its apprehension; the reader is free to explore the panel.[29] Just as Coney Island itself had multiple points of entry, so, too, does this comics page. To be sure, there *is* a central figure—the bald-headed kid with the big ears in the yellow nightshirt, whose "dialogue" was often emblazoned across his shirt front (A typical example: "Ain't I de main guy in dis parade? Well I guess dats right"). But the Yellow Kid seems more of an impresario or master of ceremonies than a "main" character: Carlton Waugh, in one of the earliest published appreciations of newspaper comics (c. 1947), wrote that the Kid "was always looking at the reader, interpreting events for him, becoming the reader's man."[30] I don't see much interpretation, but I do see mediation (and this, plus the iconographic power of this gap-toothed, broadly grinning denizen of *Hogan's Alley* [and, later, *McFadden's Row of Flats*], makes the Kid's star power very understandable). The Kid is at the center, but he is not the central figure. There *is* no center, no site where everything comes together. Annie Ronan has written that

"*Hogan's Alley*, in refusing to coalesce into an organic whole, and in neglecting to have one authoritative voice which would offer one definitive reading of the scene, embodied the anarchic spirit of its characters within its form and structure. It, thus, offered its readers an anti-authoritarian thrill."[31]

With these strips from the middle of 1896, *Hogan's Alley* comes into its own and into comics history. The assault on the propriety of the newspaper could hardly be clearer: the columnar organization of space is absent and at times is actively attacked (a page from August of 1896 features a goat butting a boy clear into the next page); the language of the newspaper is supplanted by a rich dialect; typesetting is replaced by hand-lettering; monochrome is replaced with color; and actions that might be reported more straightforwardly in the news sections (mobilization), the sports pages (cup races), or the society column (the Easter Parade) are turned upside down and re-presented in parodic form. It should almost go without saying, then, that *Hogan's Alley* belongs squarely to the tradition (or antitradition) of the carnivalesque. All the elements are there—the temporary overturning of social hierarchies, the emphasis on the corporeal over the spiritual, the generous laughter, the resistance to authority. Small wonder that the activities in *Hogan's Alley* so often referenced other holdovers of the carnivalesque: amusement parks, circuses, and dime museums.

Of episodes like the Coney Island excursion, Thierry Smolderen writes that "Outcault was transforming the printed page into a modern playground,"[32] and perhaps it is appropriate to consider the comic in relation to play, as Johan Huizinga has defined the word. Huizinga's *Homo Ludens* isolates play as a driving force of human culture, with implications for law, philosophy, the arts, myth, religion, and the rest. His task is to rescue the concept of play from analyses that see it as a training for "real" world encounters. Such analyses "all start from the assumption that play must serve something which is not play, that it must have some kind of biological purpose."[33] The emphasis on play's positive functionalism was a reaction to Puritan attitudes toward play that saw it as useless, frivolous, perhaps even harmful, but the functionalist response turned play into something akin to work—and play is work's "great complement and frequent competitor."[34] For Huizinga "the fun of playing resists all analysis, all logical interpretation," and he proposes that we respect the unseriousness of play even as we recognize that "culture arises in the form of play."[35] It's easy to spot play in *Hogan's Alley:* unproductive recreative activities taking place on a Sunday. This is chaotic, to be sure, but for the most part orderly, as well, and modeled on other orderly activities. It is alarmingly, delightfully, free.

In a famous passage Huizinga outlines the "formal characteristics of play": "We might call it a free activity standing quite consciously outside 'ordinary' life as being 'not serious,' but at the same time absorbing the player intensely and utterly. It is an activity connected with no material interest, and no profit can be gained by it. It proceeds within its own proper boundaries of time and space according to fixed rules and in an orderly manner. It promotes the formation of social groupings which tend to surround themselves with secrecy and to stress their difference from the common world by disguises or other means."[36] This is a very appealing list, and it suggests some ways in which other activities might be constituted as "play." Huizinga does not consider the role of play in the engagement with texts; his chapter on art concentrates on artistic competitions as a type of play but not artistic engagement. He does consider *performance* a form of play: "The arena, the card-table, the magic circle, the temple, the stage, the screen, the tennis court, the court of justice, etc., are all in form and function play-grounds, i.e. forbidden spots, isolated, hedged round, hallowed, within which special rules obtain. All are temporary worlds within the ordinary world, dedicated to the performance of an act apart."[37] But play can serve as an equally valuable concept in thinking about the operations—or performances—of reading and viewing. Readers and spectators are often said to "suspend their disbelief" in order to invest themselves in a text—what is this if not a form of performative play?

John Morgenstern is one scholar who, in relation to children's literature, does connect reading and play. In an interview he has argued, "The children's novel exists to provide literate children—and adults—a way to return to the phantasmagoric play that has been lost." He and play theorist Brian Sutton-Smith use the term *phantasmagoric* "because it connects play to dreaming and daydreaming."[38] Reading encourages reverie, and only children are "allowed" this kind of play. I would extend this to reading more broadly, while suggesting that comics and cartoons perhaps seem to address themselves to children, the better to allow adults to sneakily partake of such "forbidden" pleasures.

Huizinga further notes that play is "a stepping out of 'real' life into a temporary sphere of activity with a disposition all its own," and he refers to play "as an intermezzo, an *interlude* in our daily lives"—a perfect description of the comic strip and its place in the (daily) newspaper.[39] Reading comics is easily understood as a form of play. And sometimes the comic strip can itself depict an interlude, an intermezzo from the normative behaviors of daily life, and this is what occurs in McCay's *Dream of the Rarebit Fiend*. Rarebit is eaten; sleep or reverie ensues; transformations occur; all returns to normal upon waking.

Now, again, consider *Hogan's Alley* and other comic strips, other "play-grounds." It is found in the newspaper, that catalog of Things You Need to Know; it is separated from the news sections spatially (it has its own section or page) and formally (it consists of a bounded series of drawn pictures in more or less exaggerated styles with lettering that is strikingly different from that used in the news stories). It proceeds according to its own internal logic (Mary Worth *will* fix people's problems, Lucy *will* pull the football away, Ignatz *will* throw a brick—and by the same token, Ignatz will *not* fix people's problems, Lucy will *not* throw a brick, and Mary Worth would *never* pull the football away)—these characters each exist in their own universe.[40] Reading the comics does not produce value; it is done for amusement.[41] At the same time, the comics are very absorbing: circulation wars were built around procuring the most popular comics (beginning with *Hogan's Alley* itself), and readers often wrote fan letters to creators (as well as to the characters themselves). From the 1920s to the 1950s (at least), continuity strips such as *Terry and the Pirates, Little Orphan Annie,* or *Thimble Theater* unfurled months-long sagas that held readers, briefly but definitely, in their collective grip. Perhaps only the secrecy aspect is missing from this example, but I will return to this aspect much later in the book, in relation to superheroes. (The place of secrecy in play is also debatable: Roger Caillois modifies Huizinga's definition by noting that it is integral only to a particular *type* of play, which he labels *mimicry*.)[42]

Smolderen has written of what he calls "swarming" in early comics like *Hogan's Alley,* as well as the contemporaneous comic strips and children's books featuring *The Brownies* by Palmer Cox. Swarming is a phenomenon with forebears in artists ranging from Bosch and Brueghel to George Cruikshank and William Hogarth, and which he traces as far back as the illustrated Bibles of the Middle Ages.[43] Busy images such as Hogarth's led the eye on a kind of chase and appealed to our predatory instincts (which gives a somewhat more sinister cast to "Where's Waldo?"). Smolderen also hypothesizes that the marginalia in illuminated Bibles and the populous illustrations for the Brownies books provided relief from the didacticism of the text and from the remorseless march down the page of text itself: they provided a play-space for the eye and mind. In the examples of *The Brownies* and *Hogan's Alley* the swarm provides an appealing combination of regularity (dozens of children) and variety (no two exactly alike). Again, he evokes a kind of controlled chaos that encourages a free play of exploration: these images do not simply depict play; they encourage play—they are literally *playful images.* The printed page has indeed become a playground, for the reader as much as for the denizens of *Hogan's Alley.*

Brian Sutton-Smith has explored the range of rhetorics that draw on variant ideas of play and playfulness. The last of these he calls the "rhetoric of frivolity," which speaks loudly to the phenomena at the center of this book: "play is not about the building of various kinds of personal and social order but is instead a series of interruptions, inversions, and inconsistencies that effectively deflate the orderliness, hierarchy, and pretence of 'official' social structures. The player, frequently a jester or trickster, shows that there are other meanings to life from those that are publicly recognized."[44] It's easy to find jesters and tricksters on the comics page, but I would further argue that comics (and cartoons) themselves *are* the trickster. They do not simply present images of disorderly play; rather, when activated by a reader, they constitute a form of disorderly play, frivolous play. *The Poetics of Slumberland* will also be dedicated to demonstrating that "there are other meanings to life from those that are publicly recognized."

PLASMATIC AND ANIMISTIC ENERGIES

Comics and cartoons are bastions of plasmatic and animistic energies and, under the guise of their implied address to children, are one of the most significant repositories of such "primitive" beliefs in the modern world. While instrumental reason had little use for such fantasies of metamorphosis and expanded possibility, these marginal media allowed them free rein.

Sergei Eisenstein's uncompleted essay on the early cartoons of Walt Disney celebrates the liberating experience of *anima*, that sense that all objects possess a natural life or vital force.[45] In early animation everything pulsates with life—not only in the foreground, where barnyard animals, steamboats, and airplanes bounce and stretch in zesty rhythm, but, before the introduction of transparent animation cels, even the supposedly stable background scenery seemed to possess a vibrant buzz of its own.[46] Forms were dynamic and mutable; all things were possible.

Writing about the use of the term *animism* in art history, David Freedberg notes that it came to cover a broad range of cultural beliefs about the nature of matter. Sometimes it referred to a belief that inert objects possessed a soul; sometimes it referred to the attribution of "living character" to those inert objects—one was innate, the other projective. The term, he wittily notes, "acquired a life of its own."[47] The rhetoric of writing about art in the Renaissance was replete with discussions of images as "living," which could mean several things: a figure might be so realistic as to convince one of its possessing actual life, or the image could be charged with the spirit of its creator and thus possess some of the artist's life force.[48] And there was another option for thinking about the living image: the image could actually come to life—marginal images in a Byzantine Psalter might feature penitents regarding an icon of Jesus, depicted with his hand extending out from the picture plane, beyond the frame, toward them (just as Superman's hand will project from the surface of a 3-D comic to be discussed in the last chapter). Some fifteenth- and sixteenth-century crucifixes were made with moving limbs, the better to enact the resurrection in Easter ritual, an act of reanimation. Byzantine icons were understood as possessed of grace and charismatic power—worshippers left offerings before them, and they even had mobility—mobile icons were part of liturgical practice.[49] Bissera Pentcheva has further argued that, seen by the light of a flickering candle with its dancing shadows, icons were animated images.[50] We have been blinded to the prevalence of discussions of living images, Freedberg argues, because we have relegated animism to the realm of the primitive or the childish.

It's no accident that Eisenstein finds in cartoons, a medium ostensibly aimed at children, the modern repository for the animistic spirit. Children are close to anima: they have not yet learned to accept the ossification of form. For one thing, their own bodies are growing and changing and rather visibly. For another, there is a kind of play that almost depends on investing inanimate objects with a life force. Whether it's the doll playing the part of a baby or the stuffed tiger that is really a real tiger (or vice versa), the child continually accepts what many have referred to as "the secret life of things." The figure of the child Nemo serves to license the flights of fantasy that constitute *Little Nemo in Slumberland*. Similarly, cartoons, with their implicit address to the child (anthropomorphized animals, linear adventures, broad comedy), serve as a conduit for the atavistic attraction to an animistic world. What is at stake is a renewal of perception through an act of estrangement: cartoon physics depend on an understanding of actual physics and a conscious decision to "play along" with a world that operates differently. We reconnect to a self that was willing to believe in a world that operated by a different set of rules, and novel cinematic technologies can aid that reconnection. The cartoon, fairly or not, quickly became associated with children, precisely because of its predilection for talking animals and living toys.

But animism survives in the modern adult world as well. Jackson Lears has emphasized the animistic underpinnings of post–World War II advertising, which charged the objects of the world with totemic power and spirit. Advertising fed fantasies of a nurturing world of plenitude, metamorphosis, and perpetual regeneration. "Under the right circumstances, certain kinds of commodities could still carry a charge of animation, could still connect the self to the material world."[51] As advertising became more sophisticated, campaigns began to "personify" the products themselves, imbuing them with personalities, or at least reliable traits: "Calls for liveliness in copy began to boil down to a single panacea: the need for the copywriter and illustrator 'to introduce "life"' into the advertisement."[52] Comics and animation, then, are only the most obvious repositories of animist power to have persisted in the modern world.

Eisenstein finds something ecstatic in animation's metamorphic freedom. Cartoons represent "a displacement, an upheaval, a unique protest against the metaphysical immobility of the once-and-forever given."[53] Before Disney, in the early part of the twentieth century, Winsor McCay was the protean master of such plasmatic and animistic energies. McCay was an astonishingly prolific cartoonist, with as many as five strips running more or less concurrently (in 1905 he was producing *Little Sammy Sneeze, The Story of Hungry Henrietta, Little Nemo in Slumberland, Dream of the Rarebit Fiend,* and *A Pilgrim's Progress by Mister Bunion*). His draftsmanship immediately separated him from many of his peers, and in *Little Nemo* he literally transformed the representation of space in comics, moving from the fixed frame and theatrical blocking that had typified comics space to an animated realm of wildly metamorphosing objects contained in panels that expanded and contracted to accentuate and magnify the action. In *Rarebit Fiend* and *Little Nemo* all the things in the world—and even space itself—held the potential for change. Alligator purses morph (back) into alligators (Figure 2). Beds shrink; ceilings lower or turn into

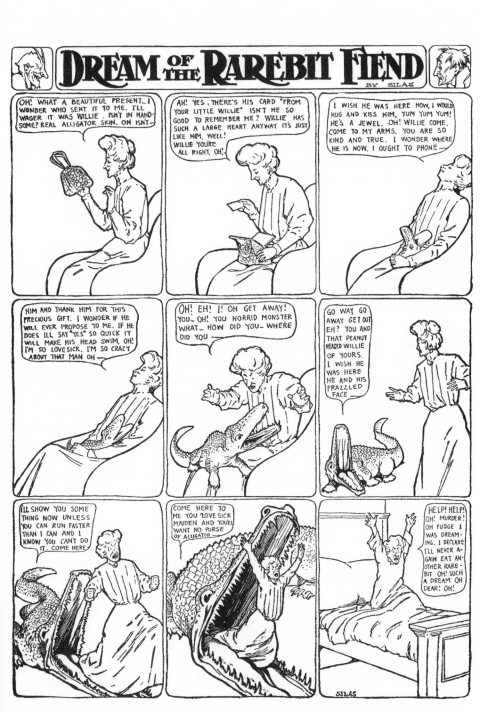

FIGURE 2. Winsor McCay, *Dream of the Rarebit Fiend*, *New York Evening Telegram*, April 12, 1905. Courtesy Ulrich Merkl.

floors; legs get shorter; noses get longer. Small puppies grow to the size of houses; people age backward. Furniture grows to mammoth proportions, dwarfing people, or people grow to the size of buildings and caper about New York. Nothing is fixed; nothing is final (other than the act of waking). Everything misbehaves; the very objects and substance of the world become disobedient.

It seems inevitable that McCay would turn to the animation of his drawings—his sequential art mapped out animation sequences before the medium existed. In 1911 he created a short animation of some of his *Nemo* characters—perhaps the second film to animate series of drawings, after Cohl's *Fantasmagorie,* but a gigantic leap beyond that film in the detail of the artwork, the sense of depth and volume, and its animistic expressiveness. McCay was already a bit of a celebrity who had a stage act as—not surprisingly—a lightning artist, and the film was originally used as part of his act. For wider distribution McCay starred in a live-action framing sequence showing him producing the drawings that made up the animation—perhaps the earliest film documenting an artist's process. The framing narratives of *Little Nemo* and *Gertie the Dinosaur* present him as a master of his craft, betting (and winning) that he can bring his drawings—and a "dinosaurus"—to life. In his first cartoons Flip and Impy squash and stretch, and an engorged mosquito swells to the size of a man's head. The giant puppy makes a return appearance, and McCay himself turns into a cartoon character, riding off atop Gertie, his own creation. His later cartoons lose this animistic zeal—and surely that has something to do with the limitations of the new cel animation technique, which produced a more stable image and disrupted the unity of objects and world that ruled the earliest films.[54]

So while this is not a book about Winsor McCay, he looms large within it for his groundbreaking work in comic strips and cartoons—which he transformed through the combination of the physical solidity of his draftsmanship and the sustained elaboration of metamorphic possibility and reflexive play—as well as his presence onscreen as artist and animator. In its continual transformation of the mundane into the marvelous, McCay's best work unleashes what one could call the madness, or the playfulness, of matter.[55] Steven Millhauser understands McCay's importance, creating, in his novella "The Little Kingdom of J. Franklin Payne," a fictional version of McCay who labors mightily, on his own time, to produce the drawings for his brief cartoons: "The animated cartoon was a far more honest expression of the cinematic illusion than the so-called realistic film, because the cartoon reveled in its own illusory nature, exulted in the impossible—indeed it claimed the impossible as its own, exalted it as its own highest end, found in impossibility, in the negation of the actual, its profoundest reason for being."[56] This master of the plasmatic bends the world to his will, creating a new set of rules to govern existence. His aesthetic remakes the world, *becomes* the world.

William Randolph Hearst, publisher of the *New York Journal,* recognized that McCay was his finest artist and took him from the world of comics to become an

THE CURSE OF CIVILIZATION!

FIGURE 3. Winsor McCay, "The Curse of Civilization," *New York Evening Telegram,* June 30, 1914.

editorial cartoonist. His drawings frequently headed articles by Arthur Brisbane, allegorical images of HOPE, THOUGHT, TOMORROW. A giant metallic dinosaur labeled TECHNOCRACY thunders through the city, crushing all in its path. A sub-human figure holding a bomb (ANARCHY) straddles the globe (CIVILIZATION) (Figure 3). The pictures are meticulously rendered, McCay's draftsmanship never more evident. They are beautiful but not playful.

In 1918 McCay produced an animated editorial cartoon, recreating the sinking of the RMS *Lusitania*. Where once he brought mischievous dinosaurs to life, now he resurrects the victims of the German attack to fan the flames of patriotism. The film is an astonishing achievement but assuredly not playful. McCay's magic has been press-ganged into the service of the real. Millhauser, writing about his fictional McCay, evokes a sadness that plays around the edges of the ephemeral escape that is the promise of the cartoon: "The animated cartoon was nothing but the poetry of the impossible—therein lay its exhilaration and its secret melancholy. For this willful violation of the actual, while it was an intoxicating release from the constriction of things, was at the same time nothing but a delusion, an attempt to outwit mortality. As such it was doomed to failure. And yet it was desperately important to smash through the constriction of the actual, to unhinge the universe and let the impossible stream in, because otherwise—well, otherwise the world was nothing but an editorial cartoon."[57]

McCay was a master of plasmatic possibility, but there were others. Another hero of the plasmatic goes by the name of Harold—if he has a last name he hasn't shared it—and he has a purple crayon.[58] Readers should remember that Crockett Johnson's 1955 work followed Harold through the night as he drew the scenery and spaces that his body would occupy. He draws the moon to see by and the ground beneath his feet, and "he made a long straight path so he wouldn't get lost." When Harold becomes frightened and his hand shakes, the wavy line his hand produces suddenly becomes real waves, beneath which Harold quickly sinks (fortunately, the stalwart fellow is a quick thinker and draws himself a boat). Harold, searching for his bedroom, draws a window around the moon (because he could see the moon from his window). "And then Harold made his bed. He got in it and he drew up the covers." (Younger readers may be forgiven for missing the puns as Harold indeed "makes" his bed and "draws" the covers.) The book ends in a reversal of Nemo, as Harold contentedly falls asleep. Harold's purple crayon is a device of awesome power, similar, in its way, to Green Lantern's power ring, which could concretize whatever the superhero imagined. Harold's crayon is not portrayed as miraculous, though; it is rather a normal tool of childhood. We were all Harolds, once.[59]

The *super*hero of the plasmatic is not Green Lantern but Plastic Man (Plate 5), created in 1941 by Jack Cole and possessed of a phenomenally malleable corporeality.[60] "Plas" snakes around an array of flying daggers, stretches upward to allow a hurtling car to pass beneath, and coils like a spring to absorb the impact of a falling safe. He makes suction cups of his feet, molds his face into anyone's likeness, and oozes through the narrowest gaps—all the while keeping up a level of patter that makes the whole thing seem easy, if not effortless. Plastic Man thematized what David Kunzle refers to as the machined body in late nineteenth-century comics. "In its more industrially conscious phase, the comic strip imagines the human body violently flattened, stretched, twisted, kinked or wrapped around a spinning drum," Kunzle writes, noting that "both fear and fascination reside in the artist's rendering of the body as machined almost beyond recognition."[61] But the tone of Plastic Man is purely euphoric—Green Lantern (in all his incarnations) is comparatively prosaic.

In "Forms Stretched to Their Limits" Art Spiegelman argues convincingly that "Plastic Man literally *embodied* the comic-book form: its exuberant energy, its flexibility, its boyishness, and its only partially sublimated sexuality."[62] Later iterations of the character, such as the Elongated Man and the Fantastic Four's Mr. Fantastic, are less giddy but still entertaining. Spiegelman refers to Mr. Fantastic as a "straight" version of Plastic Man—he, too had stretching powers, but Stan Lee mandated that he would never stretch anything other than limbs or full body. Mr. Fantastic would never extend his eye through a keyhole, or elongate an ear, whereas Plastic Man stretched and flexed in all conceivable (and a few inconceivable) ways.

Plastic Man, with his morphing morphology, also serves to demonstrate the plasmatic fantasy that underlies the entire superhero genre, with its transformative bodies, split identities, and infinite adaptabilities. Batman might not have Plastic Man's chameleonic ability to blend into the landscape (by becoming a fire hydrant, say, or a painting), but he still manages to inhabit the city's recesses, finding unexpected ways to make his appearance. And while Mr. Fantastic may be a less exuberant character, the world of the Fantastic Four as given to us by Jack Kirby and Lee, had its own plasmatic suppleness: it was replete with other worlds, Negative Zones, colorful allies and adversaries, and, at times, a cosmic energy that bordered on the psychedelic. Shape-shifters abound in superhero comics: Wikipedia (a fantastic resource for comics geeks) lists many varieties: some can morph into animals, alter their shapes and/or sizes; they can become inorganic substances, gasses, liquids, or whatever they touch. They are, indeed, so abundant that we can say that Plastic Man not only embodies the comic book but the very fantasy of the superhero.

But we can further claim that Plastic Man is a character that aspires to inhabit a cartoon, the real home of the plasmatic. The cartoon is an ecstatic celebration of "rejection of once-and-forever allotted form, freedom from ossification, the ability to dynamically assume any form."[63] Plastic Man would totally have been Eisenstein's favorite superhero.

Eisenstein found something ecstatic in animation's metamorphic freedom, but later writers have sought to locate the limits of anima. For Rosalind Krauss the technique utilized by William Kentridge in his animated films possesses a kind of inertial drag that works against the ahistorical freedom of the plasmatic.[64] Anne Nesbet finds something analogous within Disney's own films, albeit in later films than those Eisenstein favored.[65] The rotoscoped image of Snow White presents a fixed form at odds with the animistic ecstasies of the rest of the film. Joanna Bouldin, building on Nesbet's argument, finds a similar binding at work in such phenomena and phrases as "motion capture," a "capturing" that is often of racial otherness.[66] In Sianne Ngai's analysis animatedness is an "ugly feeling" assigned to racial others as an excess at odds with more normative ideologies.[67] Heather Ann Crow finds in the metamorphoses of Alice's body in Jan Svankmajer's film "not the ecstatic freedom for which Eisenstein hopes, but the profound discomfort of corporeal instability."[68] Elsewhere I have noted the dismaying erasure of history enacted by the morph, as well as erasures of racial difference.[69] And many writers have noted the passage of energy from animator to animated, resulting in the enervation or disappearance of the former in favor of the latter.

None of this is wrong, and each of the writers I have cited here has produced compelling, elegant, and essential analyses. But one wonders at the consistent backing away from the pleasures of the plasmatic. I am reminded, a bit, of the critique of representation that dominated critical theory for some years and the associated attack on pleasure exemplified by Mulvey's germinal essay, as well as the tendency of scholars to insert what is called "critical distance" between themselves and the things of their childhood (or their late-night guilty pleasures). Well, none of that for me! I come not to bury the plasmatic but to praise it. I stand with Eisenstein in defense of cartoon physics and the freedom from once-and-forever allotted form.

ANIMATEDNESS

The anti-instrumentalism represented by playful disobedience and plasmatic possibility align with *animatedness,* a central concept of this book and one adapted from the work of Sianne Ngai. As I noted above, Ngai identifies animatedness as one of the "ugly feelings" she traces throughout American literature and other cultural forms. Ugly feelings, or negative emotions, come into play when agency is blocked, and these feelings can be understood as gestures of resistance enacted by the powerless (the envious, the paranoid, the irritated). Unable to effect change, the bearers of ugly feelings exist as outsiders, refusing to perform as expected. Ngai locates a significant trope of racialized animatedness cutting through American literature and film in the nineteenth and twentieth centuries, characters defined by a surfeit of energy, an "exaggerated emotional expressiveness" that "seems to function as a marker of racial or ethnic otherness in general."[70] It is easy to see animatedness at work in the ethnically marked kids of *Hogan's Alley,* positioned as they are at society's margins and radiating frenetic energy in all directions.

With tremendous force and originality Ngai unpacks the multivalent character of the animated being: an inert object activated by another—who is often deactivated in turn—but also a lively figure taking up a position outside the norms of "civilized" behavior. To have one's body animated is to have it manipulated, subjected to external control. But, following the lead of Rosalind Krauss, Ngai points to the two meanings of automatism: industrial culture's rigidity of routine and control, yes, but also the automatism implied by the "automatic writing" of the surrealists that yields a liberation from conscious control. As Ngai points out, "this elasticity is the sign of the body's automatization (since the pliancy of an object suggests its heightened vulnerability to external manipulation), but functions also as the source of an unaccounted-for autonomy."[71] Regulation and resistance, liberation and limitation, automatism and autonomy—these are the dialectics in play. The animated body represents both the body's subjection and its freedom—Taylorist control and the "triumph over the fetters of form."

Ngai's animatedness is inscribed from the very earliest cartoons—the first two characters to appear in the *Little Nemo* animation are the ethnically stereotyped Flip and Impy (Irish and African, respectively). Once Nemo magically self-generates, he becomes a kind of ringmaster, gesturing them into a long cycle of squashes and stretches. Nemo's own normative (white) body undergoes no such distortions, neither is it subject to another character's overt control. Both aspects of Ngai's notion of animatedness are thus at work in this brief sequence: the ethnically marked body is both more pliable and more manipulated than the other bodies on display. And there is a surfeit of early cartoon characters, black and of ambiguous species (what *is* Bosko, anyway?): Felix the Cat, Oswald the Rabbit, and Mickey Mouse all appear as barely disguised black caricatures. John Updike writes, "Cartoon characters' rubberiness, their jazziness, their cheerful buoyance and idleness all chimed with popular images of African Americans, already embodied in minstrel shows and in Joel Chandler Harris's tales of Uncle Remus."[72]

While Ngai emphasizes racial representation, she also points to the ambivalence that underlies *all* animation: the tension between bodies both Taylorized and ecstatic. She argues that "animatedness and its affective cousins (liveliness, vigor, zest) . . . might also be thought of as categories of feeling that highlight animation's status as a nexus of contradictions with the capacity to generate unanticipated social meanings and effects."[73]

The rebellious characters that populate the American theatrical cartoon and its televised offspring can, like the racialized figures Ngai considers (including Speedy Gonzales), be considered marginal characters, outsiders. They are not to be taken too seriously; they are relegated to the short before the main feature or to Saturday mornings; they upend propriety and even physical law. Take the less ethnically obvious Daffy Duck. He is animated: as in, mobile and kinetic. He is animated: as in, energetic and vital. He is animated: as in, a series of static drawings imbued with motion by a labor-intensive mode of production and the cinematic apparatus. He is animated: as in, "exaggeratedly emotional." He is animated: as in, *over*animated, annoying, irritating (other ugly feelings). He is a profoundly self-conscious, exaggeratedly performative character continually doing battle with other characters, with the genre conventions of the parodies he performs, with the head of his studio, and, most memorably, with the animator "himself" in Chuck Jones's classic *Duck Amuck* (1953). He exemplifies Norman Klein's insight: "Cartoons are automata that struggle."[74] As Klein notes, the animated character is, literally, an automaton—but *animatedness* comes into play in the gestures of rebellion: Ko-Ko's refusal to go back in the inkwell. Animatedness separates the automaton from the autonomous, the regulated from the resistant.

Where my use of animatedness perhaps goes against Ngai's intentions lies in the more positive spin that I put on it. For me, animatedness is an ugly feeling but also a romantic, and somewhat heroic, condition—if the world judges the overanimated harshly, that is the price to be paid for autonomy and independence. In this, my characters are active agents, prankish and unruly. *Unruly* rather than *monstrous*—this is the tale of Gertie the Dinosaur, not King Kong. The characters experiencing Ngai's "ugly feelings" are not in positions of power; they cannot effect the kind of direct change that is the province of the powerful monster (or the monstrously powerful). The monstrous destroy the world; the unruly irritate, or perhaps bedevil, it (and I will discuss this further in chapter 4). As Bugs Bunny would say, in what could be the mantra for all these mischief makers, "Ain't I a stinker?"

ANIMATEDNESS BEYOND THE CARTOON

One might say that this is a book about the importance of *being animated.* This book will explore animatedness in different contexts to find within it a fundamental mode of being in the world, or perhaps of positioning oneself just to the side of it. The characters to be encountered here are vital figures possessed of a nearly uncontainable energy, and in this they represent little *embodied* utopias of disorder.[75] Some of them are actual cartoon characters, but—and this is important—not all. As Ngai demonstrates in her work, animatedness is not the sole province of Daffy Duck and his cartoony relatives. I find it strongly present, for example, in the artist films that I will consider: in Picasso's capricious treatment of his own images in *Le mystère Picasso;* in Pollock's refusal of traditional methods of applying paint, as seen in Hans Namuth's film; and in Van Gogh's hysterical abjection and single-minded dedication to his craft, as depicted in *Lust for Life.* It can even be seen in the slight undercranking in the scenes of Winsor McCay drawing his characters with breathtaking speed and precision in *Little Nemo.*

And animatedness marks not only the creator, artist or animator, but the creations as well. Gertie doesn't always do what she's told, and this, too, extends beyond the cartoon. When Eliza Doolittle makes her society debut at the Ascot races in *My Fair Lady,* her "unbridled" spontaneity marks both her failure (to impress the upper class through her use of programmed conversational gambits) and her triumph (as an autonomous being of infinitely greater entertainment value, she wins us over). And then there is Jerry Lewis, who is almost a tripping, stuttering, embodiment of animatedness, wreaking havoc—while meaning well—on movie and television screens in the 1950s and 1960s. The comedy sketches performed by Martin and Lewis on the Colgate Comedy Hour took an almost invariable format—Jerry, on a new job, trying, and failing, to do something properly. He, too, eludes his programming. The tension between the *automaton* and the *autonomous*, as manifested not only in the animistic spirit of the images but also in the very performance of image production, structures much of this book.

Renaissance discussions of art distinguished between *anima* and *spirito*. The former referred to a physical liveliness such as might come from the depiction of a figure in motion, whereas the latter referred to the sense conveyed of an inner life, or spirit. The figures to be encountered in this book are both animated *and* spirited, imbued with both kineticism and character.

THE CHAPTERS

The Poetics of Slumberland moves among comics, animation, and live-action cinema, locating further instances of not just animatedness but disobedient machines, plasmatic possibility, playful images, and image production.

The first chapter, "Drawn and Disorderly," elaborates on the tension between regulation and resistance. It begins with a consideration of the strong resemblance between the photographic arrays of Eadweard Muybridge and the comics, a resemblance that hides the parodic relation that really holds between them. Chronophotography was easily aligned with the rational imperatives of modernity, mapping as it did the progression of a body at precise intervals through measured space. Comics, already a going concern in Europe, change in the wake of chronophotography, not only by becoming more attuned to measured intervals of time but by replacing orderly process with a comedic progression toward chaos and/or death.

While a comic like McCay's *Little Sammy Sneeze* charts the activities of a counterproductive body, *Dream of the Rarebit Fiend,* also by McCay, offers a perceptual, hallucinatory resistance to the demands of the real. In its combination of anxious reverie and unregulated perception, *Rarebit Fiend* was as clear a response to the stresses of modern life as the comics had to offer. The chapter concludes by contrasting European and American attitudes toward creative energy, using the writings of Steven Millhauser and the figure of Winsor McCay to illustrate an American creative imagination that moves out into the world in order to remake it in its own way.[76]

The next chapter, "The Motionless Voyage of Little Nemo," develops a phenomenology of *Little Nemo in Slumberland,* a strip that greatly expanded the expressive and aesthetic possibilities of the comics. Here McCay offers immersion rather than resistance, an entrance to another, highly aestheticized world filtered through the experience of a child. The animating sensibility of the artist McCay operates through the perceptual and bodily experience of Nemo, as the malleability of space, world, and body dominates the strip, investing the solidity of objects with plasmatic possibility.

McCay's animation occupies the center of the third chapter, "Labor and Anima."

The dialectical relation of these terms has informed much animation theory, which frequently notes the transfer of energy from animator to animated, usually at the expense of the former. The chapter concentrates on two films that present the process of image making, as well as a shift in emphasis from artist to artwork. *Little Nemo* (1911), McCay's first film, was produced before the hierarchical division of labor that became animation's mode of production, while *Le mystère Picasso* (Henri-Georges Clouzot, 1955) was produced well after it. The two films position the artist-figures at their center as both industrious and magical, and both films simultaneously mystify and demystify the activity of artistic creation.

The next two chapters each take up one term of the labor/anima dialectic. "Disobedient Machines" continues the discussion of those rambunctious, rebellious cartoon characters whose every move, paradoxically, is programmed in advance. The chapter moves beyond McCay to consider animation (the creation of life) as a trope in different kinds of films—cartoons, horror, and science fiction—and it moves beyond animation to locate a similar disobedience or resistance in other genres. *My Fair Lady* (George Cukor, 1964) represents an extension of the myth of Pygmalion, as well as an Americanization of George Bernard Shaw's original text. Eliza Doolittle is both a creation of Higgins and very much her own woman, and *My Fair Lady* charts her progress from comic caricature to automaton to autonomous being. Meanwhile, the films of Jerry Lewis continually position him as a malfunctioning machine, and I posit that malfunction as a sign of resistance to order and advancing technologization.

The following chapter returns to the "labor" side of things. "Labor and Animatedness" examines both *Lust for Life,* the 1956 Vincente Minnelli biopic about Vincent van Gogh, and the contemporaneous American movement of "action painting," finding in both something very like the animatedness that Ngai has described. Animatedness might be seen as the underlying force in melodrama—*too much* emotion, *too much* emoting. In *Lust for Life* Van Gogh is presented as—at once—animated, animating, and reanimated, and some of this is also true of Jackson Pollock in Hans Namuth's 1951 film of the artist at work. In both films, as in the animated films discussed in prior chapters, the physical bond between animator and animated is emphasized, the bond between the work, the labor, of art, and the artwork.

The final chapter maps the book's concerns onto the more contemporary phenomena of superhero comics (with a particular emphasis on the whimsicality of Superman) and superhero films. The world of the superhero has darkened considerably in recent decades, and "Playing Superheroes" tries to recover the underlying sense of wonder and play that lies beneath the grim 'n' gritty. Superhero films, beginning in the 1990s, inherited much of this darkness. The films can also be understood as largely a function of CGI effects, and they present an opportunity to consider the place of plasmatic possibility in the digital age. The chapter considers the complexity of the comics-reading experience, as well as the rarebit-like reflexive play of Grant Morrison's comics, and concludes with an examination of Morrison's and Frank Quitely's reassuring and profoundly playful *All-Star Superman*.

As a whimsical figure Superman immediately summons thoughts of Peter Pan, the eternal boy, playing forever in his own private Slumberland (in his case Neverland). Both fly unaided, unencumbered by planes, wings, jet-packs, or tetherings of any kind. On the cover of the first issue of *Superman* our hero does not so much fly as *float* comfortably above the cityscape of Metropolis—quite a different picture from the one on the cover of *Action* no. 1, the comic that introduced Superman and depicts him hurling an automobile to the ground as terrified crooks scurry for cover. Superman is dedicated to fighting crime and, in those early days, ferreting out corruption, but the character also represents a fantasy of flight. In the absence of any mechanical or material aids, Superman becomes a *dream* of flight.[77] He may have more of a social conscience than the happily hedonistic Peter Pan, but that sense of mission should not blind us to their resemblance. In the 1978 film, *Superman*, Lois Lane compares them, but it's a comparison that this particular version of Superman, incarnated to perfection by Christopher Reeve, rejects. "Peter Pan," he muses. "He flew in fairy tales . . . for children." He then sweeps her off her feet and into the sky for *their* dreamily romantic flight. But let's be fair: Superman flies in fairy tales, too, albeit ones aimed at slightly older children. Peter Pan reveals the links between superpowers, children, and play; they, in fact, become concomitant with one another. That the superhero genre has effectively developed in multitudinous directions should not blind us to the child's fantasy at its core.

With an invocation of Peter Pan, the reader may become aware that for the most part, and with the very significant exceptions of Eliza Doolittle and Gertie the Dinosaur, most of the disobedient machines in this book are boys. But while rebellion may be more commonly embodied as male, I suspect that reader identification crosses gender boundaries to permit all to partake of these performances of disobedience and resistance. Of the phenomena considered in this book, only superhero comics are consumed by an overwhelmingly male readership, and I have argued elsewhere that these license a baroque performative fantasy that heterosexual boys are largely discouraged from indulging. The disobedience performed by the superhero comic takes the form of a rejection of pragmatic efficiency and the blandness of male couture and affect.[78] But superhero comics aside, the comic strips, cartoons, comedies, musicals, and melodramas encountered in this book are, and have been, happily consumed by men and women, girls and boys. Everybody, it seems, likes a disobedient machine.

David Freedberg has excavated the presence of animist concepts in the Christian art of the European Middle Ages and Renaissance; needless to say, his examples are of a higher order than those you'll find in this book. However, he notes a recurring tale, "charmingly retold" in *Miracles de Notre Dame,* about a monk painting the most hideous imaginable image of the devil. "In a fit of pique," as he tells the story, "the devil pushed him off the scaffolding, but as he fell, the Madonna stretched out her right arm, and with the help of her child prevented him from falling." Here, at last, is a character that I can relate to—not the Madonna but the devil: an animated being whose first act is to turn against his creator in a bit of cartoonish slapstick. Freedberg, unfortunately, doesn't entirely get behind this story, noting that "however delightful, it seems more than usually childish."[79] My book, on the other hand, exists to honor this mischievous image and all the others that follow.

Chapter 1

DRAWN AND DISORDERLY

"Ain't I a stinker?"
—BUGS BUNNY

COMICS, CARTOONS, AND
THE CRITIQUE OF CHRONOPHOTOGRAPHY

The saga of *Little Nemo in Slumberland* began, very auspiciously, on October 15, 1905, in the pages of the Sunday comics supplement of the *New York Herald*.[1] A lovely prose text, all the more impressive for being squeezed in beneath Winsor McCay's superb illustrations, guides the reader through that first adventure (Plate 6). In this earliest incarnation speech balloons are used minimally ("I wonder what the Oomp will say, Oh!"); the narrative is conveyed by the running (helpfully numbered) captions and the art. The page is masterfully constructed: six tiers, each with a pair of equally sized panels except for the first, in which the immense king of Slumberland overlooks all that follows, and the four-panel sequence at the bottom, as Nemo tumbles through space and, in the final image, out of his bed.

Several important and characteristic elements are at work in this, Nemo's debut. First, one might note that the dream (and the saga) begins not with Nemo but with Slumberland's king, who charges Oomp with summoning Nemo. The dream begins, then, outside Nemo's consciousness. The wide top panel provides a glimpse of Slumberland behind the king—we can make out a broad plaza, pillars, arches, arcades, and a row of columns surmounting all. The foreground space is dominated by the king's massive, bearded presence and, flanking his head, the comic strip's logo. A brick-red framing overlay divides this single broad image into three sections, producing a visual rhyme with the columns but without depth (unlike the ivy-encircled column to the left); in the center is the king. The ambiguity over whether this frame is a design or an architectural element is sustained by the position of the king, who leans casually on, and spills slightly over, the bottom frame border. Thus, through both his posture and his presence in what is really the title panel, the king is as separate from the diegetic space as he is from Nemo's dream. This is one of the two panels that do not represent Nemo in the land of wonderful dreams—the other is, of course, the final panel, in which he lies tangled in his blankets, rudely awakened. In future strips, as McCay begins to open the page to more elaborate configurations of panels, that final panel will increasingly figure as an inset—the one immutable element in the strip—an intrusion into (or carved from) the space of the dream.

McCay has infused the page with his characteristic design work. The second tier presents Nemo in bed, facing right; in the first panel the Oomp introduces himself, and in the next he presents Nemo with Somnus. In the two panels below, Nemo remains on the left side of the panel but now astride his magical mount: the Oomp promises some additional excitement ("Slumberland is the most wonderful place in the sky. You mustn't miss a single thing. See it all!"), and in the next panel Nemo and Somnus gallop through space, encountering the Oomp in the form of a huge white bird ("Gracious! What is that?"). The next four panels, across two tiers, drop Nemo into a sudden race, replete with bunnies riding pigs and monkeys atop green kangaroos, all jumping the hurdles of bursting stars that surround them. Nemo loses his mount in the last panel of this self-contained race sequence, diving headfirst through the reins, leading to his final tumble through space in the final four panels, which are arranged in a regular series of squares along the bottom tier.

Even this description misses much of McCay's brilliant detail. There is the substitution (or is it a metamorphosis?) of bed for horse. There is the increasingly extravagant coloring that accompanies the progress of the race, the muted color of Nemo's bedroom wall yielding first to a richer orange, then olive greens, sky blues, and a deep saturated red. There is the final image of a sprawled Nemo, thrown from his horse, thrown from the journey to Slumberland, and, most immediately, thrown from his bed.

And there is, perhaps most spectacularly, the evocation of *movement,* which pervades this single page. One image in particular leaps out: after we see Somnus pawing the ground, clearly eager to be off, she is depicted in full gallop, bearing Nemo toward the wonders of Slumberland. McCay has depicted the horse in what can only be described as the Muybridge position, with all four legs lifted from the ground. Nor is this the only image that recalls the pioneering work in motion capture performed by both Eadweard Muybridge and Etienne Jules Marey. Indeed, the evenly sized panels, arrayed in a graphlike configuration, presenting the successive stages of a horse's gait, could hardly be more clear. The stages of the animal's motion will provide visual continuity, dynamic flow, and, importantly, credible naturalistic detail across the six central panels. In two of the panels the beasts leaping the hurdles produce elegant arcs of motion that can be read from left to right as stages in a single movement, as in a chronophotograph.[2] And Nemo's final tumble is a backward somersault, divided into four images (with the last, back in the waking world, representing a kind of *somersaultus interruptus*) with all the precision (and perhaps more) of one of Muybridge's photographic sequences.

Analyzing the Instant

Muybridge and Marey both used photography to capture and display the stages that constitute the continuum of movement. Marey, a physician and amateur naturalist, attempted, through a series of mechanisms, to record and recreate the movements of bird and insect wings, as well as the running gaits of horses and men. He recognized the value of phenakistoscopes and other similar amusements: "This instrument, usually constructed for the amusement of children, generally represents grotesque or fantastic figures moving in a ridiculous manner." But, with images "constructed with care" that "represented faithfully the successive attitudes of the body," a more accurate understanding of physiological movements might be possible.[3]

As the story goes, and stop me if you've heard this one, the governor of California, Leland Stanford, aware of the experiments with which Marey was occupied, employed the very established panoramic and stereoscopic photographer Eadweard Muybridge in 1872 to settle a wager about whether all the legs of a running horse ever left the ground at once. Muybridge continued to experiment with sequential photography for the rest of his career, whether producing book-length studies of human and animal movements or demonstrating his "Zoöpraxiscope," which projected, and effectively reanimated, his photographic sequences.

Marey began using his "chronophotographic gun" in 1882 to take photographic sequences of birds in flight, fencing lunges, and the like. While Muybridge's technique produced individual images on a series of photographic plates, Marey's technique used an automatically advancing disk to capture the multiple vectors of motion, up and down, forward and back, in a series of exposures captured on a single plate. The chronophotograph combined the empirical weight and mimetic precision of the photograph with the plotted precision of the graph.[4] Marey's single exposures yielded evenly spaced intervals in an unambiguous sequence extracted from continuous motion.

Braun emphasizes the difference between Marey's scientism and Muybridge's formalism.[5] Muybridge's use of multiple, spatially organized cameras, as well as his characteristic array of discretely bounded, pleasingly composed images, privileged a sense of time as divisible and discrete. Contained parcels of space become analogous to contained parcels of time. Marey's single plates, by contrast, emphasized a temporal continuum, with the chronophotograph capturing instants along the axis of time's arrow. Against Marey's scientific interest in graphing movement, Muybridge was, through his discrete images, each carefully lit and composed according to acceptable aesthetic conventions, "telling stories in space."[6]

Tom Gunning does not reject the distinction that Braun carefully draws, but he argues that she may be drawing the wrong conclusion. He and others suggest that the codes of an earlier pictorialism that find their way into Muybridge's aesthetic could not dispel, and possibly even emphasized, the fascinating disruption produced by the clearly delineated sequence of movement that demonstrated the camera's astonishing ability to register what the human eye could not.[7] These are *not* the pictures of a neoclassical age, despite the semiotic cues that invite such comparison; people had never seen such pictures before. Marey's chronophotographs have an amorphous, ghostly quality that clearly separates them from the realm of natural perception, whereas Muybridge's images combine the solidity of familiar figures and pictorial conventions with the new—radically new—experience of perceived time.

Jonathan Crary also emphasizes the decisive rupture produced by Muybridge's first motion studies. He writes that "Muybridge's work obviously opened up possibilities for the rationalization and quantification of movement and time, for the mechanization of the body," but its radically "mutable temporality" suggested an *escape* from that very rationalism by offering "plural scatterings of attention and the possibility of unforeseen perceptual syntheses outside of any disciplinary imperatives."[8] Crary does not mention Marey, but the temporality of Marey's chronophotographs is clearly *not* mutable, governed as they are by the rigidity of even intervals and clearly mapped vectors of motion, and suggestive of an impossibly sustained single moment, stretched in time as it stretches across the field of the image. With Muybridge, though, the act of segmentation and the spatial display of stages of movement on a grid might generate new conceptions of the relation between image and world.[9] The organization and display of recorded moments projected the sense of temporal continuity and its relentless rationality, but it also incontrovertibly showed that time could be fractured, our awareness of it newly dispersed along a series or array of demonstrably incomplete images.

Comics became prominent as a popular medium around the same period that these motion studies were taking place, and in emphasizing the radicalism of Muybridge's work, I would argue that Crary is unknowingly *also* outlining the necessary conditions for the emergence of modern comics. Crary's comments about the temporal rupture offered by the image sequence echo Scott McCloud's discussion of the organized array of panels that characterize comics, which (in McCloud's words) "fracture both time and space, offering a jagged, staccato rhythm of unconnected moments."[10] Comics *uniquely* present a combination of static images, often infiltrated by visual cues of captured or continuing movement, arranged in temporal sequence.

In his pioneering discussion of the relation of comics and film, John Fell wrote, "By posing the dimension of time on a visible linear continuum, comics offer something different from cinema. Even after the reader has proceeded from picture to picture, the panels continue to relate to one another on the page."[11] Comics more clearly resemble what Muybridge produced than what the Edison company and the Lumières followed with. To return briefly to the issue of Muybridge's aesthetics, Phillip Prodger has pointed to some of the means by which Muybridge's sequences rupture *and* mend the usual relationship between photographic image and temporality: *Walking Elephant* is a photographic array that may be read as either a chronophotographic study of a single elephant or as a chain of multiple elephants marching in parade.[12]

These are methods that comics quickly adopt. Winsor McCay does something like it in the first *Little Nemo in Slumberland,* as the various and multihued horses, kangaroos, and billy goats are arrayed along a single, elegantly undulating arc of movement that extends across each panel and from one panel to the next (this dialectic between wild kinesis and perfectly rendered stasis has its analogue in the overarching narrative of *Little Nemo:* the cosmic journeys across time and space counterbalanced by the insistent return to the bed from which no one has moved at all—except sometimes in that brief, rude journey from bed to floor).

The rigid distinction that Braun makes—aesthetic vs. scientific dominants, Muybridge (boo!) vs. Marey (yay!)—bypasses the rich discord that arises when the mechanical marvels of instantaneous photography and chronophotography intersect with the conventions of visual and narrative representation. In the motion studies of Muybridge, Marey, and McCay the singular and the multiple compete for attention.

Comics, like cinema, depended on the work of Muybridge, Marey, Reynaud, and a host of others who experimented with recording and reproducing natural movement in the late nineteenth century. Comics and cinema offer experiences of both temporal fracturing and temporal flow, but the comics reader has more control over time than the cinematic spectator, with the freedom to look back or peek ahead. Time in comics is represented as territory in space, and the experience of the flow of time can be very carefully regulated, if not completely controlled. This dialectic between the stasis of an individual image and the spatiotemporal movement of the sequence—a dialectic that relates to the diegesis but also to the experience of the reader—is what McCloud calls "the temporal map," and it is a conceptual fundament of the medium.[13]

Modern culture from the late nineteenth century forward oscillated between the sense of time as unbound, mutable, and multiple, and time as rigid, deterministic, and most insistently bound to linear coherence. Muybridge's first studies represent a crucial moment in the "unbinding" of time and perspective, and Crary and McCloud locate in cinema and the comics—the two media that most clearly derive from these motion-capture experiments—some of that same radicalism. *Cinema* reconstituted the movement that one could infer from the sequence of still images

while *comics* retained the synchronous spatiotemporal array, or "temporal map"—
but both media were fundamentally bound to the explorations of time, rhythm, and
tempo so characteristic of modernity.[14]

The pictorial narrative had existed as a printed form throughout Europe and Asia
since the fifteenth century, but from the middle of the nineteenth century it began
to emphasize a sense of continuous movement. The closing chapter of David Kunzle's indispensable analysis of pre-twentieth-century comics emphasizes the so-
phistication with which comics became, in effect, motion pictures, influenced both
by such optical toys as the magic lantern and the phenakistoscope, as well as the
experiments associated with Marey and Muybridge.[15] In a later essay Kunzle
demonstrates how the large, complete, and "richly accoutered" compositions associated with Hogarth yielded to the line of caricature, a line that was looser, more
exaggerated, and just evidently faster, in keeping with a perception that life itself
was becoming faster paced, careening in potentially dangerous, albeit thrilling, directions.[16] Rodolphe Töpffer eschewed scenic detail to emphasize dynamic figures
trapped in chaotic circumstances. He also developed what Kunzle terms "a battery
of montage devices" to emphasize time and motion, including narrowing the frame
from panel to panel to indicate both the quickness of succession and the concomitant claustrophobia of temporal inescapability.[17]

Increasing numbers of comic artists played with image sequences that modeled
a brief, contained arc of time. An 1868 illustration by George du Maurier for *Punch*
presented three stages in the leap of a horse and rider over a fence superimposed
into a single image. Later, *Punch* published several parodies of Muybridge, such as
an 1882 "Zoöpraxiscopic" sequence of an eminent actor's histrionics (he seems to
burst into flame by the end) (Figure 4). Thus Winsor McCay's presentation of continuous time through the vehicle of animal locomotion had some significant and
precise precedents, and it is worth reviewing some of the ways that comics in the
nineteenth century evolved as a vehicle for the registration of time through the figure
of (animal and child) movement.

The extremely popular children's stories and social satires by the German illustrator Wilhelm Busch often depicted brief actions across several panels from a fixed
perspective that emphasized incremental change, measuring, with metronomic in-
evitability, the results of the calamitous pranks committed by those early masters
of comic strip mayhem, Max and Moritz, who appeared in 1865.[18] *Cat and Mouse*,
from 1864, laid the foundation for a whole history of feline-rodent (or coyote-road-
runner) conflicts in comic strips and cartoons by reducing conflict itself to a reductio ad absurdum of cause-and-effect moves and countermoves.[19] "Busch's genius,"
Kunzle argues, "lay in his ability to impose absolute linear and conceptual control
over actions and situations out of control."[20] The American illustrator A. B. Frost
took up art studies with Thomas Eakins in 1878, when the painter had become interested in using photography and chronophotography to represent movement

NEW ZOÖPRAXISCOPIC VIEWS OF AN EMINENT ACTOR IN ACTION.
(*By Our Own Zoöpraxiscopist.*)

I. FAREWELL TO EARTH!—II. THE FLIGHT THROUGH SPACE!!—III. LAND AT LAST!!!

THREE HEART-STIRRING EPISODES IN A HITHERTO CALM AND UNEVENTFUL CAREER. (DESIGNED FOR MR. PUNCH'S "WHEEL OF LIFE," BY THE GRATEFUL SURVIVOR, PARTLY FROM THE DESCRIPTION OF NUMEROUS AND RELIABLE EYE-WITNESSES, PARTLY FROM TOLERABLY VIVID RECOLLECTIONS OF HIS OWN.)

FIGURE 4. Top: *Punch*, April 1, 1882. Bottom: George du Maurier, *Punch*, 1868.

naturalistically. Frost's picture stories, again centered around animal behaviors, quickly begin to manifest a chronophotographic smoothness, again in works of vehement and hilarious sadism such as "Our Cat Eats Rat Poison," a six-panel sequence of an action and its morbid ramifications published in *Harper's New Monthly Magazine* in 1881 (Figure 5).

The visual language developed by Frost and Busch is extended in the series of strikingly elegant strips Adolphe Willette and Théophile-Alexandre Steinlen produced for the pages of the French journal *Chat noir*. Steinlen's pages demonstrated both a virtuosic display of feline body language and a new precision in the rendering of time. Charting the progress of the cat's attempts to land a goldfish, or get its head unstuck from a bucket, or its play with a ball of yarn, one marks the smooth passage of moment to moment. Here, movement is mapped at a slow, even pace, with a precinematographic (and post-Muybridge/Marey) scientific exactitude. The flexible figure of the monochromatic cat, whose adventures were usually organized in series against a blank field with no panel divisions and only the most minimal scenic detail, was a legible icon, a line of dark graphemes writing time across the space of the page.[21]

A flowing, improvisational line, the sense of an illustration as incomplete unless viewed as part of a sequence, and an increasing emphasis on what McCloud categorizes as moment-to-moment (rather than scene-to-scene or action-to-action) transitions between illustrations all contributed to the increasing association of comics and movement, often through the vehicle of animal motion.[22] So in the first episode of *Little Nemo,* Somnus, galloping across the panels arrayed on the page, is emblematic of the new representations of time and motion, but Somnus is equally a figure of arrested motion, frozen in every *single* panel, including in that one perfect posture that Muybridge first revealed to the world of human sight. With *Little Nemo* McCay demonstrated an unprecedented (some would say unmatched) mastery of temporal mapping while returning to the spatial solidity and scenic richness associated with artists like Hogarth.

Despite efforts to backdate the origin of comics, then, the medium *does* change fundamentally in the wake of Muybridge and his famed photographic arrays. Comics display a more evident interest in temporality, depicting precise moments arranged in a legible sequence, juggling a sense of both the instantaneous and the causal. And if comics are marked by a new rapidity in production (the looser line) and diegesis (smaller units of represented time), one could note a new rapidity of consumption as well. With the rise of the American newspaper comic strips and sections, a vast new audience was introduced, *on a regular basis,* to the medium. Comic strips became something to read quickly and dispose of—a part of the ephemera of modern life—which made them very different from Hogarth's prints, Töpffer's books, and even popular magazines such as *Punch* and *Chat noir* in Europe (which did not circulate as widely as newspapers). They became a medium of the *instant.*

ACT 1.—SUSPICION.

ACT 2.—THE PANG.

ACT 3.—THE FLIGHT THROUGH THE HALL.

ACT 4.—STARTLED ONES.

ACT 5.—THE BEGINNING OF THE END.

CURTAIN—REQUIESCAT IN PACE.

FIGURE 5. A. B. Frost, "Our Cats Eat Rat Poison," *Harper's Magazine,* July 1881.

Fatigue and the Regulation of Modern Bodies

McCay's *Dream of the Rarebit Fiend* often presented adult, middle-class men or women trapped in escalating transfigurations of everyday life. The strip repeatedly connected dream content to the stresses and strains of modern life, bringing to mind the tremendous emphasis that was placed on the polarities of efficient and fatigued bodies in the industrial workplace from the mid-nineteenth century forward. The metaphor of the machine was strenuously applied to the laboring bodies of the industrial age. In the discourse of production, *fatigue* replaced idleness as the enemy of productive labor; the avoidance of work was less significant than the body's productive limits. "The human motor" needed proper care if it was to function with maximum efficiency: it needed proper nutrition, improved hygiene, and a sufficient (but not excessive!) amount of sleep. Instrumental reason had to contend with the *imperfection* of the human body, a "motor" that was not fully capable of assimilating the stressful pace of modernity, the shock of industrial accidents, and the grinding repetition of the assembly line or office workplace. Anson Rabinbach writes, "Behind the scientific and philosophical treatises on fatigue lurked the daydream of the late nineteenth-century middle classes—a body without fatigue."[23]

To increase efficiency and maintain its role in a viable labor force, the human body had to be studied, its movements graphed and analyzed, its smallest motions made visible to the scientific eye. This is the context in which the scientific visualization of movement must be situated. "Marey's studies in locomotion had an enormous influence on the artists of Europe," Braun writes, "but their more enduring and pervasive effects were on the *workers* of the world."[24] Well before his experiments with photography, Marey had devised a startlingly inventive set of mechanisms for the recording and measurement of bodily activities, producing early inscriptions of fatigue.[25] For these experiments to occur, the sciences had to develop a new conception of the body: "We seem to have been traversing an immense gallery of mechanisms of greatly varied combinations," Marey wrote, "but everything here was mysterious in its immobility."[26] In Marey's shift from organic structure to dynamics and the "interplay of organs," Rabinbach locates a new emphasis on mobility: "The single thing that can be distilled from all of Marey's writing is that the body is a theater of motion."[27]

Marey's graphical data served the instrumental rationality of industrial development. Taylorism was predicated on time and motion studies that allowed every task to be disassembled into its constituent parts that could be repeated, in the same way, by anyone. The *visualization* of movement was innately bound to the *regulation* of movement within the context of industrial production.

As the nineteenth century moved to a close, the body in comics was increasingly depicted as deformed by the machineries of industrialism. A growing catalog of kinetic effects, including oscillating or blurred outlines and, of course, motion lines, conveyed a stronger sense of motion but also conjured a body reacting violently to the power of technological might. "The body is experienced as machinoid or a machinable substance, and both fear and fascination reside in the artist's rendering of the body as machined almost beyond recognition,"[28] Kunzle writes. Gunning has written that Muybridge's photography captured and made visible "a drama that would otherwise remain invisible: the physical body navigating this modern space of calculation. His images of the nude human body framed within a geometrically regular grid capture the transformations of modern life brought on by technological change and the new space/time they inaugurated, as naked flesh moves within a hard-edged, rational framework."[29]

Comics also participate in this rationalist impulse to map the moving body's navigation of graphed space. The breakdown of movement that occurs in the work of Busch, Steinlen, or McCay is part of this history, blending animal locomotion with narrative and gag structures across the pages of magazines, newspapers, or storybooks. But comics do more than replicate the fixed viewpoints and measured progress of chronophotography: the humorous, or gag, strips rather consistently parody—or perhaps caricature—the worldview that underlies the visualization and analysis of movement.

The "eminent actor" striding the stage in *Punch*'s parodic "Zoöpraxiscopic" study is an early example, but he is not alone. When Wilhelm Busch uses a fixed viewpoint to chart the stages of movement, what we find is the measured onset of chaos. The mischievous crow who stars in *Hans Huckebein* (1867) systematically leaves his tracks across the clean laundry, then knocks over a row of plates and a bowlful of eggs before spilling a pail of beer down the master's boots. The final pages of the story offer a satisfying chronophotographic sequence: in eleven images Hans takes a sip of wine, tilts his head back to swallow, samples a little more, staggers about the table, teeters into a sewing kit, and, uhhh, accidentally hangs himself (Figure 6). Leaving the Teutonic sense of humor aside for the moment, what is significant is that the visualization of animal locomotion has now been appropriated to describe the *breakdown* of order and the unleashing of the forces of entropy. Something similar comes across in A. B. Frost's "Our Cat Eats Rat Poison," in which the feline's increasingly frenzied, yet measured, contortions yield to the ultimate image of its prostrate form. While these strips revel in the chaos, the final image is often one of severely restricted movement or even its complete cessation: a crow hanged, a cat poisoned, still another entangled in (and seemingly swallowed by) a ball of yarn.[30]

The Symbolist-inflected work of Willette and Steinlen in *Chat noir* was more elliptical than the comical chaos rapturously depicted by Busch or Frost. The cat playing with the ball of yarn is first entangled, then swallowed completely (Figure 7). In another of Steinlen's strips, the *chat noir* serenades a white kitty who is seen framed by a window in the otherwise minimal and amorphous space. The seductive pleas having had their effect, the white cat leaps to join this mysterious, dark

FIGURE 6. Wilhelm Busch, *Hans Huckebein,* 1867.

figure, but the leap reveals a chasm between them. In the penultimate image the white cat hangs by a claw as the *chat noir* recoils. And in the final image, the only one from a different viewpoint, the body of the white cat lies broken on the curb. Steinlen has played with the ambiguous blank spaces of the page, juxtaposing graphic and rhythmic precision with something less mimetic that no longer belongs to the objective gaze of science.[31]

But the masterpiece of comic art that demonstrates this parodic tendency most obsessively is McCay's *Little Sammy Sneeze.* The strip is organized around an invariant structure of six panels. A delicate process is delineated, step by maddening step, over the space of four panels. Sammy occupies a fixed position as he begins the stupefyingly predictable windup to his inevitable "involuntary violent expiration of air through the nose and mouth." *Sammy Sneeze*'s tagline read, "He never knew when it was coming," but the reader knew *exactly* when it was coming—panel 5! Over the first four panels Sammy's nose starts tickling him: "UM" . . . "EEE AAA" . . . "AHH AWW" . . . "KAH" . . . and finally in the fifth panel—"CHOW!" The illustration details the immediate effects of the explosion: the puzzle pieces fly, the inkpot spills,

FIGURE 7. Théophile Alexandre Steinlen, *Chat noir*, 1884.

the dinosaur skeleton collapses in a heap (as at the end of *Bringing Up Baby*) along with the music stands, stacks of canned goods, and other fine slapstick standbys. Sammy remains where he is, a stable object against the chaotic repercussions of his eponymous discharge. The final, sixth panel features either a discussion of the aftermath (How *did* good *père* Sneeze pay for all the damage?) or, more satisfyingly, somebody kicking Sammy's ass out of the room, in a pose repeated exactly from one episode to the next. In one wonderful episode Sammy holds the candle while his father struggles to repair a broken pipe in a flooded basement (Plate 7). The sneeze blows out the candle, plunging panel 5 into darkness and hiding the ensuing disaster (although an early episode, the pattern is clearly so well established that the actual image is superfluous).[32] In the most famous episode Sammy's sneeze shatters the very boundaries of the comics panel, leaving him to gaze with complete impassivity at the viewer, no doubt wondering why his surname should condemn him to such an unhygienic and antisocial existence (Figure 8).[33]

The mechanistic, unvarying structure of *Little Sammy Sneeze* presents a meticulous time-motion breakdown, usually from a fixed perspective: the dishes are set in place, the tea is poured, the cake is served, or, in four delicate panels, a bowler moves gracefully through his swing. But in every case the rhythm of efficient motion is subverted (and I use this wildly overused word carefully) by a mighty "CHOW" that turns all to chaos. And, parallel to the main action, there is the systematic registering of the sequential phases of Sammy's sneeze, offering a powerful counterlogic to the central activity of this week's episode (in much the same way as the Roadrunner's mode of being-in-the-world will present a kind of counterlogic to the Coyote's plans). The sneeze can further be understood as a complete loss of bodily control ("He just couldn't help it!"). It should also be noted that an early kinetoscope offering was *Fred Ott's Sneeze* (1894)—a violent discharge that Linda Williams has linked to the mechanistic "attraction" of the "money shot" in filmed pornography.[34]

A more nightmarish example of bodily discipline and regulation is *The Story of Hungry Henrietta* (Figure 9), perhaps the strangest work in the McCay oeuvre and surely the only comic strip I can think of about an eating disorder. In each episode a commotion is made around young Henrietta, who proceeds from infancy through girlhood over the six-month span of the series. As people cluster around her, the child understandably begins to fuss and squirm, eliciting a torrent of advice and increasing attempts to regulate her behavior. The frantic adults can't even finish their sentences: "*I think she has the colic or something or other. I guess I had better go for the—*" "*Oh dear, what do you think ails her? I'm so—so afraid—*" "*You see you've weaned her and her stomach might be in a ter—*" In the penultimate panel, the same old coot (Grandpa, I guess) proclaims that the child is simply hungry ("*I think she's alright. Yes. She's probably hungry.*"),[35] Or the adults might caper about in ever more outlandish postures, spouting infantilizing gibberish ("*Umpt tee ump te a dey ump*

FIGURE 8. Winsor McCay, *Little Sammy Sneeze*, *New York Herald*, Sept. 24, 1905.

don't you cry"). In the final panel a tear-streaked Henrietta would be pictured, isolated in high chair or seated at the table, glumly spooning up whatever she's been given to alleviate her worries. McCay even offers a crossover episode in which Sammy Sneeze does his thing all over a dish of candies, which doesn't prevent Henrietta from scarfing them off the floor in the end.[36]

The overlap of characters points to some interesting formal distinctions between the strips. Where the panels in *Sammy Sneeze* are as equally sized and fixed in

FIGURE 3. Winsor McCay, *The Story of Hungry Henrietta*, in *New York Herald* (1905).

perspective as any Muybridge sequence, *Hungry Henrietta* is usually bracketed by
two smaller panels that present the child in relative isolation (including the occasional small group). The following four panels are wider, permitting the influx of a
set of relatives or visitors who rush about manhandling the poor kid, and, as noted,
the final panel returns to Henrietta alone, horrifically (and only partially) pacified.
Where the equal sizing of panels allowed newspapers to break an episode of *Sammy
Sneeze* into two or three tiers (and sometimes only one), *Hungry Henrietta*'s layout
demands a two-tiered presentation. Henrietta is also significantly more diminutive
in the frame than Sammy (except possibly in the first and last panels) as befits her
far more passive relation to the action. While the position of the adults varies greatly
from panel to panel, the strips track Henrietta's growing agitation with terrible precision, her body rocking back and forth from one image to the next, demonstrating her inescapable constraint. The final panels, with Henrietta literally stuck in the
corner, are particularly disturbing, not only for the implied commentary on a child-
rearing going horribly wrong but also for an unmistakable resemblance to the final
panel of every episode of *Little Nemo*. There, too, a small panel, smaller than any of
the others, contains a child sometimes frightened, sometimes disappointed, but
always with his sojourns in Slumberland disrupted. The opulence of *Nemo*'s design
cannot completely hide the fact that control, attention, and distraction operate in
each of these comics, etched upon the relatively mute figure of the child.

So in place of the graphic representation of the body that serves as prelude for
that body's incorporation into the field of industrialized labor, comics continue to
map, with an identical systematicity, a process of breakdown, a pie thrown in the
face of instrumental reason. Moving from comics to cartoons, perhaps I can introduce one final version of the tension that exists in McCay's work between the control and discipline so inherent in every line that he deploys and the resistance to
discipline so manifest in his comic characters. In 1911 McCay created a truly pioneering work: an animated film of his *Little Nemo* characters. The film was released
commercially with the addition of a framing narrative in which McCay bets his colleagues that he can bring his characters to life; he can make them move (a striking
recapitulation of the wager that led to Muybridge's initial attempts to record animal locomotion). The audience watches him draw some of his characters and gets
a glimpse of the labor that goes into the creation of a sequence of animated drawings. Finally McCay screens his film. The animation is dazzling (and I will address
it in far greater detail in chapter 3), but part of its magic derives from the contrast
with the drawings that we've watched McCay produce—all profiles or frontal poses
that have nothing to do with the colorful Flip who suddenly turns smoothly toward
us to blow a voluptuous cloud of smoke in our direction. The animated figure takes
on a playful and thoroughly profound autonomy and inaugurates the battle between
cartoonist and creation that will culminate in *Duck Amuck*. Flip, the character who
continually ruins one Nemo adventure after another, emerges from, but I would

push further and claim that he in fact *eludes,* the rigidity of the chronophotograph. Flip and Sammy—smoke rings and sneezes—mark the disobedient and undisciplined body in McCay's controlled universe.

McCay is not alone in this comic assault on the disciplined and contained body. Other masters of energetic yet carefully managed mayhem include Milt Gross as well as Cliff Sterrett, whose 1920s Sunday pages for *Polly and Her Pals* burst with a light inventiveness that led Art Spiegelman to label them one of the most emblematic expressions of Jazz Age sensibilities.[37] The best-known installment centers on a fantastically sustained chronophotograph that stretches across the central seven panels, as the hapless Paw Perkins struggles along a tortuous line of identically tuxedoed theater patrons, desperately trying to bring his wife a drink of water (Plate 8). The line of men descend a staircase, recalling Marey or Duchamp; file past a water bottle like hapless workers clocking in at the factory in a set of subdivided panels that evoke the desperately blocked passage through space; and ascend the stairs once more. When a careless elbow causes Paw to spill the water, the smooth regulation of bodies gives way to, first, a cartoonishly exaggerated attack on the uncomprehending violator and then to a panel of jagged yellow and black lightning bolts intertwined with circles and snaking forms—a dazzling abstract composition that suggests Cubist collage while anticipating Abstract Expressionism and even Op Art by decades. The final panel returns to the world of figural representation as Paw sits, glaring, in a moonlit prison cell. Order—in the form of a literal stasis—is restored. As in *Little Sammy Sneeze,* chaos leads to exclusion, getting bounced, but it's too late: the damage has already been done. The rendering of movement in a synchronic graphing is here returned to the world of moving bodies and temporal duration, resulting in a line of figures locked in step within a sequence that equally suggests both motion and its negation.

Leaping forward some decades, we find Chris Ware's *Quimby the Mouse,* which appeared in multiple formats but whose most characteristic form was a large page comprising dozens of tiny (and tinier) panels. Chronophotography is invoked through the moment-to-moment transitions, the regular array of images, the fixed viewpoint (in sequences if not the entire page). One episode ("Quimby's Travelling Blues—Part Four") is billed as an "ACME Kine-comics Cut-Out Movie (Pat Pending)," a seventy-two-frame Zoöpraxiscopic sequence featuring Quimby driving his car head-on into a pole, flying through the air, and grimacing in agony.[38] Ware's comics, which frequently reference older optical toys, perhaps chart the most minute changes of state this side of Sammy Sneeze—a traffic light changes color, a character's eyes shift to the left, a tear is wiped away. The forward momentum of comics is retarded as a new paralysis takes over.

Thus comics inherit the techniques of chronophotography but frequently deploy them to parodic effect, and this tendency continues to subtend their existence through the next century. Perhaps we can find a similar mapping of spatiotemporal *illogic* in the hurled brick bopping the bean of Krazy Kat, a sustained (thirty year!) act of violence perpetrated by Ignatz Mouse that is interpreted by the Kat as an ardent gesture of love. The agent of the law, one Offisa Pup, is constantly hauling Ignatz to jail for what he clearly recognizes as a transgression of the proper order of things. But the poor Pup is condemned to perpetual bewilderment at Krazy Kat's romantic fulfillment, while Ignatz is always free to pursue his proclivity in the next day's episode. *Krazy Kat* introduces a kind of geometric plotting—the brick's trajectory ("ZIP") and impact ("POW") often occur in the same panel, along with Krazy's reaction, a transfer of kinetic energy that often takes the radiant form of an iconic heart seemingly bursting from the Kat's chest or the image of an angelic, winged Ignatz as the answer to the Kat's prayers. In any case the emphasis on the brick's transit through space is a constant (the most constant constant in the history of the medium). And finally, what could be more similar to the sporting bodies on display in the work of Muybridge and Marey than good ol' Charlie Brown's carefully prepared run up to a football that is, always and forever, destined to be snatched away at the final instant by Lucy?

The culmination of all of this can be found in the terrible logic of Chuck Jones's Road Runner cartoons—the entire enterprise smacks of scientific rationalism before overturning it with almost equal rigor. Once again, we begin with the problem of understanding bodies in motion. A Road Runner cartoon begins with at least the titular character, and often both characters, in motion and in medias res, usually midchase, and they are little more than streaks of motion against the stylized desert landscape, moving too fast for even the cinematic apparatus to map. But it is within the power of cinema, and the chronophotographic sequence before it, to permit the arresting of movement in the form of a freeze-frame that yields a detailed view of the streamlined and single-minded form of the Road Runner, who is helpfully identified for us by both vernacular name ("Road Runner") and the mock-Latin form ("Accelerati Incredibilus"). The next few seconds allow the viewer to see the Road Runner running in slow motion, the camera tracking elegantly alongside it; as in the chronophotographic sequence, movements too fast or too detailed to see clearly are presented in such a way as to become intelligible to the human eye. As Jean Epstein argued (and demonstrated), the cinema is uniquely capable of magnifying time, thereby enabling our understanding of it. But something else is happening here: the cinematic apparatus has not *recorded* the movement of the Road Runner, the better to analyze it; the apparatus has *produced* this movement. This is a construction rather than a reconstruction. The cartoon mimics, parodies, the cinema. The still image of the Road Runner (with all feet in the air, needless to say) is not a frozen moment of movement but rather the basic unit of the animated film: the single drawing.

Chuck Jones has described the initial impetus of the Road Runner cartoon to be a sort of parody, a reductio ad absurdum of the ever-popular chase cartoon. But in stripping the form to its essentials, the cartoons achieved a perfection of form: "Donald Graham, the dean of all art teachers for cartoonists, always said that cartoons were unique in the way they established space by movement. And he said that the Road Runner series was the only case that he knew in which a form moved in 'pure' space, where the space was achieved entirely by the form moving through it."[39] This recalls (or indeed anticipates) Deleuze's concept of the movement-image, which holds that "cinema does not give us an image to which movement is added, it immediately gives us a movement-image." Deleuze himself cites cartoons as exemplary of the movement-image (although later theorists have complicated this in useful ways): the cartoon is cinematic precisely "because the drawing no longer constitutes a pose or a completed figure, but the description of a figure which is always in the process of being formed or dissolving through the movement of lines and points taken at any-instant-whatevers of their course. It does not give us a figure described in a unique moment, but the continuity of the movement which describes the figure."[40] And, as Donald Graham would have it, Road Runner cartoons are the most perfect iteration of this.

Wile E. Coyote is often depicted mired in blueprints, elaborate time-motion studies aided and abetted by materials from the Acme Corporation and its various holding companies. His plans are always eminently rational, as are the cartoons themselves—Jones elaborated a number of rules that would govern the action of the cartoon: the Road Runner remains on the road and never instigates a situation; the Coyote causes his own disasters and nearly always recognizes the impending disaster a frame or two before it strikes. The Coyote's own plans are equally thought through: "1. Carry anvil out onto tightwire. 2. Drop anvil on Road-Runner. 3. Road-Runner-Burger." Sometimes the Coyote will allow himself that luxury of a written "HA HA!!" on the plans. The scenario is mapped and plotted, and X marks the spot where the bird will meet its maker. But the wire *will* stretch under the weight of the anvil until the Coyote is standing on the road instead of far above it; the Coyote *will* toss the now-useless anvil aside; the wire *will* snap back to its initial position; and the Coyote *will* shoot upward like a guided missile. The cycle repeats, forever—from gag to gag, from cartoon to cartoon. The Coyote's body is continually "machined beyond recognition," only to appear, entirely whole and unmarked, in the very next scene.[41]

The Coyote's contraptions are animated instances of Rube Goldberg's impractical, yet seemingly workable, devices for accomplishing simple tasks. Like Goldberg's inventions, the Coyote gives us the machine as ungainly assemblage rather than harmonious whole. The filmmaking also participates in an aesthetic of assemblage—Jones was openly influenced by Buster Keaton's machine-age comedy, and as in Keaton's films, the gag—and what is a gag but a machine designed to produce laughter?—often takes place across a number of shots, edited together. The machines are designed to bring down the Road Runner, but for what purpose? In some cartoons the Coyote's motives are clearly gastronomic in nature—in *Scrambled Aches* (1957), the Coyote's mock-Latin name is "Eternalii Famishiis," but if food is the goal, dynamite seems a poor choice of weapon. Jones has described the Coyote as a fanatic, in that his quest greatly transcends any rational goal. Pavle Levi has suggested that the Coyote's manifold machines pose as utilitarian, but what they really stage is the impossibility of fulfilling desire.[42] These baroque creations become ends in themselves, as irrationality masquerades as, and thus undermines, the very image of scientific rationalism. The net effect of all the meticulous preparations is always only misdirected energy, entropy, a series of steps off a cliff, and a long slow fall into oblivion.

All of this may be most pronounced in Road Runner cartoons, but it is not limited to them. What better indication of the cartoon's resistance to the rational spaces and disciplined bodies mapped by chronophotography than the phrase "cartoon physics"? The world works differently in cartoons; how differently was first systematically explored in a 1980 article in *Esquire*, "O'Donnell's Laws of Cartoon Motion," which included such postulates as:

- Any body suspended in space will remain in space until made aware of its situation.
- Any body passing through solid matter will leave a perforation conforming to its perimeter.
- All principles of gravity are negated by fear.[43]

And so forth. This list has been amended over the years to include other facts of cartoon life, including the completely valid observation that, in cartoons, holes are movable. Cartoons reverse the production process associated with chronophotography and with the cinema: rather than recording a moving world as a series of still images, a series of still images is projected in sequence to produce movement where none existed. As if in recognition of this signal difference, cartoon logic reverses, in fact *rejects,* the logic and physics of "the real world."

So the navigation of a body through measured space is carefully mapped in the comics and cartoons that follow in the wake of chronophotography, but the instrumental reason that demanded that mapping is, in so many ways, upset.

OF REVERIES, REFLEXIVITY, AND RAREBIT

"Is it nervousness, or that Rarebit?"

A day in October 1904. An elderly gent approaches an intersection that bustles with traffic. "Why this is Broadway be gosh," he remarks to himself. "Well it's t'other side of it whar I want to go." He steps into the street, only to be run down by a speeding carriage that slices his arm cleanly off. He waves after the offending vehicle. "Say you darn cuss, see what you've done. Come back here and pay for this or I'll report ya." Unfortunately, he's still in the street and now a water wagon thunders over him, severing a leg this time. Now the man is *really* angry. "I got as much right here as he has!" Sadly, a trolley plows into him, chopping his head off at the neck. The man considers calling a constable, but a motorcar smashes into whatever is left of him. "Well! I believe I see my finish at last!" But it's all been an anxious dream, dreamt by the man's wife while he slumbers, whole and intact, beside her. "I'll eat no more rabbits," she vows. "Oh!" (Figure 10).

This horrific traffic accident took place in the pages of the October 26, 1904, edition of the *New York Evening Telegram;* as the last line of dialogue reveals, it was in an episode of Winsor McCay's *Dream of the Rarebit Fiend* (one of the earliest). In the strip people of all stripes, but primarily *urbanistes,* partake of the rich, cheesy dish and, under its influence, dream away. More than any of his other strips, *Rarebit Fiend* spoke to the anxieties of the bourgeois citizens of the industrial age. This particular protagonist—can you be a protagonist of someone else's dream?—is of an earlier time, a kind of Uncle Josh of the thoroughfare.[44] He doesn't belong in a world where speed and locomotion are the order of the day.

Dream of the Rarebit Fiend appeared in the newspaper, that most emblematic of urban forms, and Ben Singer has written of the morbid fascination that American newspapers had with grisly traffic accidents—metaphors, it seems, for the collision with modernity itself.[45] The growing role of a sensationalist press was viewed as both a consequence of, and a contributor to, the stresses of urban modernity. Gregory Shaya writes that in French culture at the threshold of the twentieth century, the newspaper was regarded as "one of the most distracting of the many distractions of modern life." He notes that George Beard, in *American Nervousness,* "pointed to the railway, telegraph, telephone and the periodical press" as the primary culprits of this modern disorder; Max Nordau, in *Degeneration,* "pointed to alcohol, the city and the newspaper."[46] The newspaper was perceived—negatively—as "a mechanism of sensory stimulation" for the urban population, and this could be seen through increasingly lurid crime reporting, the growing number of illustrations (first black and white, later color), and the popularity of the brief, punchy, *fait-divers* that observed and distilled the dynamic ebbs and flows of the metropolis. Siegfried Kracauer discoursed on the transient spaces of hotel lobbies and picture palaces for the *Frankfurter Zeitung.* Such elements, Shaya argues, "had overthrown the daily order of the newspaper." Not only did the newspaper mirror the city's "phenomenal flux" in its very form; Shaya observes that, "The problem of modern life was among the favorite tropes of the press itself."[47] Illustrations in the Sunday supplements of Joseph Pulitzer's *New York World* luxuriated equally in the construction of the new subway system and the potential Armageddon of a sudden earthquake.[48]

McCay's strip, itself a kind of *fait-divers,* began its run in the *New York Evening Telegram* in 1904 as a quarter-page feature but went through a dizzying array of format and name changes, including a run in color at the *New York Herald* in 1913.

∼ Dream of the Rarebit Fiend. ∼

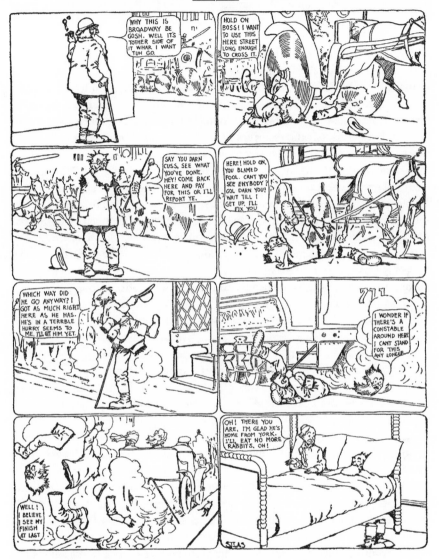

FIGURE 10. Winsor McCay, *Dream of the Rarebit Fiend, New York Evening Telegram,* Oct. 26, 1904. Courtesy Ulrich Merkl.

It was McCay's longest running strip, and versions of it appeared as late as 1924. McCay used the pen name "Silas" at the request of the *Herald*'s publisher, James Gordon Bennett, who wanted to separate this material from McCay's more kid-friendly work that was concurrently appearing in his paper.[49] The weekday strips, which appeared approximately twice a week, spun to their chaotic conclusion in about nine to twelve panels, whereas the quarter-page Saturday strips, twice as wide as the dailies, used twelve to twenty panels to extend the agony a few meticulous steps further. In later years lobster was the culprit rather than rarebit, and in other iterations of the strip the dreams had no assigned cause at all. The strip had no continuing characters, only the recurrent situation: quotidian reality gradually giving way to wilder and wilder exaggerations until the end, when the dreamer wakes.

For the most part McCay eschewed the play with panels that would characterize the slightly later *Little Nemo in Slumberland,* which I will explore in the next chapter. The frame size remains largely constant, and where, in *Little Nemo,* something growing might cause the very panels to morph and change size, in *Rarebit Fiend* the result is a more crowded frame of constant proportions. The chronophotographic influence, discussed in relation to *Little Sammy Sneeze,* remains strong: the perspective is often fixed, which emphasizes the change that occurs from one panel to the next, as objects and people variously grow and shrink, morph and transmogrify. The strip provides ample opportunities for McCay to demonstrate his prowess in depicting, in a kind of protoanimation, a smooth sequence of transitions. In this, *Rarebit Fiend* is perhaps McCay's most "cinematic" comic strip, and it was adapted to the screen by the Edison company as early as 1906.

On the comics page the rarebit fiends dream anxious dreams for an anxious age, an age of nervous disorders of all sorts ("Is it nervousness or that rarebit?" one befuddled character wonders).[50] Tom Lutz notes that neurasthenia was quite the floating signifier of fin de siècle America. It could be a sign "of either moral laxity or extreme moral sensitivity": "Whether seen as a sign of refinement and position, as a form of cultural bootstrapping, as a space for social climbers, as a disease of the shabby gentility, as a mark of distinction, a sign of social deterioration, a fearful response to modernity, or a sign of old-fashioned values, it is clear that neurasthenia helped people negotiate the large-scale changes in culture and structure which radically changed the face of social life in America between the Civil War and World War I."[51]

Its symptoms and diagnoses varied, but there was common ground; neurasthenia was readily understood as a consequence of modernity. Beard noted that modern civilization was "the chief and primary cause" of this new malady,[52] and he singled out such phenomena as noise, the telegraph, railway travel, business, "Domestic and Financial Trouble," the rapid development of new ideas, and "The Necessity of Punctuality" as contributing factors. Similarly, in Europe, Nordau observed that "even the little shocks of railway traveling, not perceived by consciousness, the perpetual noises, and the various sights in the streets of a large town, our suspense pending the sequel of progressing events, the constant expectation of the newspaper, of the postman, of visitors, cost our brains wear and tear."[53]

In Paris the first to suffer from the new breed of neurasthenic disorders were the delicate aesthetes associated with symbolism, but this "virus" was not so easily contained. Workers suffered as much as *poets maudites*. "As the typologies of the *maladies nerveuses* left the halls of the Salpêtrière and permeated the public domain," Debora Silverman writes, "the arena of susceptibility expanded; politicians, journalists, literary critics, and social theorists were faced, in the late 1880s, with the startling revelation that nervous debility was not restricted to the hothouses of literary decadence but was incubating as a collective condition."[54]

Dream of the Rarebit Fiend, although a few decades and an ocean away, expressed a similar uneasiness—or, really, a *queasiness*—about the modern world. The rarebit dreamers were haunted, it seems, by modernity, and one can find episodes that correspond to each of Beard's catalog of anxieties: A woman trails a telephone wire to find out what her late-working husband is *really* doing, betraying a suspicion of these new technologies, which both bind and separate.[55] Trains, streetcars, and automobiles are frequently encountered, oftentimes out of control: in one episode a scab worker operating an elevated train to South Ferry is unable to stop it—the train goes off the rails entirely, crashing through buildings and the Statue of Liberty before ending up in the bay.[56] In another, a man rides with a circus stunt driver and the car loops the loops, leaps over chasms, and navigates increasingly serpentine roadways as he yells to be let out: "If you were not a woman, I'd kill you!" (Figure 11).[57] Noise could be bothersome: one man daydreams of fitting his garrulous wife with a muffler designed for a riveting machine (actually, there are few strips about noise, perhaps betraying McCay's—and his medium's—visual bias).[58] Time was of the essence: a top-hatted fellow runs for his streetcar, but the street curves up around him, trapping him in a treadmill ("I do not seem to be making any headway!") in a neat metaphor for what would later be called the "rat race" (Plate 9).[59] There are new inventions, but they rarely work as advertised, or, conversely, they work too well: a woman gives her older husband a youth tablet; he regresses to handsome young manhood, but continues on through boyhood and back to infancy.[60]

Dream of the Rarebit Fiend was almost inevitably set in urban locations, at a time when anxiety about cities was rife. The city was an attractive environment, even, one suspects, for those writers who were most critical of its excesses and sought to find new rhetorics adequate to the compacted, hectic, fragmented experience of urban life. Urban populations were increasing exponentially, and in the United States and Europe this new public needed to learn the city: its scale, its pace, its relative anonymity, its fierce commercialism and congestion. And the city was often damned as the source of those nervous disorders, a site of exaggerated stimulus that defied bodily and perceptual accommodation. In his 1858 book *Paris,* Gustave Claudin

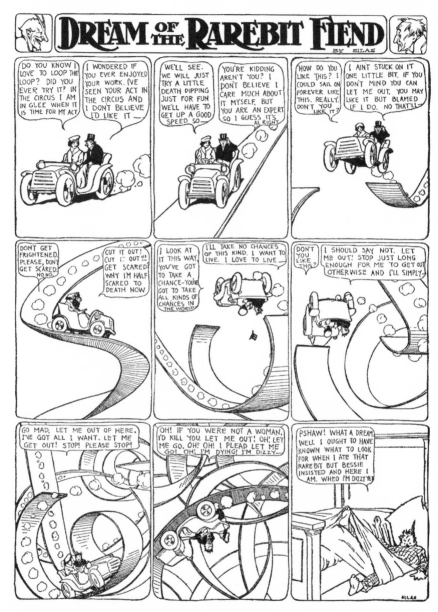

FIGURE 11. Winsor McCay, *Dream of the Rarebit Fiend*, *New York Evening Telegram*, April 19, 1905. Courtesy Ulrich Merkl.

wrote that new discoveries and technologies "bend our senses and our organs in a way that causes us to believe that our physical and moral constitution is no longer in rapport with them."[61] Ben Singer has summarized a number of distinct ways that cultural critics of the period linked the urban environment to a "recalibration of the individual's perceptual capacities": perhaps the city provided "artificial invigoration" for an exhausted populace, or maybe it further deadened the citizen's already overstimulated nerves.[62] Whatever the case—and whether or not there was any validity to the belief whatsoever—there was general agreement that the populations of Paris, Berlin, and New York were being bombarded by ever more stimuli and were thus becoming ever more susceptible to breakdown.[63]

The city was a place of business and high finance, and countless *Rarebit Fiends* detail the anxieties attendant upon those worlds. A couple is given five million dollars by Andrew Carnegie but go mad with the responsibility of it.[64] In a pointed strip that looks ahead to McCay's years as an editorial cartoonist, two men roll a gargantuan pair of dice from the roof of the stock exchange to the street below.[65] A traveling salesman dreams of hordes of eager buyers, stopping traffic and producing trainloads of orders.[66] A man rockets from New York to San Francisco to close a big deal; another has himself telegraphed to the steamship he had missed.[67] An employee goes to his boss to ask for a raise ("I must appear big and speak up"); he towers over the boss at the outset, but shrinks over successive panels while the boss looms ever larger above him (Figure 12).[68] These might be dreams of success or dreams of failure, but they are always dreams of commerce, and money, and power.

Judith O'Sullivan has pointed out that *Rarebit Fiend* featured bourgeois urban protagonists "whose fears include loss of respectability and community esteem."[69] They are frequently humiliated by the events of their dreams. An after-dinner speaker becomes more tongue-tied with every panel, while his elegant wife turns toward us in horror, buries her face in her hands, and finally rises to lead her desperately stammering, torrentially perspiring hubby away to safety, away from the public eye (This is the rare strip in which either of the main characters might be the dreamer.) (Figure 13).[70] A loose hair—a possible sign of infidelity—grows longer and longer, more and more impossible to deny, until the resulting entanglement finally swallows the couple (Figure 14).[71] And a daydreaming woman, worried whether her checkered dress is too loud for proper society, must suffer the progressive swelling of the pattern to undeniably improper proportions before she awakens in a streetcar ("I wonder if anyone noticed me! I wish I hadn't eaten that melted cheese!").[72] Writing of these anxieties around respectability and social status, O'Sullivan suggests that "These preoccupations may be in part due to the *Evening Telegram*'s practise [sic] of soliciting suggestions for 'Rarebit Dreams' from the public."[73]

Not every strip speaks immediately to the condition of modernity—many are simple metamorphosis dreams: a cute puppy grows to monstrous proportions;[74] a man in a bathtub finds himself in the open ocean.[75] Matrimonial disharmony

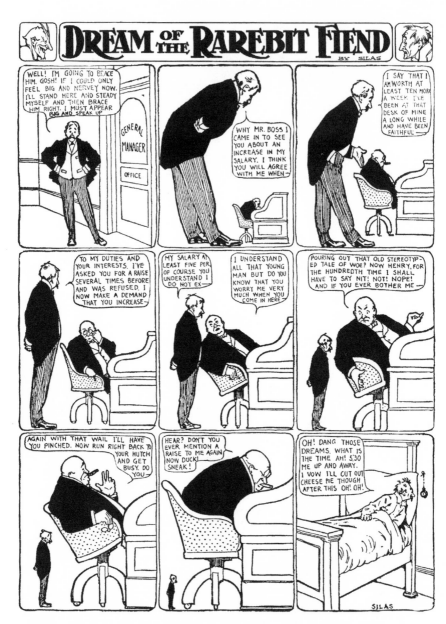

FIGURE 12. Winsor McCay, *Dream of the Rarebit Fiend*, *New York Evening Telegram*, April 26, 1905. Courtesy Ulrich Merkl.

FIGURE 13. Winsor McCay, *Dream of the Rarebit Fiend, New York Evening Telegram*, Feb. 4, 1905. Courtesy Ulrich Merkl.

FIGURE 14. Winsor McCay, *Dream of the Rarebit Fiend, New York Evening Telegram,*
March 29, 1905. Courtesy Ulrich Merkl.

was a constant theme: angry over his wife's spending, a man storms home, getting hotter and hotter until he finally bursts into some Art Nouveau–inflected flames.[76] A husband coming home late is tossed like a rag doll by his increasingly hysterical wife[77]—there are far too many to catalog. In-laws, needless to say, are incessantly targeted.

There are some happy episodes—a woman borrows millions from Morgan, Russell Sage, and Rockefeller against a mythical box of securities,[78] for example—but they are few, far between, and entirely unconvincing. More likely, a man will be tarred and feathered for revealing lodge secrets to his wife, or an increasingly desperate couple will be forced to move—to Brooklyn.[79] So much goes so terribly wrong, and so, so publicly.

Perhaps even these more straightforward strips can be seen as symptomatic of modernist ills. Neurasthenia was, after all, linked to that familiar condition of fatigue—mental fatigue, to be sure, but fatigue.[80] Beard writes that "we are under constant strain, mostly unconscious, *oftentimes in sleeping as well as in waking hours,* to get somewhere or do something at some definite moment."[81] For the rarebit dreamers, whatever the particulars of their dreams, sleep offers no respite from the day's demands; they can only struggle on.

Beard further claims that "among the signs of American nervousness specially worthy of attention [is] susceptibility to stimulants and narcotics and various drugs, and consequent necessity of temperance."[82] Nordau similarly links the disorder to addiction and narcotics: "A race which is regularly addicted, even without excess, to narcotics and stimulants in any form (such as fermented alcoholic drinks, tobacco, opium, hashish, arsenic), . . . begets degenerate descendants."[83] Why not add rarebit to that list? These are, after all, rarebit *fiends.* O'Sullivan argues that "although McCay's choice of rarebit as the dream stimulant was based on its inoffensive quality, the sophisticated nightmares thereby induced have more in common with alcoholic hallucinations than with the nocturnal terrors of childhood."[84] And it has something in common with the effects of opium: Silas himself muses at the end of one episode, "Rarebit is worse than hop!"[85]

Thomas De Quincey wrote that under the influence of opium, "whatsoever things capable of being visually represented I did but think of in the darkness, immediately shaped themselves into phantoms of the eye; and by a process apparently no less inevitable, when thus once traced in faint and visionary colours, like writings in sympathetic ink, they were drawn out by the fierce chemistry of my dreams into insufferable splendour that fretted my heart."[86] McCay, too, with his own "sympathetic ink," transformed the visible into subjective "phantoms of the eye," drawn from "the fierce chemistry" of dreams. De Quincey describes dreams in which he is "stared at, hooted at, grinned at, chattered at, by monkeys, by parroquets, by cockatoos"— an everyday occurrence for many of the eaters not of opium but of McCay's rarebit. Further, "Space swelled, and was amplified to an extent of unutterable infinity. This, however, did not disturb me so much as the vast expansion of time," and this, too, describes so many of the artist's fantasias. Small wonder, then, that like so many of the comic strip's poor dreamers, De Quincey often "awoke in struggles, and cried aloud—'I will sleep no more.'"[87]

I don't think it's too much of a stretch, then, to declare the dreamers of *Rarebit Fiend* to be, collectively, neurasthenic. The strip belongs firmly to the fin de siècle, with its concerns about overstimulation, overtaxed nervous systems, and the increasing demands of modern life. Nordau condemned the self-absorption and enervation that marked the aesthetes of his era: "With this characteristic dejectedness of the degenerate, there is combined, as a rule, a disinclination to action of any kind,"[88] and these fiends are certainly a sluggardly lot, overindulging in rich foods and dropping off, often on the job. Thus, just as Tom Lutz located various and competing understandings of neurasthenia, we can define the rarebit fiends variously: some are go-getters who continue to pursue their ambitions, even in sleep, while others are more indolent figures retreating from the demands of modernity. Nordau further fulminates: "With the incapacity for action there is connected the predilection for inane reverie."[89]

In this reading, *Dream of the Rarebit Fiend* comes off as a highly conservative enterprise, each episode exposing the protagonist to the worst excesses of modernity, as well as to the panoptic gaze of the family, the citizenry, or the constabulary (even the interested gaze of the reader of the comic strip!). The strip suggests a status quo that is humiliatingly violated, leading the protagonists into escalating agony. But there are still other ways to consider McCay's strip, ways that equally reflect the conditions of modern life and return us to the consideration of discipline and resistance encountered in the first part of this chapter.

The mechanical grind of the Fordist assembly line hardly solved the problem of fatigue, no matter how rationally organized it was. Despite the efficiency promised by the new experts, human subjects were not so easily reduced to mechanisms. Retrofitting the subject for the industrial age involved more than mapping the body; it required new means of soliciting and sustaining *attention*. The complex phenomenon of attention, understood as *directed perception*, took its place alongside the study of the body in space: controlled perception was a necessary correlate to the regulated body.

Crary takes up the phenomenon in his *Suspensions of Perception: Attention, Spectacle, and Modern Culture,* where he links the debates around the issue of attention with efforts to analyze and control the laboring body. *Suspensions of Perception* differs from his earlier *Techniques of the Observer* in its shift from visuality to "richer and more historically determined notions of 'embodiment.'"[90] In the "unbinding" of vision, new structures of obedience *and* resistance are summoned into being.[91]

As attention was being theorized by such figures as William James as pragmatic and creative, something that worked against automatism, Europe and America saw "the historical emergence of increasingly powerful technologies and institutions that would determine and enforce externally the objects of attention for mass populations."[92] The rise of Fordist production methods broke the act of labor down into a set of invariant, repetitive movements that required not thought, not the engagement of the "higher powers of mind," but precisely the mobilization of automatic stimulus-response mechanisms.

Attention and distraction provide the context for Henri Bergson's 1900 treatise on laughter, in which he wrote that "what life and society require of each of us is a constantly alert attention that discerns the outlines of the present situation, together with a certain elasticity of mind and body to enable us to adapt ourselves in consequence. *Tension* and *elasticity* are two forces, mutually complementary, which life brings into play. If these two forces are lacking in the body to any considerable extent, we have sickness and infirmity and accidents of every kind. If they are lacking in the mind, we find every degree of mental deficiency, every variety of insanity." Bergson refers to an "*inelasticity*" of character, of mind and even of body" and reminds us that "the attitudes, gestures and movements of the human body are laughable in exact proportion as that body reminds us of a mere machine."[93] Thus, well before Chaplin's 1936 film *Modern Times,* the condition of the assembly-line worker was almost innately laughable: the world of work mitigated against, selected against, elasticity in favor of a response so habituated that it hardly seemed like attention at all.[94]

Attention was constantly haunted by its dark double, *distraction.* Distraction raised the specter of breakdown, whether physiological, psychological, or technological. A careless worker could bring an assembly line to an abrupt halt, leaving the acrid stench of burning oil hanging in the factory air. City dwellers had to watch out for the traffic, the signs, and the cops, and gruesome streetcar accidents (*almost* like the one in *Rarebit Fiend*) were endemic to metropolitan life. *Distraction* was the cognitive-perceptual equivalent of *fatigue:* it posed similar problems but could also demarcate the limits of external authority. The citizen's inability to focus could be understood as passive resistance to efficiency, regulation, and the co-optation of labor, just as Anson Rabinbach later argued that the ubiquity of fatigue at the turn of the century "was evidence of the body's stubborn subversion of modernity."[95]

Distraction might also serve as the occasion for reverie. Crary suggests that the daydream constituted "a domain of resistance": regulation and discipline created conditions conducive to their own subversion.[96] For Bachelard, reverie "helps us escape time," in this case, the heavily regulated "clock time" of modernity, and this escape can be understood as a form of resistance, of liberation. The reverie exists outside clock time—it takes place in a "relaxed time" removed from the demands of production. It is "a flight from out of the real that does not always find a consistent unreal world."[97]

One last quote from Crary, then back to work—he writes that "attention always contained within itself the conditions for its own disintegration," that "it was haunted by the possibility of its own excess,"[98] and perhaps no work of popular culture spoke to that condition more clearly than *Dream of the Rarebit Fiend*. In this sense it might be productive to read these episodes less as *dreams* than as *daydreams*. A number of protagonists do awaken somewhere other than their beds (in a barber's chair, for example), and more than a few fall asleep on the job following a hefty helping of that darn rarebit. Each strip promises a metamorphosis or deformation of the real, but each is also unique—there is no "consistent unreal world," no Slumberland on the other side of the journey, no place but the place of the quotidian, newly deformed. And each provides a temporal caesura: time is indeterminate in the dream, and perhaps even more so in the daydream. A catnap might produce an epic. And for the worker zoning out on the assembly line, who can say how long a reverie lasts? These rarebit dreams might be momentary lapses or the work of an entire night. It isn't always clear. What is clear is that these dreams occur in that "relaxed time" of which Bachelard spoke.

As I have noted, the *Rarebit Fiend* strips rely on a fixed perspective (and often the characters occupy a fixed position) more than the picaresque adventures of Little Nemo, which could further suggest the fixed location of the daydreamer, whose reveries are closer to consciousness, more firmly anchored in the here and now.[99] Whether the body of the dreamer slumbers in private or public, the dreams of those rarebit fiends all begin in familiar spaces associated with everyday life. *Little Nemo* strips might open in the fabulous realm of Slumberland with the king summoning a minion to ferry Nemo or with Nemo and his friends embarked on adventures in Befuddle Hall or even on Mars, but each episode of *Rarebit Fiend* is grounded in the mundane.

The baroque fantasias of encroaching wildlife, mechanical breakdowns and the dissolution of the familiar bounds of reality, understood as reveries, begins to appear less conservative and more disobedient. Again the comic strip offers a resistance to the instrumental rationality of the waking, working life, but where *Sammy Sneeze* and *Hungry Henrietta* organized themselves around issues of *bodily* control, the hypnotic reveries that dominate *Dream of the Rarebit Fiend* enact a hallucinatory breakdown in *perceptual* control. In one episode a patient, bitten by "a mad douma," is instructed to exercise his will to resist the hallucinations that must result from the bite (Figure 15).[100] "Oh. I'll be as game as possible but it's rather tough. I am seeing all kinds of—" Meanwhile, in each image, the doctor morphs into a different fantastical beast; when he becomes a huge bird with a coiling neck and a gigantic phallic beak pointed at his patient's midsection, the patient has had enough. He can no more control his perception than Sammy Sneeze could his body.

FIGURE 15. Winsor McCay, *Dream of the Rarebit Fiend*, *New York Evening Telegram*, May 24, 1906. Courtesy Ulrich Merkl.

The fixed perspective emphasizes the gradual, if accelerating, metamorphoses. Everything is the same but for that alarmingly animate purse, or the gyrations of an automobile that moves every way but forward, or the disturbingly swelling hands that keep "Silas" from drawing today's episode.[101] From panel to panel, moment to moment, McCay builds his metamorphoses. The gradual transformation of everyday life continues, building inexorably toward chaos and breakdown. A celebrated Saturday strip from 1909 begins with a baby knocking over a small stack of blocks and culminates in whole buildings crashing into one another serially, like dominoes.[102] In its metamorphic excess the strip constantly enacts the moment when "attention inevitably reaches a threshold at which it breaks down," when "the perceptual identity of its object begins to deteriorate."[103] In many of the *Rarebit Fiend* strips a character is focused on a single object or phenomenon that grows in stature, that expands to fill the frame and the page as surely as it has filled the field of the dreamer's consciousness. There's that alligator purse that transmogrifies into an actual alligator, the tumble down the stairs that goes on forever, the stray strand of hair that becomes an impossibly tangled web.

It should be noted that most of the dreamers are unhappy with their lot—they say things like "Oh what a terrible dream!" and snarl endlessly about staying away from that rarebit. These are not quite the conscious, authored, poetic reveries that Bachelard celebrates, nor do they point the dreamer back toward the status of the child (Bachelard again). To the extent that they are real dreamers, they are helpless dreamers, as helpless as De Quincey's opium eater or any alcoholic with the DTs. Are these simply Nordau's "inane reveries," or do these reveries constitute some resistance to power's accelerating encroachment? It's not certain, and either case can be made. What is clear, however, is that these dreams and daydreams are the side effects of modernity's demands and stresses; despite their involuntarism, they operate at or even beyond the limits of external control. They are, each of them, small acts of misperception, perceptual misbehaviors.

But the fact is, they are *not* real dreamers; they are rather functions of McCay's (and his readers') playful imaginations, and we would be remiss not to consider the *playfulness* of *Dream of the Rarebit Fiend*. Johan Huizinga describes the mental play involved in mythopoesis, the "tendency to create an imaginary world of living beings (or perhaps: a world of animate ideas)," and the notion of play as an animating force tells of something about *Rarebit Fiend*'s own animistic spirit. "Which of us," Huizinga asks, "has not repeatedly caught himself addressing some lifeless object, say a recalcitrant collar-stud, in deadly earnest, attributing to it a perverse will, reproaching it and abusing it for its demoniacal obstinacy?"[104] This is the strategy of many a rarebit dream: landscapes and purses, streets and streetcars, hair and hands, all exhibit an unaccustomed willfulness that puts them at odds with their ostensible masters. But taken in toto, *Dream of the Rarebit Fiend* conveys the sense that it is the modern world itself, in its overwhelming entirety, that exhibits that "demoniacal obstinacy," putting Silas's dreamers through continuing hell but giving Silas's readers continuing pleasure.

> "I do most certainly love my wife, but oh! this guy Silas!"

Dream of the Rarebit Fiend is at its most playful when it refers to itself, which it did quite often. Ulrich Merkl catalogs thirty-two episodes of self-referentiality, and there are still more that play with the conventions of the medium of comics. This play takes several forms.[105] Numerous episodes refer to the *Rarebit Fiend* comic strip, with characters declaring that they should send their dreams to Silas. Silas himself is the dreamer in a half dozen strips—in one he gets a swelled head as a result of all the compliments he is receiving for his vaudeville act (Figure 16).[106] Not all his dreams are of glory, however: in one strip his hands become useless, jellylike appendages, forcing him to draw with his feet.[107]

A few strips acknowledge the presence of the reader. One rather chilling example has a seemingly drunken character aware that he's being observed (Figure 17). He moves into the extreme foreground, and it becomes clear that he is addressing the reader directly: "You, I mean—holdin' thu paper!" A newsie comes up, and asks him, "Have they got you in a rarebit drawing?" Then *he* addresses the reader: "I sold you that paper, eh? Didn't I?" A crowd gathers; the man grows increasingly irate. Finally he takes off his coat and threatens: "Turn over to the news part of the paper or off comes your block!" And, indeed, he punches the reader: a massive fist approaches, followed by the explosion of the blow. The dreamer wakes; he has indeed fallen asleep reading his paper.[108]

The most striking examples meditate on the material base of the medium itself. A man dreams that he is a fashion drawing illustrating men's fashion, but, thanks to a sloppy artist, he becomes increasingly ink spattered as the strip progresses (looking at the original artwork, one marvels at these impeccably drawn spatters) (Figure 18).[109] In another episode the panels collapse about a man who only wants a good night's sleep. "Silas forgot to fasten these panels," he complains, as he endeavors to tack the corners back into place.[110] There is a strip in which an ardent wooer, jealous of his fancy's love of Silas, tears the very comic strip in which they appear to shreds—the penultimate panel is just a pile of ripped up paper (Figure 19).[111] A man on his wedding day is drawn with less and less detail until he resembles a child's crude drawing (it seems that Silas has been sick).[112]

Some episodes put the creator and his creation at odds with one another. In a strip that anticipates Buster Keaton's *Sherlock Jr.* the scenery that a painter is trying to capture arbitrarily changes: it's a mountainscape, then a swamp, a city, and finally a farm. "Aw! I'm going home—I'm no lightning artist!"[113] (Of course, McCay, the tormentor, *was* a lightning artist.) In the capriciousness of these various mutations, as well as in the growing frustration of the artist, the strip also prefigures *Duck Amuck*, which begins with Daffy trying to adjust to the shifting backgrounds behind him.

FIGURE 16. Winsor McCay, *Dream of the Rarebit Fiend*, *New York Evening Telegram*, Nov. 22, 1906. Courtesy Ulrich Merkl.

FIGURE 17. Winsor McCay, *Dream of the Rarebit Fiend*, *New York Evening Telegram*, March 14, 1908. Courtesy Ulrich Merkl.

FIGURE 18. Winsor McCay, *Dream of the Rarebit Fiend*, *New York Evening Telegram*, March 30, 1907. Courtesy Ulrich Merkl.

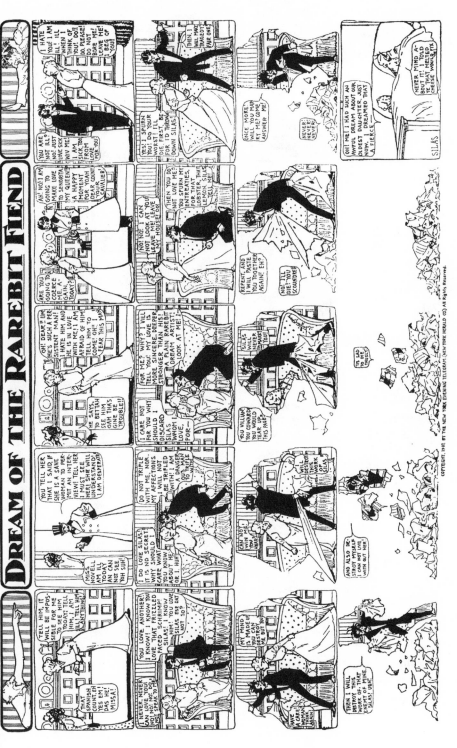

FIGURE 19. Winsor McCay, *Dream of the Rarebit Fiend*, *New York Evening Telegram*, Nov. 9, 1907. Courtesy Ulrich Merkl.

FIGURE 20. Winsor McCay, *Dream of the Rarebit Fiend, New York Evening Telegram,*
May 28, 1908. Courtesy Ulrich Merkl.

Duck Amuck is also foreshadowed in a strip in which a man peers around the panel
boundary and sees himself in the next panel (Figure 20). Each thinks the other is
someone else rather than multiple iterations of a single self, and they do battle; in
the Jones cartoon the slippage of the image frame gives us two Daffy Ducks and a
similar ontological dilemma.[114]

This lengthy review serves to demonstrate not just that reflexive gags were a prominent part of McCay's strip but that there was an almost systematic exploration of reflexivity itself. Self-reference extended from mentions of the author to his actual presence as a character, from the pen-and-ink characters to the flesh-and-blood reader, and to the various aspects of the medium of the comics. The playful images that *are* the comics now extends to images that play with their very status *as* comics.

McCay is probably not the first comic artist to play in this manner, and he is surely not the last. It seems as though reflexivity is almost endemic to the media of comics and cartoons. Certainly every medium has its share of metatextual reflection—the tradition extends at least as far back as *Don Quixote* (a coyote in the deeply reflexive Krazy Kat is named Don Kiyote) and the anamorphic insertions found in Renaissance painting. The cinema hardly wants for reflexive exercises. Yet comics and cartoons seem particularly given to this sort of play. One could provisionally offer several reasons for this predilection. The great majority of reflexive work in the comics is, well, *comical,* and comedy has always been a haven for reflexivity. Film comedy often refers to the cinematic apparatus, a kind of return of the repressed, as in many films with or by Hope and Crosby, Bugs Bunny, Mel Brooks, Frank Tashlin, and Jerry Lewis.

Formally, comics and cartoons are less beholden to mimesis than many other forms of pictorial representation. From the time of Töpffer, comics were characterized by simplified lines to be produced and consumed quickly. The anti-illusionistic devices of reflexivity, such as breaking the fourth wall or acknowledging the unreality of the drawing, are less disruptive in the comics than they would be elsewhere. The "walls" represented by the panel boundaries are evidently drawn and, as such, can be easily erased. And while there is a long tradition of what Paul Wells calls "realist" animation, which is mimetic of live-action filmmaking in its use of lighting, camera angles, and the stability of form, other traditions, including what Sianne Ngai terms "animistic animation," emphasize mutability, metamorphosis, and continual transformation.[115] McCay animated a dinosaur precisely *because* nobody could photograph one.

I would also suggest that the status of the comics image—which, since Töpffer, has been understood to be poised somewhere between writing and drawing— becomes a very personal mode of inscription. The rest of the newspaper is typeset, but the comics are the direct product of the artist's hand. In animation it is common practice for animators to use mirrors to model facial expressions and postures for themselves (more on this in chapter 3). These are very intimate modes of creation, and it's easy to understand the temptation to "put a bit more of oneself" into the work, sometimes literally.

Characters in cartoons and comics are also cursed by never being quite complete: there will be another picture of him, her, or it in the next panel (or frame), and in the next after that. They are quite obviously not the masters of their fate and exist at the behest of the constantly inscribing and reinscribing creator. Each image modifies the last; therefore, nothing is inviolate. This power is made explicit in *Duck Amuck*, as Bugs Bunny puts Daffy through his paces, and it's evident in *Rarebit Fiend*: a married man dreams that Silas is drawing him having good times with a variety of comely young women ("I do most certainly love my wife, but oh! this guy Silas!"), but the artist betrays him at the end by drawing his wife into the scene (Figure 21).[116] The hand has the power both to build a world and to destroy it.

Reflexivity also marks the inscription of the author in the work, whether as an active force (the person behind the pencil), a character in the strip, or as the creator of a widely circulating comic strip. In this, *Rarebit Fiend* prefigures his animated films, three of which show McCay producing the drawings that the cinematic apparatus will then, in his absence, animate (in a later chapter, we will consider the dialectics of appearance and disappearance in early animated films, films that insist on human creators before effacing and erasing them from the scene). Here, too, McCay continually reveals himself, reaching out to "own" the comic strip, insisting on its provenance and returning him to the scene as an active, ongoing participant in the consumption of the strip. Recall that McCay had a very popular vaudeville act (repeatedly referenced in *Rarebit Fiend*), performing as a lightning sketch artist on the New York stage. His presence in the strip, then, is something of a vaudevillian turn: the performer demonstrating, *performing*, his mastery with virtuosic flourish. This is the hand of Silas, the hand of the genius McCay, which conjures the fantastic from the mundane. Do *not* ignore that man behind the curtain. In the strip about the philandering husband Silas's hand is visible in each panel—in the first it is the only visible object, poised before the white surface (this is two years before McCay's hand will "star" in his *Little Nemo* film).

The insertions of McCay or "Silas" into the proceedings constitute a kind of vaudeville performance akin to what Neil Harris has called an "operational aesthetic"—a performance that makes the work of creating the comic strip visible (or at the very least acknowledges that the comic strip was, in fact, "made").[117] But in another sense McCay here becomes a figure not just of modernity but of modernism. Reflexivity introduces an instability into the text: it no longer follows its own rules, describing an everyday world deformed by dreams; now it exposes itself as a comic strip posing as a dream record. The imagination stands revealed, not as that of the dreamers but of the Dreamer, McCay, and the materials of production are not that gooey substance known as Welsh Rarebit, but rather the tools of the artist's trade: pen, ink, and Bristol board.

In these examples McCay permits his text to vacillate between representation and a critique of representation. This is a ludic reflexivity. Robert Stam writes, "Like gods at play, reflexive artists see themselves as unbound by life as it is perceived (Reality), by stories as they have been told (Genre), or by nebulous probability (Verisimilitude)." What they create "is not subject to the laws of sublunary nature;

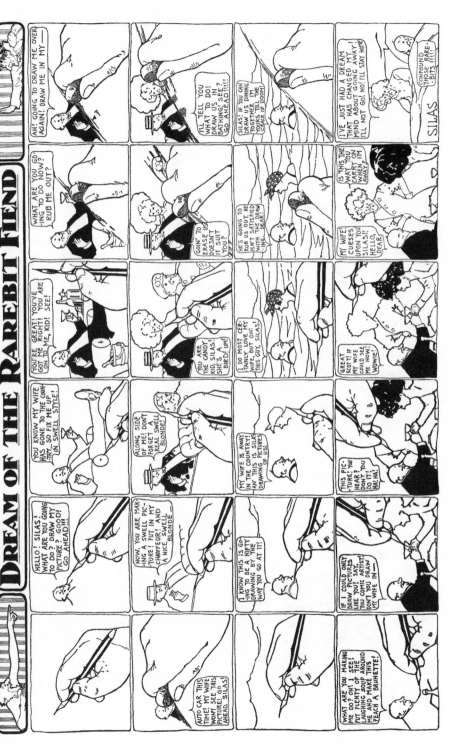

FIGURE 21. Winsor McCay, *Dream of the Rarebit Fiend*, *New York Evening Telegram*, July 31, 1909. Courtesy Ulrich Merkl.

it is subject, ultimately, only to the constraints of language itself."[118] This is not the "didactic" demystification of medium practiced (at times) by Brecht and Godard—clearly. And it is far from the "aggressive" assault on the audience that features in films by, say, Buñuel, although it *is* rather disturbing to be threatened by a comic-strip character who tries to knock my block off. Another strip uses first-person perspective to give us, literally, a corpse's eye view, from the botched operation that kills him, through the funeral procession, through the burial, all the while hearing the nasty things said by family and friends—actually, this isn't so far from Buñuel, at that.[119]

Earlier I characterized the (day)dreams of the rarebit fiends as disobedient acts, a resistance through misperception, but now it should be said that these strips are themselves disobedient, cheerfully undermining their own structures and conventions. This is what Steven Millhauser understands about McCay when he describes *Figaro's Follies*, a comic strip by his own animator/artist J. Franklin Payne. The comic strip featured a clownish monkey who would play with the panel boundaries in a different way in each strip: "In the first panel of the first strip, Figaro was shown in jail. In the next four panels, the monkey sawed through the frame of the panel and escaped; in the last panel, he stood on top of the cartoon frame."[120] *Figaro's Follies* is clearly about escape: escape from the little boxes that contain us. It reminds me of (and was perhaps inspired by) a Winsor McCay strip of unknown provenance: it depicts a clown who unravels the lines that bound his frame; finding himself now suspended in a white void, he turns away from the reader and disappears into a hole in the whiteness. *Dream of the Rarebit Fiend*, too, can be said to turn on this same set of dialectics: oscillating between waking and dreaming, stasis and metamorphosis, containment and release.

American Dreamers

The recurring appearance of "Silas" suggests that there is one other dreamer involved in *Dream of the Rarebit Fiend*, and that is its creator, Winsor McCay. In his film appearances, self-representations, and even a fictional manifestation McCay appears as a prodigious, and particularly American, dreamer—more human motor than decadent neurasthenic.

For Nordau, the European, neurasthenia was the pathology that defined the "degenerate" arts of European fin de siècle culture, whereas for Beard, as the title of his study suggests, neurasthenia was preeminently American and functioned, at least in part, as a sign that American civilization was, simply, the most advanced. Understand the disease in America, he held, and you understand it everywhere. "All this is modern, and originally American; and no age, no country, and no form of civilization, not Greece, nor Rome, nor Spain, nor the Netherlands, in the days of their glory, possessed such maladies. Of all the facts of modern sociology, this rise and growth of functional nervous disease in the northern part of America is one of the most stupendous, complex, and suggestive."[121] Some of the rarebit fiends, the indolent ones, fit neatly in Nordau's worldview, while others, the ambitious dreamers, are a more congenial fit with the more energetic and productive American nervousness.

American nervousness fed, and was fed by, American progress. The United States, after all, has always been a nation of crazy dreamers: crazy dreamers going west, inventing a nation, reinventing themselves. Here, dream stands not for indolence or sloth, escape or decadence, but for a creative engagement with the world, an imaginative engagement that has an effect on the world, that, it can be said, builds a world. Steven Millhauser's novel about the designer/world-builder Martin Dressler is subtitled, *The Tale of an American Dreamer,* and in "The Little Kingdom of J. Franklin Payne" the American dreamer is a thinly disguised version of Winsor McCay: a feverishly inventive comic strip artist and animator.

Millhauser has produced a unique body of work, although Jorge Luis Borges and Italo Calvino serve as fair comparisons. He is, like McCay, concerned less with character than with systems and structures, and his protagonists tend to be dreamers, inventors, and designers. Such eclectic and uncanny phenomena as dime museums, amusement parks, cat-and-mouse cartoons, and automaton theaters are at the center of his narratives, and his stories often take the form of dispassionate, almost clinical, descriptions of mechanical marvels and built environments—a stance that might also be said to mark McCay.

Payne, like McCay, has multiple strips running concurrently. His first successful strip, *Dime Museum Dreams,* is a neat amalgam of *Sammy Sneeze* and *Rarebit Fiend:*

> The format was invariable: in the first panel an unnamed boy was seen holding his mother's hand—nothing was shown of the mother except her hand and forearm— and staring at an exhibit in the dime museum. . . . In the next three panels the freakish creature became more and more frightening . . . until in the fifth, climactic panel the height of horror was reached and the boy shrieked out in terror. In the last panel the exhibit had returned to its original shape, while the boy sobbed against his mother's leg and listened to her words of comfort.[122]

Later, Payne introduces *Phantom of the City,* a "hymn to the city" that, with rich architectural detail, explores hidden urban spaces in each weekly episode, and *Figaro's Follies,* a reflexive enterprise featuring a monkey that played with the borders of the panels that composed the strip itself.

Payne is a noctambulist, prowling his own little kingdom while everyone else sleeps. He spends his nights producing the thousands of drawings for increasingly elaborate animated films. Taking a break, he steps from his window onto a sloping roof and, by the light of the moon, perambulates around his house and whispers, "I'm only a dream."[123]

In some ways "The Little Kingdom of J. Franklin Payne" operates as something like an American *À rebours*, J.-K. Huysmans's scandalous novel of 1884, which Nordau viewed as emblematic of fin de siècle decadence and solipsistic withdrawal. *À rebours* featured an aristocratic aesthete, Duc Jean Floressas des Esseintes, of unusual sensitivity: hypochondriac and neurasthenic, he exists in "such a state of nervous sensitivity that the sight of a disagreeable person or thing was deeply impressed upon his mind and it took several days even to begin removing the imprint."[124] Overwhelmed and "weighed down by spleen," he chooses to withdraw from the overstimulating world of human commerce and congress. He retires to a secluded villa, whose windows he entirely covers and whose interior he obsessively designs to precisely order every sensory encounter: color, smell, taste, and sight. Before his retreat he famously throws a funeral dinner in which everything—the approach to the house, the décor of the dining room, the dishes and glassware, even the food itself—is black. He creates, through the use of a porthole, an aquarium with tinted waters and mechanical fish, and assorted railway timetables and barometers, an environment suited to a kind of virtual travel that dispensed with the discomforts of the real thing—imagination providing a "more than adequate substitute for the vulgar reality of actual experience." Huysmans writes, "Artifice was considered by Des Esseintes to be the distinctive mark of human genius."[125] This quest of Des Esseintes, to establish complete aesthetic control over all aspects of his existence, represented for Nordau the most decadent of worldviews (recognizing irony is not, it seems, one of Nordau's strengths).

Payne increasingly withdraws from the world of commerce as well, reveling in the artificial worlds his pencil conjures, whether in comic strips or the drawings for his animated films. Millhauser writes of Payne's "need to escape from the constriction of physical things into a world entirely of his own devising," which echoes Des Esseintes's retreat from Paris to the carefully controlled environment of his villa.[126] But unlike his European counterpart, the American Payne equally needs the solidity of the real—reality and irreality must maintain a balance. And where Des Esseintes is singularly unproductive of anything but his own living environment, Payne does nothing *but* produce: comic strip after comic strip, and animations of increasing ambition and perfection.

Millhauser's *Martin Dressler* functions even more clearly as an American *À rebours*. The book is ostensibly a novel, but it is remarkable more for its cataloging of the various, increasingly opulent, environments that Dressler designs and builds. Dressler is characterized not by nervous sensitivity but by nervous energy, a restlessness born of the sense that he is meant to be doing "something else, something grander, higher, more difficult, more dangerous, more daring." Dressler is drawn to hotels and department stores, each of which "sought to be a little world in itself," and his aesthetic centers on what an architect refers to as "the enclosed eclectic."[127] His ever more wondrous creations—part hotel, part housing, part amusement center, part park, part theater, part commercial district—become increasingly dedicated to the unpredictable and the surprising. (I don't know whether Millhauser drew on Rem Koolhaas's *Delirious New York,* but his novel revives a similar sense of the city as fundamentally irrational.) Dressler's is a control that eludes control, that becomes something of its own, an animate space with a life of its own.

J. Franklin Payne loses everything as he sinks ever more deeply into his own obsessive act of creation, this construction of another world—his wife, his best friend, his comic strips (like McCay, his publisher presses his talents into the service of the real rather than the unreal and has him drawing editorial cartoons instead of his creations). But the production of his cartoon provides relief and release from all that: "He sank back into his black-and-white world, his immobile world of inanimate drawings that had been granted the secret of motion, his death-world with its hidden gift of life."[128] These drawings are the product of the night; while everyone else dreams, Payne creates a dream that becomes a new reality. Des Esseintes is also engaged in the creation of a substitute reality, first with opiates then without: "The secret lies in knowing how to proceed, how to concentrate deeply enough to produce the hallucination and succeed in substituting the dream reality for the reality itself."[129] They are strange bedfellows, Payne and Des Esseintes, yet they are engaged in similar projects, just spun differently. In fact, in their desire to impose an aesthetic vision upon a misunderstanding world, they both resemble protagonists in a Vincente Minnelli melodrama, and we should pause to consider just how right Minnelli would have been as the director of choice for an adaptation of *À rebours*— especially the "black dinner" sequence.

It would be wrong to say that where Des Esseintes seeks solitude, Payne has it thrust upon him—one's monomania seems as self-willed as the other's—just as it would be wrong to see one as emblematic of industry and the other of indolence. They are both dreamers, yet it is possible to understand Payne as an *American* dreamer in that his dream extends beyond himself—he creates something that takes on a life of its own, even if that life has the most profound meaning for the dreamer/ creator himself: "It was desperately important to smash through the constriction of the actual, to unhinge the universe and let the impossible stream in, because otherwise—well, otherwise the world was nothing but an editorial cartoon."[130] Whereas Des Esseintes is subject to "a whole cavalcade of dreams to which he passively submitted, without even trying to get away,"[131] like De Quincey's powerless opium eater, Payne draws, using that "sympathetic ink," to, again, objectivize the subjective in visual terms and permit fantasy to enter the world of things with a life of its own.

In the final chapter of *Degeneration* Nordau foresees the end of the decadent strain: these artists, he holds, cannot reproduce themselves and so must die out in favor of a heartier sort: "Let us imagine the driveling Zoroaster of Nietzsche, with his cardboard lions, eagles, and serpents, from a toyshop, or the noctambulist Des Esseintes of the Decadents, sniffing and licking his lips, or Ibsen's 'solitary power-ful' Stockmann, and his Rosmer lusting for suicide—let us imagine these beings in competition with men who rise early, and are not weary before sunset, who have clear heads, solid stomachs and hard muscles: the comparison will provoke our laughter."[132] Let us imagine, in other words, the European decadence that (Nordau imagines) is Des Esseintes in competition with "the human motor" that is Franklin Payne or, if we call him by his right name, the American dreamer Winsor McCay.[133]

Chapter 2

THE MOTIONLESS VOYAGE OF LITTLE NEMO

Ink, with its powers of alchemistic dyeing, its colorative life, is capable, if it but find its dreamer, of creating a universe.
—GASTON BACHELARD, *THE RIGHT TO DREAM*

THE WORLD OF PICTURES

"In one of [Hans Christian] Andersen's tales," Walter Benjamin tells us, "there is a picture book that cost 'half a kingdom.' In it, everything was alive." Benjamin faults Andersen for missing one key detail: the inhabitants of that wondrous book step from its pages to greet the child reader; in reality, Benjamin argues, it is the *reader* who crosses the threshold, who "enters into those pages." That reader "becomes suffused, like a cloud, with the riotous colors of the world of pictures. . . . He overcomes the illusory barrier of the book's surface and passes through colored textures and brightly painted partitions to enter a stage on which fairy tales spring to life."[1]

I would, in turn, fault Benjamin's faulting of Andersen's tale for, again, missing one key detail. For what I see, in something like Winsor McCay's *Little Nemo in Slumberland,* is an operation of reciprocity: the vivacious inhabitants of Slumberland solicit Nemo and, with him, the reader; they reach *out* to invite us *in* to that splendid otherworld. Fictional characters and flesh-and-blood readers are equally activated by this address.

Benjamin's brief meditation, "A Glimpse into the World of Children's Books," is also a glimpse into the practice of reading those books. Benjamin is struck by the range of activities called forth: these books demand interaction, activation, completion. There are levers to be operated, doors to be opened, questions to be answered, and, in the case of black-and-white pages, coloring to be done. The child is immersed in the book; it becomes a bit of a world, an intimate space, that is also a space of discovery, a place of safety and secrets.

In a different essay Benjamin celebrates the rich illustrations adorning older children's books, illustrations that stood apart from the pedantic lessons that the texts ostensibly sought to impart. The child was distracted, properly, by these gluttonous, sumptuous images, which fed the imagination. With more than a touch of envy, Benjamin proclaims, "This resplendent, self-sufficient world of colors is the exclusive preserve of children's books,"[2] to which I must add the later medium of the Sunday comics supplement (and, later still, comic books and, still later, "graphic novels"). And, in that comics supplement, Winsor McCay was deploying some very seductive colors and enacting some very sophisticated forms of address in his quest to draw both Nemo and the reader into the magic of Slumberland.

LIVELY BERRIES

A *Little Nemo* episode from 1908 is set not in Slumberland but seemingly in Nemo's back garden (Plate 10). It begins with Nemo talking to his mother—the first clue that Nemo is dreaming, since the parents are usually relegated to the status of off-screen voices telling Nemo to go back to sleep. Nemo is sad to be without his friend, the princess of Slumberland, and to console him, his mother sends him out back to the family's vegetable garden. Awaiting him there is Flip, his friend and nemesis from the wonderful land of dreams, who accompanies him on a stroll through the patch. Flip notices the increasing size of the vegetables: the cabbages, rutabaga, and other assorted fruits and veggies start out a bit larger than usual but finally become gigantic. In typical McCay fashion the very panels of the Sunday page grow to accommodate each new and increasingly huge plant. The final tier is dominated by Nemo's and Flip's encounter with some massive blackberries and raspberries. They tower over Flip and Nemo, forming an arbor: the panels stretch vertically above them, emphasizing the high, vaulted space. Across this four-panel tier the berries grow visibly larger from panel to panel. Flip climbs a plant to get some raspberries, and in the penultimate panel they come tumbling down, sending Flip flying and bopping Nemo on the bean. (Of course, the final panel gives us Nemo, awakened from his dream, tossed to the floor in a tumble of bedding).[3]

Throughout this episode the plants have been visibly growing behind them, but these blackberries and raspberries metamorphose most dramatically from one panel to the next, becoming as large as Flip and Nemo themselves. And although Flip announces that he will shake the plants to dislodge their fruit, we never see him do this; they actually seem to fall of their own volition. These berries are highly animated entities; to quote Alexander Nemerov, they are "very lively—too lively."[4]

Nemerov, however, was not referring to *these* berries but to *another* set of imaged berries, painted in this case by Raphaelle Peale. Nemerov devotes two chapters of his study of Peale to the *Blackberries* still life, concentrating on their strangely vivacious presence and some of the resulting phenomenological implications. More than simply an image of an animate nature, these berries, says Nemerov, citing Abrams's discussion in *The Mirror and the Lamp,* are infused with life by "the projective intelligence of the poet"—or, in this case, painter.[5] And the artistic sensibility could spread to others. Writing of a figure he named "The Rhapsodist" in 1789, Charles Brockden Brown declared: "To his strong and vivid fancy, there is scarcely a piece of mere unanimated matter existing in the universe."[6] These animated berries are a projection of an animated, animating, imaginative spirit, a spirit that was not regarded as altogether healthy. Someone's "rhapsodic imagination" was someone else's " 'ill-regulated imagination'—the property of unschooled, undisciplined, and altogether unenlightened minds."[7] Nemerov argues that "against the discourse of rationality, Raphaelle's picture, with its lively berries, introduces the irresponsible play of imaginative freedom alleged to emerge when one was alone."[8]

Despite the undeniable facts that raspberries are not blackberries and Winsor McCay is not Raphaelle Peale, I cannot resist the urge to compare Peale's berries (via Nemerov) and McCay's berries (via Nemo). While I don't pretend to know whether McCay knew or cared about Peale's work, there are some striking formal, as well as thematic, resemblances. Nemerov discusses the way the berries are arrayed in Peale's painting: somewhat more distant on the right side of the frame than on the left, giving the viewer the sense of a procession (Plate 11). The red berries dominate the right side, the black berries the left. In McCay's strip this same balance occurs, but the arrangement is reversed: the smaller (black) berries are in the left panel, and they increase in size toward the red ones on the right, providing a similar sense of composition and movement. In the painting, movement is suggested, while in the comic strip it is literal—the berries are indeed getting larger— but in strictly formal terms it is easy to see the berries as similarly arrayed from distant berries on one side to more proximate ones on the other. Nemerov points to the uncanny sense of the berries hovering, as well as a feeling that they extend outward to a space shared by the painting's spectator, and these are sensations that are amplified by the *Little Nemo* strip (McCay's berries seem to *lunge* more than *hover*).

Peale's berries are vivified by the "undisciplined" sensibility of the artist, while McCay's berries are animated by the undisciplined mind of the sleeping Nemo. The state of childhood, then, carries with it some resemblance to the character of artistic imagination, and Nemerov makes this point at the conclusion to his chapter, citing Bryan Wolf's evocation of Washington Irving's characters as "resolutely comic and undomesticated, perpetual children," a status that perhaps demarcates a site of resistance to "the encroachments of commercial society."[9] Nemerov then argues that *Blackberries* "creates the fiction of a child-like subject, a hermetic imaginer, refusing the rational standards of the new individuality. It constructs a subject whose mind, more than his appetite, is prone to ill-regulation. . . . And this wild 'fancy,' this solitary sense of play, exerts an uncanny force, giving the world of selfhood a twinkling image of the childishness it cannot express."[10]

Again, the relevance to Nemo, and, indeed, to McCay's other major fantasia, *Dream of the Rarebit Fiend* (a saga of ill-regulated appetites), is striking. While *Lit-*

tle Nemo is a product of commercial culture—a comic strip designed to showcase the color printing presses of the newspaper syndicate—it evokes the world of childhood as an escape from the earthly bonds of rationality, regulation, and discipline. These berries are unleashed by the mind of an artist creating a fiction of a child-subject whose dreams become a licensed site of playful disobediences and misbehaviors. If McCay's work belongs to a different historical moment and occupies a rather different place in the social sphere, it nevertheless seems to partake of a similar animating spirit, deployed in a similar fashion, to similar ends.[11] (A distinction should be made, however, between the "licensed" dreams of Nemo in the "proper" realm of Slumberland and the less reputable dreaming that haunts those rarebit eaters—recall that the latter frequently present nightmarish scenarios of public humiliation, and even the act of dreaming seems a source of embarrassment.)

This suspicion of the ill-regulated, playful spirit acknowledged by Nemerov, Wolf, and others coincides with Sianne Ngai's "animatedness," which she describes as an "exaggerated emotional expressiveness."[12] Again there is the somewhat suspect status of a being that offers itself up, at least in part, as an alternative to authority, discipline, and control. And of course the animated body is encountered most frequently in cartoons, which belong to the realm of childhood, apart from "adult" norms.

Nemerov continues his analysis of *Blackberries* with a discussion of the tactile vision that began to be undermined, as Crary demonstrates in *Techniques of the Observer,* in the mid-nineteenth century. Paraphrasing Merleau-Ponty, Nemerov writes that "to see is to see with our body, projecting it out ahead of ourselves, as a kind of emissary through which the world becomes palpable."[13] Subject and object cannot be entirely separable. Again, this has some relevance to Nemo's berries. While the narrative holds that the berries are growing, the visual effect is rather one of magnification. The berries become larger and larger in ways that suggest either that we are approaching them or, more disturbingly, the reverse—in any case, the change of scale is easily read as a change of proximity.

At this point it becomes necessary to point to the different sizes of Peale's canvas and McCay's comic strip. *Blackberries* is a small, intimate still life (7.24" high by 10.24" wide): the viewer of the painting must approach it, must enter, or approach, its space. *Little Nemo* was printed at full broadsheet size (about 20" by 14") and was designed to be engaged with at no more than arm's length (and perhaps a child's arm, at that). Generous selections of *Little Nemo* strips have recently been republished at their original size, and their restored scale packs a surprising wallop.[14] One does not just read *Little Nemo,* or look at it; rather, one falls into it. This is, to a degree, simply a matter of size alone, aided in no small measure by the voluptuous coloring and decorative, ornamental richness. But it also has something to do with what McCay does with that enormous space.

Thierry Smolderen has rather aptly compared the Sunday tabloid-sized comics of that early era to wallpaper: many strips featured more or less uniform-sized panels, arrayed horizontally and vertically in a set of squares or rectangles, mimicking, to a degree, Muybridge's chronophotographic arrays. The framing of these "wallpaper comics" remains largely similar from beginning to end, so the overall appearance resembles a printed pattern.[15] (Of course, there are multitudes of variations within any given comic, but as a generalized abstraction of the appearance of the Sunday comics, Smolderen's analogy is certainly valid.) A good example of this approach would be McCay's own half-page *Sammy Sneeze,* with its unvarying perspective, equally sized panels, and repeated background.

Yet the berries episode of *Nemo* (and, in fact, many *Nemo*s) offers something very different: the berries episode, while maintaining some regularities (the graduated height of each tier, the frontal perspective on the rows of vegetables, the positioning of Nemo and Flip), also introduces significant irregularities or imbalances. The eye is inexorably drawn across the page and down to the giant tumbling berries, which seem to leap outward from the surface of the page, to a third dimension (the space already inhabited by the reader). The eye thus takes an imaginary, motionless voyage across both lateral and axial spaces. Eye and berry reach across the void toward one another in a gesture of mutual exploration and discovery.

The phrase "motionless voyage" comes from Noël Burch, who has used it in connection with early cinema.[16] The "voyage" is taken by the mobilized gaze of the spectator into a perceived depth.[17] Despite the arresting sensation of a deep space experienced by the earliest spectators of the Lumière locomotive pulling into the station at La Ciotat, the staged films that followed were striking in their depthlessness. As Burch notes, the predominance of even illumination, fixed (and frontal) camera positions, painted backdrops, and performers arrayed in the style of a *tableau vivant* combined to construct a cinematic space that affirmed flatness of surface and fixed distance, establishing a gulf between viewer and scene. As his reference to the *tableau vivant* indicates, cinema's flatness had analogues in other media; what Burch calls its "popular models" ranged "from chromolithographs to strip cartoons, from shadow puppets to the *Folies Bergère,*" all of which contributed to "a superb indifference to what seems to us today the three-dimensional vocation of the cinema."[18]

Burch is hardly arguing that every one of cinema's antecedents were possessed of this same two-dimensionality but rather that there were sufficient precedents for this sort of staging as to make it an explicable, even expected, mode of representation for the cinema to adopt. Clearly, photography, painterly compositions, deep theatrical stagings, and the axial movements of vehicles also helped shape the parameters of early cinema's visuality, as is evident from the headlong rush of the train's appearance in that early film of the Lumières'. These representational modes coexist, rather uncomfortably, throughout cinema's first decades, which leads Burch to conclude that "the whole visual history of the cinema before the First World War—and not only in France—thus turns on this opposition between the Mélièsian affirmation of the surface and the affirmation of depth already implicit in *L'arrivée d'un train à La Ciotat.*"[19]

Cinematic history moves from the flatness of the early staged film to the inhabitable depth promised in the films of the Lumières and apotheosized in the complex spatialities that developed throughout the silent period. Thus, through both montage and camera movement the cinema could take the immobile spectator on a motionless voyage from distant to proximate views and from the stability of visual space to a more dynamic interplay of immersion and emergence. The question I want to pose is, do the comics restate this teleology as well?

First, Burch is quite right to identify "flatness" as a component of the comic strip around the fin de siècle. While some of the medium's most important ancestors were virtuosos of detailed, layered space (look to the serial works of William Hogarth), for the most part, comics not only had little need for depth, but their very nature somewhat mitigated against an experience of deep space. Comics privileged the sequential placement of images, and the mode of apprehending them overlaps strongly with modalities of reading in both *directionality* and the organization of signs combined in *sequence*. Perception was oriented toward a lateral, rather than an axial, movement: the eye was directed to move across or over the sequence rather than linger on, or optically penetrate, a single image. And by placing images in formation, the depth cues contained by any single image become diffused across the array, as with a photographer's contact sheet or chronophotographic sequence in which the singular and the multiple vie for prominence.

Caricature, another influence on the style of the comic strip, emphasized distortion and simplification for comic effect, and depictions of comic scenes, such as those by George Cruikshank, arrayed its humorous figures tableau-style—horizontally, in a shallow space—the better to highlight inanities of dress, behavior, and speech. The reduction of detail that marked effective comics style, beginning with Rodolphe Töpffer's picture stories of the early nineteenth century further encouraged the eye to skim from one image to the next in ways that mimicked the rather frantic, comical pace of the stories themselves (the level of detail in the pages of illustrated books varies greatly, but within comics scholarship the debate over whether these works "count" as comics rages).

Movement in early comics, whether by Töpffer, Bud Fisher *(Mutt and Jeff)*, or Frederick Opper *(Happy Hooligan)*, was also predominantly lateral, with characters entering and exiting the frame in ways that anticipate and echo vectors of movement in the early cinema (not to mention theater, an important forebear to character "blocking" in early comics). The speech bubbles in comics were arranged, first, so as not to overlap one another and, later, to aid in reading them in the correct order. And despite the subtleties possible with color engraving in the early Sunday supplements, color tended to accentuate flatness. An emphasis on shape and plane dominate the aesthetics of early comics.

Analogies between early cinema and early comics are complicated, however, by the latter's lack of verisimilitude. For many of the first film theorists, the cinema's power was tied to its photographic veracity and its automatic capturing of the visible world. Objects were magnified and animated by the camera's gaze; furthermore, they were situated within a spatiotemporally continuous world of objects, spaces, and durations. The photographic technologies of even the earliest cinema could not help but provide a richness of visual detail—comics were different. Taking Töpffer's work as prototypical of early comics, his line is sketchy, his world hastily limned; his genius is to present something more suggestively incomplete than fully rendered. Neither the objects nor the space are fully "knowable." It could be said that the resulting images, with their limited depth cues and strong outlines, draw attention to the surface of things, but it would be more accurate to say that attention is directed to the surface of the *paper* rather than to the surface textures and details of the depicted persons or objects. This idea aligns well with Goethe's sense that what Töpffer had created was something between writing and drawing, a kind of handwriting or calligraphy that combined aspects of the iconic and the symbolic. This is why it would be far more accurate to refer to the consumer of Töpffer's work (and of comics in general) as a "reader" rather than a "viewer."

In an essay on Töpffer's stories, Philippe Willems cites Eckermann's and Soret's conversations with Goethe, in which they discussed how "each small image depends upon the one before and prepares the way for the one that follows," and they praise "the way that the sketches in these wonderful notebooks pass by our eyes, page after page." Willems notes the emphasis on "quick-paced visual sequence"—the sketches themselves "pass by our eyes," dictating the pace of the reading experience.[20] David Kunzle has written of the "acute technological and social speed-up mode" that characterized the nineteenth-century fin de siècle and notes that "caricature and comic strip were always in the vanguard of a kind of graphic speedup, of which Rodolphe Töpffer is the recognized pioneer."[21] Chris Lanier expands wonderfully on Töpffer's technique: "The primal innovation was the injection of speed into the graphic narrative, both in the execution of the drawings themselves and in the time that exists between the images. He's not drawing scenes, but moments. His images don't languish in a buffer of time, adrift in temporality like islands at sea—they flow one after the other with a kind of ticking impatience."[22]

Thus the comic strip can be understood as part of the same anticontemplative modality as Benjamin claimed for the cinema, as a fast-paced experience far removed from the sanctity of the auratic. Kunzle notes that this speedup was discontinuous and that it wasn't until some decades later that comics practitioners like

FIGURE 22. Rodolphe Töpffer, *Histoire de M. Vieux Bois*, 1837.

Wilhelm Busch inherited and even accelerated Töpffer's breakneck pace, but that doesn't mean that we can't find some of this fin de siècle spirit in Töpffer's earlier example (Figure 22).

If it would be incongruous to suggest that reading Töpffer constitutes the kind of sensate bombardment associated with full-bore modernism, and, more specifically, to argue that the lateral flow of Töpffer's images is equivalent to the abrupt shifts in scale and proximity at which the cinema so quickly excelled, it would not be all that much of a stretch to make such claims of *Little Nemo in Slumberland*. Of course, comics are profoundly different from the cinema in at least one particular: the viewer does not control the flow of images in the cinema, while the comics reader can race ahead or linger at will. Nevertheless, McCay introduces variable panel sizes, magnification, instability of perspective and proximity, all of which combine to produce a more complicated, more intense, mode of address than earlier comics. *Little Nemo* was the first strip in which McCay had the entire expanse of a Sunday broadsheet page as his playground. Yet it took some time for *Nemo* to find its depth (so to speak).

In my first chapter I analyzed, in some detail, the first episode of *Little Nemo*, in which Nemo is first summoned to Slumberland to meet its princess. Nemo's bed is transformed into a magical horse named Somnus, and the journey resembles, in several ways, a phantasmagoric chronophotographic sequence. Two elements of the strip, however, went unmentioned: its impressive size, the expansiveness of the tabloid page lending itself wonderfully to the depiction of magical journeys far from the safety of one's bed. And I neglected to mention that, despite the fantastic meta-morphoses and bold color shifts, the strip is resolutely linear in its movement and planar in its organization. Only the introductory panel sitting atop the action fea-tures any significant sense of depth; otherwise Nemo is posed against bold, flat col-ors and the shallow space of his bedroom. Most of the strip consists of two columns of panels of equal width: that rhythm is crowned by the single image atop (a single space divided by columns that may or may not belong to the space occupied by the king of Slumberland), and a row of four images at the bottom, each of which is half the width of the panels above. This first Nemo is a splendid example of Smolderen's "wallpaper comics": there is a great deal of formal repetition from panel to panel but more than enough variety in colors and action to provide something more than mere patterning. But it is absolutely confined to the flatness of the page, and the fixed and frontal perspective keeps the viewer at a distance.

It doesn't take long, however, for McCay to move beyond the frontal, flat orien-tation that marks the first episode of Nemo (and the creations that preceded it)—it takes all of a week. In the two subsequent strips, Nemo again essays the journey to Slumberland: first through a forest of giant mushrooms, then across a deep chasm atop a pair of spindly stilts.[23] Both strips are similarly laid out: the top tier is a sin-gle wide panel (with architectural elements dividing the space) set in Slumberland, with some discussion about summoning Nemo; the next tier is about the same height as the first and presents the king's messenger encountering Nemo to prepare him for his voyage; and the final two tiers present the abortive journey itself. In the October 22, 1905, strip Nemo's adventure begins with his bed sinking down into the floor as though on an elevator (the caption notes that "the usual arrangement was rapidly becoming disarranged"); the rest of the strip evokes a series of down-ward steps (Plate 12). In the third tier Nemo is told that he must navigate a path that winds through a forest of giant mushrooms, which he is forbidden to touch. As he proceeds down the path and into the forest, the panels stretch downward and the vegetation increasingly towers above him. The bottom of each panel is lower than the last, continuing the downward drop of Nemo's bed, and taking Nemo both down *and into* the forest. Sadly, and, it must be said, rather predictably, in the right-most panel of the third tier, Nemo does accidentally stumble into one of the mon-umental fungi, setting off, on the bottom tier of the strip, a cascade of falling mush-rooms that sends him fleeing ("Papa! I'm getting—Oh—squashed!"). In this final tier the panels become progressively shorter (squeezed by the elongated panels in the tier above), leading to the final, inevitable square in which the dyspeptic Nemo sits up awake ("Didn't Mama tell you not to eat that raisin cake?").

There is still a strong symmetry in this bottom part of the page, but organized diagonally rather than vertically and horizontally. Strong unity of color, character-ized by the muted earthy tones of the mushrooms, gives the page a pleasingly deco-rative appearance, but there is a new sense of *immersion*. Here, in the second *Little*

Nemo, the layout of the panels begins to mimic and mirror Nemo's own phenomenological experience: the sinking bed and the downward path are echoed in the
downward-reaching panels, while the collapsing forest finds its analogue in the collapsing space of the panels around the hapless boy. The geometry of the page has
become more complex, as the eye moving across the panels (as in the first strip)
now also finds itself pulled downward to accommodate the changing space through
which Nemo moves. The strip has already moved beyond the more strictly chronophotographic array of the previous week. McCay repeats this layout in the next
episode, as Nemo tries to negotiate a chasm on a pair of stilts, only to encounter
some very affectionate long-legged storklike birds that send him tumbling onto a
bed of cactus (and, of course, out of his actual bed). The bottom drops out of the
panels in a layout once again mimetic of the space around Nemo, and, in the tier
below, the panels compress to replicate his entrapment.

These strips significantly extend the sense of immersion and participation that
was already present in the first episode of *Little Nemo.* These are still wallpaper
strips—still very decorative and strongly patterned—but there are new, dynamic
geometries in play. Over the next few years of the strip, McCay will continue to experiment with these techniques. His progress is, to be sure, neither linear nor unbroken, but it is somewhat inexorable. The strip of November 12, 1905, with Nemo's
bed tossed in a tempest at sea, involves some sustained play with perspective and
depth—the bed is, for once, viewed frontally, although Nemo continues to occupy
the middle ground of the scene. Others around the same time are organized around
a large, circular, central image: a giant turkey in one instance, a most Mélièsian moon
in another[24]—these strips are more overtly decorative than immersive. Around mid-
1906 things really start to happen consistently: McCay combines a hyperbole of detail with sustained play around perspective, panel sizes, and aspects of scale.[25] A
three-week series (beginning in May of 1906) involves Nemo changing size and
charging around Slumberland, but this series is not nearly as compelling as the
monthlong sequence in late 1907 in which the gigantic figures of Nemo, Flip, and
Inky tower over the blocks of buildings in lower Manhattan (Plate 13).

In one oft-reprinted strip a series of tall, narrow panels barely contain the gigantic elephant lumbering toward Nemo (and the reader); the final panel is all sinuous trunk, raised and extended out into the reader's space, and one barely notices
Nemo and the princess perched precariously in their small gondola atop the beast.[26]
A couple of episodes later, the elephant deposits them near a car, which takes them
on a loop-the-loop that finally launches them out into space (and again toward the
reader). "Isn't this just grand, Nemo, eh!" the princess rhapsodizes (to which Nemo
can only muster a less enthusiastic *Oh! Oh! Eh! Wha! Who! Oh!*).[27] A later visit to
the palace of Jack Frost climaxes in a "super-panel" (Will Eisner's term for a sequence
of panels that extend across a single space but represent successive moments of time)
that captures the vast breadth of the central staircase as Nemo, the princess, et al.

make their way along it.[28] And all of this comes before the strip's stylistic peak, around 1908.

The detail and scale of Jack Frost's palace is only one example of McCay's superb rendering of architectural detail, which increasingly pervades the strip in its first years. As has been widely noted, the rococo palaces and town squares of Slumberland drew heavily on the architectures of the 1893 and 1904 World's Fairs: white cities (although a bit more polychromatic than their rationalist forebears) of pillars, pilasters, sculptural domes, and ornate façades. Architecture offers a particularly immersive experience for the visitor, and World's Fairs and cities stage architecture on grander scales—it's no wonder that McCay saw these as analogous to the spatial experience of his immersive comics page. In one memorable sequence from 1909, one of these cities literally sprouts from the ground in a vertical series of five widescreen panels, much as the fairs themselves sprang up in comparatively short order.

As we saw in *Dream of the Rarebit Fiend,* McCay was no stranger to self-referentiality in his work. Really, given his interest in innovation, it would have been unnatural if he *hadn't* played with the parameters of his chosen media. *Little Nemo in Slumberland* breaks the conceptual fourth wall far less frequently than the concurrently running *Rarebit Fiend,* which more befits this extended dream of an innocent child. But even here, McCay cannot completely resist some reflexive play. Having established the volumetric solidity and immersive potentiality of *Little Nemo,* McCay could disrupt these very elements. In various episodes Flip punches through the background of the image,[29] the panel boundaries lose their rigidity (leaving Nemo helpless in a ball of crumpled paper),[30] and flat advertising images of the characters in the real-world *Nemo* operetta step off the flat billboards to become three-dimensional beings ("Be careful your majesty, don't get torn!") (Plate 14).[31] In an echo of an episode of *Rarebit Fiend,* Nemo and his friends devolve into "bad drawings" (Plate 15).[32] There is one episode in which Nemo, Flip, and Impy are washed like so many shirts: squeezed through rollers that also resemble rotary paper presses, they emerge as paper thin forms that must be hung out to dry.[33] Abandoned and hungry in an empty banquet hall, Flip, Nemo, and Impy sample the panel borders before gorging themselves on the floating letters spelling out the name of their comic strip ("It'll teach the fellow who draws us a lesson!" grumbles Flip) (Plate 16).[34]

I am dazzled by the strip from September 27, 1908, which has this same trio now at the mercy of an arbitrarily changing background (Plate 17): they seem to be in front of a *periaktoi,* an ancient stage device consisting of a row of triangular pillars with different scenes painted upon each of the three faces.[35] When the pillars are rotated, different scenes can rapidly slide into view. McCay alternates images that have stable backgrounds with images that throw the characters into disarray against backgrounds captured in midtransition. Nemo, Impy, and Flip are sent flying with each transition, and are given barely enough time to acknowledge their new surroundings before the next scene change. The effect is similar to the tour-de-force sequence in Keaton's *Sherlock Jr.,* when the dreaming Buster enters the film frame only to find himself at the mercy of what must be the cinema's most arbitrary montage sequence, serially placing him in the desert, a snowbank, a city street, and a rock in the middle of the sea. In Keaton's case the filmic medium reflects upon its own condition of being, a modernist commentary with which McCay was already familiar. Yet here, rather than finding themselves at the mercy of the artist's pen, his characters find themselves unwitting characters in someone else's stage play, adding a level of arbitrary absurdity to the whole business (and here the strip resembles Keaton's short *The Playhouse,* which grounds its oneiric transformations in a theatrical milieu).

Each of these instances plays with the structuring tension between the solidity of the depicted world and the condition of the picture plane: characters become flat drawings; flat drawings become characters; reality is but a stage set, a series of "flats." Following on Burch, Antonia Lant has discussed the mingling of theatrical flats with three-dimensional actors in the films of Méliès, citing Adolf von Hildebrand's analysis of the historical emergence of the figure from the flat pictorial plane. Hildebrand argued that "sculpture has undoubtedly evolved from drawing; by giving depth to a drawing we make of it a relief, and this relief may be regarded as the animation of a surface."[36] This trajectory, from drawing to bas-relief to sculpture, is relevant to the spatiality of *Little Nemo*. The strip that features Nemo's encounter with the poster for the *Nemo* stage show is especially interesting in this regard.[37] As images, the figures are arrayed across the poster, each looking straight ahead. Despite being part of the same picture, they are not posed in a volumetric space, and they do not interact. They do not exist in a shared space, either with Nemo or with one another. It is when they step off the poster that they begin to speak, to engage in shared behavior in a shared space (in a shameless plug for the show, the king forbids them from leaving, reminding them of their status as mere paper—should Nemo want to see the living versions, he must go to the theater!). Emergence into volume is animation of a plane; in this episode of *Little Nemo*, ontogeny recapitulates Hildebrand's phylogeny.

This oscillation between flat and volumetric image becomes the very subject of McCay's first film. The characters in *Little Nemo* perform a similar act of emergence: the figure emerges from the ground to become its own object, with its own volume, independent of the picture plane and occupying volumetric space. In the live action prologue we watch McCay draw flat figures that are posed in either frontal or profile views. These are demarcated by heavy outlines in the style of Art Nouveau, and they are outlines against a blank space without context (no backgrounds, no other figures). But as soon as the animation begins, the rules change. Flip turns toward the camera, immediately asserting the existence of a third dimension and a volumetric space. With a wave of his hand, a series of rounded slices fall into the frame, stacking up until they form the figure of Impy, who stands slightly behind Flip. Meanwhile Flip has turned around to watch this interesting process, and he and Impy change places, with Impy now moving to the *extreme* foreground. The characters tumble and twirl about, all the while demonstrating their existence in a complex, three-dimensional space despite the absence of any sort of background or setting (at the end the camera pulls back to reveal the flat, final, numbered, drawing of the sequence).

Language used by Antonia Lant, following Adolf von Hildebrand, to evoke the bas-reliefs of Egyptian culture is particularly potent with regard to the *Nemo* film: "living as it did between two kingdoms, drawing and sculpture, the flat and the full; connoting as it did the idea of transition and emergence; and operating as it did in a zone where background and foreground were rarely fully distinguishable, and often interchangeable."[38] *Little Nemo* stages the condition that marked the cinema from its inception; it recapitulates the fundamental shift that occurred in the development of early cinema in which a flat and insubstantial medium could evoke "a fuller illusion of the physicality and exactness of human beings than any prior art."[39] The Nemo animation's staging of the emergence from static to moving image further restages the earliest public screenings of the *cinématographe,* which offered up a frozen image that would spring to, if not *life,* then *liveliness.* And, in refutation of Maxim Gorky's condemnation of the cinématographe as a visit to the kingdom of gray shadows,[40] the emergence into animation in McCay's film also featured, in some prints, a transition from black and white to vivid hand-coloring.

Hildebrand observed that "all our knowledge concerning the plastic nature of objects is derived originally from movements which we make either with eyes or with hands."[41] Originally, it is the child who is animated, who animates and activates the world. But Hildebrand describes an animated viewer who can approach and circle a sculptural object, to perceive it kinesthetically, dynamically.[42] Something similar occurs in *Little Nemo*—but in reverse—now the flat drawing abruptly takes on mass and volume, emerging not only from flatness but from stasis, to address the viewer. In both cases the artwork offers itself up to a more active, kinesthetic knowledge.

What is perhaps most remarkable about McCay's accomplishment is his representational innovations that situated objects in a spatial continuum while also emphasizing their singularity and *thingness*—modes that correspond to Alois Riegl's distinction between optical and haptical spaces. Riegl tracked a teleological movement of the fine arts from a haptic to an optical subjectivism.[43] The haptic knew the world through a "close viewing" *(Nahsicht)*; the optical depended on a longer view *(Fernsicht).* The haptic spoke primarily to the viewer's tactile sense: depth and delimitation emphasized a sense of surface and the independent existence of individual objects that could each be apprehended in its turn; the optical, emphasizing such visible qualities as color and light, produced an open spatial continuum containing images of objects that *appeared to* (or could possibly) belong to the same space as the viewer. Both terms imply a certain amount of referential detail and description that were not yet present in comics images: optical space depends on a strong sense of spatial relations, while "haptic objectivism" directs attention to the surface of each individually delimited object. Early comics, in all their sketchy glory, were, I think, neither "optical" *nor* "haptical"—they solicited a rapidly scanning gaze that mitigated against either mode. The more precisely rendered *Little Nemo in Slumberland* was both (Plate 18).

Objects have a "thereness" in *Little Nemo* that they didn't have before, due not only to McCay's much-vaunted skills as a draftsman but also to his deployment of narratives that permit dramatic shifts in scale, and present an animate Nemo who explores the world. At the same time, these objects are firmly placed in a spatial continuum—always situated in a space that could potentially be shared with the reader/viewer. McCay's malleable panels, deployed across the broad canvas of the tabloid page, enhance the sense of immersion, through which the reader participates in Nemo's spatial adventures and through which a kind of "tactile vision" emerges, with the eye almost caressing the richly detailed objects on display. Objects exist simultaneously—and I'm quite aware of the paradox here—in glorious isolation, as well as within a complex spatial continuum that encompasses not only the world of Slumberland but the world of the reader as well. Vision is vision, as never before in the comics, and vision is also touch, a conduit for intimate, embodied knowledge. The arm reaches out to hold the page, or the book, and in so doing follows Nemo on his journeys, effectively reaching into Slumberland itself. Of course, this "motionless voyage" can never be complete: the reality of the page asserts the limits of the fantasy as surely as Nemo's continual waking at its bottom. There is an oscillation, most pronounced in the animation but fully present in the comic, between the flatness of the page and the fullness of the object, the flatness of the page and the fullness of the world.

"Motionless voyage" comes from Burch, but this peculiar combination of stasis and kinesis also suggests Deleuze's concept "movement of world." Writing in the second of his cinema books about dream sequences, as well as less literal instances that Michel Devillers has termed "implied dreams," Deleuze notes a condition where "the sensory-motor . . . is blocked, but movement nevertheless occurs"—this is what he calls "movement of world": "it is no longer the character who reacts to the optical-sound situation, it is a movement of world which supplements the faltering movement of the character. . . . The world takes responsibility for the movement that the subject can no longer or cannot make." His example: in a dream "a frightened child faced with danger cannot run away, but the world sets about running away for him and takes him with it."[44] Deleuze compares movement of world to

certain effects in animated films but finds its fullest expression in the films of Vincente Minnelli, where the movement of an individual dancer seems to summon up
a larger movement, a movement of world. Dance "gives a world to the image," deep-
ening the space and giving it life.

"The dancer himself begins dancing," he writes, "as one starts to dream."[45] Is it
specious to return the dream to the dreamer and to see in *Little Nemo in Slumberland* some of this same movement of world? Nemo may or may not be fleeing anything more than the boredom of waking life, but that the world runs away *with* and
for him, there can be little doubt. The world runs away *with* Nemo: in the first strip,
Nemo is summoned to Slumberland, and his bed seems to morph into the magical horse Somnus. In one of the most celebrated strips Nemo's bed grows long, sinuous legs and gallops off through the sleeping streets, carrying Flip (who's enjoy-
ing himself) and Nemo (who isn't) with it (Plate 19).[46] More typically, the world
changes *for* him: backgrounds shift; objects expand or contract, or multiply, or turn
upside down (Plates 20, 21). A bathtub becomes an ocean, crammed with animals,
ships, and icebergs; Nemo hardly moves.[47] In a refiguration of L. Frank Baum's *The
Wizard of Oz,* a cyclone rips Nemo's house from its foundations and drops it in the
middle of a city (more happily, the schoolhouse lands on the moon!).[48] There is no
shortage of examples. The extended Befuddle Hall sequence subjects Nemo and his
friends to bodily deformation (stretched and squashed), multiplication (as in a vast
hall of mirrors), and disorientation (ceilings become floors; the hall rotates around
them).[49] And one should not forget that the panels that frame and delimit Nemo's
world are themselves morphing and deforming around him all the time.

In the supremely cosmic New Year's strip of 1908, movement of world is presented with striking literalness (Plate 22). In this strip, which comprises twelve narrow panels of identical size arrayed across two tiers (plus the usual inset panel at
the bottom), we find Nemo seated on a snowy stoop, a church in the background.
In the following panels the church shrinks, and other buildings come into view and
shrink in their turn, until in the final panel on the first tier, the curvature of the
earth itself begins to be seen, to Nemo's understandable amazement. The second
tier finds Nemo now perched on the globe itself, accompanied by the old man "1908."
The world continues to shrink until it is too small to accommodate them both, at
which point the old man lets go. Nemo nearly falls, but in the final full-sized panel
a baby ("1909," naturally) saves him (in the final inset panel, Nemo has fallen from
the bed, and wakens to hear his mama wishing him a happy new year).[50]

In this strip Nemo is placed in a nearly identical position within each panel—
near the bottom of the top tier of panels, near the top on the bottom tier, and so is
effectively motionless. The world shrinks around and under him, while Nemo himself barely moves. Movement of world replaces individual movement, and, in keeping with Deleuze's own concerns, the movement that occurs is also quite literally a
movement of time, an allegorical expression of duration, as old year yields to new.

Nemo's movement in the strip is limited in three ways: he does not move at all but remains the static dreaming boy in bed; in the early years his passage to Slumberland is continually thwarted; and each episode is interrupted by his wakening. For the first years of the strip Nemo is led from one adventure to another—he is not the most willful of characters. But it is Nemo's adventures that, like the steps of the dancer, outline the movement of world—metamorphoses of objects, vectors of movement, fluctuations in panel sizes. Deleuze writes that in Minnelli's work "dance is no longer simply movement of world, but passage from one world to another, entry into another world, breaking in and exploring."[51] McCay uses not dance but dream to license the passage between worlds and even the animation of the world itself.

Excursus on Deleuze and Comics

Applying Deleuze's concept to McCay's comic strip is a fine and good thing to do, provided, of course, that Deleuze's concepts are not innately bound to the medium of the cinema. Comics and cinema are analogous in some respects but not others. The first thing to be said is that comics more immediately resemble the film*strip* rather than the projected experience of cinema; thus, Bergson's critique of cinema, which was actually a critique of the strip of still images, must be brought to bear. The comics give us a series of still images; they do not imprint what Bazin referred to as "the duration of the object."[52] Nor do they present series of those arbitrary instants that Deleuze called *any-time-whatevers:* each panel freezes characters into fixed, and significant, poses. Comics represent time, but like the filmstrip, time is figured as atomistic—a succession of discrete instants rather than a smoothly flowing temporality of persistence and duration.

This seems obvious, but it is also not quite true. It is patently *not* true that a single comics panel represents a single instant of time. Complex temporalities interweave in the comics. The characters exist in frozen poses, but multiple dialogue balloons speak to some period of passing time. Often, time takes place across the space of the panel, with time progressing as our eye scans the image, following a chain of cause and effect. Motion lines and other aesthetic cues also demonstrate duration within a single panel. Panel-to-panel juxtapositions propose a broad range of temporal relations, and the elapsed time between panels can be nonexistent (with dialogue carrying over from one panel to the next), brief (the next moment), or more pronounced (a change of scene, a leap of years forward or back). So while it's true that comics don't represent the powerful phenomenological experience of duration as does the cinema (where time leaves its indexical trace), they nevertheless seem to represent time in other ways that correspond to various temporal devices in the cinema.

Meanwhile (as they say in the comics), superhero comics might be seen as chock-full of movement-images, muscular action sequences of sensorimotor propulsion, powered by the engines of cause and effect, action and reaction. Comic strips, in their brevity and purposefulness, also have much in common with movement images; each strip could stand as a single instance of such a purposeful phenomenon. But time-images abound as well. Consider the *Peanuts* strips that feature Charlie Brown and Linus ruminating as they lean on that familiar brick wall: one four-panel strip from May 1971 opens with a silent panel: just the two of them (and the wall), facing outward. "Bob Dylan will be thirty years old this month," Linus says in the second image; aside from his open mouth, no movement has occurred. The third panel has Charlie Brown looking at Linus, saying nothing. In the final panel a visibly dismayed Charlie Brown is holding his head in his hands, saying, "That's the most depressing thing I've ever heard." Despite the self-contained joke, this strip presents an experience of any-time-whatevers (how long were they standing there? how long were those pauses?), not to mention an archetypal any-space-whatever (just where *is* that wall?).

Chris Ware, no small admirer of Charles Schulz, is a master of the time-image: an illustration he produced for a film magazine depicting three shots from *Tokyo Story* by Yasujiro Ozu (a privileged filmmaker for Deleuze) makes the link explicit. Ware's profoundly inertial work emphasizes the tiniest of moment-to-moment transitions, as well as the mundanity of any-space- and any-time-whatevers. His work is filled with complex temporal restructurings, including flashbacks and flashforwards, repetition, ellipsis, and compression, as well as the temporal mappings to be found in his great schematic diagrams tracing intertwining generational histories— time, in fact, is Ware's great subject. *Watchmen,* the revisionist superhero classic by Alan Moore and Dave Gibbons, disassociates text and image in ways that are willfully similar to the disruptions of the unity of sound and image that Deleuze discusses in the context of time-images.

To fully map Deleuze's cinema books onto comics is a task that, thankfully, lies far beyond the scope of this book; however, I think it clear that despite the evident differences in their material base and the conditions of their reception, comics comprise units, many of which are taxonomically similar to the image-signs that populate Deleuze's great study.

Riding the Line

Those "lively berries" further speak to the deep relation of McCay's work to Art Nouveau (particularly its Parisian iteration), especially its emphasis on the metamorphic possibilities of the natural world.[53] McCay has been derided for many of the same "crimes" as nouveau, criticized for being cold, overly decorative, and attentive only to surface. The otherwise brilliant Bill Watterson (creator of the comic strip *Calvin and Hobbes*) wrote: "McCay's pictures are fancy, but they lack either whimsy or guts. His palaces, cityscapes and boulevards are sterile facades, and his Art Nouveau line keeps everything flat and decorative. Slumberland, like its inhabitants, is more surface than substance."[54] Watterson is, I think, wrong about McCay and wrong about Nouveau. Revisionist scholarship has resituated Art Nouveau as a consequential early modernist style, imbricated in the rise of a new, concentrated urbanism; in the *nouvelle psychologie,* with its dialogue between interior states and the exterior modern world; and in its alignment with the more literary spirit of Symbolism. The task of Art Nouveau can be seen as nothing less than the thorough aestheticization of the built world, often with reference to processes of growth and metamorphosis in the natural world.

Paul Greenhalgh writes, "Many Art Nouveau pattern-forms are a result of nature being coaxed into the realm of artifice."[55] The dynamic flux of nature, with its metamorphoses and evolutions, was now inscribed on the urban landscape as a sign of its own vitality. Debora Silverman has referred to Nouveau as a movement "dedicated to vitalizing all recesses of the urban artifice with the evocations of metamorphic growth."[56] The city, too, was metamorphosing: it was growing, changing, and progressing in a frenzy of creative destruction. Stylized nature belonged to the artifice of the metropolitan landscape, but the motif of nature positioned urban dynamism as a natural consequence of existence. And we should not ignore the whimsy of inscribing nature as decoration upon the stolid forms of urban architecture, forms whose seeming inviolate permanence, monuments to human power over the world, was subtly derided. With this in mind, McCay's berries take on a new significance: they are, we should remember, doubly situated: diegetically, they are in Nemo's dream of a vegetable garden, but they are literally on the comics page of the Sunday newspaper—that chronicle of urban existence. In this sense they, too, ornament the urban landscape.

McCay adopts Nouveau's most characteristic figure: the sinuous line, the whiplash curve. Greenhalgh writes, "A development of the arabesque, Art Nouveau line was a sinuous, tensile abstraction of natural form, that constantly looked as though it were about to burst out of some invisible force that held it under constraint."[57] The whiplash curve, then, is about barely contained energy, a quasi-animate force awaiting release. The line is found everywhere in McCay, but my favorite appeared on April 10, 1909, as Flip, Nemo, and Kiddo decide to slide down a banister that not only lengthens and lengthens but develops sharp curves that send first, Flip, then Kiddo out of the picture (see Plate 1). Soon only Nemo remains, anxiously wondering if this stairway has an end at all. Finally it does end, and Nemo sails off the railing and out into a cosmic space where he is surrounded by multitudinous stars and a pale orb that might be the moon.

Klaus-Jürgen Sembach points out the contemporaneous emergence of Art Nouveau and the medium of cinema. They share, in his view, a fascination with movement—cinema recorded it, while Nouveau sublimated it. But, while the films of Loie Fuller's serpentine dances were an overt influence on several Nouveau creators, he is surprised to find little evidence of film getting much from Nouveau.[58] Nouveau found its way into any number of media: sculpture, glass, poster art, furniture, architecture, and design—but not film. I don't find this so surprising; if Nouveau indeed sublimates movement, then it would have little in common with the frenetic intensity of early cinema. But perhaps there is an Art Nouveau film that Sembach has overlooked, and perhaps it is an American film: Winsor McCay's *Little Nemo*. If the European artists froze movement, contained its energy, and sublimated it into elegant filigreed design work, then McCay, the American, desublimates it—he literally animates Art Nouveau and releases its energies. In *The Sinking of the Lusitania* the smoke emanating from the doomed ship takes that characteristic form—there is something radical and disturbing in the fusion of Nouveau decoration with the macabre, as the energy of the whiplash curve takes on an unaccustomed violence.

What McCay does with the whiplash curve, in both comics and films, is quite literally to animate it. Judith O'Sullivan argues that McCay's representations of movement and metamorphosis create "a compelling visual narrative, an altogether personal vision of the *fin de siecle*'s international style."[59] To animate it does several things. It gives the line a temporal dimension, where it becomes the site for narrative—it becomes part of the *Lusitania*'s death throes, and the subject of a *Little Nemo* strip. The energy that was latent in its frozen form is released (where, in *Little Nemo*, it flings the characters about). And now the line can be ridden—we can partake of its energy, derive pleasure from its dynamism. (Nor was Nemo the only one to enjoy the ride—the steeplechase ride at Coney Island took riders down an undulating track—"half a mile in half a minute!" promised the advertising—and was wildly popular. Later roller coasters exaggerated the effect.) To further Paul Klee's description of a drawing, this is not just "an active line on a walk moving freely";[60] this is a line taking Nemo for a ride.

Helen Clifford and Eric Turner wrote of Tiffany's techniques for working with molten glass that "the physical constraints to the realization of the whiplash and the sinuous curve were few, and the fertile imaginings of designers and makers could be realized with the minimum of restraint."[61] McCay, working with pencil and pen, generating architectures that did not need to comply with either building codes, the constraints of brick and steel, or even gravity, was in an analogous position of freedom.

A PHENOMENOLOGY OF CHILD-SPACE AND THE BOY IN BED

McCay created in *Little Nemo in Slumberland* an immersive and animated reality that, through its emphasis on "tactile vision" and exploration, speaks eloquently to the condition of kinesthetic knowledge. In the richly detailed world of Slumberland McCay "built" a habitable space, and he gave "life to those shadows," to use another term of Burch's, imbuing them with depth, solidity, and color. But in this work the intertwining of vision and touch is facilitated by the central figure of Nemo, the child-subject whose position licenses the operations of fantasy. This child-subject deserves more attention. What does the centrality of this figure mean to the structure of the comic strip or the design of its pages? What, apart from the generalized sense of a licensed fantasy, does Nemo bring to *Little Nemo*?

A phenomenology of child-space might prove a useful tool in our understanding of the malleable forms of *Little Nemo*, for the child surely has a different sense of space and possibilities for the self within that space than does an adult. There is no better writer on the intimate spaces of childhood than Gaston Bachelard. In *The Poetics of Space* Bachelard concentrates first on the hidden spaces of the home, the secret places that a child occupies and makes his or her own: the secret recesses of drawers and closets, the uncharted realms of attic and cellar, the safety of one's room. "For our house," Bachelard writes, "is our corner of the world. As has often been said, it is our first universe, a real cosmos in every sense of the word." Bachelard concentrates on the poet's reengagement with, and return to, the spaces of childhood because, as he proposes, "the house we were born in is more than an embodiment of home, it is also an embodiment of dreams."[62] It is the founding site of the poetic imagination: the house, for a child, channels a broad spectrum of spatial engagements that are never left entirely behind, although memories of them may be repressed.

I'd like to propose *Little Nemo in Slumberland* as representing not only a child's imaginative sensibility but also a child's experience of space, with its dialectics of safety and danger, the homey *(heimlich)* and the uncanny *(unheimlich)*. Bachelard writes that the poet or author "attracts us to the center of the house as though to a center of magnetic force, into a major zone of protection."[63] In *Little Nemo* that central zone of protection is surely Nemo's bed: in fact, it is pretty much the only part of the house with which we become familiar. The bed—with its thick comforters and walls of pillows, the safety to be found under its covers, and the possibilities for dreaming that it encourages—is a site of profound cathection. Just as, in a later comic strip, Calvin's parents can never see Hobbes as anything more than a stuffed tiger while to Calvin he is not only a real tiger but also the best of friends and most loyal of allies, Nemo's family will never see Nemo's bed as anything other than a bed, while for Nemo the bed is the vehicle, sometimes metaphorical and sometimes literal, that transports him to the wondrous Slumberland. It is his point of entry to those mobilized voyages of discovery. In a phrase that felicitously evokes the title of the strip's second iteration, *In the Land of Wonderful Dreams*, Bachelard writes that through later acts of memory "we travel to the land of Motionless Childhood"[64]— motionless, in the sense of frozen in memory, locked in the past; but we can also add the sense of the motionless childhood journey upon which Nemo embarks on a nightly basis and even Noël Burch's sense of the "motionless voyage" that the reader might take into represented realms of fantasy. Indeed, as Alexander Nemerov has noted, readers (and, I would add, comics readers) frequently set out on these imaginative journeys from their position as readers in bed, a point to which I'll emphatically return later in this chapter.

The Dutch child psychologist Martinus Langeveld, seeming to work in Bachelard's very shadow, has studied children's engagement with "secret places": "In the lifeworld of the child there exist hidden places which permit the child the possibility of experiencing in a normal manner access to strange and unfamiliar worlds around him. Where does the child find his as yet indeterminate worlds? Worlds pregnant with the possibilities of new meaningful experiences?"[65] Following Bachelard, Langeveld emphasizes the child's ability to repurpose the spaces of everyday life, places like the attic or the place behind the curtains. Here the child can engage in a state of "aimless daydreaming"—or reverie—quite in opposition to the mental attitude required in school or even family dinners. In the secret place "nothing interferes with the multiplicity of relations the objects of this world have to reality." An ordinary box can become, well, almost anything: a fortress or a cave, a boat or an airplane, even a rocket ship. And in the secret place, armed with the multiplicitous object, one can also become anyone: an explorer, an astronaut, Superman. Thus the secret place remains embedded in the familiar, while connecting to another world and another mode of being. Langeveld describes this as "a waking dream."[66] So: Nemo's bedroom becomes the staging ground, and Nemo's bed the vehicle, for an experience of transformative spaces and metamorphosing objects that highlight the strangeness of the world, the better to learn to navigate it. The child does not need to engage in the Russian Formalist project of *ostranenie* ("making strange")— the world is strange enough—but through flights of fantasy, which remain grounded in the familiarity of the secret place, the strangeness of the world can be overcome, even if not fully understood.

Langeveld emphasizes the transitional state of the child with regard to recognizing the separation between subject and world. The child he describes is equipped with a sense of self, but one not fully "split" from the world of objects. The child thus exists in a very proximate relation to the world, still very connected to the things that can be touched, grasped.[67] Returning to Bachelard, we note his contention that to recall the sensory world of childhood is to respect "the reality of toys" and the psychic investment we make in miniature worlds that we control but that nevertheless contain infinite mysteries. For Bachelard the experience of the miniature in literature returns us to the experience of the child. He likens the gaze of a botanist to the vision of a child: "The man with the magnifying glass—quite simply—bars the every-day world. He is a fresh eye before a new object. The botanist's magnifying glass is youth recaptured. It gives him back the enlarging gaze of a child," which might also give us enlarged berries.[68]

The paradoxical immensity of the miniature is a theme taken up by Susan Stewart in *On Longing*. The miniature summons up a seeming infinity of description: the meticulous intricacy of a clockwork mechanism or an exquisite dollhouse or piece of furniture is defined by their details. "Because of the correspondences it must establish," between the full-scale phenomenon and its miniature incarnation, Stewart contends, "writing about the miniature achieves a delirium of description." She cites Bachelard's observation that the emphasis on detail in these descriptions renders them "automatically verbose." But the miniature is not only known through the verbal, or even through the gaze: touch is perhaps the most important aspect: "the hand being the measure of the miniature."[69] The child remains in control of this world in which things can be touched. A series of *Little Nemo* strips has Nemo, Flip, and Impy, grown to giant size, roaming the space of lower Manhattan.[70] The city becomes a miniature; it shifts from a most unintimate immensity to a marvelous and personal object, as city blocks become something more like children's blocks to be rearranged (and knocked about) at will. Yi-Fu Tuan notes that children "are small people in a world of giants and of gigantic things not made to their scale.... Although children are midgets in the world of adults, they are giants in their own world of toys."[71] Enlarging the body or diminishing the city permits one to "grasp" it. Stewart writes: "To toy with something is to manipulate it, to try it out within sets of contexts, none of which is determinative."[72]

Langeveld compares the experience of the pubescent child to the transformations and sensations experienced by Alice in Wonderland, whose continual metamorphoses unsettle her sense of self: "Everything becomes 'curiouser and curiouser.' The whole body grows unendingly. 'It unfolds and opens like the biggest telescope. Goodbye, dear feet.' As she watched her feet, they retreated from her at 'such a rate that she lost sight of them.' This is how Alice lived the experience of discovering her own growth."[73] I would suggest, and I think this psychologist would agree, that this sense of altered scale and the shifting possibilities of body, while accentuated in puberty, predate that moment and belong quite fully to the larger lived phenomenon of childhood. The metamorphoses Alice undergoes or witnesses seem to me exemplary of a child's phenomenological experience, both in terms of the play with scale that constitutes the imaginative world of the child and in terms of the child's growing and changing body.[74] In another essay Langeveld emphasizes "the charm of all that is new" for the child, for (in his rather gentle version of childhood) "the world seems pleasant and full of promises."[75] Whether or not we accept his utopian vision, it is useful to think of childhood as "an adventure of perception," as the filmmaker Stan Brakhage phrased it,[76] and a time when touch and close, intimate viewing yield infinities of intimate, private knowledge.

In his history of children's literature Seth Lerer writes of the influence of John Locke's pedagogical theories on children's literature in the eighteenth century. In Locke's work children begin as blank slates but begin to learn through experience— experience gained through interaction with objects. Education was to shepherd children, to move them from inchoate sensual pleasure toward orderly and systematic understanding. Following Lockean principles, Lerer notes that "the job of children's literature [was] to make sense of things." Play and toys were recognized as foundational aspects of the child's life and as key to his or her maturation. Lerer notes that Locke used the word *plaything* to refer to "not just the toys of the nursery or the bedroom, but the objects of experience that teach sensible and moral action." Children's books, too, were playthings—some even incorporated the word into their titles. They could now become "objects of delight" in their own right. Children's literature became more descriptive; there was even a subgenre of biographies of (normally) inanimate objects. The pedagogical mission revealed itself in scenes of children "faced with their messy rooms, their ill-strewn closets, and a whole world of domestic spaces in need of cleaning and sorting."[77] In the animist fantasy that is *Little Nemo* (and *Rarebit Fiend,* as well), the world becomes not so much messy as disorderly—objects no longer behave as expected, and new rules are in effect.

At this point, however, it becomes important to remember that Bachelard is not necessarily writing about a child's *real* experience (or even about a real child) but about the poet's evocation of the kind of heightened experience and awareness of space that a child might have. It's on this level—evoking a memory of an imagined childhood that may never have happened but that nevertheless resonates for us—that Bachelard is at his deepest and his funniest: "Poetry gives us not so much a nostalgia for youth," he writes, "which would be vulgar, as a nostalgia for the expressions of youth. It offers us images as we should have imagined them during the 'original impulse' of youth."[78] Therefore it's not terribly important that we determine whether *Little Nemo* represents a "real" child's fantasy—the kid is, after all, named Nemo: *no one.*

For Bachelard the poetic image, "has an entity and a dynamism of its own; it is referable to a direct ontology." At work in the poetic is a reverberation that, for the receptive person, "brings about a change of being. . . . It is as though the poem, in its exuberance, awakened new depths in us."[79] The poetic image, which actually *re*awakens dormant associations, speaks first to embodied subjectivity, and in doing so it serves as an antidote to the biases of the adult mind. Evocations of childhood are at the center of *The Poetics of Space* because for a·child, perceptions remain new, and experience still has a freshness that makes each day (and each dream) a kind of adventure. The poet returns us, and here Bachelard echoes the Romantics and even anticipates Brakhage, to the world as it existed before we knew the proper places and names for everything. "Through this permanent childhood," Bachelard writes, "we maintain the poetry of the past."[80]

My point is that McCay effectively uses the figure of the child to frame a poetic vision that is part of a shared vision of what it was (or should have been) to experience the world as a child. After all, as Bachelard writes, "It is on the plane of the

daydream and not on that of facts that childhood remains alive and poetically useful within us."[81]

One more concept of Bachelard's seems particularly suited to exploring the phenomenology of the child-space of Slumberland: *intimate immensity.* "One might
say that immensity is a philosophical category of daydream," he writes;[82] it is a
category of reflection that takes the dreamer (day- or otherwise) far from him- or
herself; it is the space of an *elsewhere.* Citing Baudelaire's recurring evocation of
vastness, Bachelard finds that "it denotes attraction for felicitous amplitude."[83] Baudelaire, with reference to the music of Wagner, wrote of an "*immensity with no other
decor but itself.*" The poet feels elated by this, "released from *the bonds of gravity*"
(emphasis his, believe it or not).[84] Bachelard then notes that this "primal" value liberates the dreamer. "He is no longer shut up in his weight, the prisoner of his own
being."[85] This is therefore different from the experience of the sublime, which belongs more fully to the external world. This is rather an immensity located within
the subject, which reverberates to images of the vast in art.

Little Nemo in Slumberland might be seen as an exercise in intimate immensity.
Nemo: a small boy swept from his bed and invited to Slumberland. Slumberland is
a vast realm, and vast distances must be traversed to get there. In his shape-shifting
dreams Nemo encounters dramas of scale: immense animals and miniature cities
evince wonder. While some of these encounters are terrifying, they are still not sublime: Nemo never reflects on the power that can create such marvels and such terrors; indeed, the power might be that of his own capacity to imagine. How, though,
is *Little Nemo* intimate?

Picture the strip's "ideal reader," a small child, sprawled on the floor reading the
Sunday funnies, perhaps needing to shift position a bit to explore the panels at the
top, the middle, the bottom. All of the elements that contribute to the immersiveness of the strip—the immensity of the page, the saturated colors, the diminutive
Nemo's exploration of Slumberland and its surrounds, the metamorphosing berries,
looming mushroom forests, charging elephants, opulent architectures, the panels
that swell and contract, barely containing the action, all reaching that inevitable
point of closure in the bottom right-hand corner, as Nemo awakens in a puny little panel bereft of all the wonders and expansiveness that marked that other
realm—all this is contained within, and bounded by, the single page into which the
reader sinks so gratefully.

Each episode of *Little Nemo* was a more or less self-contained episode that took
up the entirety of a page, but only that page. (And those other adventures that are
not found on this particular page? Well, they are summoned up in the reader's memory, and the experience becomes both more immense and more intimate still.) The
entire episode could be taken in with a single glance, then explored more fully by an

act of reading and a close looking. Close looking would reveal more detail; exploration would be rewarded. Elevated perspectives, the "vastness" of the tabloid page,
and the expansiveness of Slumberland are counterbalanced by the comic strip as
miniature: "delirious" in detail, clearly bounded, and contained. Magnified objects
appear immense but remain only small objects, magnified. Stewart writes: "In its
tableaulike form, the miniature is a world of arrested time; its stillness emphasizes
the activity that is outside its borders. And this effect is reciprocal, for once we at-
tend to the miniature world, the outside world stops and is lost to us. In this it resembles other fantasy structures: the return from Oz, or Narnia, or even sleep."[86] Or,
we must add, Slumberland. "The miniature, linked to nostalgic versions of childhood
and history, presents a diminutive, and thereby manipulatable, version of experience."[87] And so, *Little Nemo* is both miniature and gigantic at one and the same time.

Little Nemo is grandly spectacular but also intimate, as reading is intimate. As I
noted earlier, the consumer of comics is considered a reader rather than a viewer:
reading is an activity whose pace, posture, and level of attention are all controlled
by the reader. The reader is proximate to the text, which is frequently held, famil-
iarly, in one's hands, or perhaps rested on a lap or a chest. Sometimes we read at night,
by flashlight, in bed, alone in the world in an island of our own making. Another
Nemerov essay, the suggestively titled "The Boy in Bed," has remarkable conceptual
and historical pertinence to *Little Nemo*. Here Nemerov reads one of N. C. Wyeth's
paintings illustrating a 1913 edition of Robert Louis Stevenson's *Kidnapped*, in which
the young hero, David Balfour, clings to a spar as he watches the ship on which he
had been sailing, the *Covenant*, sink in the darkness (Figure 23). Nemerov brilliantly
unpacks the image as connoting the very act of reading: the boy clinging to the spar
in the dark of night is aligned with the boy in his wood-framed bed. The ship in the
distance is like the book—the vehicle for his imaginative journeys into an adventure-
some world—its billowing white sails recalling the turning pages, while the entire
scene of the sinking, with its "brilliant projected illumination," can be understood
as emanating from the imagination of the boy at the bottom of the frame in a kind
of dream screen (see, for example, Frank Godwin's "The Sandman" for an analogous
composition, this time explicitly marked as a projection of the dream-work).

"What does the emanating and bittersweet power of imagination look like in
American painting in the years right after 1900?" Nemerov asks in the opening sentence of his essay. A bit further on he notes, "One of the striking facets about the
Brandywine illustrators is how often they portray children imagining in bed."[88]
Nemerov historicizes this tendency, especially in the case of Wyeth, by invoking an
anxiety surrounding the relatively inert, symbolic register of literature and the book,
around the emergence of new, more immediate and vivacious "technologies of presence" including the phonograph and the cinema.[89] In silent cinema's expressivity,
which existed despite the relative absence of the word, spoken or written, the power
of the book "as the provider of powerful hallucinations of absent entities" might be

FIGURE 23. N. C. Wyeth (1882–1945). *The Wreck of the "Covenant"* ("It was the spare yard I had got hold of, and I was amazed to see how far I had traveled from the brig"), 1913. Oil on Canvas. Illustration for Robert Louis Stevenson, *Kidnapped: Being Memoirs of the Adventures of David Balfour in the Year 1751* (New York: Charles Scribner's Sons, 1913). Collection of Brandywine River Museum. Bequest of Mrs. Russell G. Colt.

usurped.[90] Wyeth's paintings negate the feared power of these new media through their vivid, colorful, opulent presence on the page, but the paintings also serve as a tacit acknowledgment that the word is, indeed, no longer enough to capture and propel the imagination of a new generation. (Nemerov writes of "the trajectory of Wyeth's thought between 1905 and 1913: from anxious concern about the page's deadness to an exhilarated, almost bombastic defense of its rippling life."[91] In a coincidence too juicy to resist, the years from 1905 to 1914 also represent the years of *Little Nemo in Slumberland*'s initial run. Also consider the significance of these years for D. W. Griffith and the nascent medium of the cinema.)

Nemerov does point to a recurring trope in Stevenson's writing of dream or hallucination as a series of brilliant, projected images, but these are more likely references to magic lantern slides than to the nascent medium of the cinema. Indeed, Marcel, the narrator of Proust's *A la recherche du temps perdu,* had such a device as a child: "Some one had had the happy idea of giving me, to distract me on evenings when I seemed abnormally wretched, a magic lantern, which used to be set on top of my lamp while we waited for dinnertime to come: in the manner of the master builders and glass painters of gothic days it substituted for the opaqueness of my walls an impalpable iridescence, supernatural phenomena of many colours, in which legends were depicted, as on a shifting and transitory window."[92] Nevertheless, Nemerov's analysis speaks compellingly to the depiction of the imagination (or the depiction of the act of imagining itself) in the age of mechanical reproduction, in which the vividness of the printed word was feared to be losing some of its potency in the face of more vivacious, animated mediations.

But note that the young Marcel's dreams were actually a function of *reading:* falling asleep with a book in his hand, he would find that his dream thoughts "had run into a channel of their own, until I myself seemed actually to have become the subject of my book: a church, a quartet, the rivalry between François I and Charles V."[93] This particular boy in bed is almost equally enthralled by books and lantern slides, both of which are possessed of a hallucinatory vitality. Bachelard notes of "the simple experience of reading" that "the image offered us . . . becomes really our own. It takes root in us. It has been given us by another, but we begin to have the impression that we could have created it, that we should have created it." Reading becomes something like reverie, in which, for Bachelard, the mind relaxes while "the soul keeps watch."[94] Langeveld again echoes Bachelard, writing that the child, safely hidden in a secret place, is either "fully immersed in the mood of the secret place or he is observing the wide world, which, though it may be far away, is still mysteriously enclosed in this space with him."[95] From the secret place, armed with a book or an object, the child ventures forth in a state of heightened awareness and does, indeed, become one with the trigger of the fantasy.

Of course, this chapter is rather strongly concerned with still *another* "boy in bed," this one our pal Nemo, a boy who is, like Balfour, "the imaginer projected into the action" while remaining, on another level, within "the scene where the act of imagination takes place."[96] The overlap of Nemo's journey and the reader's is more overt than in the gorgeously metaphoric work of Wyeth, but for Nemo, as much as for the protagonist of Wyeth's scene, "bedroom and [the scene of] adventure coincide."[97] McCay and Wyeth (and other painters of the Brandywine school) converge in their depiction of the fantasist at one with the fantasy, the (relatively safe) dreamer and the bold adventurer bundled into the same figure. But these artists diverge in their choice of media: Wyeth and others, such as his teacher Howard Pyle, produced sumptuous paintings and illustrations for books, while McCay created comics, a medium that goes unmentioned in Nemerov's analysis (and in Kittler's, to whom Nemerov refers), a fortuitous oversight that I intend to remedy here. For the comics occupy a fascinating niche within the history of media that Nemerov presents: they are a print medium, like the book, but they were printed in that emblem of all that was ephemeral in the modern world, the newspaper. One can also provocatively position *Little Nemo* as appearing in the interstice between the dominance of the magic lantern and the cinema.[98]

Little Nemo, though, was published only on Sundays, when McCay could partake of the color engraving of the Sunday newspaper supplements: the adventures of his other characters—the rarebit fiends, sammy sneezes, poor jakes, hungry henriettas, and others—could be found in the daily newspaper or perhaps (in larger incarnations) in the Saturday edition, but Nemo lived solely in the pages of the gorgeously rendered Sunday supplements. So while it was part of the newspaper, it was not quite as quotidian as, say, *Mutt and Jeff.* Despite its presence in the newspaper, McCay's rendering of Nemo and his world unmistakably evokes the luxuriant detail and unbridled imagination associated with the illustration of children's literature (not only from the Brandywine artists but also such figures as Maxfield Parrish and Jesse Wilcox Smith, for example).[99] He was not the only cartoonist to evoke this tradition—see Lionel Feininger's *Wee Willie Winkie's World,* for another example—but he is the only one who seemed to fully partake of, and even extend, the projective fantasy depicted in works by the Brandywine artists, giving us the dreamer and the dream and ushering the reader to join the protagonist on a journey while remaining safely ensconced in a chair, sprawled on the floor, or tucked up in bed.

Little Nemo's status as a comic strip, though, suggests some differences from his Brandywine contemporaries. There is, of course, the reduced function of language. *The Wreck of the "Covenant"* is a wordless image, but, despite its beauty, it is incomplete without the accompanying text describing Balfour's plight. Words are both more and less important to Wyeth's image than to a page of McCay's *Little Nemo.* Early in its history, the strip is a somewhat text-heavy exercise, blending images with sparse word balloons and extensive captioning (the caption/picture relation also ties the work, in its earliest incarnation, to children's literature, in the same way

as the later *Prince Valiant* by Hal Foster resembles an illustrated book more, perhaps, than what we generally call "comics"). But the balance shifts irrevocably over
the first years to the image. As I've shown, McCay begins to bend the structure of
the page and the layout of panels to create an increasingly immersive environment
that mimics the hallucinatory otherness of Nemo's experience.

With *Little Nemo in Slumberland,* then, Winsor McCay does more than open up
new possibilities for the comics page. Following Nemerov, it's possible to see Mc-
Cay's strategies as producing his own allegory of reading. For, just as the quotidian
setting of Nemo's room becomes the staging ground for his adventures in Slumberland, and just as Nemo finds himself immersed in this realm of strange metamorphosing things and spaces, so does the reader, that other boy-or-girl in bed,
sink in to the rich descriptiveness of text and image, immersed in an adventure of
imaginative projection into the printed page. The image of the boy in bed, the reader
of adventures, is again the image of the motionless voyager, here projecting an animating sensibility onto the static images of a page that now opens out (or in) to
permit that projective imagination. The reader becomes Nemo, at one and the same
time tucked up in bed and afloat in the ur-imaginative realm of his own private
Slumberland.

And the motionless voyager again suggests a connection with Deleuze's movement of world, demonstrating that it might be even more fundamental to the cinema than Deleuze allows. The position of the dreamer can also be understood as
the position of the film viewer, relatively immobilized before a screen that offers up
kinetic spectacles of all sorts. Similarly, this is not only the condition of the dreamer
Nemo, around whom the world continually transforms, deforms, and reforms itself, but it also describes the condition of *Little Nemo*'s reader, comfortably positioned to enter—but only perceptually—the realm of Slumberland.

Little Nemo in Slumberland, then, works as a sustained depiction of imagination—
flights of fancy licensed by the dreaming figure of Nemo, the child who is not a child
but rather a conduit for these motionless voyages of exploration, this phantasmagoric play. Nemo's weekly forays into Slumberland present a charming, but also
restless and relentless, movement outward into encounters with the world made
strange, an exploration that is also, profoundly, an act of reading:

> . . . you were wholly given up to the soft drift of the text, which surrounded you as
> secretly, densely, and unceasingly as snow.[100]

Chapter 3

LABOR AND ANIMA

"Cartoons are automata that struggle."
—NORMAN KLEIN, *7 MINUTES*

DIALECTICAL TENSIONS AND
AMBIGUOUS INTERPLAYS

In Sergei Eisenstein's uncompleted essay on the cartoons of Walt Disney—the ur-text of animation studies—the filmmaker proclaims that the animated film, such as it existed in its early manifestations, was possessed of a kind of primordial essence. Disney created "on the conceptual level of man not yet shackled by logic, reason, or experience." Eisenstein referred to a primordialism both as it exists in the mind of the child ("the period when sensuous thought predominates") and in the fact of human evolution ("man brought back, as it were, to those prestages that were traced out by . . . Darwin").[1] At the heart of the Disney cartoon stands a celebration of metamorphosis and a delight in animism.

Eisenstein's writing emphasizes the liberating experience of *anima*. His notebooks record his interest in the word, with its implication that "all objects possess a natural life or vital force." His discussion of animation is strongly evocative of the complexities of the uncanny:

> The degree to which—not in a logically conscious aspect, but in a sensuously perceiving one—we too are subject every minute to this very same phenomenon, becomes evident from our perception of the "living" drawings of none other than Disney.
> We *know* that they are . . . drawings, and not living beings.
> We *know* that they are . . . projections of drawings on a screen.
> We *know* that they are . . . "miracles" and tricks of technology, that such beings don't really exist.
> But at the same time:
> We *sense* them as alive.

We *sense* them as moving, as active.
We *sense* them as existing and even thinking![2]

For Eisenstein animism spoke to an inherent dynamism of form: everything was in the process of becoming something else; the world was *mobile,* in all senses of the word.

Eisenstein finds a long history of what he calls "plasmaticness," a malleability of form, with folktales, circus, and Lewis Carroll predating cartoons (and to this list I would add the comic strip). "You can't help but arrive at the conclusion," he writes, "that a single, common prerequisite of attractiveness shows through in all these examples: a rejection of once-and-forever allotted form, freedom from ossification, the ability to dynamically assume any form." He goes on to note the phenomenon of this freedom's expression within a product of industrial capitalism. "In a country and social order with such a mercilessly standardized and mechanically measured existence, which is difficult to call life, the sight of such 'omnipotence' (that is, the ability to become 'whatever you wish'), cannot but hold a sharp degree of attractiveness."[3]

Eisenstein resists the charge that these cartoons enable nothing more than "obliviousness" to the real conditions of material, political, existence. For one thing, they are too simple, too brief, too evidently fantastic to truly blind one to the prison of the real: "because of the fleeting ephemerality of their existence, you can't reproach them for their mindlessness."[4] Rather, at least at this point in his writing (c. 1940), Eisenstein is content with the near-constant reminder of our polyformic potentialities, with the preservation of folk traditions, with the return, not to a childlike *innocence* but to a childhood state in which immutability of form is not yet a given, in which change is still a possibility. For without an acknowledgment of the possibility of change, how can one conceive of revolution? (Other interpretations of some of these same phenomena are less generous. Recall David Kunzle's description of the body in nineteenth-century comics as "machined almost beyond recognition."[5] Attraction and anxiety reside in these representations, and their comical tone does not obviate that ambivalence.)

For Eisenstein, then, Disney's cartoons offered an escape from the rigidity of industrial modes of production. And yet, ironically, the production of the cartoons themselves increasingly exemplified assembly-line procedures. As Paul Wells writes, "Whilst Eisenstein championed the *aesthetic* principles inherent in the language of animation, and most particularly in Disney's early works, Disney himself became more preoccupied with the development of animation as an *industry*."[6] An almost absurdly labor-intensive exercise, the creation of animated films of any duration or complexity was well beyond the capabilities of a single draftsman. Instead, labor had to be divided among teams of artists arranged hierarchically. The adoption of assembly-line modes of production was rapidly accomplished, from about 1913 to

1915.[7] A supervising animator would provide a set of character poses and oversee the production of hundreds of "in-between" drawings, all of which had to be transferred from paper to celluloid, painted, placed atop painted backgrounds (usually produced by an entirely different team of artists), and then photographed, frame by frame, drawing by drawing. Despite earlier devices such as zoetropes and phenakistoscopes, sustained animation is really a product of industrial culture: thousands of carefully aligned drawings, produced on an assembly line, are identical except for some carefully measured, nearly imperceptible changes. The clockwork regulation required of the animated image, coupled with the strict hierarchies of labor that structure its production, has led many to discuss the medium in relation to issues of Fordism or Taylorism.[8]

Labor and anima, then, might be regarded as the elemental forces creating a dialectical tension that informs the early history of animation, a dialectic that centers on the energy of the onscreen animated characters.[9] Whose energy is this, and from where does it spring? Is the animator a godlike figure, with the power to endow images with life? Or is energy not propagated but transferred, with the creation of energized creatures occurring at the price of the animator's enervation or supersession? Donald Crafton argues that the cartoon character is the animator's surrogate, or amanuensis, while Sianne Ngai, in her analysis of animatedness and animation, notes an "ambiguous interplay between agitated things and deactivated persons."[10] In one early film, to take but one of dozens of similar examples, the tools in a magical carpenter's shop come to life and work on their own; such films lead Ngai to suggest that "one could argue that what early animation foregrounds most is the increasingly ambiguous status of human agency in a Fordist era."[11] Writers on animation continually circle around the tension between the anarchic polymorphous perversity that it presents and the hyperregulated mode of production that produces it. Animation as an *idea* speaks to life, autonomy, movement, freedom, while animation as a *mode of production* speaks to division of labor, precision of control, abundances of preplanning, the preclusion of the random.

And at the intersection of all of this stands the animator. The presence of the animator in early animated films has been explored by a number of theorists and historians of animation, but it might be useful to consider these films as relevant to a broader consideration of the status of the artist within industrial culture. A new emphasis on documenting craft occurs in American art around the beginning of the twentieth century, speaking to the condition of the handmade in a moment of its—perhaps feared—obsolescence. This was also a period when what Neil Harris has termed an "operational aesthetic" manifested itself in such popular entertainments as Barnum's freak shows and vaudeville performances that emphasized rapid transformations onstage, in full view of an audience. The presence of the animator, or, more accurately, the animator's *hand,* figures in early animation as an image both of work and its erasure.

This chapter will concentrate on two films that occupy different positions in relation to the intersection of labor and anima: Winsor McCay's *Little Nemo* (1911) and Henri-George Clouzot's *Le mystère Picasso* (1955). The earlier film, one of the first to animate drawings, precedes the period when the production of animated films became fully industrialized; its animated sequence is produced by only one pair of hands. The later film exists on the far side of that divide and presents a rejection of the factory system of production, returning to both the figure of the singular artist and the animistic vitality of the images themselves. Both films purport to present art-making as labor, yet in both, labor is elided in favor of images that seem to generate themselves. What begin as avowed attempts to document the process of producing images instead become arenas for the image's liberation; labor is superseded by a created world invested with a thoroughgoing animism.

LITTLE NEMO IN MOVIELAND

The animator appears frequently in early animated films, almost inevitably as the generator of an image that comes to life. Sometimes the full figure of the artist is visible—as in J. Stuart Blackton's *Humorous Phases of Funny Faces*—but often only the hand of the animator is revealed—as is the case with Emile Cohl's *Fantasmagorie* (1908). That hand may indeed be filmed in the act of drawing (as in the cases of Cohl or McCay), but sometimes it is a cutout image of the hand that is animated in stop-motion in advance of the appearance of the cartoon's characters in moving drawings (as in the Fleischer cartoons). In fact, in the hugely metamorphic shifts that define *Fantasmagorie* or McCay's *Nemo* animation, the only stability in the animation *is* the hand of the artist, which brackets or intrudes upon the animation, which owns it, but which finally disappears from view (Figure 24). In this, early animation is innately reflexive, meditating on the conditions of its own production.[12]

Animation was too new, and perhaps too mysterious, to simply emerge fully formed onscreen. It lacked the naturalism of live-action cinema, the indexicality, the reality effect that audiences were able to grasp almost intuitively from the start. Animation was a trick of some kind, and a trick requires a trickster. In time the characters themselves would become the tricksters, eluding the control even of their creators, who would, historically, no longer intrude on the diegesis. This is the trajectory that Donald Crafton traces in his indispensable history of the early cartoon industry, and as excellent as Crafton's history is, there is perhaps still more to be said about this image of work and its erasure, something about this performance of image making, that articulates something regarding the place of the artist within industrial culture, as well as the place of animation in the cinematic imagination.

Little Nemo begins with credits grandly announcing the significance of what is to come. McCay is billed as "The Famous Cartoonist of the *New York Herald*" as the film prepares to present "His Moving Comics." And, lest there be any doubts as to

FIGURE 24. Winsor McCay (center), *Little Nemo,* 1911.

McCay's stature, the credits (incorrectly) declare that he will be "the first artist to attempt drawing pictures that will move." McCay is famous, a cartoonist, an artist, and an innovator, and all this is given to us on a single title card. McCay is immediately presented to us as belonging to society: we see him playing cards with "his artist friends" at what seems to be a gentlemen's club of some sort. He and his comrades are gathered around a foreground table, boisterously debating his claim to be able to create pictures that move (Figure 25). Amid the general hilarity, and to no discernible purpose, McCay demonstrates his drawing ability on a large and convenient sheet of drawing paper. So McCay is immediately established as a celebrity, a social figure, a member of a community, and a commercial artist who derives enormous satisfaction from performing and drawing for others.

A brief cut frames McCay against the white paper as he begins to sketch a figure in the center of the page. The following shot moves to an over-the-shoulder perspective, and the movement becomes somewhat more jerky (a result of undercranking). The diegetic audience has vanished from the scene, and there is little concern for spatiotemporal continuity in general: the camera seems to be looking down rather than across; the drawing has shifted to the left, and the artist, when he leans into

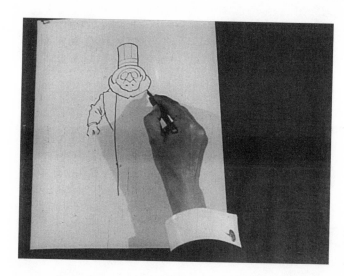

FIGURE 25.
Winsor McCay,
Little Nemo, 1911.

view, is now wearing a hat. An audience would be unlikely to notice these ruptures in continuity, however, as McCay's deftness with the pen is mesmerizing. McCay does not sketch or rough out his triptych—he simply, with a quick hand and a firm line, draws them, section by section. Impy's kinked hair and grass skirt, Nemo's dandyish attire, and Flip's cigar and circuslike garb emerge fully formed from McCay's skilled hand. On repeated viewings one is struck by the way each character is a kind of assemblage of constituent parts: a forelock, a collar, a row of buttons, all rendered in the heavy smooth outline one associates with both McCay and Art Nouveau.

Little Nemo speaks intriguingly to the place of the artist in the age of industrial modernity. As Emily Shapiro has argued, within American painting of the late nineteenth century there emerged a new emphasis on depicting the working hands of such craftspersons. Shapiro connects this concern with clock makers, weavers, and etchers with a resistance to the tyranny of industrial time. As Thorstein Veblen wrote, industrial production depended on an "unremitting requirement of quantitative precision [and] accuracy,"[13] which reduced the creativity and autonomy of individual workers. For Shapiro, images of skilled manual laborers spoke not simply of a bygone era but to the skilled hands of the artist engaged in the production of unique images. Yet, in this period, Shapiro finds "conflicted assertions of manual skill."[14] The methodical processes David Chalfant used in his painting *The Clock Maker,* for example, "erased any visible trace of the artist's own skilled labor and 'de-humanized' his living subjects, who were depicted with the same reproductive accuracy and utter lack of affect as the inanimate props that surrounded them."[15] Chalfant went so far as to paint on a copper surface, which accentuated the machine-crafted appearance of this and other works. Conversely, the expert draftsman Thomas Eakins emphasized "representational precision" in his depictions of inanimate objects while employing a less regimented, less mechanical style in rendering the human body, enacting what Shapiro calls a "visual manifestation of a body/machine split" across his oeuvre.[16] The tension in the arts between the aesthetics of the hand and the machine had been largely resolved in favor of the latter by the end of the first decade of the twentieth century, but development, as we know, is unequal, and it is not surprising to see it occur as "late" as 1911, the date of the *Little Nemo* film.

The audience of 1911 (or 1910, for those who saw the film as part of McCay's live act) must have marveled at the dexterity of McCay's hand (abetted only slightly by the undercranking) as it limned those figures, but I also imagine that they were doubly impressed by the perfection with which he summoned forth the characters so familiar to them from the Sunday comics supplement. They would have been wowed not only by his skill as an artist but by his absolute fidelity and exactitude. The hand of McCay would thus be both individual and industrial, artist and assembler, master craftsman and machine operator—at once a tool of both *production* and *reproduction*. Here Shapiro's "conflicted assertion of manual skill," which she tracked through the fine arts of the late nineteenth century, plays out in the field of popular culture in the early part of the twentieth.

The lightning-sketch artist of vaudeville could be seen as another response to the shock of the machinic new, and McCay was a dazzling lightning-sketch artist. Onstage, before a paying audience, an illustrator would produce work after work of either documentary fidelity (portraits of famous figures or audience members) or metamorphing wonder (the transformation of one figure into another, e.g.). In the context of American painting, Shapiro writes of "the intersection of preindustrial craft traditions rooted in manual skilled labor and an industrialist ethos that demanded of human workers nothing less than the efficiency and reproductive exactitude of the machine,"[17] and the lightning-sketch artist stands at just such an intersection. One of McCay's first jobs was as a sketch artist for a local newspaper. Such work called for instantaneity and fidelity—the same traits later valued in photojournalism.[18] Later, of course, came McCay's blizzard of comic strips, culminating in both the breathtaking expansiveness of *Little Nemo in Slumberland* and the astonishing detail of the editorial cartoons he produced for Hearst. His popularity permitted him to develop and perform a lightning-sketch act for the vaudeville stage in New York, and it was to accompany this act that he produced his first animated films.

McCay's abilities as a sketch artist are fully on display in *Little Nemo*. Crafton has linked the presence of the animator in early cinema to the tradition of the lightning-sketch act, and he has identified the most common tropes of the lightning-sketch film. The performer-sketcher is frequently attired in evening wear, which Crafton notes was also the attire of the stage magician, the sleight-of-hand artist. These magicians conjure their characters with a few deft, dexterous strokes. But he also points out that all of these films augment the innate "magic" of the performance with elements drawn from the repertoire of the trick film—specifically, under-cranking and stop-motion—further enhancing the artists' status as magicians.[19]

The hand of the animator is presented as a figure of magic and an agent of entertainment, but it should also be understood as an image of *work*. Matthew Solomon has discussed the lightning-sketch act as part of a theatrical tradition of rapid transformation that included "shadowgraphy," "chapeaugraphy," and quick-change artists.[20] Solomon links the popularity of these forms to their foregrounding of Neil Harris's "operational aesthetic," in which the spectator is initiated into some of the ways that illusions (or deceptions) are engineered.[21] Despite the mystification involved in the sudden animation of static images and the myriad transformations and mutations they undergo, there is, in *Little Nemo,* a semblance of this operational aesthetic, an emphasis placed on the processes of both image making and filmmaking, a gesture, or at least the appearance of a gesture, toward a demystification of process.

The next scene involves some comedy. Workers deliver supplies to McCay: bales of drawing paper (marked "DRAWING PAPER") and barrels of ink ("INK") are lugged into his studio—an abundance that invokes a sense of this man as a dynamo who requires industrial amounts of raw materials to keep up with his output. Crafton has written of the "extraordinary, materialist conception of animation" evident in McCay's—and only McCay's—work: the continual emphasis on the vast numbers of drawings and innumerable hours of labor.[22] McCay, in that studio, becomes something of a cartoon character himself, surrounded as he is by all those cartoonishly labeled supplies, not to mention stacks of drawings, some racked into a mutoscope. He looks at a sequence and seems satisfied, pleased, in fact. An office boy enters, clutching a feather duster; the viewer feels some sense of foreboding, and—*yes!*—the kid trips over something and sends piles of drawings spilling to the floor (even this bit of humor draws attention to the artist's prodigious productivity).[23] Fortunately for the kid, one of McCay's buddies shows up, and McCay shows him some of the individual drawings that he has produced.

Norman Bryson has written that much Western representational painting is predicated on the "disavowal of deictic reference"—the *deictic* being the labor and temporality of image production.[24] The emphasis on the presence of the animator, and the animator's hand, in early animation—especially in the first films of Winsor Mc-Cay—could be seen as a rare revelation of, or at least an allusion to, the deictic, to the time of work, of image production.

In all of these manifestations and contradictions McCay becomes an exemplary human motor, that figure that Rabinbach located at the center of numerous utopian ideologies of the early twentieth century: "All of these movements, though in different ways, viewed the worker as a machine capable of infinite productivity and, if possessed with true consciousness, resistant to fatigue."[25] Indeed, McCay will need to be resistant to fatigue, given the task he has set himself in producing thousands of drawings featuring all the main characters of his Slumberland universe. As I mentioned in chapter 1, this sequence, which records McCay's movements with scientific fidelity, evokes the early apparatuses of Marey's experiments, and as I also noted there, *mapping* movement was the first step toward *controlling* movement. The hand of McCay is an artist's hand, exerting control, but at the same time it becomes something of a mechanism, a motor, laboring efficiently and with startling, machinic precision. Ultimately, not even this human motor could keep up with the unique production demands of the animated film. But he'll give it a go, here, in his first film.

Eisenstein finds not only "attractiveness" in animation's metamorphic freedom but also something ecstatic. Animation speaks to a "lost changeability, fluidity, suddenness of formations—that's the 'subtext' brought to the viewer who lacks all this."[26] Freud proposed that primitive peoples and children hold a characteristic belief in the "omnipotence of thoughts," but he clearly believed that these fallacious beliefs should be left behind. Eisenstein, always more utopic, wants to reclaim them. The new film hero, unnamed in Eisenstein, but whom we might call Mickey Mouse, is now "an unstable character" in that he is "the kind of character for whom a changeable appearance is . . . natural."[27] It is not necessarily an expressive, emotional fluidity that is articulated through a fluidity of physical form; mutability is rather a simple condition of being. We are fascinated by these "polyformic" traits because we seem to lack them; except through our cartoons, we have lost contact with our "primal plasmatic origin," and thus cartoons represent "a displacement, an upheaval, a unique protest against the metaphysical immobility of the once-and-forever given."[28]

McCay's early films serve as rather perfect exemplars of the pervasive animism to which Eisenstein felt such devotion, especially, I think, in his first film, in which he endowed his *Little Nemo* characters with movement and, therefore, life. *Little Nemo* is one of the first sequences of animated drawings, and McCay drew every one of those thousands of images. With his next cartoon, *Gertie the Dinosaur,* an assistant traced the background scenography (there were no backgrounds in *Nemo*), and very shortly after that John Bray patented a technique for animation using transparent cells that could be layered atop a single background image, breaking both the image and the movement down into constituent parts.[29] With the advent of cel animation—the division of labor that it permits, as well as the newly stable image that results—the animism of early animation, in which every element of the image fairly pulsates with life, becomes less evident, although it reveals itself in other ways.

Simply by limning them, McCay's hand magically endows his famous creations with existence even before the animation begins; it is an agent of the uncanny. Anthony Vidler understands the uncanny as a kind of slippage: "it is, in its aesthetic dimension, a representation of a mental state of projection that precisely elides the boundaries of the real and the unreal in order to provoke a disturbing ambiguity, a slippage between waking and dreaming."[30] In the cinema the slippage between waking and dreaming is also one of the most familiar modalities in which Deleuze's movement of world occurs. In this case a slippage between waking and dreaming is enacted in the slippage between animator and animated, between labor and anima. This is not a slippage between dichotomous states but a slippage between and among ambiguities: the animator is controller and mechanism, the creation unruly and regulated (I will pursue this further in chapter 4); the animator is enervated or animated by the process of animation, a human motor producing human (or animal) motors. The hand is godlike, endowing the inanimate with life, but it is also a servant, a tool that disappears once its labors are complete.

The final scene in the prologue brings the viewer into the projection room, as McCay's animation is unveiled. Early animation links the industrial medium of cinema to the handmade, reintroducing the innate uncanniness of the medium while adding a new, paradoxical layer of undecidability. Laura Mulvey writes, "As new technologies are often outside popular understanding when they first appear, the most advanced scientific developments can, paradoxically, enable and revive irrational and superstitious beliefs in an animate world."[31] The film-within-a-film begins with an image of Flip that uncannily draws itself (in stop-motion) as if in response to the cranking movement of the projectionist, as if the projector was actually a kind of drawing machine (which, in a way, it is). Here, in an Eisensteinian sense, is animation at its purest. Eisenstein begins his exploration of animism with the fact of animation itself: drawings themselves, lines on paper, are animated and given "life." In other words, animation is about its own condition of being before it is about anything else.[32] One could argue that animation releases the movement that lies dormant in the still image. Paul Klee, after all, referred to a drawing as "an active line on a walk moving freely, without goal. A walk for walk's sake."[33] Klee bestows upon the line an autonomous character, and early animation is populated by these autonomous lines, seemingly self-generating or generated within that most animistic of all media, the cinema. And, indeed, the Nemo animation begins with a line taking itself for a walk, a line and an image in the process of becoming.

This "magical" sequence is followed by a kind of explanation: another over-the-shoulder shot of McCay's hand turning out a very similar picture.[34] The resulting picture (now labeled "No. 1" at the bottom) is then slipped by someone's hand into a vertical frame, presumably to be photographed (the camera is the one part of the apparatus that we never see—we get drawings, a mutoscope, the animation stand, and the motion picture projector, but no camera). The camera tracks in, the image takes on color, and the animation proper begins.

Everything in the narrative has apparently prepared us for this moment when the characters that have been painstakingly drawn again and again become possessed of an ineffable life of their own. The audience has seen, to this point, a demonstration of the mechanical perfection of McCay's artistry, paper and ink delivered, images arrayed in towering stacks, the workings of a mutoscope, and explanatory intertitles, all proclaiming the miracle to come. Yet all of this turns out to be something of a setup, a rather brilliant sleight-of-hand through which the audience is entirely *un*prepared for what actually transpires. McCay has heretofore drawn all the characters either in profile or facing outward; they thereby enunciate a rhetoric of flatness, a two-dimensionality that is completely belied in the instant that Flip suddenly turns toward the spectator. The animated world immediately takes on a depth and volume that the individual static images actively denied. Flip blows an insouciant smoke ring in our direction, a gesture that imbues the character with an autonomy, an immediacy, that seems not fully subject to the authority of the animator's hand.

The sequence that follows continues to dazzle, a century later. True to its status as an attraction, it is not about anything so much as its own existence and the possibilities that it unleashes on the world.[35] It takes place in no place, a blank white field in which purpose and logic are, for the moment, suspended. Everything here exists solely to move and to morph, indulging in—no, reveling in—that "freedom from ossification" that Eisenstein enjoyed so much. As Flip waves the cigar smoke away, a series of slices fall into the frame atop one another to become the caricatured African known as Impy, and the two figures begin to cavort, moving smoothly from foreground to background. Flip takes a tumble, to Impy's great, wide-mouthed amusement, and the hot-tempered Flip retaliates with a poke. The two spin and tumble as an agglomeration of fine lines congeals to reveal the foppish form of Nemo. Playing the ringmaster of this little circus, Nemo gestures at his two flanking compatriots who begin to squash and stretch in obedience to his movements (Plate 23). This sequence repeats several times, anticipating the cycling images that defined the "limited animation" television shows of a later generation but also recalling animation's provenance in the rotating phenakistoscopes and zoetropes of an earlier moment.

What immediately distinguishes McCay's animation from that of Cohl or Blackton is the quality of the drawing. McCay's virtuosic draftsmanship and sense of design are a world apart from the stick figures and chalk drawings of his contemporaries. The animation is detailed and lifelike, with a strong sense of depth and, despite the absence of backgrounds, perspective. Hand-coloring provided a further level of sensuous detail (and also connected the work to its Sunday comic strip forebear).

After this interlude of squashing and stretching, Flip and Impy squash their way into nonexistence as a floating wand appears to be grasped by Nemo. This turns out to be a drawing implement, and Nemo, his back to the camera, limns, from the top down, a life-size image of Slumberland's lovely princess, an image that then comes to life. Nemo has thus become McCay's surrogate in posture and animistic power.[36] Significantly, Nemo is not the product of McCay's hand but, instead, coalesces from an array of disconnected lines in what seems an act of self-generation. And while McCay disappears with the onset of the animation, Nemo and *his* creation, the princess, interact with one another (in his next film, of course, McCay will interact with Gertie). Nemo, then, is blessed with a persistence within the diegesis that eludes McCay himself. The animated figure represents an uncanny doubling of the creator: its questionable status (alive or not?) allows it to usurp its own author.

Nemo plucks a magically growing rose to bestow upon the princess as a massive dragon enters the scene from offscreen. The dragon's mouth opens to reveal a gilded throne on which the two can sit. Nemo and the princess wave to us, and then the dragon bears them off, his sinuous body snaking smoothly into the distance in a masterly display of perspectival animation. And then, in something of a charming afterthought, Flip reappears, chauffeuring Impy in a primitive automobile (labeled "HONK HONK"). Flip aims to follow the dragon, but the car explodes in a riot of smoke, sending Flip and Impy sailing upward and out of sight. Doctor Pill runs onscreen, sensing perhaps that his presence is needed, but sees no one, at least not until Flip and Impy land on him. As they begin to help the good doctor to his feet, the motion ceases. The shadow of a thumb appears, the camera tracks back slightly, and the hand is again visible at the edge of the picture (labeled "No. 4000"). The end of the animation brings the return of the hand, of everyday reality, and the end of miracles. It also brings the end of the film. We see none of the presumably astonished reactions of McCay's comrades; we do not even glimpse the artist himself. (The ending is reminiscent of the end of a *Little Nemo* comic strip—the fantasy abruptly interrupted. But the ending is also *not* like the strip in that we never fully return to the everyday world.)

Once the projection begins, McCay only figures as a drawing hand, and once the animated sequence begins (following the image of Flip labeled "Watch Me Move"), he vanishes completely. It is as though the animator has brought about his own demise, as though the animatedness of the images, and the liberation it represents, comes quite literally at the expense of the human creator. The drawings are produced by the hand, but the mechanism of their animation is hidden, so their passage into movement transcends the hand's operation. McCay's "deactivation" even precedes his literal disappearance from the film. The slight speeding of the film of McCay drawing already begins to make him seem like something of an automaton, a kind of drawing machine, a literal human motor. The hand is unwavering, its precision nearly dumbfounding. There is no hesitation, no sign of decisions being made or options considered.[37] The hand simply draws and, having drawn, moves on. It seems at once a machine and something possessed of its own anima. Thus McCay's hand becomes both a synecdoche and a substitute for McCay himself.

The animistic spirit that pervades early cartoon films not only gives us the autonomy of characters and the deanimation of the animator; it also, and perhaps most fundamentally, gives us the autonomy of the image itself.[38] In this, too, it recalls the overturning of expectations experienced by spectators of early cinema. Screenings of the Lumière brothers' earliest films began with the projection of the initial frame as a still image. "You anticipate nothing new in this all too familiar scene," Maxim Gorky reported in 1896, "for you have seen pictures of Paris streets more than once. But suddenly a strange flicker passes through the screen and the picture stirs to life."[39] The still frame lulls the viewer, while movement assumes its powerful immediacy against the ground of that stillness (for all viewers, it seems, *except* Gorky, who referred to the *cinématographe* as a "Kingdom of Shadows"). In *Little Nemo*, sixteen years later, the passage into animation recapitulates the shift from still to moving image that marked those screenings by the Lumières: the still frame lulls the viewer, serving as the ground against which the figures of movement assume their powerful immediacy. What would have perhaps most surprised the 1911 viewer of *Little Nemo* is the *recognizance* of the moving image at a time when narrative had increasingly incorporated spectacle within its naturalizing structures.

Noël Carroll has written of the horizon of epistemic expectation that the spectator brings to bear upon different sorts of images. It would be irrational to expect a photograph to suddenly move, he points out: "one commits a category error if one expects movement," and, concomitantly, we have come to understand that "movement is a permanent possibility in the cinema."[40] But of course the wonderment experienced by the earliest audiences of the cinema *was* partly the wonder of expectations overturned (Gorky's gray images of Paris yielding to a new kind of real-time movement). At a time when Winsor McCay was best known as the artist behind the detailed, precise, static images of Slumberland or for his command as a lightning sketcher, the apparently autonomous movement of Flip, Impy, Nemo, the princess, and Doctor Pill surely must have involved some of the delight of a categorical redefinition. McCay's comic strips were meticulously rendered, the very completeness of each image rendering them resistant to movement and change even as his elaborate graphic matches and magic lantern–like dissolves imbued his comic strip world with elaborate, endless metamorphosis. The animated version of *Little Nemo* transposes the metamorphosing world entirely onto the meticulously rendered characters, operating against a blank field that can be understood as the artist's drawing pad, a lightning-sketch chalkboard, or perhaps even the movie screen itself.

LITTLE NEMO MEETS PABLO PICASSO

There is a striking echo of *Little Nemo* in a film made some decades later, *Le mystère Picasso* (1955), directed by Henri-George Clouzot. Each artist, McCay and Picasso, outlines a trio of figures: a large central figure facing outward is flanked by two smaller figures in profile (Figure 26). It is a seductive rhyme, although a brief one— the pictures move in radically different directions from that single momentary rhyme—but it does underscore the homologies between these films.[41] *Little Nemo* is

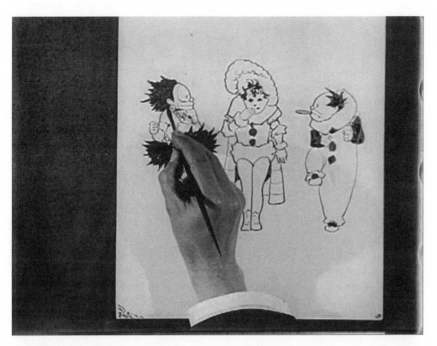

FIGURE 26. *Little Nemo,* 1911 (top); *Le mystère Picasso,* 1955 (bottom).

historically positioned just before the onset of the factory system of animation, while Clouzot's film serves as a conscious rejection of such a system and a return to both the figure of the individual artist *and* the animism that permeated early cartoons. *Le mystère Picasso* and *Little Nemo* can reciprocally inform one another, and André Bazin's analysis of the later film is almost equally applicable to the earlier one.[42]

The films have remarkable formal and structural similarities: each features a black-and-white live-action prologue that introduces the artist and his genius, followed by a series of colorful, seemingly self-generated images that thwart our expectations.[43] The tension between labor and anima that structures early animation is rediscovered and made explicit by Clouzot and Picasso, in ways that might have broader relevance to the depiction of artistic creation in the cinema. I am thinking of the Hans Namuth film of Jackson Pollock working, in which, again, the recording of the artist's process yields to a more autonomous image, in this case animated by the movements of the camera across and toward its surface.

The film is a collaboration between Clouzot and Picasso for which the painter created some twenty works in an avowed attempt to capture the creative process of an artist at work. Rather than film Picasso painting, however, Clouzot and Picasso seek to "demystify" the creative process by concentrating solely on the marks made by the hand of the artist, at the moment they are made. The hand becomes a physical manifestation of the artist's consciousness. At first Clouzot films Picasso drawing behind a semitransparent surface using bold inks that bleed through, but Picasso was dissatisfied with the relatively monochromatic results, and after a few images they switch over to oil painting captured with stop-motion exposures. The film, which purports to reveal real-time process, in fact becomes something of a trick film—the creation of the final painting, which takes about five minutes of screen time, actually took eight days to complete—but in these earlier sequences, it is as though Picasso was drawing on the surface of the screen itself, recording his marks directly onto the surface that we are now watching (and in this the film bears an affinity to Namuth's film of Jackson Pollock, dripping paint on a glass surface mounted above the camera). Some of the images that Picasso produces are simple: an eggplant on a plate, a pitcher, a window (or is it a painting within the painting?); others are more elaborate: simple outlines giving way to swathes of color; layer piled upon layer obscuring those below; cutout shapes in collage; the final product unpredictable. Wipes, suggestive of the flipping of a page, serve to transition from one work to the next. The images include monochrome drawings, polychrome drawings, oil paintings, and collages—there is little sense of an underlying system—just enough, really, for the film to confound.

Juxtaposed to *Little Nemo, Le mystère Picasso* can easily be seen for what it is: an animated film with a live-action framing sequence and some live-action inserts. Bazin himself situates Clouzot's film within the tradition of animation that extends back to Cohl's *Fantasmagorie* and through the work of Oskar Fischinger, Len Lye, and Norman McLaren. "This tradition does not make of the animated film an *a posteriori* animation of a drawing that has a virtually autonomous existence. Rather, it turns such a film into the evolution of the drawing itself or, more accurately, its metamorphosis."[44] I would argue that McCay's *Little Nemo* is also part of that tradition, and its emphasis on the performative figure of the artist makes for an especially pertinent comparison. Much of what Bazin notices about *Le mystère Picasso* is present in *Little Nemo*.

As I've argued, the emphasis on the hand of the animator in early animation, and especially in the films of McCay, could at least be seen to allude to the deictic, to the time of work, of image production, and this is part of the argument that Bazin advances with reference to *Le mystère Picasso*. Bazin has described the film as a suspense film. The film consists primarily of a largely invisible Picasso creating drawings and paintings for the camera. Lines of ink and swathes of paint appear on the canvas, seemingly of their own accord. By deemphasizing the actual figure of the artist, Clouzot purports to explicate the way the artist thinks with his hand. But, as Bazin quickly points out, the film "doesn't explain anything." The film provides no insight into the thought-process behind creation. Any point in the visual field has an equal likelihood of becoming significant, "for during this work not a single stroke, not one patch of color appears—'appears' is the right word—in any way to be predictable."[45] The viewer tries to predict not only the order of the pen/brushstrokes but also the moment of completion. This anticipation generates much humor in the film: Picasso is clearly uninterested in the products of these improvisational exercises (he stipulated that they be destroyed upon the film's completion), and he consistently works to defy not simply one's momentary expectation but the paradigm of expectation itself. It is in this sense that Bazin wants to call *Le mystère Picasso* "a Bergsonian film." "Each of Picasso's strokes is a creation that leads to further creation, not as a cause leads to an effect, but as one living thing engenders another." As a film that enacts "a pure and free metamorphosis," it instantiates a particularly pure image of Bergsonian duration.[46]

What first links *Little Nemo* to the Picasso film is primarily the sustained attention to McCay as an artist. McCay, like Picasso, is introduced as the star of his film; an illustrious creator turning his particular genius to a new medium. Both films give us the artist as genius, and both seemingly work to demystify the process of creation by detailing its various stages and by simply making it visible. As Bazin argues in his analysis, however, Clouzot's film explains nothing, and the same can be said for *Little Nemo*. McCay's ability to produce his familiar characters rapidly and precisely does anything but demystify his creative ability. And because Picasso is hidden throughout most of *Le mystère Picasso*, either behind the screen or off-camera, the images seem to generate themselves. The hand is simultaneously venerated and hidden, recording the presence of the artist while also, through camera trickery, creating a record of the artist's supersession.

The argument that Bazin advances for Clouzot's film is not historically specific: the film is presented as a somewhat idiosyncratic examination of a somewhat idiosyncratic artist. But when his argument is applied to McCay's film, considered as both early animation and relatively early cinema, a historically important dimension emerges. The idolatry of the hand as an explanatory force in Clouzot's cinematic treatment of Picasso, and the revelation of duration, can be retrofitted to contribute to an understanding of the hand of the artist, the individual, within the context of mass production that defined industrial culture.

As I have noted, the two films begin by introducing their artist-stars, but the terms of that introduction could not be more different. Where McCay is surrounded by hale and hearty fellows, Picasso is seated alone in a black void. An iris out situates him in a bare space evocative of the film noirs of Anthony Mann and John Alton. Three pools of light break the darkness, creating a triptych of isolated objects: on the left is Picasso, seated on a wooden box; on the right is a wooden easel, holding an image that is turned away from the camera; and, between them, almost suturing them together, is a rough wooden panel, hinged in the middle, on which two of Picasso's images are hung (Figure 27). The artist, clad in undershirt and shorts, puffs on his cigarette, contemplates the panel, and moves to consider it more closely. This visual introduction is overlaid by a narration concerned with the unknowable mysteries of artistic creation ("We'd love to know that secret process, guiding the creator through his perilous journeys"), a mystery that the film will claim to partially solve, as watching the hand of the artist will reveal something of that process. The visible hand will translate the invisible workings of mind.

A reverse shot gives us Picasso, now approaching the camera, his eyes transfixed by his own works, which now lurk, beyond our gaze, on screen right. He pauses, his eyes shifting slightly from left to right. A further cut gives us Picasso's point of view, revealing two characteristic post-Cubist works pinned to the unfinished wood. The next shot has moved us further around the space: behind the panel, blocking our view of the great man. The easel faces toward the camera to screen left, its surface an unbroken white void, a blank canvas whose luminous whiteness contrasts with everything else within the scene. A cloud of cigarette smoke billows from behind the panel, and Picasso now moves again into view, receding from the camera to confront the canvas/screen/void.[47] He picks up a brush. The narration likens the act of creation to a walk on a tightrope as Picasso sketches a face. "If he slips and loses his balance, everything's lost." The face grows wings. "The painter stumbles like a blind man in the darkness of the white canvas." The face becomes a dove. The narrator informs us that Picasso has allowed us to witness his tightrope walk. This ends the precredit sequence of the film.

Both films thus begin by introducing the artist as a somewhat miraculous figure. McCay is positioned as *social,* a commercial artist drawing for a diegetic and nondiegetic audience. He engages in dialogue with other characters, produces a

FIGURE 27. *Le mystère Picasso,* 1955.

number of drawings for them, and is seen in his studio turning out the thousands of images required for the animation.[48] McCay "conjures" a piece of magic by making his pictures come to life. He is at once artist, entertainer, and magician. Picasso is positioned differently, as a solitary genius in an existential void, yet, the imperious playfulness that he will subsequently display will turn the artist Picasso into the entertainer Picasso, in a rather highfalutin vaudeville act of prestidigitation and showmanship.

Picasso now disappears from the screen, replaced by the series of images he produces from the other side of the surface. In the first (I won't describe them all), a slightly squeaky sound of the pen accompanies the appearance of black lines: a bearded figure, crouched with arm outstretched; the bust of a woman, then to the left of a bisecting line, the woman's body; an inset figure with a horse (Quixote on the wall?); spotted blacks and patterning—ultimately, a portrait of an artist painting a model. But it's not done. Heavier blacks obscure more and more of the image. The inks bleed. Only some of the original figures survive in an ocean of black (and the two inset figures floating above). The sound stops. The camera holds on the image. A wipe, white space, and the next picture begins, the action set to music this time. Now colors appear. Each image seems to introduce some new element or thwart any expectations that might carry over from an earlier production. One of the sequences runs backward so that the image is unproduced as we watch. The line drawing is supplemented by the stop-motion appearance of swathes of color and pattern. The whole thing is playful and very funny.

Eighteen minutes later Picasso reappears, shirtless now, behind his latest canvas, declaring his profligacy, machismo, and indefatigability, all at once: "I can go on all night." A huge Picasso nude dominates the black background. Then begins the film's most comedic sequence, as Picasso races the clock to produce a canvas within five minutes (the amount of film remaining in Claude Renoir's camera). Picasso expresses his desire to work in color ("It's more fun") but otherwise informs his waiting crew that the resulting picture will be a surprise. Now the camera is placed looking over Picasso's shoulder, just as McCay was filmed four decades earlier, as he begins the picture, a vase; only then does the camera return to its usual position on the far side of the image, which now becomes a fish.

This sequence, the most traditionally suspenseful sequence in this "suspense film," involves much cutting among shots of Picasso, his creation, Clouzot, the cameraman (Claude Renoir), and a still photographer. In this sequence alone do we hear the actual sound of the pen on the drawing surface, the instructions passing from director to star, the time counting down. Some dialogue has informed the audience that this is a color sequence, but Picasso spends a few minutes working monochrome—then switches to color with only two minutes left (actually, the sequence, filmed with two cameras, cuts between color and monochrome stocks). He races the clock, but the situation is less fraught than Picasso, and the audience, suspect: "I need more time," Picasso tells Clouzot, who responds, "I cheated to allow you more time!"[49] The cutting becomes more intense, as we move from a penetrating close-up of the artist's intent gaze to the image of a face—so it was a face!—that he has just completed.

Picasso makes another appearance about ten minutes later, declaring his satisfaction with another drawing and that it is finished. But, he says, "I need to make another one, with a different approach. I want to go deeper . . . and take more risks. I want to show all the different layers." The filmmakers move to Picasso's studio so he can work in oils, but the opacity of the standard canvas will require a different technique: stop-motion exposures from the artist's side of the canvas rather than continuous filming from the other. It is here that the film becomes more properly an "animated" film.[50] The images now appear to paint themselves; there is no longer a man behind the curtain, or screen, or paper. The hand of the artist now appears in the invisible interstices *between* frames. The exposures are not made after each stroke of the brush (as many descriptions of the film would have it) but rather after each action. So, as before: sections of the background suddenly change color. Now patterns appear. The bull gets stripes, then spots. Here are some lines—a bit later they have petals—they become flowers. Musical crescendos announce each anticipated-but-unexpected change until the painting is complete. The loss of real time clearly disturbs Clouzot: "It bothers me that people will think you did this in ten minutes." "How long has it taken me?" "Five hours." "Well, now people know."

Picasso demands a bigger canvas, and the film expands to CinemaScope proportions to accommodate him. The imp has co-opted the cinematic apparatus itself; Ko-Ko has escaped the inkwell and taken over the studio. A new scale, a new medium, really. Picasso now shifts to collage, as cutout shapes of fabric and paper (perhaps wallpaper), appear in stop-motion. Picasso moves to mixed-media, drawing and painting over his collage with a palate that evokes his Cubist period. Picasso paints a woman reclining in an odalisque (the perfect pose for the Cinema-Scope frame). He changes her pose, adjusts her expression; the picture acquires layers of erasures and a mutability that suggests the animated films of William Kentridge.

So, while McCay entirely vanished from *Little Nemo,* replaced by the animated product of his own hands, Picasso continually reappears, asserting his will and willfulness. He hardly seems enervated by the endeavor; indeed, he seems rather animated himself. Picasso embodies both labor *and* anima here: he is animator and animated, creator and creation. He morphs chickens into faces, changes the mode of production, and breaks the (academy ratio) frame. Flip was the mischief-maker in *Little Nemo,* but in *Le mystère Picasso* it is the capricious Picasso who plays that role.

Clouzot's stated intention was "to make a pedagogical film for those interested in art." " 'And to think that I wanted to make a cartoon!' sighed Picasso" (according to the film's promotional material anyway).[51] Picasso is not only the artist/creator, the controlling hand that makes the cartoon; he is also what Norman Klein has called the controller figure *within* the film, the mischievous imp with shifting tactics who keeps the viewer (and even the filmmakers) off-balance, the disobedient machine that wages war against the cinematic machine itself.[52] His last appearance before the camera comes at the end of the film. He walks across the screen, signs his name (and thus, the film) on a sheet of paper, and declares, à la Porky Pig (sans stutter), "This is the end."[53]

Of course, Picasso's strengths as a cartoon character, the pronounced presence he brings to his performance, implies that the "animated" sequences are somewhat less autonomous than in more traditional cartoons. In some ways it is as impossible to *forget* that Picasso is behind that screen, making every mark, as it is impossible to *remember* that McCay drew every stroke of that two-minute animated tour de force. Picasso produces images, not characters—his human figures are only occasions for aesthetic play, not figures of identification or narrative function. And the images are largely drawn from Picasso's well-known iconography: if he doesn't have a Gertie or a Nemo, he has his nudes, his artists, his toreadors, his Cubist distortions. But in another sense Picasso disappears into his images as surely as does McCay.

What disappears—surprisingly, given the film's mandate—is, first of all, the hand of the artist. After the opening scene, for the first few pictures, that hand was hidden but present. Yet the instant Picasso stops making lines in real time, opting instead to work in stop-motion, painting whole sections between exposures, the "thought process" that the hand was to reveal is elided in favor of a new mode of production that seems more like instantaneous thought. It is as though the artist thinks, "This should be blue," and in having the thought, suddenly it is. Or—perhaps it is now the *image* that thinks. No longer a recording of production, then, but a shift to an image that seems not simply to draw but to *think* itself. Animism in *Le mystère Picasso* is thus not as much about movement as it is about thought. The inanimate possesses a consciousness, which manifests itself in metamorphosis. It comes to life in a different way: it thinks itself into being.

So the images pulse with *something,* even though it's something different, and why not call it animistic spirit as Eisenstein did: "a rejection of once-and-forever allotted form, freedom from ossification, the ability to dynamically assume any form." What began as a professed desire to understand the process through which an artist produces an image becomes an arena for the image's liberation; the created world on canvas and onscreen becomes invested with a thoroughgoing, bewitching animism.

Sianne Ngai reserves the term *animistic animation* to refer to the type of animation that Eisenstein celebrates, the animation that represents "a triumph over the fetters of form."[54] I would slightly tweak Ngai's term to include animation that privileges, as both the Picasso and McCay films do, metamorphosis over movement, mutability over character. Animistic animation presents a continual morphing of forms; it is less concerned with movement through space than with change over time. It speaks to duration.

In his analysis of the film, Bazin notes that paintings are always accreted duration[55]—the time of viewing a painting has little correlation to the time of its production, which corresponds to Bryson's conception of the deictic. The initial thought-process, the small studies, the palimpsests of painted-over surfaces and reconfigured compositions, the abandoned directions—most of this is invisible to the viewer of the finished work. While museums might display some of the preliminary studies or provide X-rays of the underlying layers, all of this is supplemental to one's experience of the painting-object. In Clouzot's film, however, a painting is something that exists in time, better apprehended in its process of becoming than in its final state—as Bazin writes, "only film could make us see duration itself."[56] What we perceive is a strikingly literal version of what Bergson called our sense of a "thickened present": "a continuous flux . . . a succession of states each of which announces that which follows and contains that which precedes it."[57] The thickening layers of ink or pigment are only the concretization of that thickened present: it consists primarily of our memories and anticipations of what the image was, is, and might be.

It is in this revelation of process and accreted time that *Le mystère Picasso* becomes, for Bazin, Bergsonian, and this aspect is closely related to his sense of it as a suspense film as well. McCay's film is also Bergsonian—it, too, gives us images that are never "finished," that are always in the process of becoming, and so, on another level, *Le mystère Picasso* becomes significant for its rediscovery of some of the "primitivism" of early animation, with its dual emphasis on handiwork and mechanical process.[58] Indeed, the resemblance of Clouzot's film to an earlier tradition in the history of animated films was also noted, though in negative terms, by Bosley Crowther of the *New York Times,* who wrote that "the swift evolution of [Picasso's] drawing has about the same novelty as did the old out-of-the-inkwell movie cartoons."[59]

Through Bazin one can understand the film as a particularly clear instance of Deleuze's time-image: an image that speaks to duration over completion, suspension over resolution. The alignment of such a film with the time-image is interesting, for Deleuze himself wrote about cartoons in the context of the movement-image, and most cartoons are probably most easily understood in that way. This tradition emphasizes movement over metamorphosis. Characters exhibit strong visual continuity (despite the exaggerations of stretching-and-squashing bodies, eyeball-popping double takes, and similar effects) and inhabit a world strongly informed by mechanisms of cause and effect (coyotes, cats, and Elmer Fudd all deploying elaborate plots to achieve a simple, stated goal—to, for example, "kill da wabbit"). Such cartoons are predicated on the existence of a world in which discrete actions take place. A common technique in animation is to draw the first and final poses of a figure's action and then fill in the intermittent stages between those poses. This betrays a predilection for the purposive, causal, completed actions that constitute the movement-image. But within the history of animation lies a tradition that privileges metamorphosis over spatial trajectory, that emphasizes the *time* of becoming over the *space* of action, and it is to this tradition that both *Le mystère Picasso* and *Little Nemo* belong.

Both *Little Nemo* and *Le mystère Picasso* could safely be classified as animistic animations.[60] So if *Le mystère Picasso* is a "Bergsonian film," as Bazin would have it, then so is *Little Nemo,* and they are also, and for the same reasons, Deleuzian films. But I also want to claim that animistic animation represents more than an inscription of duration; it also belongs to Deleuze's movement of world.

Movement of world and animism would hardly seem to go together—they belong to utterly different systems of thought—and yet they overlap in their fascination with energies of motion and the animatedness of worlds. Most of the writings on enervated or deanimated animators concentrate on the animated body that inherits the movement of the animator (and this is a very direct inheritance—*this* set of movements by the animator yields *that* set of movements for the character). But, as I noted above, the animism of early cartoons frequently permeates the entire onscreen world. Of *Little Nemo* and *Gertie the Dinosaur,* Crafton observes, "McCay's restless moving lines are part of the excitement of the films."[61] It is not only the characters that take on the attributes of life but the image itself. And if the world inherits the animatic condition that once belonged to the animator, then we have a situation remarkably similar to what Deleuze labels movement of world.

This category of image posits the world as taking up the movement that was once the province of the film's protagonist—in films produced in the wake of the Second World War, the human is deactivated, living a purposeless existence in a world of any-space-whatevers, and the world moves to compensate for the loss of mobility experienced by this postwar subject. In, fact, all those Fordist critiques that track the transfer of energy from enervated animator to energized image link up rather nicely with the condition of Deleuze's time-image, which is, after all, situated within a postwar environment in which the ability to purposefully act has been severely truncated, hence: "it is no longer the character who reacts to the optical-sound situation, it is a movement of world which supplements the faltering movement of the character. . . . The world takes responsibility for the movement that the subject can no longer or cannot make."[62] The Fordist critiques of Eisenstein's utopian anima are also rooted in a historical shift, this time in modes of production (from artisanal handcraft to industrial division of labor)—in both cases there is a crisis of agency that is expressed in the passage from deactivated person to activated image-world.

It must be said that Winsor McCay and Pablo Picasso do not perform deactivation readily. Both *Little Nemo* and *Le mystère Picasso* go to great lengths to celebrate the artists' genius and their uniqueness. Their labors are visible, their hands sure— they are marvelous beings. As with McCay, Picasso is simultaneously, if contradictorily, presented as wizard and worker. In his indefatigable ability to turn out work after work, Picasso is something of a human motor, as was McCay, and arguably even more so. McCay, after all, clocks out after completing his four thousand drawings, while Picasso tells Clouzot, "I don't mind being tired. I can go on all night if you want."[63] (He is, however, a rather more *bohemian* human motor than McCay.) Preceded onscreen by puffs of cigarette smoke, Picasso appears as something of a "painting locomotive"—a phrase Van Gogh used to describe his own manic productivity in a letter to his brother, Theo. In the promotional literature for the film Clouzot wrote: "Picasso, a *magician* in spite of himself, transforms a flower into a bird. With everyone exhausted by the pace, Picasso *tirelessly* sparked forth veritable fireworks of lines and colors, reflecting all the themes of his lifetime. As the bloody corridas, still lifes and nudes streamed forth endlessly from his fertile brain, he made one think of an old *wizard* waving brushes and paints."[64]

Picasso is another lightning-sketch artist, and like McCay he is a machine and a magician, a laborer and a conjurer. This conflation of magic and industry is not unique to these two artists. Thomas Edison, who described himself as a dynamo, was also known as "The Wizard of Menlo Park." George Lucas's special effects company is called Industrial Light and Magic. Rhetorics of industry and alchemy, labor and anima, abut one another unselfconsciously. One resembles the other too much to ignore; both produce marvels. As Arthur C. Clarke's famous dictum holds, "Any sufficiently advanced technology is indistinguishable from magic."[65] But it also speaks to the persistence of the uneasy relation between handcraft and industrial production that Shapiro identified in the fine arts around the end of the nineteenth century: an industrial level of production, a machinic efficiency, but at the same time, the products of a single hand—an artist, a conjurer. To be a machine yet not a machine, to be machine and human and superhuman at once—there is surely something alchemical at work. Is this undecidability, this slippage, animation's first uncanny valley?

Little Nemo and *Le mystère Picasso* share significant structural, formal, and rhetorical elements. Both films celebrate the handmade in the age of industrial production; both reveal, yet elide, the process of creation; both alchemically transform labor into anima; both slip between the rationality of production and the irrationality of production. The artist in each film becomes a kind of preternatural force. At the same time, neither is completely unpredictable: McCay draws the stars of his renowned comic strip, and Picasso dwells extensively upon his own personal iconography. But, finally, real differences emerge in their respective relations to industrial culture. McCay's film celebrates precision, mass production, meticulous timing, and a craftsman-artist who is also something of an automaton. Clouzot's film celebrates improvisation, variant and unpredictable temporality, and an industrial technology that must conform to the caprices of the idiosyncratic artist. Picasso, the artist, may draw on his trademarked iconography, but every picture he creates is unique, the results of each endeavor unpredictable. McCay, however, recreates the familiar characters of Nemo's universe with breathtaking precision and fidelity. McCay becomes an almost literal human motor—a craftsman who nevertheless exemplifies the machinic precision of the industrial age—but Picasso, shirtless and contemplative, becomes the artist existing apart from the machineries of production—a unique figure alone in a universe of his own making.

THE ANIMATOR VANISHES

As the history of animated film progresses, the animator, whose presence informs the films of Cohl, McCay, the Fleischers, and others, begins to vanish from the screen. This is hardly a continuous process, however, and it's amusing to compare the treatment of the animator in a handful of films produced between 1918 and 1931.

In 1918 McCay produced his most ambitious film, in both length (it was the longest cartoon produced to that time) and seriousness—it chronicled the sinking of the RMS *Lusitania*. Using a strikingly more realistic style than he employed either in his earlier animations or in the allegorical editorial cartoons that he was now producing, McCay's work still retains an almost documentary-like immediacy and intensity. "From here on you are looking at the first record of the sinking of the *Lusitania*," an intertitle declares. In this film McCay is presented as neither wizard nor laborer—and he is never shown producing a drawing. We see him meeting with someone to get "the details of the sinking—necessary for the work to follow," and, after a further title informs us of the twenty-five thousand drawings that will need to be produced, we see him presiding over a studio of half a dozen artists (and what looks like one researcher or archivist). Somewhat strangely, considering his self-presentation in earlier films, McCay is wearing his hat and coat and appears to be *leaving* the studio. He is the credited author of the film, but the production process is more familiar, less prosaic—it requires *workers,* not human motors or magicians.

Before Max Fleischer's Out of the Inkwell cartoons there was Bobby Bumps, from Bray productions. Each Bobby Bumps cartoon was introduced with the animator's hand drawing, first, the main characters (Bobby and Fido) and then the scenic elements for their latest adventure. In *Bobby Bumps Puts a Beanery on the Bum* (1918) the hand draws Bobby lying on his back with his eyes closed. Bobby obligingly lifts his leg so the animator can draw the rest of his foot. He looks rather like a corpse, so the effect of his sudden animation is more startling than perhaps intended. The animator then issues a set of instructions by writing them next to Bobby: "HAT OFF"—so he can ink Bobby's hair. "TURN OVER"—so he can finish coloring in his shorts. Bobby mischievously hops aboard the hand, leading to the next instruction: "GET OFF MY HAND." After drawing Fido ("YOU FORGOT HIS TAIL," Bobby helpfully points out in a speech balloon—a feature associated with comics that was frequently deployed in silent cartoons), the hand outlines the front of a beanery displaying a help wanted sign, a bottle of ink pours over the scene to provide an attractive wash, and the story begins.

The hand will return at various points—to break up a fight between Fido and a nasty little cat and to aid Bobby, who is being chased by the irate proprietor of said beanery. "HELP," says Bobby, and the hand enters the scene to provide a ladder as a means of escape. After Bobby and Fido climb up, the hand erases the bottom of the ladder, leaving the perplexed beanery-owner below. One last act of assistance: Bobby is given a realistic inkwell, and he pours ink down over his adversary, drowning the screen in a flood of black, which ends the cartoon. The Bobby Bumps cartoons point back to McCay's work earlier in the decade, in their depiction of the presence of the animator as well as in the interaction between animator and character, and point ahead to Crockett Johnson's *Harold and the Purple Crayon.*

Disney's Alice comedies belong to a more baroque period of this history. Disney inverted the "out of the inkwell" formula, placing a live figure into an animated world. Nevertheless, the first of these, *Alice's Wonderland* (1923), retains an emphasis on production. This "Laugh-o-gram" begins with young Alice ("chuck full of curiosity") visiting a cartoon studio. A frighteningly young Walt Disney, seen putting the finishing touches on a picture of a doghouse, invites her over to watch him work. He shows her the picture, which abruptly begins moving about and emitting cartoonish symbols of a struggle taking place. A small dog flies out the door backward, then charges back in, engaged in a losing battle with one pissed-off cat. Alice is predictably delighted and tours the rest of the studio. Cartoon cats are playing music and dancing about on a drawing table, and an animated mouse is tormenting a live-action cat (a nice effect). One young animator sits before a picture of two boxing dogs; he beckons his coworkers (presumably Hugh Harman, Rudolph Ising, and Ub Iwerks) over to watch a couple of rounds of the canines pummeling one another. Here the labor of producing a cartoon is entirely elided. The animators have become observers, rather than producers, of animated antics. The rest of the cartoon takes place in Alice's subsequent dream, in which she travels to Cartoonland as an honored guest—a narrative that gestures as much toward Winsor McCay as to Lewis Carroll.

The inevitable apotheosis of all this is the 1931 Van Buren cartoon *In a Cartoon Studio*. Here cartoon characters produce cartoons, as repetitive cycles of drawings depict cartoon characters producing repetitive cycles of drawings. Office boys carry tottering piles of drawing paper and giant bottles of ink (McCay's spirit hovers here). A model moves through each incremental stage of movement as an animator draws her—as he flips through his drawings to check his work, the model dances in synchrony with her drawn counterpart. An anthropomorphic movie camera skips through the scene, hand-cranking its own head to record the various sequences being created. The film culminates with the premiere of the cartoon, which the cartoon characters thoroughly enjoy.

And so the animator fades from view. The onscreen production of images, a production that fully established the authority of the artist, is superseded by an increasing emphasis on autonomous characters.[66] The Out of the Inkwell cartoons of the Fleischers and films from the Bray Studios frequently presented the relation between animator and animated creation as something of a battle, with Ko-Ko, for example, engaging in a swordfight against Fleischer's pen wielding hand. "The playful struggle between the animator and his creation that typifies the plots," Crafton argues, "is an allegory expressing the shift in importance away from the artist to the work."[67] The cartoon character comes to provide the continuity and centering function once furnished by the figure of the animator. But, despite their becoming "agents of his will," what Crafton elides is that this transition in emphasis from animator to character also serves to repress the animator—now *animators*—as producer. When animation was no longer the product of a single hand, after the single creator had become something of a fiction, the onscreen animator perhaps *had* to be erased. The images and the life they possess begin to seem self-generated, springing spontaneously into existence with no evident progenitor.

But the disappearance of the animator also raises the questions posed at the outset of this chapter regarding the energy and vitalism of the animated character: whose energy is this? Crafton, writing about the special status of the animator, the bestower of anima, the spirit of life, states, "For an artist to be able to bring something to life bestows upon him the status of a privileged being."[68] This notion of the animator as conscious, powerful, and of almost divine agency stands in notable contrast to the figure described by Sianne Ngai, who notes the "unexpected mechanization of the human animator by the inhuman object he animates."[69] In this view life is not simply bestowed by the animator upon the inanimate; it is transferred, and this transference occurs at no small cost to the animator. (Nor is this specific to the cartoon film. Susan Stewart wrote of a considerably earlier technology that "the automaton repeats and thereby displaces the position of its author.")[70] The animator becomes less of a divinity and more of a cog in the wheel of industrial production, churning out image after image, pouring days of labor into a few seconds of film. The human motor is dehumanized, deanimated, mechanized by the process of animation. This Fordist tension perhaps explains more thoroughly than Crafton does the battle between creator and creation that subtends the history of animation. All those imps and sprites escaping out of the inkwell like genies from their bottles escape the very automatism and mechanization to which their creators have been consigned.[71]

Rosalind Krauss offers a further complication: "Is there not a sense," she writes, "in which Disney's 'triumph,' along with that of the other Hollywood cartoonists, is not a revolt against the rationalization of the human body, but its cast shadow, its dialectical underside now made to surface as comical?"[72] She finds in a Tom and Jerry gag (Jerry's legs turn to wheels to aid his getaway) an expression of, rather than a rejection of, a Taylorist conception of the body. The plasmatic becomes the shadow of instrumental reason. There is, in Krauss's question, an echo, probably unintentional, of Terry Castle's discussion of the uncanny as a "kind of toxic side effect" of "the aggressively rationalist imperatives" of the eighteenth century.[73] Both Krauss and Castle discover an oasis of disorder lurking somewhere within the vast deserts of reason and industrial capitalism, but they choose to understand its presence differently, Krauss emphasizing (or at least pointing to) the ideological constraints on the plasmatic imagination. She seems fully aware of this literal ambivalence in thinking about the plasmatic when, later in the same paragraph, she proposes that there is little difference between the two "opposed" views of Disney espoused by Eisenstein and Stanley Cavell, between the former's idea of Disney's cartoons as exemplars of anima and the latter's "condemnation of the weightlessness of cartoons."[74] Liberation, or a further mark of containment? Ossification, or its opposite?[75]

There are still other ways to come at this issue. As Art Spiegelman has noted, "Cartoonists 'become' each character in their comics, acting out every gesture and expression."[76] Using somewhat different language, William Schaffer notes, "The animator finds himself reanimated in turn by the characters he animates and feels himself becoming a cartoon. Resonances of influence are conducted back through the pencil into the vibrating network formed by the strings of the artist's nervous system."[77] The linearity of cause and effect is replaced by a self-modifying feedback loop. Who animates, and who is animated? Chuck Jones subtitled his memoir, *The Life and Times of an Animated Cartoonist*. Furthermore, the process of filming a person (Winsor McCay, let's say) breaks continuous movement into discrete units, the same units that when projected reproduce movement. Animator becomes animated (or animation material) then reanimated.

Keith Broadfoot and Rex Butler argue that "the direction of the metaphoric transferral cannot be established in animation for the simple reason that animation is the very presentation of the metaphoric—the transferral—itself."[78] In this, they note, Eisenstein recognized that Disney had done him one better in the treatment of metaphor. For them the appearance of the animator in these early films suggests that "the two characters—the animator and the animated—and the two gestures— the gesture of the animator's hand and the gesture of the character's figure," constitute an absolute resemblance. "But this resemblance itself can never be actually given: it would be only the moment of animation which connects them. The animator is trying to depict the equivalence between the movement of his hand and the movement of the character, but the enigma of his art is that this equivalence can never be seen. This moment of equivalence, although the animator must always anticipate it to begin to draw at all, must also be unexpected, a product of chance."[79]

So, again, the animated figure doubles the movement of the animator, who must disappear, but in Broadfoot and Butler's formulation of this transfer the animator remains invisibly present—for the movement of the character remains the movement of the animator—the gestures and poses as the animator acts out the scenario, and the movement of the hand that renders the stages of movement. The cartoon becomes the indexical trace of the animator's movements, they note, as surely as swirling lines of a Jackson Pollock canvas represent the movements of his now-absent body, but it is an equivalence that must remain equivocal.

Schaffer and Broadfoot and Butler provide a less linear, less deterministic model of the process of animation, but it works best for the early films, the *Fantasmagories* and *Gerties*, when the single animator really does double himself in onscreen animated forms, than it does for the fully Fordist mode of production that quickly dominates animation production. And, within that mode, it works to varying degrees for the directors and animators at or near the top of the labor hierarchy. Below a certain point, however, we run smack into the realities of factory production, when Popeye's punch would be the product of the labors of directors, designers, lead animators, assistant animators, in-betweeners, and painters, not to mention sound recordists and voice talent ("resemblance" might still hold for those highest in the hierarchy of labor—the directors and lead animators).

Here, as ever, Sianne Ngai's parsing of these oppositions is helpful: she notes that the cartoon body's elasticity is the sign of *both* "the body's autonomization (since the pliancy of an object suggests its heightened vulnerability to external manipulation)" *and* "the source of an unaccounted-for autonomy."[80] Flip might be something of an autonomous prankster, but watching Flip and Impy repetitively squash and stretch like a phenakistoscopic illusion, it becomes evident that these animated figures are little more than clockwork mechanisms, automata really, whose every movement and function has been timed to the fraction of a second. McCay could therefore be seen as a different kind of human motor—not a dynamo, not a source of power, but simply a properly functioning machine—a human motor producing quasi-human motors (and thus *re*producing). His labor yields a body or bodies that are as fully regulated as bodies can be. But even this is too simple—remember that they squash and stretch at Nemo's command, and Nemo is clearly serving as McCay's onscreen surrogate, exercising the animator's will and demonstrating his virtuosic control. In this sequence, activation and deactivation, autonomization and autonomy, coincide (that it is the racialized characters who submit to Nemo's will has already been noted).

But, to some degree, the plasmaticness of the animated drawings *does* speak to a new freedom. Flip and Gertie possess an autonomy, a presence; they at least *appear* as no longer subject to the authority of the animator's hand. As in the myth of Pygmalion, the creation takes on a life of its own (or perhaps even leeches life from its creator).[81] Thus begins a long tradition in the history of animation: the creation that gets away from its creator—the subject of the next chapter. Is it a coincidence that the character that inaugurates the Nemo animation is the mischievous Flip, who is surely the prelude to the more openly disobedient Gertie (accused by McCay of being a "bad girl")?

But if labor produces an anima that compensates for its own enervation, is it a compromised anima, produced through the precise calibrations demanded of the machine age? Whether anima is truly lost to the instrumental forces of control is a question to be taken up in the next chapter.

Chapter 4

DISOBEDIENT MACHINES

Disobedience, in the eyes of anyone who has read history, is man's original virtue.

—OSCAR WILDE, THE SOUL OF MAN UNDER SOCIALISM

The preceding chapter emphasized the intimate bond between the animator's labor and that labor's product. This chapter will explore the trope of the *disobedient machine*—the animated creation that turns its back on its creator to pursue its own agendas, fulfill its own desires, or perhaps just fail in its own way. Such figures enact complex tensions among the terms *animation, automatism,* and *autonomy,* and—as the second part of the chapter will demonstrate—they don't need to be cartoon characters at all. There are ways in which Eliza Doolittle is to Henry Higgins as Gertie the Dinosaur is to Winsor McCay—a virtuosic creation that demonstrates the creator's abundant skill, a creation rooted in a wager or a dare, a creation that must pass a test on its creator's behalf. Both Eliza and Gertie have their moments of compliance and their moments of resistance. The first part of the chapter will consider versions of disobedient machines encountered in animated films—cartoons, of course, but also horror and science fiction films that use animated models and/or whose narratives turn upon the animation of inanimate matter. The second part will turn to disobedient machines of the human variety, works that feature vivacious, "animated" characters who, like their cartoon forebears, are not so easily, or thoroughly, contained.

ANIMATED DISOBEDIENCE

As discussed at length in the preceding chapter, the Fordist mode of animation production mitigates against the spontaneous and the uncontrolled. "And yet," Norman Klein adds, "so much anarchic energy is possible." Klein, in analyzing the Hollywood short cartoon, brilliantly describes cartoon characters as "automata that struggle." I have already suggested that cartoon physics are actually a function of animation's reversal of the filmic production process, in which movement is constructed rather than reconstructed. Klein, too, locates in the narrative content of the Hollywood cartoon an allegorical relation to its mode of production that manifests itself in the continual narrative tug-of-war between animator and animated, between the characters he labels the *controllers* and those he calls the *overreactors* (the functions often shift between the characters in the seven minutes of gags—from Jerry to Tom and back again).[1] Narrative replaces the animistic spirit that the process took out, producing situations of propulsive anarchy, mutability (mutable anarchy?), and endless struggles to determine who controls and who eludes control.[2] Following Klein, William Schaffer proposes that "animation implies a singular *experiment* in the possibilities of perception and a profound *allegory* of the relationship between humans and machines."[3] In essence, cartoon characters don't rebel because they *can* but almost because they *have to.*

The anarchic spirit of these cartoons is, I think, a continuation of the animistic energy that Eisenstein lauded, but it is an energy that now manifests itself more strongly as performance rather than as a given within the medium itself. Here we see the need for the disobedient animated creation—the Gertie who, despite McCay's promise that she "will do everything I tell her to do," insists, from her first moments onscreen, on doing things her own way. *Gertie the Dinosaur* provides anima on two levels: first there is the appealing oscillation of all the lines that compose her and her world, and then there is the *performance* of anima in her reluctance to follow instructions, her refusal to submit to the regulation that undergirds her very existence. It goes without saying (I hope) that Gertie's disobedience has been carefully timed, to allow for her interaction with the live McCay onstage.[4]

Sublime Monsters; Uncanny Automata

Cinematic narrative has, from its inception, been intrigued by tales of the unnatural creation of life, an unnatural creation that often allegorized the cinematic apparatus itself. The literary historian Michelle Bloom argues that the cinema was the locus for a reinvigoration of a "Pygmalionesque" desire that transcended any particular narrative iteration. "The very medium," she writes, "embodies the long-standing human desire for the animation of the inanimate. Even when the Pygmalion paradigm fails in film [narrative], the medium itself succeeds in creating the illusion of movement."[5] The cinema quickly discovered the mysteries of stop-motion trick films and films that animated a series of drawings, and animation has persisted (and arguably has become the dominant mode) in the era of digital production, although it remains associated most strongly with fantasy and children's entertainment.

In tone, films like *Pinocchio* (1940), *Gertie the Dinosaur,* and the Out of the Inkwell cartoons of the 1920s and 1930s are quite different from other tales of synthesized life, such as *Frankenstein* (1931), *Metropolis* (1926), and more recent science fictions, including *2001: A Space Odyssey* (1968) and *Blade Runner* (1982). All these works tell of the creation of a being or beings that, at some moment, begin to act autonomously; Nemo, Gertie, the robot Maria, Pinocchio, Frankenstein's Monster, Hal, and the various replicants all become disobedient machines. But while some creatures, Gertie and Pinocchio among them, are allowed their trespasses, for other disobedient machines the consequences can be dire. (I will concentrate on relatively early instances of the creation of synthetic life in the cinema, works that are, not coincidentally, most devoted to detailing the act of creation itself.)

Perhaps these tales can be usefully distinguished from one another by their alignment with two rhetorical modes: the uncanny and the sublime. Some of these disobedient machines are uncontainable, *sublimely* terrifying rather than *uncannily* disturbing. The sublime and the uncanny are closely related: both stage a confrontation with the limits of human power and agency, and both are heavily freighted with the weight of the unknown. And yet they operate at different scales, raise different questions, play through different conflicts, and align with different aesthetics. The sublime figures the unknown as excess; the uncanny presents the familiar in terms of estrangement. Both inaugurate crises for the subject: the sublime appears and is resolved as an epistemological crisis around the limits of human knowledge; the uncanny instantiates an existential crisis centered on the unknowable interiority of the self. The uncanny is preoccupied with undecidability, the porous boundaries between human and nonhuman, organic and inorganic.

Anthony Vidler has pointed to the close relation between the two modes: "Aesthetically an outgrowth of the Burkean sublime," the uncanny is "a domesticated version of absolute terror, to be experienced in the comfort of the home and relegated to the minor genre of the *Märchen* or fairy tale."[6] In the uncanny, argues Tzvetan Todorov, "events are related which may be readily accounted for by the laws of reason, but which are, in one way or another, incredible, extraordinary, shocking, singular, disturbing or unexpected, and which thereby provoke in the character and in the reader a reaction similar to that which works of the fantastic have made familiar."[7] The uncanny is rooted in conundrums of logic and rationality, while the very nature of the sublime pushes beyond those boundaries.

The creation of artificial life, in both literature and film, is often fraught with elements of the sublime. Such stories nearly always engage the discourse of *things man was not meant to know;* not for nothing is *Frankenstein* subtitled *The Modern Prometheus.* Synthetic creation narratives are about, among other things, the harnessing of power—perhaps an inappropriate power—a power that dazzles and seduces. In these stories, as elsewhere, the sublime stages a confrontation between man and the limits of his power. The creation of life becomes an occasion for sublime excess. The arcing lights and bubbling beakers involved in the creation of the robot Maria recur in the storm-tossed skies and the crackling of lightning that

FIGURE 28. *Metropolis,* 1926.

presage the animation of Frankenstein's Monster and his ineffable Bride in James
Whale's two *Frankenstein* films (immeasurably aided by Franz Waxman's florid or-
chestrations). And there is King Kong: the synthetic creation of animator Willis
O'Brien. The narrative presents Kong as *discovered* in nature rather than *created* in
a laboratory, so he might seem out of place here, yet the film is obsessively centered
on its own spectacle of synthetic life (does the film's advertising slogan, "The Eighth
Wonder of the World" refer to the giant ape or to the miniature model brought to
life through cinematic magic?). Sublime excess pervades *King Kong.* The shrouded
mysteries of Skull Island speak for themselves, and after his capture he is, just like
the robot Maria before him (Figure 28), "premiered" before a cosmopolitan crowd.
The staccato popping of blinding flashbulbs in this sequence replaces the atmospheric spectacle and the montage of scientific contraptions found in the other films,
and, just as the first evidence of life in *Frankenstein* was the monster's twitching hand,
so it is Kong's arm that first breaks free of the onstage constraints that bind him.
The spectacle of the inanimate creature "coming to life" cuts across these films, accompanied by as much *Sturm und Drang* as the filmmakers can muster.

Mad scientists are sublime; or they at least venture into the territory of the sublime. There is alchemy at work, or sorcery: some kind of transgression against the

laws of matter and man. The mad scientist operates on that border between a properly scientific knowledge and taboo theories and methods. The films fairly crackle with demonic energies, energies that also seem to be the lifeblood of the creators themselves. Henry Frankenstein frantically scrambles about his cavernous laboratory, a manic gleam in his eye, in the sequence that culminates with his hysterical shriek of "It's alive!" Carl Denham pontificates at breakneck pace throughout the first half of *King Kong,* verbally flattening everything in his path. And the mad inventor Rotwang in *Metropolis,* already partly artificial, masterfully manipulates the switches and levers like a symphony conductor. Indeed, there is another sense in which we can see these figures as "conductors": in that their own demonic energies seem to be transferred to their very creations. Denham and Rotwang virtually disappear from the scene after the birth of their creations, and Henry Frankenstein lies catatonic. In every case the somewhat problematic animatedness of the creator seems to infect, or is somehow conducted into, his creation.[8] The opening of *Bride of Frankenstein* gives us Lord Byron speaking of the lovely Mary Shelley as the mind that conceived a Frankenstein—authors are mad scientists, too.[9]

Compared with these demagogues and demigods, Winsor McCay cuts a rather more benign figure. Yet in some ways his *Little Nemo* film is an exemplary creation-of-life film (*Gertie* even more so). The film, after all, begins with McCay making the ridiculous claim that he can make his pictures, his characters, move, a claim to which his friends respond with warm mockery. Like Frankenstein and Rotwang, McCay wields the power to bring the inanimate to life. Here, too, the creator's own ferocious energy seems to transfer to his drawings—as we saw in the previous chapter, after the Nemo animation begins, McCay disappears. The drawings not only take on properties of life but seem to obviate the necessity of a creator at all. Gertie is even more alchemical—McCay wants to restore life to a prehistoric being, after all. Oddly, there is no cinematic apparatus: after making his thousands of drawings, McCay appears before his cartoonist friends and draws a picture of a rocky landscape with a cave from which he will summon Gertie. Of course, this is meant to recreate the live-action performance in which an onstage McCay interacted with his animated Gertie. But when you stop to think about what's going on here, it appears less like a playful cinematic experiment, like *Little Nemo,* and something more like sorcery.

But it is difficult to imagine spectators reacting to the animation of the trickster Flip or the adorable Gertie with the same terror inspired by Frankenstein's Monster or the robot Maria. Nor does one hear about McCay's films producing the sort of shock that presumably greeted the film of a train arriving at La Ciotat as recorded by the Lumière *cinématographe.* Instead, it seems likely that the effect was of something playful, marvelous—remarkable, surely, but hardly the stuff of a paradigm shift. These characters belong more firmly to the realm of the *uncanny* than the *sublime.* If artificial life narratives frequently reference the rhetoric of the sublime through their invocation of the dark realms beyond everyday reality, they also, almost inevitably, summon a sense of the uncanny. The doubled figure of creator/creation, the shadow figure that haunts the original, the familiar returned in the guise of the unfamiliar: these are common tropes of uncanny representation. After all, as a character remarks in Karel Čapek's 1920 robot saga *R. U. R.*, "nothing is stranger to man than his own image."[10]

Wilhelm Jentsch posited that a feeling of uncanniness could arise in an encounter with clockwork automata: "In telling a story one of the most successful devices for easily creating uncanny effects is to leave the reader in uncertainty whether a particular figure in the story is a human being or an automaton."[11] The double belongs to the field of the uncanny, but the automaton belongs to the technological uncanny—specifically, a *mechanical* uncanny. While automata might deceive the eye or ear, their motive force is neither mysterious nor alchemical but rather a matter of clockworks. They are engineered creations, often produced by a solitary figure who is something more of a tinkerer than a man obsessed: Jacques de Vaucanson; *Pinocchio's* Geppetto; Spalanzani, the inventor in E. T. A. Hoffmann's tale "The Sandman"; the fictional Edison of *The Future Eve*. These are not mad scientists; they do not tap demonic or sublime energies.

The sublime as a phenomenon is aligned with the gigantic, while the uncanny is more easily aligned with the miniature. Kong, Maria, and Frankenstein's Monster all bear the mark of excess and gigantism in their very beings as well as their sites of origin: the gargantuan Kong and the tribal rites of his Skull Island home; Maria's mesmeric powers, which she shares with the vast and glittering Metropolis itself; the Monster's horrific visage, and the mountaintop laboratory where he is given life. As Susan Stewart has written, "the gigantic represents infinity, exteriority, the public, and the overly natural. . . . The gigantic unleashes a vast and 'natural' creativity that bears within it the capacity for (self)-destruction."[12] The monster is gigantic, while the automaton is something more of a miniature. The miniature is characterized by "clockwork precision," Stewart notes; it "represents a mental world of proportion, control, and balance," while the gigantic "presents a physical world of disorder and disproportion." The miniature further represents "closure, interiority, the domestic, and the overly cultural."[13] The sublime is expansive, large-scaled, cosmic; the uncanny is an altogether quieter and more intimate mode (Freud's own example, of course, was the childhood home). Its operative mode is less slack-jawed wonder than a subtle frisson. The sublime is best appreciated from the safety of distance, while the uncanny is an altogether more proximate and intimate phenomenon.

Fundamental to Jentsch's description of the uncanny is a state of undecidability. Following him, Vidler writes that the uncanny is, "in its aesthetic dimension, a representation of a mental state of projection that precisely elides the boundaries of the real and the unreal in order to provoke a disturbing ambiguity, a slippage between waking and dreaming"[14]—or, I suggest, between material and immaterial, organic and inorganic, human and almost-human. Here is the ultimate instance of the *unheimlich*: we are no longer at home in our own bodies.

The cinema, with its phantasmic doublings of the real world and the people in it, is a fundament of the technological uncanny. Early cinema produced its sense of the uncanny in varied ways that could be aligned with the ideas of both Freud and Jentsch. Laura Mulvey writes, "If the contemporary response to the Lumière films aligns them on the side of Freud's ghostly uncanny, Méliès transfers to cinema many characteristic attributes of Jentsch's uncanny, exploiting technological novelty as well as the cinema's ability to blur the boundary between the animate and the inanimate with trick photography."[15]

As I noted earlier, Michelle Bloom traces the history of a Pygmalionesque imagination and its translation from the failed Pygmalion tales of nineteenth-century literature (such as Hoffmann's "The Sandman") to its twentieth-century rebirth in the cinema, where some of the earliest films were of artist's models coming miraculously (and harmlessly) to life. Gaby Wood finds a similar translation in the trick films of Méliès: "In Méliès's workshop, you might say, automata gave birth to the movies."[16] Much of this original novelty disappeared or went underground as the cinema became more familiar, but perhaps one place where the medium's originary uncanniness (and animistic spirit) continued to lurk was in the realm of the animated film.

If cinema presented itself as life's uncanny double, it could be argued that animation was the fantastic, refracted double of the film; the uncanny's uncanny. As Lev Manovich notes, "Once the cinema was stabilized as a technology, it cut all references to its origins in artifice. Everything that characterized moving pictures before the twentieth century—the manual construction of images, loop actions, the discrete nature of space and movement—was delegated to cinema's bastard relative, its supplement and shadow—animation. Twentieth-century animation became a depository for nineteenth-century moving-image techniques left behind by the cinema."[17]

For Mulvey, however, it was live-action cinema that epitomized the uncanny properties of the medium precisely because it moved animation *away* from the realm of drawings: "From the perspective of the uncanny, the arrival of celluloid moving pictures constitutes a decisive moment. It was only then that the reality of photography fused with mechanical movement, hitherto restricted to animated pictures, to reproduce the illusion of life itself that is essential to the cinema."[18] In this view the cinema is fundamentally connected to the "undecidability" of the moving figure, and most fully in its most realist incarnations. Perhaps the fundamental uncanniness of the cinema is repressed via animation by being safely relegated to, and contained within, the realms of childlike fantasy and cartoonish unreality—analogous to those "minor genres" to which Vidler saw the uncanny confined.

Some tales of synthetic life are playful, others nightmarish.[19] What distinguishes these two registers? A central issue for these protagonist-creators and the beings they've generated is *control*: does the creation elude the creator's control, and if so, in what way? And what are the consequences of this slippage for the creator and his creation? The synthetic being can demonstrate its autonomy by behaving unpredictably: most obviously through overt disobedience, perhaps running amok across the landscape *(Frankenstein)* or refusing orders *(Pinocchio)*. The creator might be at risk at the hands of his creation *(Frankenstein)* or might suffer indirectly for the creation's behavior (*Pinocchio* again).

Apart from the special case of cartoon characters, automata don't rebel: their very name precludes the rebelliousness that signifies the beginnings of autonomous being. If they are mistaken for human, this is usually the result of human error. (The creators themselves rarely make that error, of course, but may encourage others to do so, as in the case of "The Sandman's" Spalanzani.) Automata *enchant* through their resemblance to the human: in "The Sandman" Olympia beguiles the gullible Nathaniel, just as the animated drawings of Gertie have beguiled audiences for nearly as long as cinema has existed. Thus the distinction between the darker, more sublime tales of synthetic life and the more playful iterations of uncanniness can be fairly well aligned with the contrast between *misbehavior* and *misperception*.

Outside the realm of fiction, automata do not quite fool us—they only threaten to. The first time one beholds the breathing Sleeping Beauty at Mme. Tussaud's in London, one looks, then looks again, surprised by the barely perceptible motion of the figure's chest, but the illusion is quickly detected and after testing one's assumption (perhaps by surreptitiously poking it) one can feel amused and then move on. Similarly, flat animated characters like Gertie and Pinocchio, marvelous as they are, do not resemble the human *too much*. Despite the uncanny pleasure derived from viewing an automaton with some of the properties of a living being, the viewer's sense of real and unreal is never truly in question. On the other hand, the narratives of *Metropolis, Frankenstein, King Kong,* and more recent films such as *Blade Runner* all present worlds in which automata (robots, monsters, and replicants) coexist with humans. Here they become the kinds of beings that Mary Douglas and Noël Carroll have referred to as "categorical mistakes" that literally cross over from, transgress, the field of representation and take up a place in the realm of being.[20]

One emblematic shot stands out: during Kong's New York rampage he is seen through a window, looking in at a sleeping woman who just might be the one he seeks. Kong is framed in the window like something from a Freudian dream-screen. In the next moment, however, Kong's giant paw enters from the side of the frame (presumably through another window), seizing the poor brunette and dragging her off. What this quite literal transgression of the screen space demonstrates is that these figures are not just disobedient in their behavior; they are disobedient in the

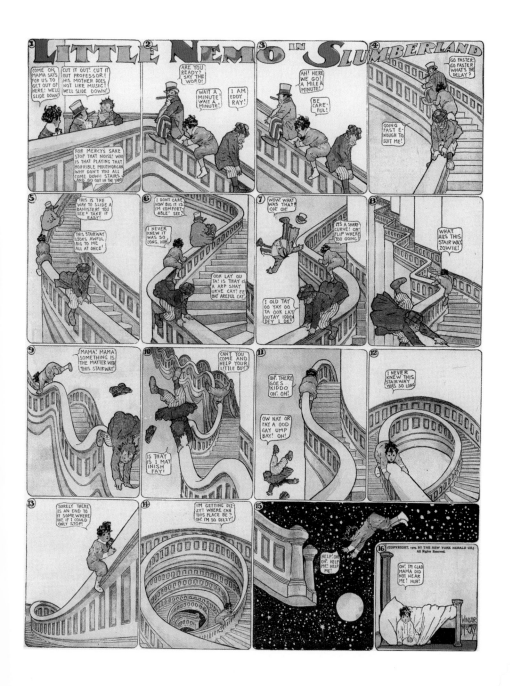

PLATE 2. R. F. Outcault, "The Horse Show as Reproduced at Shantytown," *New York World,* Nov. 17, 1895. San Francisco Academy of Comic Art Collection; the Ohio State University Billy Ireland Cartoon Library and Museum.

PLATE 3. R. F. Outcault, "The Residents of Hogan's Alley Visit Coney Island," *New York World,* May 24, 1896.

PLATE 4. R. F. Outcault, "An Old-Fashioned Fourth of July in Hogan's Alley," *New York World*, July 5, 1896.

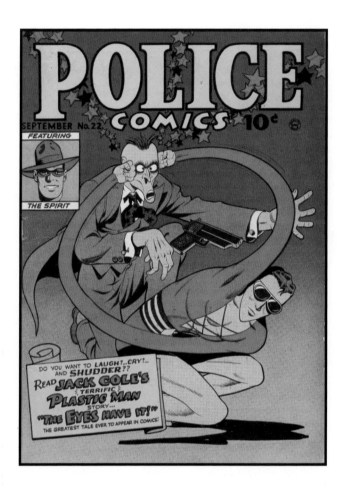

PLATE 5. Jack Cole, *Police Comics,* no. 22 (Sept. 1943). Copyright DC
Comics.

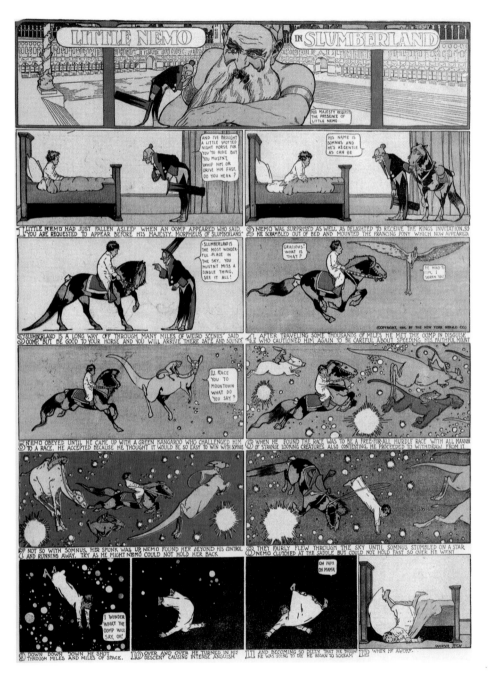

PLATE 6. Winsor McCay, *Little Nemo in Slumberland*, *New York Herald*, Oct. 15, 1905.

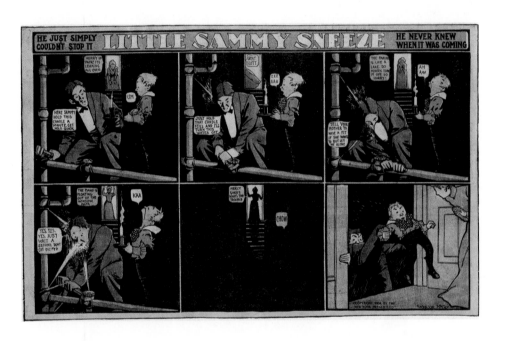

PLATE 7. *Little Sammy Sneeze, New York Herald,* Oct. 9, 1904. Courtesy of Peter Maresca and Sunday Press Books.

Polly and Her Pals

PLATE 8. Cliff Sterrett, *Polly and Her Pals, New York Journal,* Jan. 30, 1927.

PLATE 9. Winsor McCay, *Dream of the Rarebit Fiend, New York Evening Telegram,* Feb. 9, 1913.

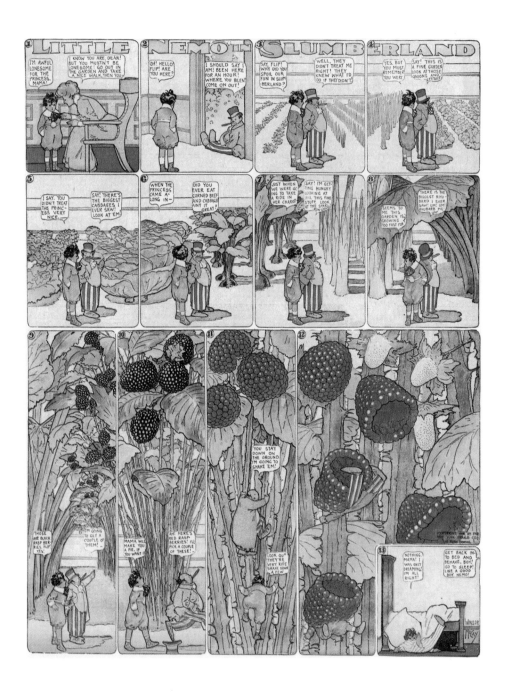

PLATE 10. Winsor McCay, *Little Nemo in Slumberland, New York Herald,* July 19, 1908.

PLATE 11. Raphaelle Peale (American, 1774–1825). *Blackberries,* ca. 1813. Oil on wood panel, 7¼ × 10¼ in. (18.4 × 26 cm). Fine Arts Museums of San Francisco, gift of Mr. and Mrs. John D. Rockefeller 3rd, 1993.35.23.

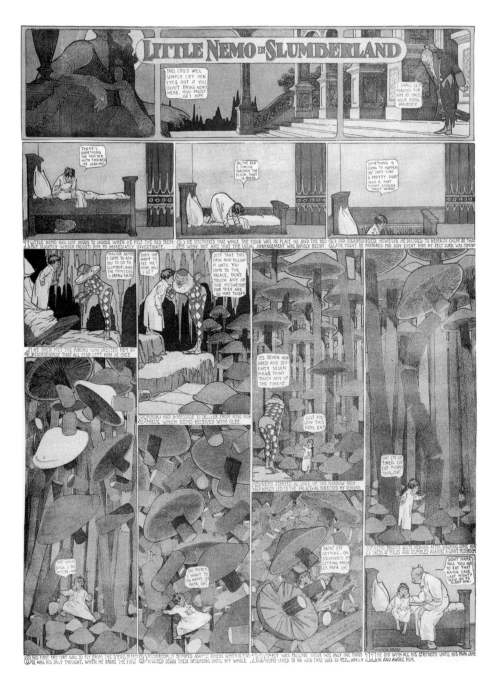

PLATE 12. Winsor McCay, *Little Nemo in Slumberland, New York Herald,* Oct. 22, 1905.

PLATE 14. Winsor McCay, *Little Nemo in Slumberland*, *New York Herald*, Nov. 15, 1908.

PLATE 15. Winsor McCay, *Little Nemo in Slumberland, New York Herald,* Dec. 1, 1907.

PLATE 16. Winsor McCay, *Little Nemo in Slumberland*, *New York Herald*, May 2, 1909.

PLATE 17. Winsor McCay, *Little Nemo in Slumberland, New York Herald,* Sept. 27, 1908.

PLATE 18. Winsor McCay, *Little Nemo in Slumberland*, *New York Herald*, Jan. 19, 1908.

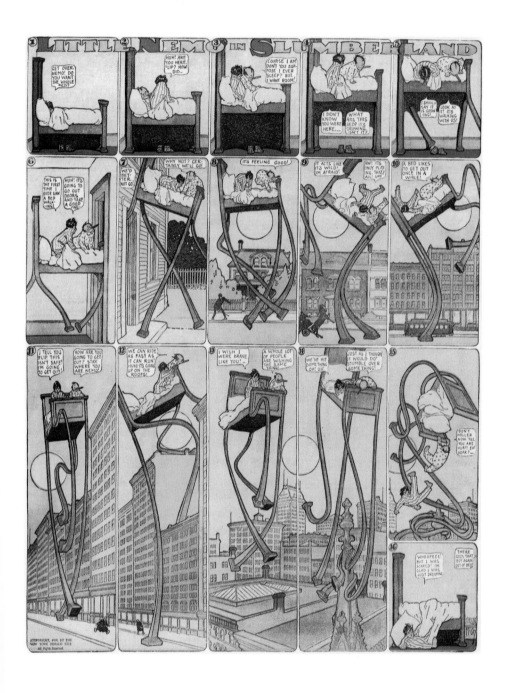

PLATE 19. Winsor McCay, *Little Nemo in Slumberland, New York Herald,* July 26, 1908.

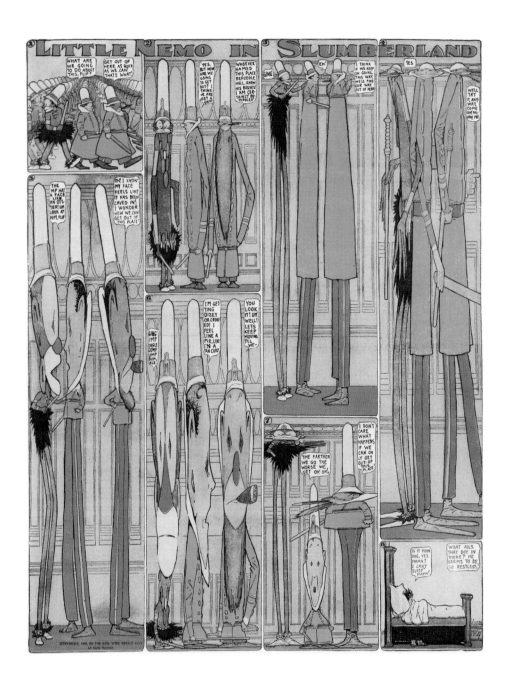

PLATE 20. Winsor McCay, *Little Nemo in Slumberland, New York Herald,* Feb. 2, 1907.

PLATE 21. Winsor McCay, *Little Nemo in Slumberland, New York Herald,* Jan. 26, 1907.

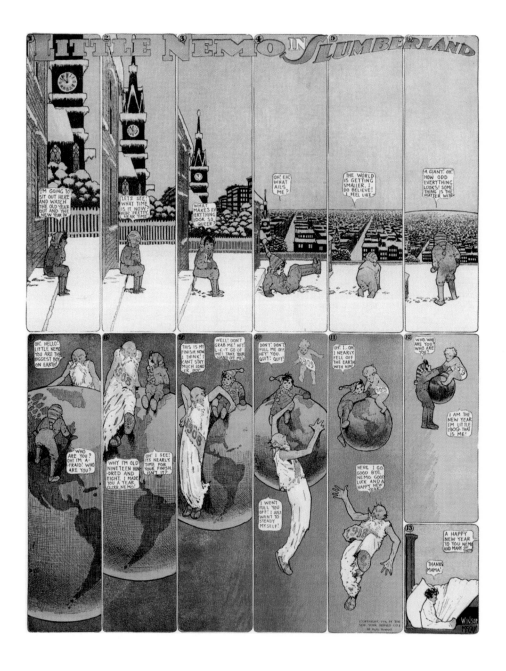

▲ PLATE 22. Winsor McCay, *Little Nemo in Slumberland*, *New York Herald*, Dec. 27, 1908.

▶ PLATE 23. *Little Nemo*, 1911. Hand-colored film frames. Courtesy John Canemaker.

PLATES 24 and 25. Images from *Lust for Life,* Vincente Minnelli, 1956.

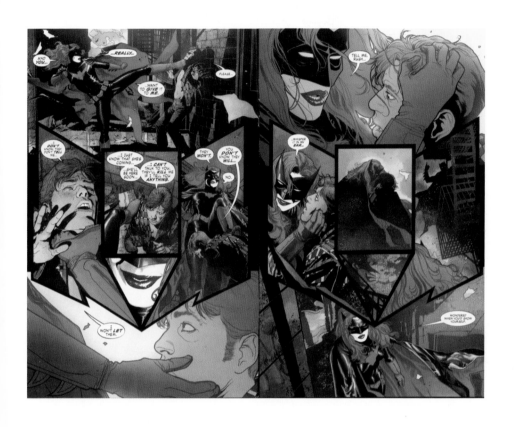

PLATE 26. Greg Rucka (writer) and J. H. Williams (artist), *Batwoman: Elegy* (2010). Copyright DC Comics.

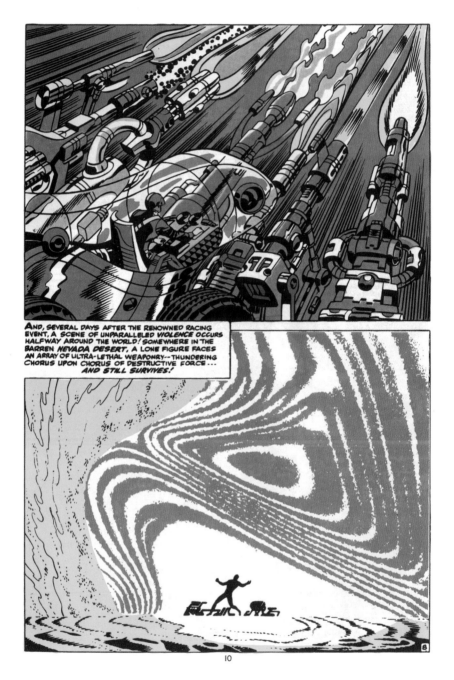

10

PLATE 27. Jim Steranko, pages from *Nick Fury: Agent of Shield,* ca. 1968–69. Copyright
Marvel Comics.

PLATE 28. Brian Bolland, *Animal Man* covers. Copyright DC Comics.

PLATE 29. Grant Morrison (writer), Chris Weston (artist), *The Filth* (2004). Copyright DC Comics.

PLATE 30. Jack Kirby, *Fantastic Four*, no. 77 (August 1968). Copyright Marvel Comics.

PLATE 31. Frank Quitely, *All-Star Superman,* no. 1 (Jan. 2006). Copyright DC Comics.

very fact of their being, which precludes their being trained, constrained, or contained. They must, instead, be destroyed, leaving the borders restored.[21]

That these are categorical mistakes fits nicely with Mulvey's sense that live-action cinema was a new instantiation of the uncanny. While moving drawings could be safely relegated to the realm of toys and handicraft, too unreal to matter, the cinema represented something both more *automatic* and more *phantasmic.* Cinema demanded of its audience a continual (and almost willful) misperception on the most fundamental level: illusions of movement, depth, and presentness.

Those synthetic life narratives that introduce fantastic characters into the midst of a world of humans might, then, be seen to stage *a recuperation of that misperception.* These stories stage the possibility of the misperception turning out to be correct. *I know very well but even so* . . . is the formula for fetishistic satisfaction (and it should go without saying that automata serve as exemplary fetish objects). By subverting the safe remove of *"I know very well"* in favor of that haunting *"but even so,"* these fictions give us an excess of presence, a plenitude that is, seemingly by definition, monstrous. This might begin to account for the slippage between the uncanny and the sublime in narratives of synthetically created life: while the cinema may be innately uncanny, tales of synthetic life frequently borrow the trappings of the sublime, as I have demonstrated. The undecidability of the uncanny, then, is resituated within a narrative context that asserts—against logic—the reality of the illusion, replacing uncertainty with a more sublime and transgressive terror.

Disobedience at Disney

So early animation is filled with creations that disobey their creators, as early as Flip, the mischief-maker, and Gertie, the "bad girl." The uncontainable Ko-Ko the Clown emerges out of the inkwell at the start of each cartoon, an inkwell to which he often has to be forcibly returned by the cartoon's producer, Max Fleischer. The time has come to explore the prevalence of these misbehaviors. If the godlike animator can create a figure that can do his precise bidding, and make it jump through as many hoops as he pleases, why create something that immediately rebels?

We have seen that the rambunctious creations of early animation not only *disobey* their creators; in many cases they actually *replace* them. The onscreen production of images, a production that fully established the authority of the artist, is superseded by increasingly autonomous characters. But to borrow Gunning's language again, perhaps the animator does not entirely disappear but rather "goes underground." Here two works from the Disney studio might illustrate the continuing concern with the illusions of animation, the desires of animators, and the autonomy of disobedient beings. In *Pinocchio* the studio perhaps achieved its realist masterpiece: a film rich in visual and kinetic details, with a greater unity and consistency than its predecessor, *Snow White and the Seven Dwarfs* (1937). The film featured enormously detailed backgrounds, sophisticated lighting and atmospheric effects, and superb character animation, but it still retained some heterogeneity: cartoony animation for most characters but rotoscoping for the Blue Fairy (a detail to which I'll return).

While it is something of a commonplace to criticize the Disney studio's sanitized adaptations of classic children's literature, the best of the films, and *Pinocchio* is surely one of those, can be fascinating in their own right. What makes *Pinocchio* so compelling is not simply its hallucinatory realism (is that an oxymoron?) but its profound reflexivity. This tale of a little wooden boy becomes a metaphor for the aspirations of the Disney studio itself and a longer standing dream of animation in the sense discussed above. This is entirely in keeping with Eisenstein's sense that Disney represented all that animation could do. What, after all, is Pinocchio *about*? Geppetto is a master craftsman who wants to accomplish something more: he wants his creation to be real. What was the goal of the Disney animators? To create animated characters that could generate identification and empathy from an audience, as well as *belief*. Geppetto's workshop is filled with clockwork automata that erupt in a riot of limited but cacophonous action. The automata, in their repetitive, mechanical actions, are reminiscent of the simple looping image sequences of an earlier era's optical toys, while Pinocchio himself, with his greater range of movement, motivation, and expressivity, is more properly cinematic, from the moment the Blue Fairy animates him ("What they can't do these days!" Jiminy Cricket slyly observes), well before he becomes a "real" boy (Figure 29). It's worth observing that Pinocchio is "real" for us from the get-go. As soon as he can move and talk he becomes a figure of identification, so from an audience standpoint he doesn't need to become any realer, demonstrating that the combination of animateness and voice is a sufficient indicator of life. In fact, I'm always slightly disturbed when he does become a real boy at the film's end—I miss that little wooden boy (I confess to a similar disenchantment at the end of Cocteau's *La belle et la bête*).

The Pinocchio who stars in the book by Carlo Collodi is rather different from Disney's version. (He is, not to put too fine a point on it, kind of a prick—after the Talking Cricket warns him to be a good and obedient boy, Pinocchio throws a wooden hammer at him and kills him.) The most significant difference between the book and the Disney version is that literature's Pinocchio is already sentient even before he is carved into the form of a puppet, when he is nothing more than a log. The film's Pinocchio begins as an inert marionette who is animated only by the combination of Geppetto's desire and the Blue Fairy's intervention (just as the cinematic Pinocchio begins "life" as a series of inert drawings, to be granted life by the cinema itself). It is significant that the means of realizing Geppetto's desire within the diegesis is the aforementioned Blue Fairy, who is herself rotoscoped—she's a hyper-real hybrid of live action and animation who embodies an uncanny blurring of boundaries.

FIGURE 29. *Pinocchio,* 1940.

What is it that makes Pinocchio *a real boy?* The easiest answer, for both book and film, is *morality*—morality defines the human. The ostensible moral is that disobedient boys will come to no good in the world. The human is not defined by the ability to *reason* (lying, after all, involves pretty good reasoning) or *emote* (he can emote right away) but by the ability to make (or want to make) correct *moral* choices. What keeps him from being a real boy, by this reading, is therefore his disobedience.[22] But I'd like to propose a different reading, one that would put Pinocchio into a longer history of "disobedient machines." I want to propose that it is precisely Pinocchio's *mis*behavior that makes him real, that makes him human.

Misbehavior and disobedience link Pinocchio to the earlier characters in the Disney films that so captivated Eisenstein, and in this we might see in *Pinocchio* a return of the repressed barbarism that was so effaced in the studio's first feature-length animated film, *Snow White and the Seven Dwarfs.*[23] Anne Nesbet has written of the "inanimation" of the Snow White character—a rotoscoped Marge Becher (later Marge Champion). Where that first feature seemed more geared to the kiddies, with its pedagogic songs on how to wash your face, *Pinocchio* gave audiences Honest John and Gideon, the terrors of Pleasure Island, and jokes about actors.[24]

Here we return to the determinedly disobedient creatures of early animation—

why must they disobey? Perhaps it is precisely because something that simply follows its programmed instructions will never be anything *more* than an automaton. The spark of life that separates automaton from living being is precisely its assertion of autonomy. The creation that disobeys does not just come to life: it takes on a life *of its own*. That is, the machine behaves autonomously and *proves* its autonomy by misbehaving. Rebellion is an assertion of self, an assertion of free will in more or less playful terms. As Pinocchio sings in defiance of Geppetto and school and Jiminy Cricket and responsibility in general, "There are no strings on me."

In the introduction to her edited volume *Genesis Redux: Essays in the History and Philosophy of Artificial Life,* Jessica Riskin discusses Michelangelo's representation of the creation of life on the ceiling of the Sistine Chapel, with Adam's outstretched arm nearly touching the hand of God: "There, between the two fingers, one aiming, the other waiting, is Michelangelo's representation of life itself, reaching from God to Adam. It is, quite simply, a gap."[25] The "understated drama" of this gap articulates, for Riskin, something of the mysteriousness of the life-force, but one could also say that this gap, this separation, between creator and creation is fundamental on another level. Adam himself is, after all, a little like Pinocchio, who had to remove himself from Geppetto, had to cut the strings that bound him to his creator, to become an autonomous being. Here is the human, a figure created in the image of god, the creator, who is seemingly predestined to disobey. Original sin, the fall from grace, is the fall *into* humanity. This fallibility, this disobedience might be what makes man less than god, but in other contexts, such as *Pinocchio,* or *Frankenstein,* or *My Fair Lady,* it makes creations into something more than mere machines.

We can therefore find a three-part division in *Pinocchio:* there is Geppetto, the divine creator; the slavish automata that populate Geppetto's workshop; and Pinocchio, the disobedient individual. Intriguingly, one can find this identical structure in another Disney saga from the same period, *Fantasia*'s adaptation of "The Sorcerer's Apprentice," also from 1940, featuring Disney's biggest star, Mickey Mouse. That the animated creature is something uncanny, irrational at its core and perhaps even a bit magical, lies at the heart of "The Sorcerer's Apprentice" section of *Fantasia.* While most cartoons play out the creation/creator duality on the most playful levels, "The Sorcerer's Apprentice" operates on a darker plane. Mickey Mouse, once the exemplar of the unruly, animistic spirit so celebrated by Eisenstein, and a character voiced at first by Walt himself, plays the hapless apprentice, in over his head. Putting on his master's hat, Mickey commands a broom to fetch water, but then is unable to stop his enthusiastic servant, who tirelessly lugs bucket after bucket, flooding the room. Splintering the broom with an axe only multiplies the problem, as each piece becomes a new broom, equally dedicated to its task. Only the return of the sorcerer returns the world to its proper order—again, the omnipotent creator, able to bestow the spark of life; the automata, marching in lockstep, forever completing a task that is already complete; and the misbehaving creation, played by that onetime avatar of animistic freedom, Mickey Mouse. Here he is an apprentice, engaged in being schooled, and even the magisterial sorcerer is finally forgiving of his apprentice's trespass, with a hint of an indulgent smile and a swat on the *tuchus*.

"The Sorcerer's Apprentice" belongs squarely to both the uncanny *and* the sublime. (The brooms belong, at least at first, to the former, the magisterial wizard and the growing sense of terror to the latter.) It's worth noting that the brooms, despite their compelling anthropomorphism, function only as mindless drones, quite the obverse of the attentive and independent Gertie or Ko-Ko. It's also interesting that multiplicity, the very foundation of frame animation's operations, is revealed (the one broom, itself constructed of a series of drawings, breaks apart into a series of brooms), only to become an object of fear. It also stands as something of a conservative tract regarding the Disney studio's own mission statement: animism is powerful stuff and should remain under the control of seasoned professionals. How far we have come from *Steamboat Willie*.

DISOBEDIENT HUMANS

My Fair Lady

For reasons that will become clear, the object under scrutiny here is neither George Bernard Shaw's play nor the stage version of *My Fair Lady* but George Cukor's 1964 film version, which costarred Rex Harrison and Audrey Hepburn. This book has been strongly informed by that Pygmalionesque desire of which Michelle Bloom wrote, but *My Fair Lady*'s connection to Pygmalion is rather more direct: it is a musical adaptation of George Bernard Shaw's play of that name, which itself updates the myth most familiar to us from Ovid's telling. In that version Pygmalion, a sculptor disillusioned with women's wanton ways, sculpts an ideal woman from ivory with which he falls in love. Making an offering to Venus, he wishes (or, really, *wishes* he wished) that she could bring his statue to life, and Venus sends Cupid to accomplish this.

In Shaw's retelling the setting is contemporary London circa 1913; Pygmalion becomes Henry Higgins, a renowned linguist; and his statue, named Galatea in later versions, becomes Eliza Doolittle, a Cockney flower girl.[26] Eliza is one of the great disobedient machines, and the musical is one of the great works about the performance of disobedience. Gertie the dinosaur must demonstrate a life of her own if she is to be more than an automaton, but in the live-action *My Fair Lady*, the stakes center on developing a *voice* of one's own.

My Fair Lady is a passing narrative, in which Higgins proposes to introduce Eliza as a member of society simply by teaching her to speak "properly" and present herself well. It is, in essence, a *Frankenstein* with gender politics. Richard Gladstone

FIGURE 30. Rex Harrison as Henry Higgins, *My Fair Lady,* 1964.

points out that Shaw's "position in relation to class was not that society should elim-
inate the concept of ladies and gentlemen but that the status of lady or gentleman
might be attained by anyone with intelligence and character who *aspired to the part.*"[27]
This represents a strangely democratic attitude toward class, which becomes a function of successful performance rather than dynastic succession or monetary value.

Alan Jay Lerner took swathes of dialogue right from Shaw, and one is awestruck
by his ability to turn such lines as "I can do without you" or "I have grown accustomed to your voice and appearance" and turn them into songs while preserving
the Shavian sensibility. The work gives us Henry Higgins, the creator—a man of
science, with a home laboratory filled with apparatus, who joins the long history of
gynophobic myths, fables, horror stories, and science fictions that feature a man
out to create an idealized female being (Figure 30).

Indeed, with Higgins teamed with Colonel Pickering, *Pygmalion* anticipates, and
My Fair Lady recalls, the repeated filmic trope of two men engaged in a quest to
create a woman: Higgins and Pickering flanking the figure of their creation, Eliza,
at the ball that is the film's centerpiece, are visually identical to shots of Rotwang
and Federer flanking the robot Maria in *Metropolis,* or Henry Frankenstein and
Doctor Praetorius flanking the newly wakened Bride of the Monster (Figure 31).
In Shaw's play Higgins's mother remarks: "You certainly are a pretty pair of babies,
playing with your live doll," to which they reply:

> *Pickering:* We're always talking Eliza.
>   *Higgins:* Teaching Eliza.
> *Pickering:* Dressing Eliza.
> *Mrs. Higgins:* What!
>   *Higgins:* Inventing new Elizas.

FIGURE 31. *My Fair Lady,* 1964 (top); *The Bride of Frankenstein,* 1935 (bottom left); *Metropolis,* 1926 (bottom right).

Overall, however, Higgins is more tinkerer than mad scientist, a man of strong idio-syncrasies rather than one channeling truly demonic energies (although, admittedly, he does celebrate his "spark of divine fire"). The agony of the tortured creator in such works as *Frankenstein* is parodied here, as the house staff sing about "Poor Professor Higgins" as we watch Eliza suffer a range of torments.

And what of their creation, Eliza? First, it should be noted, that Eliza is, in fact, not their creation: unlike filmdom's Frankenstein's Monster, stitched together from various cadavers, or the Golem of legend, fashioned from ordinary clay, Eliza Doolit-tle is already human but is not what society would term "a lady." In fact, one can identify what we might call the Four Stages of Eliza: a child at the outset, given to simple wants ("Lots of chocolate for me to eat") and needs (early on, she is forcibly given a bath by Mrs. Pearce and the household staff); an imperfectly programmed machine at the Ascot Races; a perfect "talking doll," passing at the ball; and, after the ball, finally an independent, autonomous being. One hugely unresolved question that hovers over *Pygmalion* and *My Fair Lady* concerns the role of language in this maturation—has language allowed her access to deeper feelings and introspective knowledge, or is it simply the vehicle for the communication of those latent elements?

The film not only gives us Shaw's version of the Pygmalion myth; it also firmly adheres to what we might call "the Audrey Hepburn plot," as encountered in such starring vehicles as the films *Roman Holiday, Funny Face,* and *Sabrina,* as well as a stage adaptation of *Gigi:* it is the story of an "ugly" duckling who comes into her own under the tutelage of a (considerably) older man. But what is striking in the relation between Higgins and Eliza is not simply the gulf that separates powerful creator and powerless creation but the ways in which they double one another. Higgins asks the musical question, "Why can't a woman / Be like me?"—announcing his narcissistic desire to produce his own double. After the ball, her triumph becomes his ("You did it!" Pickering sings to Higgins). If Eliza rather spectacularly fails to fit in at the Ascot races ("Come on, Dover! Move yer bloomin' arse!"), then so does Henry, attired in his usual brown tweeds where everyone else is bedecked in monochromatic Cecil Beaton finery. Eliza's revenge fantasy ("Just you wait, 'Enry 'Iggins") is replaced by his ("In a year or so / When she's prematurely gray"). Higgins accuses Eliza of lacking emotion ("That shows a lack of feeling") and calls her "a heartless guttersnipe"; she similarly accuses him of having "no feelin' heart in ya." They are more aligned, these two, than either would like to think.

Much like Mary Shelley's *Frankenstein*—a work, we should remember, by a woman about a man creating a subjugated creature—*My Fair Lady* is about the need for the creator to take responsibility for his creation. Henry refers to Eliza as "this *thing* I've created," and variously refers to her as a creature or baggage. "Does it occur to you, Higgins, that the girl has some feelings?" asks the somewhat more humane Pickering. "Oh no, I don't think so," Higgins replies. But when he—briefly—treats her as human, when he discourses on the magic of the English language and all the expressions it is capable of, when he refers to their mutual quest, the result is the incandescent shared triumph of "The Rain in Spain." He has not, however, thought one moment beyond the ball at which he will pass her off as a member of society—following the celebrations of *Higgins's* triumph, Eliza is left prostrate on the floor, in the dark, crying "What will become of me?"

Higgins cannot recognize Eliza as an independent being, either before her makeover ("Does it occur to you that the girl has feelings?") or after—"There isn't an idea in your head or a word in your mouth that I didn't put there," he thunders at her. Recognition is to accept the other being as a being, as something more than protoplasm or machinery. The roboticist Rodney Brooks has written that the body is a "mass of biomolecules . . . a machine that acts according to a set of specifiable rules," but this basic fact of physics and physiology has no bearing on our actions: "I believe myself and my children all to be mere machines. But this is not how I treat them. I treat them in a very special way, and I interact with them on an entirely different level."[28] Eliza understands what Brooks is getting at: "You see Mrs. Higgins," she explains to Henry's mother, "apart from the things one can pick up, the difference between a lady and a flower girl is not how she behaves but how she is treated. I shall always be a flower girl to Professor Higgins because he always treats me as a flower girl and always will. But I know that I shall always be a lady to Colonel Pickering because he always treats me as a lady and always will." Autonomy has something to do with recognizing another's autonomy. Rodney Brooks continues: "It is this transcendence between belief systems that I think will be what enables mankind to ultimately accept robots as emotional machines, and thereafter start to empathize with them and attribute free will, respect, and ultimately rights to them."[29]

To Higgins, Eliza is first subhuman, then an automaton. In fact, to Higgins, Eliza resembles Hadaly, the android at the center of Auguste Villiers de l'Isle-Adam's 1886 novel, *L'Ève Future,* in which a mythical Thomas Edison constructs an artificial woman for a friend of his who is engaged to a woman who is beautiful, but coarse.[30] Edison, in real life "the phonograph's papa," had himself tried to market a talking doll in France just a few years earlier—it was a nasty-looking thing with a fragile mechanism, but there wasn't a word in her mouth that he didn't put there.[31] Eliza, however—the *"live* doll"—is another story—she continually asserts her autonomy: "I'm not *dirt* under your feet," she tells Higgins, marking her immediate difference from the Golem of Jewish legend. Her song, "I Can Do without You," denies the godlike power of this ersatz "creator"—"Without your pulling it / The tide comes in," she sings. "Without your twirling it / The Earth can spin." Even this, however, is met by Higgins's triumphal reproclamation, "I did it!" Even her autonomy, it seems, was his beneficent idea, as well as something in his power to bestow. But Eliza repeatedly signals her independence by deliberately mixing Higgins's elegant English with her own Cockney slang.

It seems clear that Higgins had little intention of creating an autonomous Eliza—what he had in mind was something more along the lines of a chatbot, one of the first of which was Joseph Weizenbaum's creation, named, yes, Eliza (Eliza became operational in 1966; two years after the film of *My Fair Lady*). Chatbots are virtual automata programmed to provide a simulation of conversation, and Eliza simulated the discourse of a therapist: reflecting statements back to the "patient" as questions, eliciting further detail, attuned to mentions of family members and mental states. Eliza and other chatbots followed in the wake of Alan Turing's 1950 essay "Computing Machinery and Intelligence," which proposed that if a machine could fool a human into believing that it was, in fact, not a machine, then from a functional standpoint it could be said to be very like a human. *My Fair Lady* is not just *Frankenstein* with gender politics; it is also the Turing Test set to music, and at the ball, as Miss Doolittle fools one and all into believing that she is an aristocrat, she becomes the perfect chatbot, passing the Higgins test (a variation of Turing's) with ease. It is in the aftermath of the ball that Eliza (Doolittle) exceeds her programming, becoming, effectively, a fully psychologized character with an inner life and complex desires, and not simply an automaton parroting a script.[32]

There *are* automata lurking in *My Fair Lady*, however, and they are to be found at the races, dancing the Ascot Gavotte. Beaton's set and costume designs trend heavily toward grays for the men, starker whites and blacks for the women's elaborate gowns. The patrons move as if on tracks, gliding past one another while emotionlessly intoning about their racing pulses and flushing faces. They resemble the clockwork mechanisms in Geppetto's workshop, moving through their limited repertoire of programmed moves with metronomic and monochromatic precision. The elegant choreography of near-collisions and frictionless motion is sullied by Higgins's willful ignorance of social niceties but demolished by Eliza's spontaneous, animated pleasure at the track ("Come on Dover!"). Once more, spontaneity and animatedness are hallmarks of the human. Even before this, Eliza's missteps in performing her assigned role ("Them she lived with would have killed her for a hat-pin, let alone a hat," she elegantly declaims) have provided the audience, and her future suitor Freddie, with no small pleasure. Not surprising, then, that the subsequent ball, while more successful, is so much less resonant: in her white, flowing gown she fits smoothly into a world that has little connection to ours, in which dishonesty rules and emotions have no place. She has joined the monochromatic set and, lovely as she is, she is not our (or her) Eliza.

Despite some sense that Shaw's play has been simplified and romanticized, *My Fair Lady* is infinitely more sympathetic to Eliza, whose point of view and experience with Higgins are given far more attention than they received in *Pygmalion:* I find it the more emotionally complex and balanced of the two works. In fact, it is the introduction of a romantic dimension, decidedly and deliberately absent in Shaw's version, that helps to establish some parity between the two protagonists; Stanley Cavell has demonstrated the ways that Hollywood romantic comedies became elaborate negotiations of the terms of a relationship, negotiations between equals (in this, then, Lerner and Loewe have, to good effect, Americanized Shaw).[33]

Still, *My Fair Lady* has been castigated for its gender politics: despite Eliza's rejection of Henry, she returns to him at the finish, and rather than welcome her back, Higgins simply calls for his slippers. This criticism, however, misses the point. Higgins is presented throughout *My Fair Lady* (and *Pygmalion*) as a man ready for his comeuppance—not for being a "modern Prometheus" but for being a socially obtuse bully who takes no responsibility for his "creation." One is encouraged to identify with his grandiloquence and humor at the start, and Eliza begins as a broad Cockney caricature, well suited to serve as the butt of his jokes. As the work deepens, however, we come to identify with Eliza—a shift that is finally punctuated by Mrs. Higgins's "Bravo, Eliza!" in support of her rejection of Henry. In fact, the women of *My Fair Lady* are not nearly as scattered as Higgins and Pickering, and at least two of them are models of good sense as are none of the men. Higgins is overtly mocked: when he sweetly lilts, "I'm a very *gentle* man," the audience has more than enough evidence to the contrary. The work ends with Higgins performing his customary role of obstinate autocrat, but—on the heels of the achingly direct "I've Grown Accustomed to Her Face," he, she, and we know better. The script from the 1956 stage production reads:

> Higgins straightens up. If he could but let himself, his face would radiate unmistakable relief and joy. If he could but let himself, he would run to her. Instead he leans back with a contented sigh pushing his hat forward till it almost covers his face.
>
> Higgins (softly): Eliza? Where the devil are my slippers?
>
> (There are tears in Eliza's eyes. She understands.)
>
> The curtain falls slowly.

It's that *slowly* that tells all, brilliantly maintained in Cukor's film, where the two of them hover on the brink of whatever it is they're going to do from here as the scene fades out. But let us note that she makes no move to get him his damned slippers.[34]

All of this is not to say that the gender politics of *My Fair Lady* are unproblematic: language is the tool of reason and therefore the province of men, emotion that of women. Not surprisingly, language looms large in *My Fair Lady*—what Shaw and Higgins refer to as "the divine gift of articulate speech"—although it must be said that Higgins wields this gift like a weapon. Eliza's most overt resistance comes in the form of the song "Show Me!," which concerns the limits of language. The first word of the song, sung with juvenile earnestness by Freddy is "Speak"—following his paean to the language of love, Eliza cuts him off:

> Words words words
> I'm so sick of words
> I get words all day through
> First from him now from you
> Is that all you blighters can do?

Eliza's rebellion takes the form of a rejection of language—even the language of the love song:

> Sing me no songs
> Read me no rhymes
> Don't waste my time
> Show me!
>
> Don't talk of June
> Don't talk of fall
> Don't talk at all
> Show me!

This song—Eliza's song—has no equivalent in Shaw, whose faith in language is unshakable, and it is the clearest sign that *My Fair Lady* is not *Pygmalion* and that this Eliza is not entirely Shaw's creation.

Pygmalion is not only a treatise on language but on voice, and *My Fair Lady* carries things one step further, although unintentionally. Eliza has a voice, but it's one that marks her class and limits her social mobility. Higgins gives her a new one, which allows her to do two things. First, she is able to "pass" at the ball; in other words, she is able to pretend to a higher station—and here *My Fair Lady* intersects with *Blade Runner,* as it enacts a kind of Turing Test, where performance of something (thought, for Turing) is functionally tantamount to the thing itself. But, second, language also seems to allow Eliza access to deeper emotions—indeed, her mastery of language *does* seem to make her human. Her trauma in the aftermath of the ball stems from her sense of erasure ("What will become of me?") and also from her helplessness in the face of feelings that she can only now begin to articulate.

Higgins finally accepts that Eliza has a voice of her own. Following his rejection, he storms home, glad to be rid of the baggage, but his feelings overtake him: "I've grown accustomed to her voice," he sings—note: *her* voice (which is why his final line about the slippers—only moments later—doesn't fool me for an instant). But what *is* Eliza's voice? She begins the story as street-urchin Eliza, played by the aristocratic Audrey Hepburn with the broadest of put-on Cockney accents; in her later, more alienated, incarnation she sounds like, well, she sounds like Audrey Hepburn. And, of course, if this work is about speech and voice, we need to discuss the fact that Hepburn's voice is dubbed in most of the songs by Marni Nixon, about whom Wayne Koestenbaum has written so well: "The voice of Marni Nixon, ghosting for Audrey Hepburn in *My Fair Lady* and for Deborah Kerr in *The King and I,* told me everything about singing in the dark, singing without a body, singing from an erased, invisible place in the universe. No one saw Marni Nixon's body; invisibility made her voice operatic, characterless. Audrey Hepburn lip-synched 'I Could Have Danced All Night': like Eliza, I listened but didn't sing. I opened my mouth, in a wide, vapid O of awe and shame, while women's voices streamed from my green Magnavox record player."[35] And in all the songs, but especially I think in "I Could Have Danced All Night," both Nixon and Hepburn could be said to be channeling Julie Andrews, who first played Eliza on the stage. Meanwhile, Harrison not only performs his songs with his own voice, but—at his insistence—was recorded live while filming, rather than using the standard playback system that musicals had depended upon since 1929. Harrison/Higgins thus achieves a unity of body, self, and voice that Hepburn/Eliza cannot.

So the creation exists as a kind of ventriloquist's dummy, not so unlike Edison's talking doll after all. When Pickering admits that he'll miss Eliza, Higgins has an easy solution, one that recalls the fictional Edison's solution with Hadaly: "we'll get her on the phonograph so you can turn her on whenever you want." With the phonograph, the voice can be "captured," separated from one body and installed in another. Later, Eliza remarks that "the phonograph has no feelings to hurt." At the end of *My Fair Lady,* however, Higgins sits alone in his domicile, listening to those very phonograph recordings as Eliza, unseen, removes the needle from the record and continues her speech in person: "I washed me face and hands before I come, I did." The phonograph is superseded by Eliza's presence—not as an automaton but as an autonomous human being—possessed of feelings that Higgins must acknowledge. To have a voice—to give voice to one's feelings or beliefs—is to exist in a social world; it is to be given a place in the symbolic system that is language—it is to become an "I." Spoken language emanates from the body, as a "natural" form, while written language belongs more clearly to a system of signs and syntactical rules.

So in *My Fair Lady* we are given two women: Eliza, a woman whose voice is replaced but who is able, at the end of the work, to have a voice of her own (rather than the voice of/on the phonograph), whose mind and body are finally unified, and Audrey Hepburn, a woman who has no voice of her own (when singing), who must mouth the words that others have said/sung, who is devoiced (rather than disembodied), whose body and mind (in the form of voice) are divorced, ripped asunder. This is the unresolvable irony at the heart of the film version of *My Fair Lady,* which complicates the stage version that preceded it, which itself complicated George Bernard Shaw's original conception.

Jerry Lewis: Malfunction as Resistance

Jerry Lewis is a disobedient machine of a different order, less *disobedient* than *malfunctioning,* a jerking automaton performing spectacular breakdowns in the midst of America's postwar complacency, a period that also saw something of a seismic shift in technological paradigms. The malfunctions and maladaptation's that recurred in *Dream of the Rarebit Fiend* were squarely of an industrial era, while the body of Jerry Lewis is poised—though *poise* seems exactly the wrong word here—between the competing demands of industrialism and the new world of the electronic.

At this point it should hardly need to be said that Jerry Lewis enacts the ugly feeling of animatedness. Lewis's own characterization of his role in the Martin and Lewis comedy team is telling: "The handsomest guy in the world and a monkey."[36] (To what extent Lewis's Jewishness is a part of his self-perception is unclear, but ethnicity was a constant reference point in Martin and Lewis's club performances, although it is absent in the films).[37] Jerry's abjection before Dean could as easily reverse, however, as in all the routines where Jerry hijacks the orchestra to sabotage Dean's song. Jerry is an inert object (a "lump") activated by the addition of Dean (and this is how Lewis tells it as the story of his career), but he is also hyperbolically autonomous, careening about the stage in unpredictable ways. ("Dean, I adlibbed!" he suddenly exclaims in the middle of a sketch, "Don't you *love* me!" and kisses Dean full on the lips.) Where Dean is the embodiment of unflappable cool,

Jerry is marked by, in Ngai's words, "exaggerated emotional expressiveness"[38] (a trait still in evidence in his annual telethon), laughing or crying or shrieking with abandon. He is, in his younger days, possessed of an astonishing physical elasticity that performs a "triumph over the fetters of form," to return to Eisenstein's language. At once a pitiable object (skinny, whiny, abject) and a figure of raucous autonomy, he is a figure of divine animatedness, a frenetically embodied utopia of disorder.

It's also easy to posit Jerry as an animated character, as many of his best films were directed by Frank Tashlin, the one director from the Warners cartoon unit to move to live-action filmmaking. Tashlin's cartoons were largely typical of Warner's justly celebrated output: crazed, anarchic comedies featuring an array of zany characters (mostly voiced by Mel Blanc) who remain firmly entrenched in comedy's pantheon. It is difficult to watch *Porky Pig's Feat* (1943), with Porky Pig and Daffy Duck trying to figure out how to sneak out of a hotel without paying their exorbitant bill, and not see it as a seven-minute version of a Hope-Crosby film, or a trial run-up to Martin and Lewis.[39] Tashlin's animated work often featured baroque camera angles and inventive editing, and he has said that he was trying to break into feature films at the same time that he worked on these cartoons.

If Tashlin's animated work contains relatively few prefigurations of his foray into live action, it's no secret that his live-action films fully bear the marks of his history in the exaggerated and satirical realm of cartoons, featuring an eye-popping embrace of Technicolor and CinemaScope, grotesque visual and performative cartoonishness, and a faux-sophisticated mockery of Hollywood, Madison Avenue, and the female form. Outrageous sight gags abound: in *It's Only Money* Jerry stops his truck alongside a tight parking spot, and pushes it laterally into place. In the exquisite *Son of Paleface* Bob Hope holds up one axle of his car as he drives, and even remarks that what he's doing is impossible. And frequently, Tashlin's leading players seem like transposed cartoon characters—there's a hell of a lot of Daffy Duck in Bob Hope, and the examples of Jerry Lewis and Jayne Mansfield speak for themselves.

Jerry Lewis and Dean Martin were a well-established act by the time Tashlin directed them in *Artists and Models,* but the case could be made that they had incompletely transformed themselves into film comedians, remaining at heart vaudevillians.[40] In *Artists and Models,* though, the first of the collaborations with Tashlin, Jerry becomes a cartoon character: a masseuse begins to stretch and twist his legs in directions human limbs were never meant to go (Figure 32). He even spends a good portion of the film disguised as "Freddy Fieldmouse," a cartoonish character from a children's book (I like to think that the actual illustration of Freddy was drawn by Tashlin, but I can't prove it). Cartoonish exaggeration continues in the later films directed by Tashlin (which included *Hollywood or Bust* [also with Martin], *Rock-a-Bye Baby, It's Only Money, The Disorderly Orderly,* and *Cinderfella*). It's not unreasonable, then, to see Jerry Lewis as not only a cartoon character but as the creation of the animator, Frank Tashlin—Jerry (the created) even doubles for Tashlin

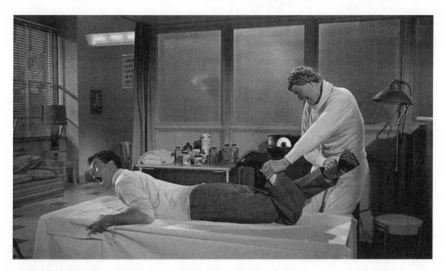

FIGURE 32. Jerry Lewis in *Artists and Models,* 1955.

(the creator) in the tellingly titled *Artists and Models,* playing an aspiring children's book author—Tashlin had published three children's books in the 1940s.

But Jerry was not content to remain a cartoon character for long, and he wanted to do more than rebel—he wanted to direct. Much as the animated Nemo conjured a pen to draw an image of his own that then came to life, so Jerry wanted to take control of the apparatus of production to become what he termed, in the title of his 1971 "textbook," "the total film-maker."[41] Lewis the filmmaker would control and produce Jerry the character; the animated would now become both creator and creation but fractured versions of both. As I've argued elsewhere, the films within this "total" discourse are consistently organized around Lewis's struggle for self-control and for a stable position within the socially constructed definitions of masculine behavior and desire.[42] The career of Jerry Lewis is therefore marked twice over by a continuing struggle for control: control over the production of the comedic discourse and the complementary comic struggles enacted by that Jerry character, Lewis's alter ego, or, better, his alter id.

But if Jerry Lewis is a machine, then he is a machine that appears at a significant moment in the history of technology, a moment being analyzed nearly contemporaneously by Marshall McLuhan. *Understanding Media: The Extensions of Man* appeared in 1964, tracking the complex ambivalences produced by a series of media—*media* as understood in both traditional terms (radio, telephone, film, television) and in McLuhan's new expanded definition (electricity, typewriters, advertising). Lewis goes unmentioned, but he is clearly relevant: in films from the late 1950s to the mid-1960s the body of Jerry Lewis channeled anxieties surrounding the pervading aspects of the very electronic technologies with which McLuhan was grappling. In describing Jerry as an automaton trapped in a twitchifying feedback loop of an electronic circuit, Gilles Deleuze argued something similar to what I am proposing, and his brief observations can be effectively expanded in the context of *Understanding Media*.[43] Against the ground of McLuhan's argument, Jerry appears as a more problematic figure of the electronic age than Deleuze suggests—one caught in the moment of transition between mechanico-industrial and electronic paradigms of technological being, a body trapped in the "critical pressures of the new electric environment."[44]

At the same moment that McLuhan theorized the transition from industrial age to electronic culture, Lewis was performing a body racked between these two paradigms. His subjectivity, played out on the surface of his body (including his voice), is no longer capable of being defined against the unitary concentration of The Machine but is not yet comfortable with its dispersal into global circuitry and information circulation. He spins, tilts, and stammers, but he keeps on ticking and talking. His is an unrelenting synesthesia without the relief offered by the state of shock—he is jolted (shocked) but never numbed (state of shock). If the rarebit fiends of an earlier day were oneirically responding to the pressures of the hyperregulated machine age, Jerry is hung up on the transition from visible machine to nonvisible electronics. No one, I would suggest, embodied the trauma of what I have elsewhere called *terminal identity* as effectively as Jerry Lewis.[45]

One of Lewis's earliest forays into professional entertainment was with something known in the biz as a "dummy act," a tour de force of animatedness in which he performed "outrageous mimes to phonographic records."[46] The phonograph, the technology at the center of *My Fair Lady*, makes a return appearance. McLuhan cites John Philip Sousa's prognostications on the medium of the phonograph: "With the phonograph vocal exercises will be out of vogue! Then what of the national throat? Will it not weaken? What of the national chest? Will it not shrink?"[47] McLuhan amplifies Sousa's argument: "The phonograph is an extension and amplification of the voice that may well have diminished individual vocal activity."[48] Jerry's dummy act looks like a significant example of the Sousa doctrine: the chicken-chested performer appears as an automaton whose movements and behavior are entirely determined by the prerecorded, precedent status of the phonograph record. In *You're Never Too Young*, Jerry lip-synchs to a record by Dean: a ventriloquist act in which Dean is the voice, Jerry the dummy.[49]

This determinism is nowhere more clear than in the inevitable breakdown of phonographic technology, as the record player winds down, or the record skips, or the wrong record is played. In *The Patsy* (Lewis, 1964) the staff of a dead comedian decide that they should use their combined talents to create a new star; their new "patsy" (Jerry) will be, in other words, programmed. Perhaps they should have beta-tested—Frank Krutnik describes the scene when their big-hearted ex-bellboy patsy performs their material: "Stumbling onto the stage, he knocks the microphone off its stand and then proceeds to decimate the polished routines that have been taught to him. . . . Stanley presents a spectacle of maladjustment."[50] Maladjustment or malfunction. Even the dummy act, perhaps a metaphor for this entire performance of middle-management ventriloquism, goes awry, awfully.

These scenes have earlier analogues in the 1932 film *Horse Feathers,* as the Marx Brothers—including Harpo—use a phonograph recording to masquerade as Maurice Chevalier, and in *Shall We Dance* (1937), where Ginger Rogers steals the balancing weight from Fred Astaire's turntable, causing his responsive tap dances to skip and wind down accordingly. Fred, however, is always more comparable to Chaplin, as we cannot help but marvel at the inventiveness of his routines, the grace with which he "collapses" into a sullen sitting position. How different a figure Jerry presents in these moments, dumb and dumbfounded, raging against the machine that was meant to compensate for his own disability. Jerry performs a breakdown that is manic and inelegant.

The skillfully disastrous performance in *The Patsy,* the performance of performance as a disaster, should also be seen as a chaotic and inchoate resistance to programming and control—Jerry's Stanley Belt will, ultimately, *of course,* emerge triumphant by performing in his own way. Jerry's "own way," a sentimental pantomime routine, unfortunately looks to the nondiegetic spectator a lot like Charlie Chaplin's or Red Skelton's "own way." The routine is a cardinal example of what Dean Martin disgustedly referred to as Lewis's "Chaplin shit"[51]—Jerry has returned to a dummy act but doesn't know it.

McLuhan writes that without the "hot" medium of the phonograph, especially when entwined with radio, "the twentieth century as the era of tango, ragtime, and jazz would have had a different rhythm." From serving initially as a "talking machine" whose primary function was transcription, the phonograph imposed new rhythms of mechanical reproduction and influenced the emergence of ragtime's syncopations. Early 78 rpm records, in McLuhan's view, were similar to presound, early narrative film: they "produced a brisk and raucous experience not unlike that of a Mack Sennett movie."[52] In contradistinction to Adorno, who regarded commercial recording as antithetical to the performative improvisation that quickly came to define jazz as a musical form, McLuhan labors mightily to regard recording as crucial to any dialectical understanding of popular music in the twentieth century, not only as something popular but as music.

Wayne Koestenbaum's evocation of listening to soundtrack albums in the private space of the family rec room is relevant here as well. The doubly disembodied Marni Nixon is his privileged example, but Jerry's channeling of Dean Martin's voice through the medium of his own body demands its own kind of attention. Imperfectly Dean, perfectly Jerry—perhaps the performer of this dummy act is no dummy after all but a dialogic subject possessed of a new kind of self.[53]

McLuhan finds something similarly performative in the speech acts of the 1960s disc jockey; the voice of the DJ "alternately soars, groans, swings, sings, solos, intones, and scampers, always reacting to his own actions." Furthermore, it moves "entirely in the spoken rather than the written area of experience." For McLuhan, the spoken word "does not afford the extension and amplification of the visual power needed for habits of individualism and privacy."[54] It implies a public space (of speaking and hearing), and it fully occupies only the present moment of its utterance. Speech is responsive to nuance and capable of modulation, and it encourages a performed response in a way that the written word does not. It always allows the possibility of improvisation.

Of course, Jerry's own speech is characterized by its free association, syncopated rhythms, and slightly Tourette's-like set of nasal stutters, stops, and extended lines—a speech both smoothly improvised and stutteringly stuck. In *Artists and Models* the superhero-obsessed Jerry encounters a young woman (Shirley MacLaine) posing in a Bat Lady costume for her comics artist roommate. Jerry thinks she's the real deal and verbally spills all over the place in an inspired bit of scatted improvisation: *Ba-ba Ba-ba Ba-ba Ba-ba Bat-Lady!!!* And so, actually, what the dummy act presents is what we should now recognize as the characteristic Jerry dialectic between an obliteration of self through subservience to the playback's determinism and an assertion of self *against* that automatonistic determinism through the real-time responsiveness of performed improvisation. Riffing against the machine, let's call it, or malfunction as disobedience.

The films of Jerry Lewis are filled with that staple of film comedy, the tug-of-war between man and machine—a topic of significant interest to McLuhan. It's a kind of generational marker that McLuhan's dominant point of reference within cinematic comedy should be Chaplin: the rediscovery of Buster Keaton's comedy of automatism and adaptability would not occur until about a decade later, while Lewis and Tashlin were surely *too* contemporary, *too* vulgar to warrant consideration. Jerry embodies the end of that modernism exemplified in Chaplin's comedy. In *Modern Times* (1936) Charlie cannot control the spasmodic, repetitive movements endlessly required on his assembly-line job: on a break or outside the factory "he repeats his compulsive twitchings with an imaginary wrench."[55]

Charlie is defined through a division of labor and the crudest kind of use-value, but the pathos of his performance and the clarity of the visual metaphors (swallowed by the factory machine, e.g.) reinstate the character as an embattled soul in jeopardy. As McLuhan writes of Chaplin, "The clown reminds us of our fragmented state by tackling acrobatic or special jobs in the spirit of the whole or integral man" (an idea superbly illustrated by the animated, cutout Charlot figure that opens and closes Léger and Murphy's *Ballet mécanique* [1923]),[56], and this was just as true of other solo film comedians including Keaton and Lloyd.[57] Noël Carroll argues something similar of Keaton's work, finding the diminished role of the craftsman in American culture to be effectively recalled not only by Buster's symbiotic, solitary relationship to a locomotive engine in *The General* but by Keaton the filmmaker's always evident craftsmanship as well.[58]

This brings us to Jerry's own "compulsive twitchings." Unlike Chaplin, Keaton, or Astaire, all of whom subjugated technology through displays of balletic or athletic mastery, every spastic movement of Lewis's takes him toward his own oblivion (and this extends to the lack of control that the "total filmmaker" Lewis continually reveals).[59]

American modernity of the 1920s figured the machine as somewhat more discrete from the organic and human than did its European counterpart. While fusion with the machine was a source of anxiety (hence the protection offered within Benjamin's state of shock), separation was nevertheless imaginable: Keaton's engineer *must* leave his engine to effect his girl's rescue; Chaplin's Tramp *will* kick his feet and walk off down the road, free from the cares of the assembly line. There is the possibility of world and self existing unencumbered by the prosthetics of industrial technology. The mass media, however, as McLuhan theorized it in the mid-1960s, presented itself as an all-pervading, self-referential, and totalizing experiential "reality." We could fail to acknowledge this condition of being, but in doing so, McLuhan argued, we would amputate what was in effect part of ourselves, our very nervous systems, thereby leaving ourselves blind, deaf, dumb, and stupid. The global village, by definition, offered no hiding place.

Under these conditions Jerry Lewis becomes something other than an updated version of Chaplin's "mechanical doll, whose deep pathos is precisely to approximate so closely to the condition of human life."[60] While Buster Keaton adapts to the world, and Charlie Chaplin transforms it, Lewis is assimilated to the machine, becoming, in effect (almost literally), a machine himself (a "human motor" that differs from others we've encountered in these pages). "He's a human Dispos-All," Phoebe Tuttle (Agnes Moorehead) acidly observes in *Who's Minding the Store?* "All that's missing is a switch!" Later Mr. Quimby (Ray Walston) notes, "This boy is a dynamo!"

When not actually being defined as a machine, Jerry is often cast as the mere servomechanism of the machines that seem to work *him* (over): the exercise equipment that squashes and stretches him in *The Nutty Professor,* for example, or the Exercycle in *Who's Minding the Store?* There's that team of masseuses that treat him like a rag doll in *Artists and Models.* The mise-en-scene of *Who's Minding the Store?* is dominated by stem-to-stern product placements, and the branded objects in the department store become more autonomous and animated than the human characters. Despite one *Weekend*-like multiple-car pileup and a truly apocalyptic encounter with an overinflated vacuum cleaner, the consumerist clutter buries the anarchic impulses of the comedy. This is so very different from the pristine factory set of *Modern Times,* which facilitates the Tramp's oneiric performance in which he takes the space over, dominating that which had dominated him.

Keaton's characters are marked by an initial automatism that must be replaced by active human adaptability; his characters are machines that fail at first because they can't respond to changing information or circumstances. Jerry is more frequently cast as a machine that just plain *doesn't work* (the telling title of a later film is *Hardly Working*)—hence what he describes in *Hollywood or Bust* as the "jerking and the twitching," not to mention the spilling and the falling and the stammering and the whole thing with the lack of bodily control.[61]

But note further that while Jerry is constantly at war with the Mechanical, stuttering to a screeching, spastic halt in a constant enactment of technophysical breakdown, he is also always (and at the same time) becoming Media. He "becomes" a typewriter in *Who's Minding the Store?* and a television in *Rock-a-Bye Baby.* Lewis's character in *Artists and Models,* Eugene Fullstack, is "a little retarded" example of comic books' nefarious influence, dreaming of Vincent the Vulture and loudly spewing out superhero narration and secret rocket formulas. He seems to have become a receiver, or perhaps a transmitter, or perhaps a receiver of the transmissions of his own unconscious.[62] Or, as *he* explains to a psychiatrist on a televised panel discussion, "My subconscious was battling against my conscious and the basic intelligence of my mind wouldn't allow myself to comprehend some of the problems that were forethought prior to sleeping and at the same time not having any rest because of no sedation whatsoever to make my rest and dreams any brighter or smarter than they were when I was much younger!" This is automatic speech: a breathless chain of free-association in which the mechanical operation of generating words supersedes its semantic function.

In *Who's Minding the Store?* Jerry challenges the power of the psychoanalyst (not to mention the transcriber) when speaking to Mr. Tuttle, the department store president: "Your brain must be very busy to be a president with a CLICK-CLACK BIH-SHTOOM SHTOOBIDOOM—Like an IBM machine!!" Deleuze wrote, "This is no longer the age of the tool or machine. . . . This is a new age of electronics, and the remote-controlled object."[63] And Jerry, that servomechanism for every mechanism, becomes the comedian for the information age. Citing Jerry's dismaying jerking and twitching when he gets "that lucky feeling" in *Hollywood or Bust,* Deleuze figures Jerry as a primitive cyborg—a slapstick Stelarc twitching in desperate response to constant and conflicting commands. Like a *malfunctioning* IBM machine!![64]

It's of course appropriate that Eugene is possessed by comics, which in the 1950s were at the center of a witch hunt, following the publication of Fredric Wertham's *Seduction of the Innocent.* Comics were a little suspect, and while Wertham and those who followed in his wake went rather too far, comics perhaps *should* be a little suspect. In my first chapter I described how comics of the late nineteenth and early twentieth centuries offered up a graphic resistance to the rationalist imperatives mapped in chronophotographs, a breakdown of order in the face of encroaching order. One would (OK, *I* would) love to see a chronophotographic sequence of Jerry Lewis, lurching unpredictably and uncontainedly against all the regularities of Muybridge's grids.

What one constantly witnesses in the films of Jerry Lewis is not a simple automatism but a full-bodied resistance to the unnatural stimuli of technologies in transition—his body spasms rather than glides, crashes rather than operates. In McLuhan's terms the comedian performs a failed autoamputation for the audience: his body serves too evidently as the servomechanism of machinic and electronic forces. The agony of Jerry Lewis lies in his proximate intimacy to these "extensions of man"—a pathetic proximity that precludes the comfortable possibilities of satire to be found in Chaplin, Jacques Tati, and even Tashlin; precludes the comfortable illusions of self-sustaining selfhood; or precludes the comfort of any coherence at all. The individual is reduced to an automaton—but a malfunctioning automaton, a marionette with tangled strings.

Chapter 5

LABOR AND ANIMATEDNESS

"All that I have is really yours, my lust for life and my energy, too, for I am able to keep going now with your help and can feel my capacity for work flowing back."

—VINCENT VAN GOGH (LETTER TO THEO VAN GOGH)

Sianne Ngai's "animatedness" is "the exaggeratedly emotional, hyperexpressive, and even 'overscrutable' image of most racially or ethnically marked subjects in American culture," but, as I hope to have demonstrated by now, it's a valuable concept in other contexts as well—even beyond the realm of the animated film, as shown by the preceding discussions of *My Fair Lady* and Jerry Lewis.[1] *Lust for Life* (Vincente Minnelli, 1956) could be said to present Vincent van Gogh as an animated figure who, indeed, suffers for his hyperexpressive overscrutability. Van Gogh, after all, was an artist, and, as we saw in the second chapter, artists have often been posited or represented as undisciplined figures, existing suspiciously beyond the borders of acceptable behaviors—Alex Nemerov describes "the irresponsible play of imaginative freedom" that the artist had grudging license to indulge. The artist could be said to suffer from an animatedness of imagination; furthermore, the artist, Nemerov reminds us, *animates* through "a presence that enlivens the world."[2] The somewhat suspect figure of the artist animates the world, while representations of the artist, here in a Hollywood biopic, depict him as an animated figure, whose animatedness bespeaks, enacts, and enforces a separation from polite society. The portrayal of the artist *as* animated being can be seen to stand in for the *animating vision* of the artist him- or herself. It is the singular accomplishment of Minnelli's *Lust for Life,* however, to give us *both* the animatedness of the artist *and* his animating vision.

Ngai has pointed to the "unusual immediacy between emotional experience and bodily movement" in a reader "animated" by a text, and *Lust for Life* presents a similar immediacy, here located in the protagonist rather than the reader.[3] The very title of the film speaks to a lively, perhaps too lively, engagement with the world—the phrase comes from a letter from Vincent to Theo, in which he writes, "You see,

FIGURE 33. *Lust for Life,* 1956.

brother, I think of you a very great deal these days, in the first place because every-thing, all that I have, is really yours, my lust for life and my energy, too, for I am able to keep going now with your help and can feel my capacity for work flowing back."[4] A lust for life, energy, the capacity for work—all this speaks a passion marked by melodramatic excess.

In *Lust for Life* the intimacy of Vincent van Gogh's easel painting (Figure 33) is enlarged to epic, CinemaScope proportions. Through the amplification of these brushstrokes, which now stretch across the wide screen, the film revels in both the materiality of the paint and the physicality of the act of painting. These magnified marks, fervently testifying to the presence, if not the very soul, of the painter, fur-ther align the film strikingly with the intensity of the American postwar painting grouped under the heading of Abstract Expressionism—the large-scale, gestural art of Jackson Pollock, Clyfford Still, Willem de Kooning, and others. Perhaps sur-prisingly, the Irving Stone novel on which the film was based was not contempo-raneous with its MGM adaptation but was first published in 1934. Even so, Stone's image of a primitivist, self-destructive Van Gogh seems attuned to the romanticiz-ing of a particular kind of artist in 1950s America.[5] In fact, however, the novel did not become a sensation until its reissue in 1946—just as postwar American art was beginning its ascent. It was not the art of Europe but of America that was then be-ing mythologized; Abstract Expressionism was a large part of how America gained prominence in modern art in the postwar era.[6]

In 1952 the art critic Harold Rosenberg had famously described contemporary American painting as "action painting," a mode that, he argued, more than any-thing else memorialized the gestures of the artist. "At a certain moment the canvas began to appear to one American painter after another as an arena in which to act—rather than as a space in which to reproduce, redesign, analyse or 'express' an object, actual or imagined. What was to go on the canvas was not a picture but an event"[7] (really, an *animated* event). Action painting was understood as an "event" and a "performance"—a record of a kinetic event more than of preconsidered, reflective creation.

The cinema, too, is a medium dedicated to the recording of action, of movement, whether the movement of the objects of the world, the movement of the camera itself, or even the movement of the film through camera and projector. And by the mid-1950s, with the rise of widescreen processes like the multiprojector Cinerama and its anamorphic single-projector offshoot, CinemaScope, film had also moved toward becoming more of an "event." When postwar outdoor recreations such as camping, car touring, do-it-yourself home improvements, and trips to Disneyland began to leach off the motion picture audience, and as the rise of the domestic medium of television began to make its presence felt, Hollywood reinvented itself as an engaged form of entertainment. As John Belton argues, Cinerama, CinemaScope, 3-D, and other newfangled gimmicks were all marketed as "participatory events" for the viewer, and huge road-show adaptations of Broadway hits aligned cinema with the special event of theater.[8] Thus American film became something more participatory, and something more of a performance, just at the moment that American painting entered the gestural, performative moment of "action."

The alignment of *Lust for Life* with Abstract Expressionism, and in particular with "action painting," points, as well, to the fundamental animatedness of the Abstract Expressionist artist, as exemplified by Jackson Pollock. Here, after all, is a movement defined, for Rosenberg, by the physical activity of the painter, the generative gestures and kinetic performances, as much as (or more than) the appearance of the paintings themselves. The fundamentally physical connection of painter to painting, the means by which the paintings pick up and continue the movement of the artist recalls the transfer of energy and the intimacy of the bond that exists between animator and animated, as discussed in chapter 3.

"Anything that has to do with action—psychology, philosophy, history, mythology, hero worship"—is relevant to these paintings, Rosenberg argues. "Anything but art criticism. The painter gets away from art through his act of painting; the critic can't get away from it. The critic who goes on judging . . . as if the painter were still concerned with producing a certain kind of object (the work of art), instead of living on the canvas—is bound to seem a stranger."[9] Therefore the action painter is closer to the world of action than to the world of art. The artist's technique takes him from the ethereal realm of culture and toward an earthy, unmediated and unmeditated primitivism.

The primitivism of Minnelli's Van Gogh is commensurate with Michael Leja's contextualization of Abstract Expressionism in terms of what Leja calls the "Mod-

ern Man" discourse, which gained considerable traction in postwar American culture. The template for the new primitive could be found in Modern Man nonfic-
tion of the postwar era, guides to the Organization Man and other bloodless configurations of the day. Leja has argued that "Abstract Expressionism had much more
in common with the mainstream culture than some of its aggressively elitist de-
fenders would allow." One did not have to look far to find other contemporaneous
"cultural manifestations of fascination with the primitive and the irrational. They
turn[ed] up repeatedly in Hollywood films, newspaper and magazine articles, radio
programs, and books of all sorts."[10] Set against the effete Modern Man was a more
brutal, self-destructive, more mythic archetype, and some Abstract Expressionists
(a.k.a. "action painters") played this role for all it was worth, setting an American
brutalism against its more effete European counterparts.

Indeed, for T. J. Clark, the only Abstract Expressionist canvases that matter are
those "truly consumed with their own empty intensity, with painting as postur-
ing, with a ludicrous bigness and lushness and generality."[11] Abstract Expressionism was characterized by a *too-muchness: too much* paint, *too much* effort, *too much*
artistic persona. Clark describes the color schemes of the most popular works by
Mark Rothko: "the ones where a hectoring absolute of self-presence is maintained
in face of the void; with vulgarity—a vulgar fulsomeness of reds, pinks, purples, or-
anges, lemons, lime greens, powder-puff whites." A good painting by Hans Hof-
mann, he writes, is "tasteless to the core—tasteless in its invocations of Europe, tasteless in its mock religiosity, tasteless in its Color-by-Technicolor, its winks and nudges
toward landscape format, its Irving Stone title, and the cloying demonstrativeness
of its handling."[12]

Lust for Life (an Irving Stone title, yes, but taken, as we've seen, from one of Van
Gogh's letters) exhibits not just some but *all* of these characteristics (and many of
them also apply to the rest of the extravagantly vulgar Minnellian melodramas of
the 1950s). It could be said that both Abstract Expressionism and widescreen melodrama sought "to devise a form of modernist visual representation that could accommodate and enrich developing models of the human individual, models that
attributed new importance to irrational others within human being."[13] The "action"
in both depended on the precarious balance between control and excess; the net
effect was a willful vulgarity, a rudeness that bespoke petty-bourgeois aspirations
and limitations.

I want to argue that Minnelli's *Lust for Life* turns Vincent van Gogh into something of an action painter, not simply in its presentation of the painter-as-hero[14]—
and an American hero at that—but also in the scale and even the vulgarity of its
spectacle. The new emphasis on the physicality of painting, the way the canvas
becomes a record of the moment, of embodied movement, is appropriate to the ferocious physicality of *Lust for Life*: a physicality that can be found in the hunched
tension of Kirk Douglas's performance, the veracity of place produced by its well-

publicized location work, the sumptuous material excess of its widescreen expansiveness, the lushness of Miklos Rozsa's score, and the vibrancy of its Ansco Color palette. To posit an analogy between the film's Van Gogh and action painters is to move beyond a consideration of Abstract Expressionism as a significant contextual sidebar to the film, to an argument more concerned with the physicality, even the mythos of physicality—the animatedness—on which both *Lust for Life* and "action painting" depended.

BIOPIC, EPIC, MELODRAMA

Lust for Life is a fascinating amalgam of three Hollywood genres: biopic, epic, and melodrama. Like all Hollywood biopics about artists (or writers or musicians), it flatters the audience without shame; each time a character proclaims Van Gogh's paintings to be worthless, an audience member, with the benefit of hindsight, can pat him- or herself smugly on the back, free to believe that he or she would surely have recognized the man's genius from the get-go.

Where the biopic is pedantic, the historical epic has a more pedagogic function. Vivian Sobchack has theorized the phenomenological impact of this genre, whereby *temporal* excess (the sweep of history) is encoded as a *material* excess (widescreen, thousands of extras, gargantuan sets).[15] In *Lust for Life* the "epic" sweep encompasses approximately ten tumultuous years in Van Gogh's life; they are also the *last* ten years of his life, but the artist's death has no finality since it opens onto the immortality of Van Gogh as myth. The material excess of the epic is summoned by the film's slightly excessive length, the ten-year sweep, the grandeur of Cinema-Scope, and the passionate score by Miklos Rozsa (like *El Cid,* which Rozsa also scored, the film chronicles a journey past death and into immortality—these are not "sad deaths" but epic deaths). The film adds to the condition of spectacle by making much of the "wantonly expansive"[16] use of the real, historical locations.

The use of Van Gogh's actual paintings—photographed in large-scale format with brief strobic flashes—with the intense magnification of the brushstrokes and layers of thickly applied oil paint, further speaks to the film's "epic" excess. The material excess represented by the medium of oil paint itself connotes luxury and solidity; it was a medium well-suited to the depiction of mercantile wealth.[17] The same might be said of the lustrous product that MGM was producing in the 1950s. James Naremore argues that in *Lust for Life* "the visual experience offered to the public by MGM, in which we see beautifully photographed montages of Van Gogh's canvases and dozens of undetectable forgeries spread across the sets in casual abandon, is in part a spectacle of *wealth,* roughly equivalent to the thrill of watching the cozily massed extras in a DeMille epic."[18] *Lust for Life* is therefore certainly steeped in what Sobchack calls the "eventfulness" of the epic.[19]

Part biopic, part epic, *Lust for Life* is primarily a melodrama. According to

Thomas Elsaesser, in his influential essay "Tales of Sound and Fury," at the center of melodrama lies an abyss of inarticulateness, an insufficiency of language that he links to the symptomology of hysteria.[20] Melodrama presents a precarious world of individuals grappling for control in a world resistant to (their) understanding or change. That world is objectified through aesthetic and performative excess—an oppressive, stylized mise-en-scène and exaggeratedly emotive acting. The protagonists' failure is manifested in a failure of language: a halting and painful speech that cannot say what it must or a torrent of words that only seem to hide the impossibility of true articulation. This social paralysis often manifests itself in an excessive animatedness, whether in performance (think James Dean in *Rebel without a Cause*) or in filmmaking (as in the hysterical camerawork and mise-en-scène accompanying Georgia Lorrison's wild ride in *The Bad and the Beautiful*).

Michael Leja rightly contends that Abstract Expressionism had much in common with Hollywood cinema, but he emphasizes film noir, which I think is the wrong genre. It is true that "like Mythmaker painting, *film noir* attributes a complex, layered, conflicted subjectivity to its protagonists. . . . Sometimes mysterious inner compulsions are portrayed as the principal factors in [that protagonist's] destructive actions."[21] But noir is hardly the only genre to provide such a correlate.[22] Leja seems almost to *repress* melodrama (not "tough" enough, perhaps?). While both noir and melodrama challenge a powerful, self-knowing masculinism, the former frequently displaces sexual anxiety onto the safe remove of a femme fatale, whereas in melodrama the feminine is internalized, yielding far more tormented, self-contradictory protagonists. Dean in *Rebel without a Cause* and *East of Eden* comes to mind, as do Marlon Brando's more classically masculine Stanley Kowalski in *A Streetcar Named Desire* and Douglas's tormented Jonathan Shields in *The Bad and the Beautiful*.

Melodrama may be a somewhat clichéd approach to the telling of an artist's life. Typically, the artist articulates himself not with language but through an art that is misapprehended for much (if not all) of the artist's lifetime; the artist is, almost by definition, misunderstood. But melodrama is particularly appropriate to Van Gogh's life—not only because his tragic life is the very stuff of melodrama but because his own writings reveal something of a melodramatic imagination. The words of his cousin's rejection, the deliciously fevered "*Never, no, never!*" echo through Vincent's letters just as they do in the film (as a slightly variant "*No, never, never!*"). And he recognizes his own problems of self-expression: explaining one of his outbursts to Theo, he writes that "what I say at such times is what I've been bottling up for a long time and then blurt out, sometimes quite bluntly."[23] Stone's novel is similarly melodramatic: "A great inarticulate surge of grief welled up in his throat."[24]

And, of course, the Hollywood melodrama has become recognized as a fundamentally antirealist genre, one that sacrifices physical accuracy and verisimilitude in favor of a distorted, intensified mise-en-scène reflective of emotional tensions and subjective states. In this context Van Gogh's comments about his favorite painters have some resonance: they "are the true artists, because they do not paint things as they are, examined in a dry analytical manner, but as they . . . feel them to be. . . . I long most of all to produce those very inaccuracies, those very aberrations, reworkings, transformations of reality, as may turn it into, well—a lie if you like—but truer than the literal truth."[25]

THE WORLD OF THE IMAGE

It's possibly heretical to advance this claim when discussing a film by Vincente Minnelli, but the image track of *Lust for Life* seems at first somewhat superfluous, serving the literate script and the performances of the actors. But as the film progresses and Van Gogh moves toward his own mastery of the image, the film's images become increasingly sumptuous and autonomous. At the height of Vincent's passion (a passion both euphoric and destructive), the film's images and Vincent's become one, and they come to constitute a world of their own—indeed, take on a *life* of their own.

Minnelli's film effectively adapts a novel that has not aged well, and the initial restraint of the image at first seems due to the film's status as a literary adaptation. Elsaesser has written of the effect of narrative compression in Minnelli's work, a compression that results in the piling of climax upon climax, accentuating the overall tone of simmering hysteria, and this is certainly true of *Lust for Life*.[26] Vincent's disastrous, abortive love affairs, his break with both the ministry and his family (except, of course, with Theo), his emotional and physical struggles and debilitations, and his fiery battles with the Impressionists all take place in the film's first hour. The script was written by Norman Corwin, an important writer for radio who had produced relatively few screenplays (a good deal of the dialogue comes straight from the novel).[27] Corwin distills and largely dispenses with the interminable sections of the novel devoted to the all-star roster of Parisian artists drinking and arguing about the nature of art, and he is adept at providing backstory unobtrusively but effectively.

In fact, a great deal of information is conveyed by the soundtrack: in dialogue, in Theo's voice-over readings of Vincent's letters, and in Rozsa's underscoring. There are few stretches devoid of either words or music. We are told about the horrors of the miners' life in the Borinage and of Vincent's desire to understand and help them. Rozsa's score emphasizes the drama of life down in the mines and the exhilaration of Vincent's first encounter with the paintings of the Impressionists. The palette in the early parts of the film contributes to this deemphasis of the image. The scenes at the Borinage and at the Hague, even at the family home in Nuenen, are presented in muted earth tones: somber olives, grays, and browns. At this point Vincent is only drawing, not painting, charcoal and chalk monochromatic studies on brown paper. The image becomes more vivid at the beach in Scheveningen, a richer palette whipped by wind and captured in oil paint, but this is a brief interlude; and even in Vincent's studio the paintings are few and scattered, still surrounded and swallowed by the plethora of monochromatic drawings. Up to this point the image has served a primarily illustrative function, operating with restraint and with that almost Bazinian realism (long takes, deep space, and moral uncertainties) that characterizes many of Minnelli's melodramas.[28] The film seems at risk of becoming a series of tableaux vivants, an episode of *Masterpiece Theater*, even, perhaps, an issue of *Classics Illustrated*.

But with the image relieved of the burden of narrative, it is freed to do something else. In Paris the palette begins to shift to lighter, brighter colors; significantly, this does not happen through depictions of sun-drenched landscapes or broad boulevards but through Vincent's encounter with an exhibition of Impressionist painting.[29] Work by Renoir and Monet rivets Vincent's attention, and in an epiphanic moment, the first of many for him, the camera holds and tracks in on a Monet, a painting of a woman in a field. Then, more words. Vincent argues with Theo; Vincent is lectured by Pissarro, but finally, finally words begin to fade, replaced now by a slow montage of Vincent's paintings, which move surely toward the liberated colors and thick dabs of paint that are recognizably "Vincent's." Yet another lecture follows, this one by Seurat, and Vincent briefly tries his hand at pointillism, painting a sun-drenched garden while closeted by night in Theo's apartment. But through Vincent's frustrations and travails something has been added to the filmic image: a vividness, a luminosity, a bright clarity from which Vincent's paintings, and the film, will never return.

The image track crescendos with Vincent's arrival at Arles. He arrives at night, dumped in a creaky bed in a squalid room. Beyond the shutters all that is visible is an inky void; there is literally *nothing there.* But, come morning, Vincent is awakened by twittering birds. Wiping the sleep from his eyes, he rises and throws open the shutters. Here, exactly one hour into the film (precisely halfway through) the image erupts in a manner not unlike Dorothy's arrival in the Technicolor land of Oz. The intense color of the peach trees blossoms forth, not with the saturated candy colors of Oz but the subtler tones of Ansco-inflected nature (Plate 24). But this is more than the emergence of color—the film has already gone there—it is the addition of emphatic camera movement to vibrant color that summons a feeling of delirious, utopian plenitude. A montage sequence of moving shots takes us beneath the spreading trees, follows their upward reach to the sky, and seamlessly merges with a tilt down a painted landscape. The world experienced by Vincent has become, through montage and movement, one with the world created by his paints.

As his life in Arles continues, and Vincent works himself increasingly into a state of nervous exhaustion, the colors become feverish, hallucinatory. The close-ups become more intense, the canvases more magnified upon the CinemaScope screen. By the time he collapses in the cafe, Vincent has come to inhabit his paintings. "In my picture of the Night Café," he wrote in a letter to Theo, "I have tried to express the idea that the café is a place where one can destroy oneself, go mad or commit a crime. In short, I have tried, by contrasting soft pink with blood-red and wine-red, soft Louis XV–green and Veronese green with yellow-greens and harsh blue-greens, all this in an atmosphere of an infernal furnace in pale sulphur, to express the powers of darkness in a common tavern."[30]

It is not at all surprising that this very café becomes a hallucinatory setting—part reality, part painting, part dream—in Minnelli's film. Vincent rouses himself from an alcoholic stupor, and his bloodshot eyes absorb the unrelievedly flat reds, the sulfurous lamps, the slow clack of the billiard balls: a saturated, immersive setting more truly expressionist in its saturated colors than the black-and-white nightmare settings of *The Cabinet of Doctor Caligari.* Subjective reality has become the *only* reality, and naturalism has no place here.

Vincent's awakening in *The Night Café* is part of a series of shots that frame him within his own paintings. The shot begins with a striking dissolve from a close-up of his 1888 canvas *Starlight over the Rhone* that momentarily superimposes Vincent's brushstrokes on the photographed figure of Vincent himself. For that instant the artist himself seems a painted creation, a product of his own fevered vision (Plate 25). Earlier in the film, while discussing matters with his sister in Nuenen in a static two-shot, Vincent is framed by his first major painting, *The Potato Eaters,* as though he were at a table with the peasant family he is celebrating. While painting outdoors in Arles he is filmed in close-up before one of his canvases of blossoming trees, the painting filling the background. And, convalescing after the severing of his ear, he is awakened in his bedroom by the sensation-seeking crowd outside. The bedroom set is a careful copy of the room in his famous painting, which has been emphasized in an earlier scene, in happier times, by a cut from the painting to the identically framed set. Now, though, the room has become his prison: the creator is trapped in the confines of his own aesthetic creation; there is no reality beyond the one he can create.

Parker Tyler wrote of Jackson Pollock's swirling brushstrokes: "If one felt vertigo before Pollock's differentiations of space, then truly one would be lost in the abyss of an endless definition of being. . . . But we are safely looking at it, seeing it steadily and seeing it whole, from a point outside."[31] I wonder if this is also true of the hysteria and excess of Minnelli's own vertiginous crescendos—if they do not edge up as closely to the abyss, then neither do they, in their widescreen synesthetic immersiveness, offer the viewer the same safety of "a point outside."

PERCEPTION AND PERFORMANCE

But that first morning in Arles is indisputably celebratory: the discovery of a productive vision capable of *remaking,* indeed *animating,* the world. Griselda Pollock's analysis of this same scene, however, emphasizes the power of *nature* to inspire the creative vision of the artist. She argues that the film mythologizes artistic creation as grounded primarily in an act of perception. "Art is at once direct visual experience and the personal filter through which nature passes."[32] By returning to the actual locations in which the life was lived and the paintings produced, and by following his rejection of the overcultured artistic debates of Paris for the sun-drenched fields of Arles, the film proposes that Van Gogh was able to introduce "Nature back into Culture." Following Elsaesser's essays on Minnelli, Pollock writes that the only way for Van Gogh "to cut through the resistance of the world around him" is through "his gaze as an artist. Vision thus provides a moment of lyrical liberation when the artist looks at nature."[33]

Pollock links the epiphanic vision that accompanies Vincent's arrival at Arles to the Central Park sequence of *The Band Wagon* (1953) in its negotiation of "the relation of the popular and natural to the cultural and elite." In *The Band Wagon*, Astaire's Tony Hunter and Cyd Charisse's Gabriel Gerard stroll past a small group of dancers to a solitary spot. There, "in the park, close to Nature, without choreography, true art is presented as something which is neither commercialized popular dance nor formalised high art, but a direct overflowing of feeling into freely expressive movement."[34] There is something to this, but I cannot accept *The Band Wagon*'s version of Central Park as nature, when it is a happily stylized MGM set. In Minnelli's films the idea of nature is always already mediated: this remains more Tony's world than either Gaby's *or* nature's.

It is again nature that informs Pollock's understanding of Vincent's epiphany in Arles. She argues that when Vincent first looks from his bedroom window, the subsequent montage represents his point of view through a classic reverse shot, but she further suggests that the montage actually is not grounded in any precise point of view but rather with what she calls an "all-overness." "The camera's movements feed a nostalgic fantasy of the total freedom of the eye," she writes, a notion of a "disembodied eye" familiar to readers of Jean-Louis Baudry. These shots of the real landscape of Arles "then dissolve into painted images while retaining the same upward and downward movement," and thus: "Pure perception slides effortlessly into art, signifying by this sleight of photographic representation that art is merely the optical register of pure individual perception." The "innocence or intensity of his artistic vision" gives us "not only his vision of nature, but Nature itself. . . . What is elided is of course [of course!] the fact of both film as a production . . . and art as a graphic and material production process."[35] Oddly, then, Pollock holds that this montage, the first vivid and stylized sequence of the film, where filmic technique is most evident, is where the work of the signifier is most transparent, most effectively hidden.

I would counter that the bleed between individual perspective and this "all-overness" rather *marks* the site of—the work of—production, not its elision. That the paintings are animated by the camera with the same pans, tilts, and dissolves used on the "natural" landscape (as natural as CinemaScope and Anscocolor could allow) suggests that Van Gogh's vision gives us a performance *unleashed,* not that "art is merely the optical register" of a pure perception. What is celebrated in this sequence, what I believe the spectator identifies with, is the movement beyond an extravagant *seeing* of the world to a productive vision that *remakes* and *animates* it.

The bountiful region of Arles facilitates *performance,* a performance of creation, for Vincent. In that context the opening of the shutters might be seen to correspond not to liberation of vision and nature but to the raising of a theatrical curtain (not unlike Judy Garland singing "The Boy Next Door" while framed by the window and curtains of her home in *Meet Me in St. Louis* [1944]). In Minnelli's hands the arduous work of production, Vincent's frantic workings of paper and canvas, can easily be seen as analogous to the rehearsals that go on in *The Band Wagon,* while the paintings themselves, in sumptuous color and widescreen, made kinetic by camera and editing, achieve the perfect performative synthesis of the musical numbers themselves.[36]

Lust for Life is not about the purity of perception so much as the necessity of performance and the imperative of creation. "Bring me some red," the painter Derain said on his deathbed, "some red and some green." This line is quoted by Stevie, the young artist-patient at the outset of Minnelli's 1955 melodrama *The Cobweb,* and the terror evoked is a terror of whiteness, the absence of color; the absence of color speaking to an absence of passion, of the Minnellian decor that is an extension of self, of life, of humanity. The mute (or perhaps shrieking) whiteness of the blank canvas must be filled; it summons performance, intervention, action (the same can be said of the blank page that terrifies the writer Jeffrey Moss in Minnelli's *Bells Are Ringing* [1960] or even the blank fields that McCay and Picasso obsessively fill in their own orgies of productivity). Painting becomes not the transcription of nature but a performance of energy that brings color to the world. The array of paintings carelessly strewn about the yellow house in Arles or framed as Vincent's legacy at the film's end offers a plenitude that is testament to the obsessive work of their production.

A PAINTING LOCOMOTIVE

Serge Guilbaut notes that during the postwar period "the United States was generally seen as a culturally dry, unsophisticated, crude, antihumanistic, and cold land. The country was young, violent, and technological, good for the movies but not fit to participate in the old traditional discourse of painting." Guilbaut further identifies some of the self-identified clichés by which America and France defined themselves and each other: "America was violent, brutal, and free, while France was overcultured, suave to the point of decadence, and riddled with inner contradictions.

One was rough, the other was slick. Interestingly enough, both sides agreed on the validity of these clichés for differentiating their two cultures. The catch was that each country saw its characteristics as positive compared to the negative qualities of the other."[37]

The physical work of artistic production occupied the center of Rosenberg's category of action painting, displacing other aspects of the creative process such as contemplation, reflection, sketching, and reworking. Tactically, this proved significant—painting was now a man's activity in keeping with America's image as a place that was "violent, brutal, and free"[38]—something altogether different from what was perceived as the effete, mannered, and bloodless modernism being produced over there in Europe. Jackson Pollock was the archetype of the American Abstract Expressionist, his notorious drinking binges, his violence, his impropriety, and, not least, the seeming inarticulate physicality of his mode of painting, all contributing to his fame both inside and well beyond artistic circles. Rosalind Krauss captures the self-consciousness of his posture when she refers to "that dissolute squat, in his James Dean dungarees and black tee-shirt," a comparison that suggested itself even before their similar deaths by car crash (a variation of what Bataille has termed "automutilation"). Pollock was a kind of method actor, a performer who seemingly tapped into the culture's most atavistic urges.[39] J. Hoberman writes, "The brutish Marlon Brando who galvanized Broadway in the 1947 production of *A Streetcar Named Desire* reminded more than one member of the New York art world of Pollock; two years later, *Life* introduced Pollock to America as something like the Brando of abstract art."[40]

Lust for Life Americanizes its European protagonist—Van Gogh becomes, via Kirk Douglas, an American in Paris (and Nuenen, and Arles). Theo was portrayed by the British actor James Donald, and it is Theo's voice that reads Vincent's letters on the soundtrack, as though Vincent's reflective, learned, and articulate persona had to be separated from his more primitive, intuitive, and physical self. But Guilbaut's observation that the clichéd European artist was "riddled with self-contradiction" is also figured in *Lust for Life*'s presentation of Van Gogh. While Vincent shares some of Pollock's brutal primitivism, it is Anthony Quinn's Gauguin who has the swagger and hard-drinking machismo ("Two absinthes!" he shouts to a bartender).

The self-contradictions of Vincent's character are most pronounced in the film around the dialectic of *work* and *emotion*. As is often the case with postwar American melodrama, the male protagonist is feminized, primarily by a hyperemotionalism that distinguishes him from other men in the film. This hyperemotionalism is pronounced in *Lust for Life:* Vincent doesn't work—even Theo calls him an "idler" and supports him financially. Repeatedly, he is accused of shirking his responsibilities, of being unable to provide for his spouse (be it Kee or Sien), or, indeed, even feed himself. His idleness is often linked to his perceived weakness: Gauguin says that while he might have some of the same problems as Vincent, "I don't whine about it!" Kee's father accuses him of being unable to withstand pain or disappointment without "whimpering." In Arles Vincent proves to be a very happy homemaker: when Theo takes a wife, Vincent takes Gauguin. He has decorated the room for Paul, giving him *Sunflowers.* "I painted them for you," Vincent says, to which Paul bemusedly replies, "That's very friendly of you, Vincent . . . very friendly." If Vincent can now provide a home, it is nevertheless in the guise of a wife, albeit one who can't cook. Just as he did with the women in his life, Vincent throws himself tumultuously into his relationship with Gauguin, demanding complete attention, his ardor manifesting itself in obsession, unrestrained verbiage, and "whining." Vincent is a classic hysteric. As with other male protagonists of postwar melodramas, a torrent of words cannot hide the character's inability to articulate the deepest feelings, to confront the existential despair of ultimate loneliness.

But at the same time that Vincent is presented as an unemployed idler, he is also portrayed as the most industrious of workers. He journeys down to the mines, tends the sick, and educates the young at the Boringe; in Nuenen, surrounded by his charcoal studies, he resembles the unflaggingly industrious Jonathan Shields of the *Bad and the Beautiful;* Van Gogh's actual letters continually stress the fact of labor—hard labor—in the constructing of art. "To get to the essence of things one has to work long & hard. . . . Art demands dogged work, work in spite of everything and continuous observation."[41] In conversation with Theo, paraphrased in the film but here quoted from Van Gogh's original letter, Vincent argues:

> Then there is the other kind of ne'er-do-well, the ne'er-do-well despite himself, who is inwardly consumed by a great longing for action, who does nothing because his hands are tied, because he is, so to speak, imprisoned somewhere, because he lacks what he needs to be productive, because disastrous circumstances have brought him forcibly to this end. Such a one does not always know what he can do, but he nevertheless instinctively feels, I am good for something! My existence is not without reason! I know that I could be quite a different person! How can I be of use?[42]

In Arles Vincent becomes another human motor—in the film he writes that he is "working like a steam engine"—in his own letters he refers to himself as "a painting locomotive." Later, in the asylum at Saint-Remy, he writes that he works "like a miner who knows he is facing disaster," but, more hopefully, he describes one of the characteristic, somber silhouetted figures in a painting as "any man, struggling in the heat to finish his work." Despite being a symbol of impending death, the sister ministering to him notes that "it doesn't seem a bad death," to which Vincent replies that it isn't—to "work, boldly and joyously," is the best, and the most, that a man can do.

Thus Vincent is fractured, an incoherent figure: an "idler" in a world of working men, he is also the man who works the hardest, who is never, ever not working. To live is to struggle for definition, and that struggle is work of the highest, most demanding order. As it was, to some degree, in the Picasso and McCay films, art is here presented as *work, labor*—the activity of remaking the world in the terms of one's own aesthetic that is a hallmark of Minnelli's films. These paintings do not come easily to Vincent: it's difficult to imagine describing a Van Gogh painting as "effortless"; rather, the canvas manifests labor in its layers of paint, the sense of frantic haste, the pigments squeezed directly from tube to canvas, the quest for a visual language adequate to the intensity of the experience (as well as to the autonomy of the medium).[43] This is why Kirk Douglas is so perfectly cast: the hunched yet expansive physicality of his performance—what Naremore calls Douglas's "crouched energy and muscular, tormented gestures"—is similarly "effortful."[44]

There is, therefore, some breakdown of the dialectic with which Vincent is constantly being upbraided: Vincent, indeed, suffers from an excess of emotion but also from an excess of industry. He is a man possessed, obsessed, driven endlessly by the imperative to create. "Must you persist in the face of everything?" Theo asks, already knowing the answer. Yes, he *must*. And in persisting he both finds himself and goes mad. Jean Douchet has described "the problem of the artist" at the center of Minnelli's work, "confronted by the work of art which absorbs him, but which also menaces him in his very existence as soon as he has created it."[45] "My pictures come to me in a dream, with a terrible lucidity," writes Van Gogh. It is at this point that the film begins to resemble a canvas by Van Gogh; it is at this point that he almost literally inhabits the frenzied intensity of his paintings. In one of his own letters he writes that he is "in a constant fever of work."[46] When he is finally committed to the hospice at Saint-Remy, the bureaucratic head of the facility notes in his dictated report that his patient suffers from "excesses of work and emotion." The rest of the world may distinguish between these two states, but in Vincent, principles associated with the masculine and the feminine commingle, and the clichéd constructs of "American" and "European" are not easily separated.

PERFORMING PAINTING

A hallmark of Minnelli's style is the explosion, at moments of emotional epiphany and breakdown, into a more unrestrained, hysterical stylistic realm that sweeps the spectator into a heightened sensorial emotionalism. *Lust for Life* features an abundance of such moments: the awful awakening in *The Night Café* and the scene of self-mutilation are but the two most dramatic. But the film is punctuated as well by epiphanic montage sequences of Van Gogh's work. In the transformation of painting to cinema that occurs in *Lust for Life,* the magnification of the brushstroke moves us beyond the *materiality of the medium* to the *physicality of production.*

At first the camera keeps a respectful distance—a zoom in or out on a complete canvas—but the montage becomes more rapid as Vincent becomes more animated, an array of frenetic details. Closer shots of sinuous brushwork displace the earlier emphasis on composition and location—now it is the *inner* landscape that dominates. In the scenes at Saint-Remy the camera lingers more as the brushstrokes become more lustrous. The camera, accompanied by Rozsa's melodic theme, pulls out to reveal the glorious *Starry Night,* but two abrupt cuts, punctuated by the music, isolate the central swirl of the Milky Way and a jagged array of moon and stars. The thickness of the paint, the clashing colors, and the vertiginous brushstrokes fill the CinemaScope frame, pushing out at the edges, threatening to overwhelm everything. Now the film has pushed figural painting into the realm of abstraction—a characteristic task of modernist painting—the giant brushstrokes summoning the arabesques of Jackson Pollock's painting.[47]

In 1951 a short film of Jackson Pollock painting, produced by Paul Falkenberg and photographed by Hans Namuth, premiered at the Museum of Modern Art in New York (the film was soon followed by the publication of a portfolio of Namuth photographs of Pollock).[48] The film helps make evident the link between cinema and action painting. There, onscreen, is the performing body of the artist, making the broad gestures that send his paint through space and onto its receiving surface. Pollock's body is in constant motion; the film does not depict a contemplative mode of creation. Elizabeth Frank writes that the film reveals "a sense of immediate, intuitive decision,"[49] but, as she notes, the film was also instrumental in creating the sense of Pollock as a spontaneous performer, for whom acting and painting are one and the same. Rosenberg's "The Action Painters" appeared the next year.

The film aligns intriguingly with *Le mystère Picasso* and even with *Little Nemo.* Just as Picasso worked from a new position—*behind* the work—and with unfamiliar inks, so does Pollock find himself painting, for the first and—emphatically— only time, on a glass surface through which he is filmed. In each case the artwork literally comes between the artist and the viewer. But there is a crucial difference: in the Pollock film, artist and art are innately connected, simultaneously visible, while the image of Picasso is divorced from the images he creates (the artist and the images rather alternate screen time). Curiously, *Little Nemo* gives us both: first an onscreen artist who creates an onscreen drawing, then the animated drawings that exist apart from McCay, who disappears entirely.

The indexical relation between gesture and painting (what Rosalind Krauss refers to as "making an image by means of an airborne gesture through which one could see the body of the artist himself")[50] now becomes iconic. In this transformation Pollock becomes one with all the myriad performers whose gestures have been inscribed on celluloid. There is little difference, to paraphrase the lyric of "That's Entertainment," between the indexical trace of Fred Astaire's choreographed routines and Jackson Pollock's choreographed production of abstraction. This precise point is made by Morton Feldman, for whom the film represented a very early commission: discussing his process, he said that he "wrote the score as if I were writing music for choreography."[51] One extended take presents Pollock virtually dancing his way across the canvas, the camera following as tightly as it followed Astaire and Charisse through *The Band Wagon*'s Central Park. Rosenberg's language summons a kind of choreographic spirit: "The painting itself is a 'moment' in the adulterated mixture of his life," he writes, "whether 'moment' means the actual minutes taken up with spotting the canvas or the entire duration of a lucid drama conducted in sign language."[52] Namuth's filming of Pollock's performance makes that connection evident, but it was always there in the emphatic, existential relation between the artist's body and his production.

There is also, in the gestural performance of Pollock's technique, an evocation of the intimate, reciprocal bond that exists between animator and animated, in which each can be seen to animate the other (see the previous chapter). Keith Broadfoot and Rex Butler find similarities between Pollock's process and the any-time-whatevers that characterize movement in the animated film. "Pollock comes not simply at the end of figuration but also at the beginning of a new figuration in which the figure is no longer opposed to its dissolution but only given, as Deleuze says of the figure in cartoons, in or as its very dissolution."[53]

Lust for Life and the Falkenberg-Namuth film, and the other artist films considered earlier, not only represent the performance of painting; they frame painting as performance—again, as surely (and as sure) a performance as Astaire's in *The Band Wagon*. The trace of Vincent is recorded not only on the surface of his canvases but on the surface of the film: the grimacing, the hysteria, the animatedness that marks the abjection of Vincent's self, as well as the frantic acts of artistic production. In the 1951 film Namuth's camera follows the animated Pollock as he works a large canvas laid on the ground outside his studio, accompanied by his laconic commentary ("my painting is direct . . . I enjoy working on a large canvas . . . "). Then the technique of the film changes: Pollock hangs his work on the wall, turning the painting into a product, inert and complete, and the camera suddenly becomes more active: providing close-up details and animating the work by zooming, tracking, dissolving, and panning across the surface of the broad canvas.[54] This is precisely how the camera treats Van Gogh's canvases in *Lust for Life,* moving from wide views to magnified details in which the concretized movement of the work's creation is revivified through an array of cinematic effects.[55] And it is also a restatement of the structure of *Little Nemo*—animated artist yielding to animated artwork.

So Rosenberg's conception of action painting does not simply posit a deep, *expressive* relation between the artist and the work (how could it be otherwise?), but rather emphasizes the *physical* relationship. "The act-painting is of the same metaphysical substance as the artist's existence. The new painting has broken down every distinction between art and life."[56] *Lust for Life* takes on the same task with regard to Van Gogh, suggesting not only that the paintings are expressions of Van Gogh's emotional torments and euphorias but that the paintings are literally extensions of Vincent. "I want to get to the point," Vincent wrote to his brother, "where people say of my work: that man feels deeply, that man feels keenly."[57] But the strategy of the film is to animate, make *physical,* Vincent's emotion. The simian posture, the wheedling voice, the violent outbursts—all of these make the life of the heart legible on the surface of the body. The frenzied painting does much the same thing— Vincent rails against the world and the canvas, his self-loathing (and megalomania) directed against his work.

The performance of painting is thus part of the film's strategy of corporealizing Vincent, forging an existential bond between his excesses of emotion, the physical symptoms of that agony, and the paintings as productions of that excess. It becomes impossible to consider these brushstrokes apart from the labor or action of producing them. Naremore proposes that *Lust for Life* is "more interested in dramatizing [Van Gogh's] behavior than explaining or justifying it,"[58] and this observation speaks to a valuation of temporal immediacy and the moment over psychology and interpretation; this immediacy, too, is fundamental to the performance at the center of Rosenberg's conception of action painting. Rosenberg writes, "A painting that is an act is inseparable from the biography of the artist"[59]—the biography and body of the artist—and this has some relevance to the immersive biopic that is Minnelli's *Lust for Life.* In fact, in action painting's physicality, its immediacy, and its vulgarity, and with *Lust for Life* and Namuth's film of Pollock firmly in mind, perhaps it can be said that action painting aspired to the condition of cinema.

THE REANIMATION OF VINCENT VAN GOGH

Lust for Life can be said not only to animate Van Gogh but to *re*animate him as well. The Picasso, McCay, and Pollock films gave us real artists in real time, but *Lust for Life* provides a retrospective, postmortem, vision of its artist. Where the other films present an artist imbuing a picture with life, with liveliness, *Lust for Life* reverses the valence: Van Gogh's paintings paradoxically summon their creator into existence (and, to a great degree, influence the aesthetic of the film itself). But the film's conclusion returns us to those images, which have outlived Van Gogh, and the circumstances of their creation. The film ends with Vincent motionless in bed, his life ebbing in the aftermath of his suicidal shooting. Theo sits beside him and lights his brother's pipe. "Theo," Vincent says, "I'd like to go home." These are his last words. His pipe falls from his mouth, and Theo falls to embrace his brother one last time. The shot dissolves to a close view of his painting *Wheat Field with Reaper,* which we saw him painting at St. Remy. There is the figure of the reaper, whom Vincent had explained as a picture of death. The camera pulls back, accompanied by a voice-over repeating his words—that the death happens with the sun flooding everything, in a light of pure gold. The canvas is now flanked by others: a self-portrait, sunflowers. The camera continues to pull back, and now new canvases appear above and below as Rozsa's score swells. As the ending credit appears, there are at least fifty of Vincent's canvases visible onscreen—some that we recognize thanks to the film that is now concluding, many that it seems we've always known.

Here, in perhaps its ultimate manifestation, is Deleuze's movement of world, a concept Deleuze already linked to Minnelli's work. Recall that Deleuze describes the circumstance of the image taking on the movement that is somehow denied the film's protagonist—and consider this scene, with the image of a stilled Van Gogh (death is the ultimate cessation of movement, no?) yielding to a dramatic reverse tracking shot that floods the screen with a deluge of his paintings. That final shot is a literal version of Deleuze's concept, as the images inherit the movement now denied their maker, but it is also clear that the paintings live on—they move through space, to museums and collections around the globe; they move through time, at least to our own present moment; and they move, ultimately, into the *Weltan-schauung* of the Western world. And, needless to say, those images move *us*.

And so there is a fascinating circuit of reciprocal vivification at work in *Lust for Life*. Van Gogh (like any animator) creates works that take on a life of their own. The fame of the pictures summons a biopic, reanimating Van Gogh, and his biography further animates the pictures, making them more vivid for the viewer. The film marks Vincent as overly animated, suffering from excesses of work and emotion, but at the same time it portrays him as possessed of an animating vision that ultimately seems to animate the film itself, bringing it to vibrant life.

Chapter 6

PLAYING SUPERHEROES

What happened to the good old days? The heroes and villains, the team-ups and dream-ups?

—GRANT MORRISON, *FLEX MENTALLO #1*

SUPERMAN IN SLUMBERLAND

I'm not sure whether comparing Superman to Little Nemo makes immediate sense or no sense whatsoever. For someone not versed in the world of comics, the comparison would hardly raise an eyebrow—they're the protagonists of two comics aimed, seemingly by definition, at younger readers. They are both equally a part of "popular culture," functionally and fundamentally equivalent. But to the comics reader the two might seem—literally—worlds apart. Little Nemo belongs to the Sunday funnies of an earlier day—a comic strip that served as a wondrous showcase for the virtuosity of its creator, but one without a strong mythos, with a protagonist marked by no great distinction (it's never clear just why the princess so desires his company) who never seems any the wiser for his experiences. He is a largely passive agent. Superman, on the other hand, is a fully fledged character with a rich history, both in terms of his origin story (so familiar that it can be summarized in the first pages of *All-Star Superman* in eight words: *Doomed planet. Desperate Scientists. Last Hope. Kindly Couple.*)[1] and in the rich continuity that has accrued over the course of seventy-plus years of stories. He is an exemplar of physical and moral force, an upholder of values, a citizen of the cosmos who masquerades in the guise of human frailty. He represents the best that we can aspire to (although to Lex Luthor he is a walking, flying reminder of all that we can *never* be). While originally a child's fantasy figure in the nascent medium of the comic book, as that medium has matured, so has Superman. He is no Nemo.

But I want to make a more nuanced case for seeing Superman as of a piece with Little Nemo, recognizing their similarity as agents guiding us through playful realms of plasmatic promise—it's a case that depends on ignoring swathes of the continuity mentioned above but, still, a case worth making.

Let me begin by noting that Nemo is, in his way, as exceptional as Superman—they are both "strange visitors to another planet," or world, or land. Superman is a Kryptonian ensconced on our Earth (and several others); Nemo gets to be a regular visitor to the wondrous world of Slumberland. They are both benign figures on the side of "the little guy": Superman began his exploits in 1938, tackling corrupt bosses and slumlords; in an extended sequence thirty years earlier Nemo, garbed in a most foppish raiment, visits "Shantytown" armed with a "wonderful wand" that will make his wishes come true.[2] Rather than wishing things for himself, our plucky hero—yes, *hero*—quickly starts to better the lot of the slum's residents. He begins modestly, and even a bit condescendingly: "I wish you dressed in clean clothes!" But two panels later he restores the sight of a blind woman, quickly moving from the crusading territory of Jacob Riis and Superman to something more messianic (and here we should mention the oft-noted parallels between Superman's story and Christ's).

Leaving aside the "grim 'n' gritty" Superman stories of the 1980s and 1990s, Superman is something of a whimsical figure, especially from the postwar years into the 1970s. He is a nearly omnipotent being whose "best friend" is a cub reporter named Jimmy Olsen; has a "super-dog," Krypto; has time for seemingly every charity event Metropolis can think of holding; and fights villains with names like "Toyman." Comics covers featured things like Lois Lane dropping a fresh-baked biscuit on The Man of Steel's foot, causing him to hop about in (mock?) distress, or Superman surreptitiously helping a sweet old lady blow out a multitude of birthday candles, or Superman—no lie—juggling. "Imaginary" stories allowed readers to see Superman's Super-baby, or the Superman of the far future, or Superman as one of the Knights of the Round Table (I think I just made that last one up, or maybe it was a Batman story). Superman is playful, wisecracking, and confident—neither terribly violent nor evidently tormented. Just as in Nemo's dreams, there is never any real danger.

Both Nemo and Superman lead double lives: Superman's life is divided between being Superman and being the more earthbound Clark Kent, while Nemo's life is divided between waking and dreaming. The greater parts of both narratives feature the more wondrous aspect—Superman and Slumberland are ascendant over Kent and the waking life. But despite their colorful exceptionalism, in their more fantastic aspects or realms Superman and Nemo serve as the reader's normative surrogate or avatar in encounters with the bizarre or plasmatic. Superman encounters shape-shifting aliens and Phantom Zone criminals; Nemo stumbles over magically growing mushrooms and improbably large blueberries—he even sojourned on Mars for a while in 1910. And in the *Little Nemo* animation, remember, it was Flip and Impy that were subjected to squashing and stretching—not Nemo.

This is not to say that Superman and Nemo are exempt from bodily deformation or reformation. On Mars Nemo's body is rolled as flat as a piece of paper; on
Earth he grows to the height of a small building. And Superman used to encounter
something called Red Kryptonite. This convenient substance, clearly a writer's best
friend, would not kill Superman (the green kind did that) but would affect him in
unpredictable ways, never the same way twice, for twenty-four hours. There are so
many fabulous examples—fortunately, a website has gathered the "9 Dumbest Effects":[3] Red K gave Superman long hair and a beard; it gave him a toddler's body
with his adult mind intact; it gave him a "rainbow face" that changed color to correspond to his moods; and—my favorite—it gave him the head of a red ant (which
allowed him to communicate with some giant alien red ants [Figure 34]; and—oh,
never mind). It even pushed Superman further into *Little Nemo* territory, giving
him terrible nightmares. In fact, Red Kryptonite does not so much summon
thoughts of the boy Nemo as much as other characters of McCay's, who, after ex-
posure to a strange substance, became deformed in unpredictable but temporary
ways. Yes, Red Kryptonite is but another flavor of rarebit, and it is the vehicle for
plasmatic possibility in the Superman multiverse.

It's not the only such vehicle, however. Superman has a nemesis in the figure of
Mr. Mxyzptlk, the Imp from the Fifth Dimension. This puckish, prankish figure's
sole delight lies in making Superman's life as difficult as possible. Not quite malev-
olent, but hardly benign, he is the trickster complement to Superman's stolidity, presenting him with a series of challenges that at the very least try Superman's patience
(he became a "super-headache" in a 1946 issue) while inadvertently presenting
greater dangers to our world. Mxyzptlk is a derby-hatted, cigar-smoking little man
who bears more than a passing resemblance to the derby-hatted, cigar-smoking
trickster of Slumberland, Flip. Introduced in March of 1906, Flip was a "bad and
brazen brat," an "awful disturber in the ceremonies held in this beautiful place." In
the early months of *Little Nemo in Slumberland* Flip served as the great spoiler, continually thwarting Nemo's attempts to reach Slumberland. Both Flip and Mxyzptlk
were a little delusional: Mxyzptlk thought that Superman looked forward to his pe-
riodic playful visits to our dimension, since he livened things up, while Flip "believed the princess would fall in love with him once she should see him, when the
truth was the sight of him with his big cigar and his impudent face was shockingly
frightful."[4]

Mr. Mxyzptlk and Red Kryptonite are only the most blatant examples of Superman's alignment with the whimsical, and they belong to a period of comics history known as the Silver Age—a period when superhero comics experienced a renaissance after the doldrums of the postwar years.[5] New heroes, redesigns of older
heroes, and, at Marvel, new sensibilities were put into play. But Superman, bless his
invulnerable heart, got sillier.

The Superman of the Silver Age was the inadvertent result of the postwar

FIGURE 34. Curt Swan, *Action Comics*, no. 296 (Jan. 1963). Copyright DC Comics.

censorship within the comics industry, in which strong restrictions, or outright bans, were placed on depictions of crime, cruelty, violence, and sexuality. Under the strictures of the Comics Code Authority, which placed its seal of approval on every comic book, those that had been poised to target more adult markets (homecoming GI's were avid comics readers) were once again ghettoized as children's fare, and rather bland children's fare at that. Funny animals and kids dominated the stands, as superheroes faded from view (other reasons for the decline of the superhero genre might be a postwar fatigue—superheroes had become strongly identified with the war effort—or just the ebb and flow of the market). Those that survived were the most iconic, but even they had their (already minimal) rough edges softened.

The writers of Superman's adventures, under the creative editorship of Mort Weisinger, found new kinds of stories to tell, and, in retrospect, the Superman they presented is refreshingly human, even a bit dull in an appealing sort of way. Superman was surrounded by a growing cast of characters, and stories even returned him to his home planet of Krypton (actually, a whole city full of other Kryptonians survived, but that's another story). Mermaids and magic were allowed, along with Red Kryptonite, imps from other dimensions, and "imaginary stories." Grant Morrison, writing of the "world of dreams" (a fortuitous phrase) that constituted Superman's Silver Age, finds in these tales something more symptomatic, and emphasizes their expanded emotional range. "No longer shackled to the rules of social realism, the stories themselves were liberated to become what a generation of young readers demanded: allegorical super-science stories about how it felt to be twelve."[6]

But even more was going on. Morrison notes that not only Superman but his "entire supporting cast . . . was subject to inhuman forces of transformation on a monthly basis" and suggests that they are fairy tales for an anxious age. If rarebit was the cartoon vehicle through which the anxieties of the industrial age made themselves manifest, then the endless transformations visited upon Superman and his pals, the continual undermining of superheroic certainties, "embodied every human terror" of the Atomic Age. "These stories liquified the armored hard body of the wartime supersoldiers and patriotic strongman," Morrison writes, and in doing so, equally allegorized the bodily anxieties of their adolescent readers and the national anxieties of postwar America in playful, yet emotionally resonant, ways.[7] Whether read allegorically or not, the Superman comics of the Silver Age became a repository of mind-bendingly odd conceits and a spirited, anything-goes sensibility.

Thus, certain similarities of character and narrative bind *Little Nemo* and Superman, and, by extension, superhero comics, but there are other connections between the comic strip and the genre. Superhero comics have an oneiric quality that further aligns them with McCay's great work. What is a superpower, after all, but a fantasy, the kind of fantasy that we might find expressed in our dreams—dreams of flight, of strength, of invisibility, of suddenly transporting to another place, another time, dreams of animals, dreams of scale- and shape-shifting. That superhero comics explain these fantastic abilities through references to gamma rays, alien interventions, or cosmic power does not obviate their true origins in dreams and play. Umberto Eco finds "a kind of oneiric climate" in the way each Superman story existed utterly apart from all the others; nothing that happened in one had any effect on another.[8] Scratch the surface even a little bit, and superhero comics can be seen to exemplify Bachelard's *irreality function,* the creative imagination that liberates us from the strictures and logics of the real.

And the origin story is a further locus of oneiric energies. In comic after comic, film after film, origin stories are told and retold (*origin*—a word I learned from superhero comics). Every supercharacter has one, or gets one eventually. The movement into the origin story, often in the form of a flashback, can also be seen as a movement into dream, into dream-space.

In the first place the origin story frequently takes the form of a dream, or at least an unquiet reverie. The interpolated origin story in Frank Miller's *The Dark Knight Returns* is exemplary. It is a hugely elaborated retelling of the familiar tale—indeed, it is its very familiarity that permits the kind of baroque embellishment Miller provides. The episode takes five pages, each divided into a four-by-four grid, making sixteen identically sized panels per page (the sequence begins on two facing pages, so the reader is actually confronted with a metronomically regular thirty-two panels in one spread). The now-aged Bruce Wayne accidentally comes upon *The Mark of Zorro* on television—the very film he had watched with his parents the night they were gunned down. He is immediately plunged into a memory, marked at first by bright color before settling into the sequence's dominant blue-grays, browns, and blacks. The panel breakdown—a horrific chronophotographic sequence—moves the action forward in excruciatingly slow motion: two panels for the trigger to be pulled, another three for the cartridge to eject. Bruce is frozen with the memory but manages to change the channel, each KLIK of the remote providing evidence of new horrors on the streets of Gotham. One strip of panels on the third page subdivides each frame, alternating between partial views of Bruce's agonized space and the talking heads of television news. He staggers out into the night—a comparatively vast space spilling across the panel divisions of the page's top half—still flashing back to isolated moments of that traumatic night. Lightning flashes; dark panels alternate with light. A bat approaches the window, and it's no longer clear whether this is a flashback to the night when an errant bat provided Bruce with inspiration ("I shall become a bat!") or if this is some new bat, a compulsive repetition underscoring the continuing rightness of Wayne's/Batman's mission. At the bottom of the final page the bat crashes through the window in a single panel stretching the width of the page, smashing through the panel boundaries—boundaries that have so confined Bruce in his torment—in a gesture of vengeful liberation.

Much has been left out of this description: the graphic rhyme between a broken string of pearls and the ejecting shell cases, and a further rhyme between the pearls and the small caption boxes that deploy across the space. Language is devalued in favor of a heightened emphasis on page and panel, design and color. The sequence borrows from the toolbox of the cinematic dream sequence: the magnification of time, the emphasis on subjective experience, the metonymic relations among objects, the highlighting of graphic relations over causal. Bruce's paralysis transmutes into a movement of world, as the images flow unbidden through his consciousness, and a bat acts to break the pattern, which allows Bruce to return to action as "The Batman." (The end of the dream brings the beginning of action here, whereas in *Little Nemo in Slumberland,* the end of the dream is the end of adventure.)

I would also suggest that the compulsive retelling of the origin—and, trust me, it is compulsive—is already oneiric, in its continual return to the primal scene of trauma. Furthermore, the origin story is always the narration of a metamorphosis. Whatever powers and abilities the hero exhibits arose then and there. The origin story as dream, then, is the place where the "ossification of fixed-and-forever form" is overcome; in the superhero comic it becomes the same site of plasmatic possibility as the dreams of both the rarebit fiends and the more innocent Nemo.

Before returning to the topic of play, it's worth briefly acknowledging that the superhero genre is also a modern repository of animist sensibilities. Superheroes often manifest animal powers—Hawkman can fly like a bird, Aquaman can breathe underwater like a fish. More recent versions of some characters connect the superhero's power to more primal forces: Alan Moore's version of Swamp Thing was not a monstrous hybrid of human and swamp goo but a plant elemental who could tap into "The Green," a psychic realm that bound together all plant life on Earth; Jamie Delano's version of Animal Man created a similar realm that connected all animal life. The superhero's mask frequently references the animal world, evoking spiders and wolverines, hawks and bats. For some African tribes, animal masks allow communion with the spirits of the animal world and embody atavistic beliefs about humanity's relation to the natural and supernatural worlds. The mask of shamanistic ritual confers identity, while in modern societies, masks function to conceal it—the superhero mask combines these functions. Batman wears a mask as a disguise but also for ritualistic purposes—the bat-totem becomes a simile for his nocturnal mysteriousness, and its exaggerations frighten criminals, "a cowardly and superstitious lot." Despite the sense that superheroes constitute some kind of "modern mythology," they playfully tap strongly into older traditions of animistic power and possibility.

Superman might be the most blatant example, but I think superhero comics more generally can be characterized as playful, despite overwrought attempts at relevance and "mature" content. I'm convinced that the overt concern with issues of law and order is something of a red herring in the superhero cosmos—these flamboyant figures are more easily aligned with a pleasurable chaos than with restrictive order.[9] They present a space apart, a magic circle, as Huizinga would have it, within which difference is something devoutly to be wished rather than a social burden. Roger Caillois's work on play and games-playing can shed further light. Superhero narratives might not be games for the characters in the stories—often worlds or entire multiverses are at stake—but the stories are frequently built around ongoing, seemingly endless, competition between superheroes and their designated nemeses, and so might fall under the heading of *agon* (competition games) for Caillois. I would argue, however, that superhero comics connect most strongly to Caillois's play category of *mimicry*.[10] There is a strong element of role-playing in the world of superheroes—who among us has not tied a towel around the neck to serve as an ersatz cape? (Or is that a boy thing?) Reading superheroes is a form of playing superheroes. Reading, I enter another realm with its own rules and conventions (once, Green Lantern's ring was powerless against anything yellow, and for some reason every city had its own seemingly designated superhero). The time spent reading was unproductive (just ask my parents for confirmation), and (despite my pretended hopes for paying for college with my comics collection) it created no wealth—these are two important conditions of play for both Huizinga and Caillois. Most urgently, it involves acts of fantasy that may be knowingly set against what is sometimes called "real life."

In my introduction I set aside one element of Huizinga's definition as not germane to understanding comics as play; Huizinga wrote that play "promotes the formation of social groupings which tend to surround themselves with secrecy and to stress their difference from the common world by disguises or other means."[11] For Caillois this aspect of play is integral only to games of mimicry. It is rooted in an "incessant invention" in which the player or spectator (who is a kind of player) "forgets, disguises, or temporarily sheds his personality in order to feign another,"[12] and it seems hugely relevant to the appeal of superheroes, with their secret identities and Justice Leagues—and relevant to comics culture, with its Merry Marvel Marching Societies, Comic-Cons, and guardians of continuity. It's provocative that Caillois finds an abundance of mimicry in the world of animals, especially insects, in which a mask or guise (an illusory appearance) serves to "change the wearer's appearance and to inspire fear in others,"[13] given the proclivity of superheroes to take on the appearance or attributes of animals (Wolverine) and insects (The Blue Beetle).

Games, for Caillois, can exist as combinations of categories, and if superhero comics represent an instance of mimicry, then it is *mimicry* combined with *ilinx,* the latter being games or forms of play "which are based on the pursuit of vertigo and which consist of an attempt to momentarily destroy the stability of perception and inflict a kind of voluptuous panic upon an otherwise lucid mind."[14] Examples might include roller coasters and spinning games. I don't think it's a stretch to claim that many of the best artists of superhero comics induce something very like this. Steve Ditko's oblique angles and abstract forms, the shattered layouts of Neal

Adams or J. H. Williams III, the psychedelic overload of Jim Steranko and Jim Starlin, and the cosmic imagery and photo-collages of Jack Kirby all push perceptual experience across a threshold (Plates 26, 27). And the heroes themselves sail through the cities, hanging from webs or bat-threads or, like Daredevil, bouncing acrobatically off the walls in an act of *parkour, avant la lettre*. One of the few things that superhero films do right is to capture, and push, this vertiginous kinesis. Secrecy, make believe, vertigo—all of these are elements of play identified by Huizinga and Caillois, and all are endemic to the superhero genre and, to an extent, the fan culture that surrounds it.

And then there is the metatextual play within the texts themselves. The role of the reader has been the subject of much modernist and postmodernist play in literature, and comics are no different, particularly in the work of the British writers who followed Alan Moore *(Watchmen, V for Vendetta, From Hell)* into the world of American comics. The comics writer most engaged with a consideration of the reader is surely Grant Morrison, part of that generation. Morrison is as reflexive a writer as mainstream comics can probably handle; and, like Winsor McCay, he toys with a range of elements that create the comics experience. The cover of the fifth issue of his revisionist version of *Animal Man* even featured a most McCay-like hand, engaged in drawing the titular figure (Figure 35).

Animal Man was a reboot of an earlier, nearly forgotten, character who, thanks to an alien encounter, could take on the attributes of any animal. In Morrison's version the aliens proclaim themselves "agents of the power that brings your world into being," and when a villain outlives his usefulness, they proclaim him "A minor character. Old-fashioned and melodramatic. Best forgotten. Your story ends here." A gesture, and the character devolves through the stages of drawing—color vanishes, followed by the inked lines, leaving only the pencil drawing, which itself devolves to a roughed-out version, a stick figure, and, finally, nothing (Figure 36).[15] Recall an episode of *Rarebit Fiend* in which a character dreamt that he was only an increasingly simple drawing.

The alert reader will realize that the "power" that the aliens serve is the author of the comic book, as it turns out, one Grant Morrison. Unnamed until the end, the author shows up as a recurrent character in the fiction, musing on the nature of the universe and the act of writing. "What'll it be next? Choice extracts from the Oxford Dictionary of Quotations? Trotting out the Nietzsche and the Shelley and the Shakespeare to dignify some old costumed claptrap? Probably." He reflects upon David Bohm's implicate order theory, which presents "a vision of a vast, interconnected universe where every part contains the whole." In such a universe fiction and reality become equally valid, equally reflective of "the whole." "Sometimes you wonder, in an interconnected universe, who's dreaming who?"[16]

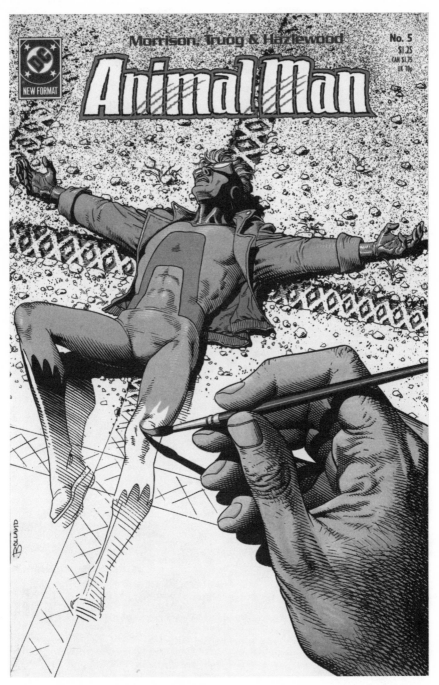

FIGURE 35. Brian Bolland, *Animal Man*, no. 5 (winter 1988). Copyright DC Comics.

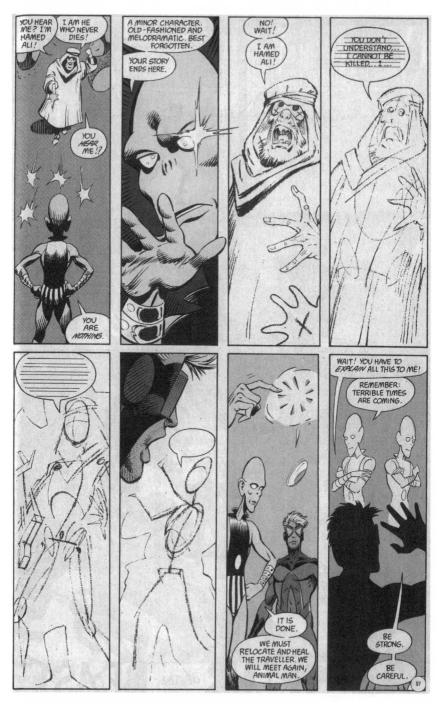

FIGURE 36. Grant Morrison (writer), Chas Truog and Doug Hazlewood (artists), *Animal Man*, no. 12 (June 1989). Copyright DC Comics.

Some of the characters in *Animal Man* know that they're fictional characters. A Mad Hatter figure in a sanitarium observes, "We're all just words on a page. I just thought you ought to know." As they drag him off, he begins to rave: "Some cheap hack is writing our lives!" "Ignore him," is the doctor's advice.[17] The climactic story arc, set in that same asylum, features a "breach in the continuum" between "our reality and the higher world out of which we are unfolded"—in other words, between the comic book universe and ours.[18] Animal Man is very close to meeting his maker. Brian Bolland's inspired covers for the series distilled its themes: the hand drawing Animal Man, and, on another cover, a hand (the same hand?) unraveling him. Buddy standing outside the comics page, reaching into it to tap a startled comics character on the shoulder. The Hatter, now a costumed character, leaks superhero comic books from his eyes (Plate 28). A monkey types the script of the comic you're about to read. And, on the cover of the final issue, the figure of Buddy/Animal Man is drawn against a photographed background, lying at the feet of a mysterious figure; a computer terminal seems to display a script.

The superheroic adventures of Animal Man moved through some of the narrative beats that seemed de rigueur in the 1980s as the comics "grew up." The casual fun of the early issues of the narrative steadily evaporated, animal rights polemics multiplied, and Buddy's wife and children were killed. In the final episode Buddy/Animal Man, trying to understand the nature of his existence, a quest that has led him to an unprepossessing house in The City of Formation, meets his maker. The writer, "Grant" now, shows him all the *Animal Man* comics in which Buddy has been appearing and explains the formulaic nature of the genre and the reasons for his narrative choices. Mourning the death of his cat, Grant has killed Buddy's family—besides, it makes for easy drama.[19] Grant thanks all of his collaborators, family, and friends as Buddy struggles through an arbitrary and generic battle sequence in the background. But there is a happy ending. In what will become a signature moment for Morrison, the writer, weary of the heightened violence of "realistic" and "adult" superhero stories, writes a new ending for Buddy/Animal Man—his family restored, oblivious of his fictional status, his universe coherent and closed once more.[20] Compared with Alan Moore's deconstruction of the superhero genre, Morrison offers something more like *re*construction—an acknowledgment of the nature of fiction, accompanied by a belief in the virtues of its "escapist" possibilities.

What is finally striking, though, is less the Pirandellian inclusion of the *author* in the work than the acknowledgment of the *reader* by the fictional character. There were many *Rarebit Fiends* featuring or referring to "Silas," but only one that addressed the reader of the strip. There is an infamous moment in *Animal Man* with Buddy in the desert, experimenting with altered states of consciousness—something that his animal powers have already started him on. He's blissfully trippin' when he becomes aware of something, some other presence, behind him. He turns to look over his shoulder—his face fills the page (at nearly life-size)—his eyes widen—and he gasps, "I CAN SEE YOU!"[21] The superhero has pierced the veil and seen the very reader of the comic book in which—he is becoming aware—he is featured. It is a disconcerting moment and justly celebrated—few superheroes grasp their nature as fictional constructs.

Morrison has become one of the caretakers of the most iconic superheroes at DC Comics, but his earlier work was more overtly indebted to surrealism and the Theater of the Absurd. Such works as *Doom Patrol* and *The Invisibles* were dense weavings of intertextual references and conspiracy theories, and Morrison occasionally returns to this more overtly trippy material. In his limited series *The Filth*, with art by Chris Weston, a rather pathetic little man turns out to be a powerful figure in a reality behind our reality. In an early issue, during a superhero battle above a city, the fleeing bad guys "engage inksuit gutter interface," which allows them to flee "beyond the page wall." They make their escape into a "void freefall between pages," while poor Ultra-Humanitarian smashes "against the fiction wall," leaving a nasty red smear (Plate 29).[22] Here, then, is another "breach in the continuum," and the metatextual sense of a self-aware fiction—another reality playing out in two-dimensions, a reality that literally exists on the space of the page. One character's thought balloons carry an inordinate amount of narration; it turns out that he has developed a superpower: "a consciousness so focused and so disciplined, it can actually manifest words in a cloud above my head." In that later chapter of *Animal Man* Buddy also managed to travel between planes of reality, breaking the panel wall just as McCay's clown—discussed in chapter 1—unraveled the lines that contained him.[23]

The culmination of Morrison's direct address to the reader shows up in a Superman comic. *Superman Beyond!* was a part of Morrison's *Final Crisis* event, in which Superman teamed with other super-incarnations from other planes of reality to save the cosmos from an all-devouring energy vampire named Mandrakk (it plays better than it sounds).[24] Much of the comic is rendered in 3-D in order to depict the "4-D vision" that Superman needs to employ "to truly comprehend" what he experiences. The interdimensional ship on which he rides, when seen in 3-D (for us) and "4-D vision upgrade" (for Superman), hovers in front of a series of oblique planar surfaces depicting different scenes—once again, we are in a "void freefall between pages" in order to represent the "arteries between universes."[25] And, a bit later, Superman, learning to perceive the complexity of the multiverse, reaches his hand outward, and in 3-D it extends elegantly toward the reader—a sequel to Buddy's "I can see you!"

Final Crisis becomes a treatise on stories. The story-devouring Mandrakk is in danger of being "believed into existence," but against him the Monitor has "found a better story; one created to be unstoppable, indestructible! The story of a child rocketed to earth from a doomed planet." Superman is the story that will save the multiverse from the limbo that comes when the stories die, and this he understands, instinctively: "I've never known such certainty. This is my reason to be. My purpose is simply to stop him." Superman even finds himself in the realm of Limbo, introduced in *Animal Man*, the place where all the old and forgotten characters wind up—here it is the place in which no stories exist.

The incursion of the comics story into the "real" world and the hand of the artist both appear elsewhere in Morrison's work. A more recent series, *Joe the Barbarian*, presents both: the very first panel of the first issue frames a close-up of a hand drawing; the view widens to reveal the youthful protagonist drawing a fantasy figure. Joe soon finds himself transported to the world of his toys, simultaneously stumbling about his room and becoming immersed in an epic adventure in which his toys, his action figures, and his pet rat are all involved. The reference to Nemo's sojourns in Slumberland seems clear, but this Nemo cannot waken.[26] We learn that the figure he was drawing earlier was one of his action figures, a member of the "Action Elite." Joe, then, is more consumer than creator, more reader than author. Again, the world of fiction has encroached on the world of the reader, but by beginning with Joe sketching, Morrison has demonstrated the permeability of these categories: readers are also creators, and creators are animated by their creations.

Wolfgang Iser refers to the text as "a living event" in its unfolding, an event that generates a sense of "lifelikeness."[27] He even attributes a consciousness to the text, or rather, he proposes that the text constitutes a consciousness itself, one separate from the generating consciousness of the author or the receiving consciousness of the reader. The text's consciousness is a kind of hybrid of both of these (which implies that there are as many "text consciousnesses" as there are readers). Iser's language stresses the dynamism of the textual encounter, its kineticism: "The reader sets the text *in motion*"; "the reading process always involves viewing the text through a perspective that is continually *on the move*"; and there are always "*actions* involved in responding to [a] text."[28] We should recall that *action* is the word Rosenberg used to describe a set of painters whose corporeal performance was strongly inscribed upon their canvases, and *action* is what *Action Comics* promised and delivered—kineticism and physicality wrapped up in that word. The first issue of *Action Comics* gave the world Superman, who was said to move faster than a speeding bullet.

The child—and I think most comics readers begin as children—is a particularly absorbed reader, I think, with a commitment not just to reading but to rereading, and this returns us to Nemerov's consideration of "the boy in bed," stealing some nocturnal time to pore over a few more pages of Stevenson by flash- or candlelight. With comics we move from *the boy in bed* to *the kid on the floor* surrounded by comics—either a collection of *Fantastic Four*s or the spread-out pages of the sprawling Sunday funnies. Iser locates the genesis of literary theory in that experience of total absorption: "when we have been particularly impressed by a book, we feel the need to talk about it; we do not want to get away from it by talking about it—we simply want to understand more clearly what it is that we have been entangled in. . . . Perhaps this is the prime usefulness of literary criticism—it helps to make conscious those aspects of the text which would otherwise remain concealed in the subconscious; it satisfies (or helps to satisfy) our desire to talk about what we have read."[29]

Readers are animating forces, activating a text by engaging with it, playing with it. But to play with a text is to allow oneself to be activated and animated by it in turn. The cartoonist Lynda Barry has written, "I believe a kid who is playing is not alone. There is something brought alive during play, and this something, when played with, seems to play back."[30] There is a reciprocity between readers and texts, no less than between creators and creations, though the tension between reader and text may be less fraught. Animating and animated sensibilities have been central subjects of this book—artists are animated by the world, and their perspective animates it in return. Cartoon characters are animated but animate their viewers in turn, who imaginatively enter a world of cartoon physics and the overturning of "once-and-forever allotted form."

Reading comics is an intense activity. Geoffrey O'Brien, discussing the experience of consuming Marvel comics in the 1960s, notes that "what is hard to recapture is the trancelike absorption with which these comics were read."[31] And Iser writes, "It is only by leaving behind the familiar world of his own experience that the reader can truly participate in the adventure the literary text offers him."[32]

Some recent writings about popular music are rather effective at evoking the once-fugitive pleasures of reading superhero comics—pop music and superhero comics having much in common. Sasha Frere-Jones, for example, wrote in an issue of the *New Yorker* that "popular music is good at using speed, physical sensation, and unmediated language to articulate the experience of life."[33] And this finds an echo in O'Brien's evocation of late-1960s culture (including Jim Steranko's comics): "Wherever you looked there was the possibility of finding the aesthetic essentials—urgency, immensity of perspective, speed, depth, improvisational ecstasy, and unwobbling balance—if possible, all at the same time, packed into a single image or a single note."[34]

Speed is, of course, central to comics. Since the days of Töpffer, the medium itself has scanned quickly. The iconography of comics has a number of ways to represent rapid motion. And superheroes possess speed in abundance—the Flash is not alone. Vast speeds and scales, fundaments of the sublime, structure the superhero universe. In the words of Reed Richards of the Fantastic Four (who ought to know), "Everything is moving faster now! The universe has become a vast kaleidoscope of light and sound!"[35] *Speed and scale*—but right now I want to emphasize a different speed and scale; *not* the scale of Negative Zones and multiverses; *not* the speed of the Flash, Superman, or the Silver Surfer. Instead, as you will see, the *speed* is 45 rpm, and the *scale* is the pop single of the 1960s.

O'Brien has written wonderfully about film, fiction, music, and comics. A strong autobiographical streak cuts through his writing, but not only is this typical in writing about comics; it's practically required. Sean Howe's anthology *Give Our Regards to the Atomsmashers!* is at least as dedicated to the contributors' encounters with comics as to the comics themselves. It's interesting to compare two of O'Brien's writings that only *seem* to be about different topics—his *Atomsmashers* piece on the insistent grooviness of Steranko's *Nick Fury: Agent of Shield,* and his earlier essay on the insistent grooviness of the songs of Burt Bacharach.

The essay on Bacharach is partly about the pop single itself. While long-form recordings had significantly reshaped the ambitions of composers and performers, O'Brien notes that the 45 returned to the aesthetic of an isolated song. With albums, "Listeners could go about their housework or their lovemaking for as long as half an hour without having to change the music," while the brevity of the 45 forced one's attention.[36] An appealing analogy can be drawn, I think, between the 45 and the single issue of a comic book. O'Brien discusses them in similar terms: the 45 represented "a fragile metaphysic" in which "the gossamer speculations of a stretched-out and mostly pleasurable afternoon—was sustained, perhaps provoked, by certain chord changes,"[37] while comics "came and went like those otherwise uneventful summer afternoons that the reading of them so thoroughly occupied."[38] The similarity is not too surprising given that they belong to the same time—not just summer afternoons but the mid-1960s (or thereabouts), as well as *adolescence* (or thereabouts . . .). Like a couple of teenagers sprawled on the floor in their pastel Capris, spinning platters on a portable player with a mass of black disks and garishly colored sleeves arrayed about them, comics readers, too, are often pictured surrounded by the latest hits, pursuing their pleasures with a similarly alluring informality.

The 45—like the comic book—"could be held in the palm of the hand yet contained immeasurable depths and reaches, a perfect mystical object made of cheap plastic"—or even cheaper pulp paper. And, like a comic, the 45 "focused attention unwaveringly on a solitary object of desire. . . . If the B side turned out to be worthy of attention that was merely a gratuitous extra fillip"—a welcome bonus that I might compare to discovering a surprisingly compelling backup feature about Asgard, or the Elongated Man, or the Bizarro World.[39]

O'Brien returns repeatedly to the self-contained space carved out by the 45: "Listening to a 45 was a separate act, preceded by careful selection and attended by reverently close attention. Each was judged by how completely and unpredictably it mapped a reality in its allotted playing time. The best carved vast stretches out of that limited duration, while the worst felt interminable even at a minute and a half."[40]

I think that in this formulation of O'Brien's *listening* constitutes something more totalizing than *reading,* but I would argue that the compactness of the comic book—its brevity, pace, and punch—turn the reading experience into something akin to listening: a sensory engagement more than a purely cognitive processing. Of course, listening to singles (or even albums) also contains aspects of looking and reading: liner notes, lyrics, photos, and other desiderata were central to the experience (and distinguish it from today's iPod culture). Comics lacked the sonic dimension—for which they compensated with the bombast of lettered sound effects—but were as textural as they were textual. Nearly any issue of *Fantastic Four,* which I began reading somewhere around 1967 or 1968, certainly "carved vast stretches" out of their "limited duration." I'm looking at the awesome cover of *FF #77* (Plate 30), with Psychoman wielding (or merged with) a Kirbyoid machine whose intricacies mark the architecture of the composition, within which we see glimpses of all the action somehow contained on the twenty pages within. Lo, even the mighty Galactus and the mercurial Silver Surfer are but small elements of the burgeoning whole! (Stan Lee's rhetoric really is the only language adequate to these images.)

O'Brien evokes comics as "a dream that could be shared, passed around, that did not dissolve on waking."[41] Comics and pop music need to be shared; to listen or read is to participate in a community of implied or actual like-minded connoisseurs, like the guys hanging out at the record shop in Nick Hornby's *High Fidelity.* Songs perhaps have a more intimate edge than comics, linked as they are to the heady dreams of pure love and love lost. "The song is the place where perfection stays," writes O'Brien, "a shared space"—shared between lovers this time rather than chums—"one degree removed from this world."[42] But one should not entirely underestimate the intimacy of the superhero comic, and Marvel's in particular, which whispered and buzzed with uncontainable emotions and energies. Christopher Sorrentino, in his *Atomsmashers* essay, describes the private/public realm of superhero readers: "the satisfaction of identifying with the lone heroes of Marvel, of embracing their stark emotional seclusion, shoulder to shoulder with a group of fellow adherents."[43] DC Comics had recurring villains and occasional crossovers, but Marvel built a *universe* of superheroes and true believers. And washing over it all, the voice of Stan Lee, the "Murray the K" of the comics industry, the babbling disc jockey whose alliterative patter bound the whole megillah together and cajoled the willing reader into a sense of participation.

In a 2005 review/essay, John Updike discussed the child-centered novels of Steven Millhauser, Jonathan Lethem, Jonathan Safran Foer, and others who "have devoted their most ambitious and energetic efforts to detailing the fervent hobbies and the intoxicating overdoses on popular culture, the estrangement and the dependence that characterize contemporary American childhood." Updike proposes that "childhood's new viability as novelistic ground may signal a shift in the very nature of being a human being, considered anthropologically as a recipient and continuer of tribal myths, beliefs, and strictures. Older novelists . . . portrayed the pained shedding of this traditional baggage; the newer novelists, having inherited almost no set beliefs from their liberal, distracted middle-class parents, see childhood as the place where one invents the baggage—totems, rituals, lessons to live by—of a solitary one-person tribe."[44] We move to adulthood, passing among the signifiers of popular culture, choosing or being chosen by certain images that offer certain (or uncertain) possibilities, that resonate within the one-person tribes as well as larger communities of fanboys, friends, and readers.

What Updike identifies as the need to invent the baggage of one's later life also lies at the core of the comics themselves, especially through that already noted obsession with the origin story. Origin stories are told and retold, often by the characters themselves (and often *to* themselves). "If the bildungsroman is the passage from childhood to maturity," John Hodgman wrote, with characteristic dryness, "then the origin story is a shorter trip, from childhood to a prolonged immaturity."[45] This is a bit mean, but it isn't wrong. Maturity is held in abeyance by the superhero comic, perhaps nowhere more so than with the "adult" superheroes of the 1980s with their more emphatically traumatic "origins." Hodgman notes that all readers of superhero comics, which he refers to as "the still disreputable muscle that drives the medium," know "the seductions of the origin story. There are many strengths of serialized storytelling, but resolution is not one of them. Death, of course, is never final in a comic." Thus, "beginnings are where it's at, where the story hums with the irony and compact power of the novel."[46]

Perhaps it was Jules Feiffer's *The Great Comic Book Heroes* that began weaving the web that connected the actions on the page to the adventures of reading or creating them. The book recalls acts of reading within a savvy community. Jonathan Lethem has described a shift from a slightly older generation of writers' interest in the metamorphic possibilities of comic *strips* (writers such as Jay Cantor, Millhauser, and Tom de Haven) to the more recent fascination/obsession with comic *books*, superhero comics in particular, in novels by Michael Chabon and Lethem himself,[47] not to mention Junot Diaz, whose *Brief Wondrous Life of Oscar Wao* was in part a love letter to Jack Kirby and Gilbert Hernandez. With this generation—somewhere between boomer and X'er—the superhero comic becomes an axiom of childhood (or boyhood), a crucial scenography against which one's own origin took shape (or flight). Comics become a crucial site of escape *to*, rather than escape *from*, a protected terrain of self-definition (assuming one is a certain kind of adolescent boy), and this extends beyond literary figures and the essayists of *Atomsmashers* to the "alternate universe" of academia. David Carrier's *Aesthetics of Comics* features a charming kid on the cover absorbed in a comic book; it's a picture of Carrier in earlier days. Will Brooker's dissertation on Batman is partly a saga about writing a dissertation on Batman. Henry Jenkins has discussed the death of his mother in the context of his world of comics reading. And my own writing on superheroes remains heavily invested (*over*invested, they tell me) in an autobiographical questing—discovering new territory, taking flight, moving (if not moving on).[48]

Meanwhile, autobiographical comics, which had arisen as a virulent rejection of the monomythical irreality of the superhero universe, began to edge back toward the world of caped crusaders and supermen.[49] Superman returns in Chris Ware's work as a despairing figure gone to seed and possibly suicide.

O'Brien writes that "we appreciated the liberty that comics gave us: we were free to move in and out of what we could see was an illusion. We could allow it to be as real as we wanted it to be; we could dissolve it at will."[50] The opulent fantasy realm of superhero comics was a realm of play, play both solitary and communal (even if the community was more implied than actual). Superheroes offered not just escape but a *phenomenology* of escape. "What they were supposed to be about dissolved if you thought about it too much: the mysteries of secret origins . . . the possibility of suddenly acquiring an alternate body or entering a parallel dimension."[51] Comics provided a place, in other words, of plasmatic possibility, of Bachelardean reverie, of intimate immensity.

THE INTOLERABLE LIGHTNESS
OF THE SUPERHERO FILM

And so superhero comics can be read as playful texts that revel, in their way, in plasmatic possibility and freedom from once-and-forever allotted form, as were the cartoons that Eisenstein was so drawn to. What of the superhero film? One can see them occupying the intersection of comics and cartoons—they do, after all, depend to a large extent on CG animated bodies to replicate the bodies in the comics (it's been joked, with some validity, that Hollywood has only now become capable of producing images like those Jack Kirby turned out forty years ago). And yet the superhero film feels, for the most part, like something less than the sum of its parts.

While I've been a devotee of superhero comics for a significant part of my life, my relationship to superhero *movies* is more ambivalent, more unsettled. Superhero films remain something of a provisional genre, still very much in a state of becoming. In a way, I feel like an aficionado of Broadway musicals pontificating on the inadequacy of the film musical in 1930; a time of ponderous, static films with lousy sound reproduction—but, a scant three years later, one of the most dynamic of film genres. The superhero film genre in the first decade of the twenty-first century yielded a glut of nearly identical films, which seemed like dumbed-down versions of the characters still appearing, to better effect, in the comics, just as the early musical films out of Hollywood dumbed down Broadway song lyrics for a nonurban and nonurbane audience.[52] So I'm far from certain that superhero movies have discovered their real voice.

By rights, I should be enamored of the superhero film. It offers a range of phenomena that I've spent my career celebrating—kinesis, immersion, weightlessness, bright colors, urban locations, fluidity, kaleidoscopic perception, and masquerade—in spades. It is a place of expressive bodies and the eroticism of human movement. In that, it is like the musical. The heightened rhetoric of the musical took the form of exaggerated color, costume, cinematic technique, and performance style. The musical number became a space of liberation, of masquerade, a place where, as Richard Dyer brilliantly observed, emotional authenticity and theatricality—usually regarded as dichotomously opposed categories—combined. For Dyer this act of combination is at the heart of queer responses to the musical—the musical becomes a place of resistance to a culture that continues to insist, absurdly, on dualistic oppositions.[53] Utopia is thus defined as a place of movement, of border crossings and crane shots, of choreographed transgressions and performances of liberation. So much of this applies to the superhero movie—Catherine Deneuve swinging down the street in an extended take in Demy's *Les demoiselles de Rochefort* is rather different from Spider-Man swinging above the street in a single take from Raimi's *Spider-Man*—but, in their kinetic exuberance and transformation of the quotidian urban environment into a space of play, they are also quite similar.

So what's my problem? First, there's the fact that all superhero films are really blockbusters; big-budget films with gargantuan resources. Unlike the genres that were taken up by European critics (westerns and crime films), superhero films are not B movies made in the backwater backlots of smaller studios. There are no "little" or "quirky" superhero movies apart from direct-to-DVD animated films and, long ago, *Mystery Men*. Furthermore, superhero films are blockbusters that seem to stake out the safest or most familiar version of the character. The franchise comics are different: Marvel and DC will often use one title to hold down the "official" version of the character, while other titles can be aimed toward narrower audiences, and there are definite auteurs among comics writers. The remarkable range of the superhero comic finds no real analog in superhero films, which seem to be one of two things: light or dark. There is no room for the distinctiveness of a Grant Morrison or a Garth Ennis, or even a pulp aficionado like Ed Brubaker, much less such idiosyncratic works as Paul Pope's *Batman Year 100,* or Jonathan Lethem and Farel Dalrymple's *Omega the Unknown*.

For the comics fan in me, then, the superhero film generally feels like an impoverished version of superhero comics. And the film buff in me is also left wanting. Here it might be instructive to bring some other genres and filmmakers to bear upon the superhero film.

Anthony Mann's westerns are characterized by a strong identification with the body of the protagonist (particularly when that protagonist is played by James Stewart). The films obsessively revolve around the body fractured, punctured, trampled, and wounded. In no other westerns, and perhaps no other cinema, is the pull of gravity so inexorable, so determining. So many Mann westerns take place on the edge—not just the frontier, but the timber line, the limit-point. In *The Naked Spur,* when the bounty hunter Howard Kemp climbs a rock face to confront Ben Vandergroat, chipping notches in the rock with his spur, we *feel* the strain on his body, pitted against the elementalism of surging water and barren rock; we *feel* the downward pull of gravity toward abyssal failure. Kemp's protracted struggle speaks to the need for the character to transcend his spiritual and emotional history—this is literally an attempt to raise or uplift oneself, posed in resolutely physical terms. The struggle reveals itself in Kemp's absolute physical exhaustion and the spectacle of his body brutalized, sweating, and frenzied.

Compare this to another vertical action scene, this one a battle taking place against the wall of a building between Spider-Man and Doctor Octopus in *Spider-Man 2*. Doc Ock's mechanical arms can punch holes in the brick wall, holding him up with apparent ease, while Spidey's powers allow him to cling to walls. The camera careens about their careening figures, at times even turning their vertical arena into a horizontal plane. The only figure endangered in this scenario is Aunt May, hanging on by the skin of her umbrella. But her fall is interrupted by a rescue, and then the battle continues. The figures are, in many shots, entirely computer-generated, and the net effect is of some vaguely rubberoid action figures harmlessly bouncing each other around. There is nothing at stake—this is neither the first nor last time these characters will confront one another—and the only emotion in the viewer is the pleasure (and, make no mistake, it *is* pleasurable) provided by the vertiginous kineticism of the sequence.

I've proven perhaps precisely nothing here, other than the fact that *Spider-Man 2* is not *The Naked Spur,* and that the all-ages superhero film is not the adult western. *Spider-Man* is a thrill ride; the emphasis is not on a moral journey presented in physical terms (although, as in many a superhero film, trauma and guilt serve as background to the action, there is nothing of this in the wisecracking body-flinging ensuing onscreen). It's a lighter film. So let me bring another genre to bear and consider Fred Astaire's astonishing dance in *Royal Wedding,* the one in which he, like Spider-Man, climbs a wall. Using nothing but a rotating set with a camera mounted on it, the scene produces the illusion of Astaire dancing up the wall, across the ceiling, and down again, in a single glorious, giddy take. Seen on a large screen, the scene produces an awareness of one's corporeal being in much the way that Annette Michelson claimed for *2001: A Space Odyssey* (and note that Kubrick's film used an identical rotating set for some of its weightless effects).[54] One is confronted by a body transcending bodily limits, defying gravity, mocking the real. It is lighter than air, liberated from earthly constraints. But, and this returns me to Michelson again, it is resolutely *a body in space;* it is a body that belongs to the space that it masters. We watch a body go from prosaic and inexpressive, bound by gravity's laws, to marvelous and profoundly expressive of the exuberance of new love. In *Spider-Man 2,* by contrast, we have encountered "bodies" in "space"—phenomena generated, composited, or rendered by computer. Roger Ebert similarly complains of the first Spider-Man film: "Not even during Spidey's first experimental outings do we feel that flesh and blood are contending with gravity. Spidey soars too quickly through the skies of Manhattan; he's as convincing as Mighty Mouse."[55] These films give us corporeality without a *corpus*.

The superhero film, then, provides neither the psychological weight of the adult western or the ineffable lightness of the musical. It speaks to nothing but its own kinetic effectiveness. By removing the body from space, it removes meaning—lived meaning—from the body. My previous book of essays, *Matters of Gravity*, was something of an ode to weightlessness, but perhaps, I'm stunned to discover, there's such a thing as being *too* weightless.

The central problematic of the superhero film involves the integration of live-action and CGI—and the word *integration* summons up the notion of the "integrated musical," which integrated song and dance with narrative and character. The rise of the integrated musical is usually presented as the moment of the genre's maturation. But it must be said, as Gerald Mast has, that the dominance of the "integrated musical" wasn't necessarily a good thing—it also meant the submergence of the attraction, the sacrifice of diversity for unity, of pleasure for drama. Yet even the integrated musical maintained a magical heterogeneity in the passage from speech to song, from mundane walking to ecstatic dance—a passage from an *inexpressive* to an *expressive* body. By contrast, after Tobey Maguire's Peter Parker pulls Spider-Man's mask over his face and swings into action, the figure onscreen literally ceases to be Tobey Maguire. This has the unfortunate effect of severing the connection between the inexpressive body and the liberated, expressive one.[56] The films give us not a passage between states of being but rather a *rupture* that denies the connection between them. Thus the superhero film is an exuberant, performative, embodied genre that, in many ways, inherits the giddy, sensual power of the musical but without the, um, *actual bodies*.[57]

In an earlier essay I discussed the fantasy of the morph—a profound manipulation of surface that elides the history accreted beneath that surface.[58] Racial identity is repeatedly referenced but neutralized through the endless state of mutability that characterizes the world of the morph. The word isn't used much anymore, but superhero films have become the site of the morph. Shape-shifting characters like Mystique in the X-Men films recall the liquid Terminator of the second film of that franchise, and extended morphing sequences detail the transformation of, say, Flint Marko into Sandman in the third Spider-Man film.

The central fascination in the superhero film is with the transforming body, whether of hero or villain. Much attention is given to the body's discovery of its own transformation, which explains why superhero films are even more obsessed with origin stories than the comics themselves—the first film always features the hero's origin, and subsequent films treat the emergence of each villain's metamorphologies with loving care. As in the comics, the origin story is the real site of plasmatic possibility, and it is always the most intriguing part of these films. The character, and perhaps the audience, does not yet know how the bite-of-a-radioactive-spider, gamma-rays, particle-accelerator, mutant-gene, or what-*ever* will manifest itself within or, more importantly, upon his or her body. This is the moment when, rarebit-fiend style, everyday reality will yield to something more, the moment when the constraints of the mundane world will evaporate, forcing a new awareness of corporeal possibility as the body is rethought, radioactively (within the diegesis) and digitally (on the level of production).

From there, however, the conventions of the genre quickly produce new constraints—the character is either permanently transformed or can shift back and forth; rarely are there further surprises. A bank might get robbed or a weapon stolen; a battle will ensue; conflagration will be narrowly averted; there will be noisy explosions. A new normal has taken hold. We have left the plasmatic freedom of Slumberland far behind.

In the absence of a "real" body, the cinematic superhero becomes an incarnation of electronic technology, a digital being embodying the fact of being digital. It's no accident that this wave of superhero films followed the development of ever-more convincing CGI technologies. Whatever they are within the plot, these are bodies that are newly adequate to the malleable conditions of digital culture. Una Chung has noted of *Avatar* that "the film does not suggest that embodiment is not essential, but rather that embodiment is not singular."[59] Subjectivity requires *a* body but not necessarily the one it started with. The superhero film proposes something similar but frankly in less interesting terms—after all, Jake Sully's consciousness radically changes as he assimilates to Na'vi culture; superheroes and villains only become a bit more noble, venal, or bathetic. Perhaps, as in the case of *The Dark Knight*, the hero's voice changes. Really, superhero films are—and I'm fully aware of what I'm writing here—*Avatar*-lite, but they do capture and convey a sense that bodies are no more inviolate than any other form of coded information.[60]

The digital, after all, bears no scars and no history, and perhaps this begins to explain why the narratives are so obsessed with trauma: the death of Spider-Man's Uncle Ben, which leads to Spidey's acceptance of the dictum, "With great power comes great responsibility"; Batman's Shakespearian anguish around the murder of his parents—so so much Oedipal crap.[61] *X-Men* even brought Auschwitz into the mix (actually, that kinda worked!). Of course, all of this comes from the comics themselves, but there the material served more as backdrop to the colorful fantasies unfolding in every issue. Batman wasn't haunted by the murder of his parents until the 1970s and didn't become the psychological equivalent of his nemeses until the grim 'n' gritty 1980s. Spider-Man was always more neurotic, but the weight of his "great responsibility" didn't seem *quite* so heavy in earlier years—Peter Parker arguably bore more of that load, looking after, as he did, his aging Aunt May. His alter ego mostly seemed to enjoy the gig. But the films make a fetish of trauma, the better to compensate for the painlessness and weightlessness of digital being.

There is some pleasure in all this morphing and CGIing—superhero films deliver the goods on vertiginous sensation—but they finally present a constrained plasmatic. The creators of digital special effects are too absorbed in replicating the physics of the real world to revel in the possibilities of cartoon physics. Origin sequences aside, the characters metamorphose predictably; the films present more order than chaos.[62] And there is that rupture, which finally separates human-space from plasmatic-space. The only rupture in an early Disney cartoon like *Plane Crazy* comes at the end, when the film is over and the real reasserts itself. (This is the "secret melancholy" of the animated film to which Steven Millhauser refers.)[63] Until then, one is immersed in an animistic world of metamorphosis, flexibility, and possibility. But the superhero film is a bifurcated form—not even hybrid—bifurcated between actor and action figure, between live-action and CGI (and the climax is inevitably overdependent on CGI, even in the otherwise sublime *Iron Man*), and between plasmatic possibility and the limitations of not only the real but the inflexible conventions of genre. By substituting a digital body for a physical one, and rupture for continuity, the genre ends up speaking to the *impossibility* of bodily liberation and the foreclosure of potentials.

"LAST HOPE": *ALL-STAR SUPERMAN*

But superhero comics are still out there, and writers and artists continue to find new ways to spin the material, often with very satisfying results. The Silver Age of Superman has been summoned and recuperated by Grant Morrison and Frank Quitely's twelve-issue series, *All-Star Superman*. Their Superman is a profoundly serene figure—the now-iconic cover to the first issue features him sitting on a cloud, elbows on knees, overlooking Metropolis; it is either sunrise or sunset (Plate 31). Superman is devoid of any hint of machismo—his eyes are half-closed, perhaps in reverie, or perhaps he's squinting from looking toward the sun (which would be improbable but lovely); he is smiling a small Buddha-smile, and he is looking back over his shoulder at the readers, inviting us in—a very different acknowledgment of the reader than the one in *Animal Man*.[64] Where most superhero comics covers present bombast, heroic postures, and splashy scenes of threat and destruction, Morrison and Quitely give us, as they described it in numerous interviews, the most *relaxed* being in the cosmos—and why not? He's Superman, after all. "If nothing can hurt you, you can afford to be cool," Morrison has said.[65] Without homage, irony, or parody the character has been reconnected to his more benign postwar incarnation, in which his adventures were as apt to be comical as adventurous, where imagination was allowed free rein, and within which the reader felt safely cocooned.

Superman may well have been born of anxiety—Jerry Siegel and Joe Shuster were well aware of the stormy rise of Nazism, with its own talk of *uber-Menschen* and power. Their version of a superman was an altogether sunnier figure, but he was nevertheless a man of unparalleled strength and steel. In other essays I have discussed Superman as, variously, an American superman, a boy's superman, and a figure of the modern age—only the Man of Steel had the "power and abilities" appropriate to the rigors of the Machine Age.[66] Born of anxiety, yet a profoundly reassuring figure, Superman was out of place in the darker superhero stories of the 1980s and 1990s, which suited Batman far more. The gentleness of the Silver Age suited him better, and this is what the creators of *All-Star Superman* have realized.

Morrison's Superman exists on the other side of the Comics Code divide. The cultural shifts of the late 1960s demonstrated the obsolescence of the old standards, while the rise of direct market comics shops, which bypassed newsstands and other traditional sales outlets, removed comics from the disapproving eye of community watchdogs. Publishers could cater to older—and more devoted—readers, and the late 1970s and early 1980s saw an explosion of talent and a corresponding rise of diversity. The success of *Watchmen* (Alan Moore and Dave Gibbons) and *The Dark Knight Returns* (Frank Miller) created a vogue for more adult approaches to superhero comics, with varying results. The stories became more violent, the heroes more troubled (shading from the neuroses of Marvel's superheroes of the 1960s to the near-psychoses of their later brethren). While striking work continued to appear, the grim 'n' gritty approach had become a cliché, a cliché that continues to inform the trauma-laden superhero film.

As I mentioned earlier, the first page of *All-Star Superman* summarizes the character's history in four panels, two words per panel. Turning the page immerses the reader in a double-page spread filled with the roiling surface of the sun—the dimensions of the page are smaller than the broadsheet on which *Little Nemo* was printed, but there is still an experience of both a space opening out and a sinking in on the part of the reader. Flying serenely—I know I used that word already, but really, it's the *only* word—beneath its massive curvature, arms extended and slightly back—a gentle posture—and with a calm smile playing on his face, is Superman. Several things are going on here. First, this is presented as something of an *emblematic* image of the hero (Noël Burch's term for the insert shots of early narrative cinema that introduced the characters outside the diegesis). It actually isn't an emblematic shot—the next pages show us that Superman is on a rescue mission here—but it feels like one, part of the prologue presented on the preceding page. And, it will transpire, the level of solar radiation Superman is absorbing here is such that it will ultimately lead to his demise. This fact should, retrospectively, transform this image into a cruel and ironic joke, but it doesn't. Superman is doing what Superman does. And the series will end, twelve issues from now, with Superman performing his final labor: after the sun is attacked by Solaris, The Tyrant Sun, Superman flies off to repair it (a labor in which, it's suggested, he's still engaged, and not dead at all).

Along the way Morrison will revisit the characters and iconography of the Silver

Age Superman. Krypto is back, and so is Bizarro. In one particularly silly story from the late 1950s, Superman developed an unwelcome power: a tiny Superman would shoot from his fingers, save the day, and steal Superman's thunder. In Morrison's recuperative revision, Superman takes "microscopic Kandorian super-doctors" into his bloodstream so they can learn to cure his sun-induced cancer. When it transpires that it's too late to save Superman, he returns to the children's cancer ward, which he'd visited at the start of the issue. "I brought some friends to meet you," he tells the kids, as tiny Supermans, their salvation, fly from his fingers.[67] What reads as treacly in summary made for very effective comics. Quitely's art presents Superman with his arm outstretched toward the reader, while the tiny supermen fly beyond the boundaries of the panel, as though they are coming to save *us* (Figure 37).

What is perhaps most striking in this sequence is its profound understatement. The discussion with the super-doctors and the visit to the cancer ward take up a single page, and the actual visit takes up two panels. The stricken children are only visible in the background of one, their shaved heads the sole marker of their prognosis. But the faces on these children register pleasure and excitement—not about their possible cure but about the presence of Superman in their ward and in their lives. An entire issue could have been devoted to this selfless action of Superman's. Close-ups of the children could have driven home the seriousness of their plight, their anguish and that of their parents and doctors. *All-Star Superman* gives us none of that. Morrison assumes his readers know about cancer, the absence of a cure, and the Make-a-Wish foundations—he doesn't sidestep the anxiety about the disease, but neither does he overwhelm the reader with it. What he does is allow himself, and us, and even the fictional children on his ward, a fantasy of someone not only with the powers and abilities to help but with the desire to do so as well. The scene is simultaneously playful, whimsical, and moving.

Just as McCay did not ignore the seriousness of traffic accidents by treating them comically in *Dream of the Rarebit Fiend*, *All-Star Superman* recognizes that comics can treat anxious topics with a light yet sensitive touch. The historyless digital superhero body in the films cannot admit anxiety and trauma, and so must have them imposed on it, but the lightness of the superhero comic does not necessarily come at the expense of the real. Meanwhile, Morrison has cleverly recuperated a goofy Silver Age conceit and idealistically returned Superman to his do-gooder status (at his outset, in 1938, he was something of a New Dealer, always fighting for the little guy). All this in one page.

Morrison's Superman is an amalgam of all the versions of Superman, from comics, cartoons, and films, distilled to what the author refers to as "the essential 'Superman-ness.' "[68] Each episode presented another example of a superpowered being, an "alternate Superman," if you will, which further served to underscore what makes this superman *Superman*. Our Superman can repair the sun but also has time to visit cancer wards and save little Goth chicks from suicide (after his super-hearing

FIGURE 37. Grant Morrison and Frank Quitely, *All-Star Superman*, no. 10 (May 2008). Copyright DC Comics.

reveals that her worried doctor is held up in traffic). "You're much stronger than you think you are," he tells her. And that's it, isn't it? Superman is a set of values and a confidence in those values. Morrison describes him, paradoxically but logically, as an Everyman.

But not your everyday Everyman. Morrison's work on *All-Star Superman* was heavily informed by his fascination with Giovanni Pico Della Mirandola's fifteenth-century text *Oration on the Dignity of Man.* Pico argued that humans have the unique ability to possess ideals and to aspire to them. We observe and try to imitate—the flights of birds, for example. And we should aspire to the highest orders, the angels, rather than indulge the most brutish aspects of our natures. For Morrison, Superman is of the order of angels. "We live in the stories we tell ourselves," he says, and therefore those stories should feed our noblest aspirations.[69]

Morrison's obsession with the reality of stories fueled his four-issue miniseries *Flex Mentallo*—a psychedelic celebration of the power of the superheroic imagination and an earlier collaboration with Frank Quitely.[70] In this four-issue saga superheroes are real but manifest themselves as fictions in our reality: "They bypassed the death of *their* reality by becoming *fictional* in ours."[71] Nevertheless, they continue to have an impact: "Since we came to live in the imagination, we've been creating and transmitting certain ideas directly into your reality."[72] The emphasis is on the ideas that germinate in readers—ideas that seem to come from the archetypes themselves rather than from individual artists and writers. As the story ends, just before the return of the *real* superheroes, a caption informs us, "You have been inhabiting the first ultra-post-futurist comic: characters are allowed full synchrointeraction with readers at this level."[73]

All-Star Superman handled things with fewer postmodern flourishes than *Flex Mentallo,* but the net effect is similar. In the seminal tenth chapter the dying Superman creates a miniature Earth with greatly accelerated time within the "barely beating heart of the sickly infant universe of QWEWQ," in order to study what a world without Superman would be like.[74] As he continues about the business of his day, we observe the rapid evolution of life and civilization on Earth Q—gods and religions arise, a German philosopher muses on the concept of "the superman," and finally—on the penultimate page of the story, at 11:59:59.998 P.M., we see the hand of an unidentified artist sketching an earlier, rougher version of a now-familiar comics character with a big *S* on his chest (Figure 38). (This is perhaps the most profound iteration of the artist's hand in Morrison's oeuvre.) "This is going to change everything," he tells his unseen partner. In the absence of Superman, it seems, humans would have to invent him. Earth Q, then, is *our* Earth, the world on which two boys from Cleveland "created" Superman.[75] Superman, real in one reality, is manifested as a fiction in ours.

Despite that dramatic conclusion, I think that the emphasis is less on the boy-creators than on a culture's need for stories—stories about Superman. To create Su-

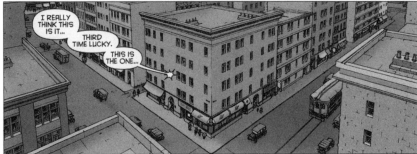

FIGURE 38. Grant Morrison and Frank Quitely, *All-Star Superman*, no. 10 (May 2008). Copyright DC Comics.

perman is to unleash decades of stories, a blizzard of stories, stories that are still being told and retold today. The point is made a bit less directly than in *Flex Mentallo,* but the message is the same: we *do* live in a world with Superman, and it matters not whether he is flying in our skies or in our comic books.

While telling a larger story, one with its share of dramatic beats and conflicts, Morrison and Quitely recaptured the sense of whimsy that must have underlay the creation of this character by two midwestern Jewish kids.[76] Seriously, how cool is

Superman? "He's from another planet!" "He's bulletproof!" "He can jump really far!" (He couldn't fly, at the beginning.) What has returned is the feeling of *play*. The happy strangeness of the Silver Age was the by-product of cultural anxieties around mass culture's effect on children, while Morrison's recovery of its tropes was designed to remind adults that superhero comics could be an oasis of whimsical fantasy—a new Slumberland, but with really cool capes.

NOTES

INTRODUCTION

1. These are the years of its initial run. A later and less dazzling incarnation, *In the Land of Wonderful Dreams,* ran from 1924 to 1927.

2. Bachelard, *The Poetics of Space,* 16.

3. Ibid., 26.

4. Bachelard, *The Poetics of Reverie,* 14.

5. In some ways Bruno Bettelheim has already told it. See Bettelheim, *The Uses of Enchantment.* It actually surprises me that Freud is so often posited as useful with regard to *Little Nemo.* Yes, these are "dreams," but, really, Slumberland is just Wonderland transposed to a new medium, a space of imaginative play, and Freud is rarely invoked in relation to Lewis Carroll's great work.

6. For more on this conjunction see Sutton-Smith, *The Ambiguity of Play,* esp. chap. 8, "Rhetorics of the Imaginary."

7. Deleuze, *Cinema 2,* 59.

8. Pierre Couperie has discussed these media as strongly related, noting that "the animated film, the movie, and the comic strip were born simultaneously; although each appeared independently of the other, they embodied in three related forms the single deep-seated trend underlying the entire nineteenth century" (Couperie, *A History of the Comic Strip,* 9).

9. In this book *cartoons* should be understood as referring to animated cartoons rather than humorous illustrations that appear in print.

10. Examples include *Little Nemo, Krazy Kat, Bringing Up Father,* and *Mutt and Jeff.*

11. See Millhauser, "The Little Kingdom of J. Franklin Payne."

12. Lears, *Rebirth of a Nation,* 226.

13. Ibid.

14. Ibid., 225.

15. Ibid., 232.

16. Nestrick, "Coming to Life," 303.

17. See Burch, *Life to Those Shadows,* 6–22 ("Charles Baudelaire versus Doctor Franken-stein"); and Bloom, "Pygmalionesque Delusions and Illusions of Movement."

18. Wood, *Edison's Eve,* 189. The myth of Pygmalion, Shelley's *Frankenstein,* Carroll's *Alice in Wonderland,* and Hoffmann's "The Sandman" are constant reference points in writings on animation.

19. The vitality of the cartoon character might even be something to aspire to. Lears cites a 1902 ad for Shredded Wheat that promised "BOUNCE!" The ad copy read: "If you want to be rid of that stomach heaviness after eating breakfast and in its place have that 'feeling of bounce'—an elastic step—a bright eye—an alert mind and the spirit to dare and do—try this simple yet satisfying dish for breakfast" (*Rebirth of a Nation,* 269). Henri Bergson held that humans could adapt to a changing world by combining an attentive attitude with an *elasticity* of body and mind (see Bergson, *Laughter,* 18), and that's exactly what the Shredded Wheat Company was selling. Elasticity is also the hallmark of the cartoon body, and we could also say that the cereal transforms the consumer into an animated character squashing and stretching his or her way to work.

20. My thanks to Heather Warren-Crow for suggesting this elegant connection to me via email.

21. Thanks to Dana Polan for this observation.

22. Bachelard, *The Poetics of Reverie,* 13.

23. For a compelling account see Campbell, *The Year That Defined American Journalism.*

24. Writing of the modern distraction, Siegfried Kracauer noted that it "demands and finds an answer in the display of pure externality; hence the irrefutable tendency . . . to turn all forms of entertainment into revues, and, parallel with this tendency, the increasing number of illustrations in the daily press and in periodical publications" (Kracauer, "The Cult of Distraction," 325–26).

25. Michael Schudson has presented American journalism, from the fin de siècle forward, as a dichotomy between "journalism as information," exemplified by the *New York Times,* and "journalism as entertainment," as promulgated by Joseph Pulitzer's *New York World* and Hearst's *New York Journal* (see Schudson, *Discovering the News*). The *Times* is most clearly aligned with Bachelard's reality function; it even eschews *comics* (and what clearer indication could we have of the alignment of comics with the irreality function?). The problem is that this dichotomy is overly reductive. Campbell argues what any careful newspaper reader can easily recognize—that these two approaches to journalism—information and entertainment—were always mixed. "As readers readily discern in moving from the news sections to the sport pages, newspaper content is, and has long been, an amalgam of news *and* entertainment" (Campbell, *The Year That Defined American Journalism,* 18). One doesn't even have to move to another section—the mixture occurs on almost every page.

26. See Baker and Brentano, *The World on Sunday.*

27. Baker and Brentano imagine the editors, illustrators, and writers of the *World*'s Sunday supplements "cackling to themselves as every week they published another vaudeville revue of urban urges and preoccupations" (ibid., x).

28. There was a popular song of 1882 called "McNally's Row of Flats," which may have inspired the feature's new name. Later iterations were *Around the World with the Yellow Kid,* which delivered what the title implied, and then *Ryan's Arcade.*

29. Cf. *Hogarth's Gin Alley* as a predecessor.

30. Waugh, *The Comics,* 2.

31. Ronan, "Shoot at Any Ole Ting."

32. Smolderen, "Why the Brownies Are Important."

33. Huizinga, *Homo Ludens,* 2.

34. Henricks, "The Nature of Play," 177. The discussion of the history of play as functional is found on pages 166–67.

35. Huizinga, *Homo Ludens,* 3, 46. There are echoes of Bachelard in Huizinga's study. Huizinga writes that "to understand poetry we must be capable of donning the child's soul like a magic cloak and of forsaking man's wisdom for the child's" (119). Bachelard muses that "poetry gives us not so much a nostalgia for youth, which would be vulgar, as a nostalgia for the expressions of youth. It offers us images as we should have imagined them during the 'original impulse' of youth" (*The Poetics of Space,* 33). For Bachelard poetry puts us in touch with the nonrational parts of our being: "To the *function of reality,* wise in experience of the past . . . should be added a *function of unreality,* which is equally positive" (*The Poetics of Space,* xxxiv), and this corresponds nicely to Huizinga's sense that it is the unseriousness of play that gives it value: "You can deny seriousness," he writes, "but not play" (3).

36. Huizinga, *Homo Ludens,* 13.

37. Ibid., 10.

38. Morgenstern, "The Children's Novel as a Gateway to Play," 393.

39. Huizinga, *Homo Ludens,* 8, 9.

40. There have been crossovers between strips, either for purpose of homage or parody, but these are stunts with their own temporary logic.

41. Unless, of course, you're writing a book on the subject.

42. See Caillois, *Man, Play, and Games,* 19–23.

43. Smolderen, "Why the Brownies Are Important."

44. This pithy summary of Sutton-Smith's chapter comes from Henricks, "The Nature of Play," 175.

45. See Eisenstein, *Eisenstein on Disney.*

46. Paul Hammond locates this quality even earlier, in the trick film: "Not only statues but scarecrows, snowmen, dummies, skeletons, figures in paintings, posters, photographs, playing cards and book illustrations, pulsate with life, through the camera's stop-motion capability" (Hammond, *Marvellous Méliès,* 90).

47. Freedberg, *The Power of Images,* 284.

48. See Jacobs, *The Living Image in Renaissance Art.*

49. See Belting, *Likeness and Presence.*

50. Pentcheva, "The Performative Icon," 631. This is a point made earlier by Michelle Bloom with reference to the flickering candles that reanimate the portraits of the dead in a shrine in Francois Truffaut's *The Green Room* (see Bloom, "Pygmalionesque Delusions and Illusions of Movement," 27–28).

51. Lears, *Fables of Abundance,* 126.

52. Ibid., 290.

53. Eisenstein, *Eisenstein on Disney,* 33.

54. See Thompson, "Implications of the Cel Animation Technique." Thompson actually argues that there's something radical in this disruption of unity, which may be true, but the net effect is a more stable image.

55. This phrase, "ludilo materije," comes from Munitic, *Alisa Na Putu Kroz Podzemlje I Kroz Svemir,* a sustained exploration of *Alice in Wonderland.* (The title translates as "Alice on a Trip through the Underground and the Cosmos.") My colleague Pavle Levi translates the Serbo-Croatian phrase as "the madness of matter," but it could also mean "the playfulness of matter."

56. Millhauser, "The Little Kingdom of J. Franklin Payne," 107.

57. Ibid. Vivian Sobchack points to a similar melancholy "between the impossible—and immensely appealing—dream of plasmatic freedom and, constituted as momentary nostalgia, the specific cultural poetics of its loss" (Sobchack, "The Line and the Animorph or 'Travel Is More Than Just A to B,'" 262).

58. Johnson, *Harold and the Purple Crayon.*

59. Harold's opposite number is Daffy Duck in *Duck Amuck.* Here the wielder of plasmatic power is the animator rather than the protagonist.

60. The superhero of the *ecto*plasmatic is Dr. Strange, Sorcerer Supreme.

61. Kunzle, *The History of the Comic Strip,* 2:357.

62. Spiegelman, "Forms Stretched to Their Limits," 80. Spiegelman's article has been archived and is available in an electronic edition at www.newyorker.com/archive.

63. Eisenstein, *Eisenstein on Disney,* 21.

64. See Krauss, "'The Rock.'"

65. See Nesbet, "Inanimations."

66. Bouldin, "The Body, Animation and the Real."

67. Ngai, *Ugly Feelings.*

68. Crow, "Possessions," 89. Crow's emphasis in her chapter on *Alice in Wonderland* is on films in which a live-action Alice is both integrated with animated imagery and subject to animatic manipulation.

69. See Bukatman, "Taking Shape."

70. Ngai, *Ugly Feelings,* 94.

71. Ibid., 117.

72. Updike, "The Mystery of Mickey Mouse," 388–89.

73. Ngai, *Ugly Feelings,* 124–25.

74. Klein, *Seven Minutes,* 75.

75. I take this phrase from Alex Nemerov's review of my book proposal, and I thank him kindly.

76. Thanks to Dana Polan for this observation.

77. In the first issue of Kurt Busiek's *Astro City,* that comic's equivalent of Superman actually does dream of flight: unfettered freedom of movement that occurs in a space apart from the world's massive demand for his superheroic capabilities. See Busiek, Anderson, and Ross, *Astro City,* no. 1.

78. My argument: *Superheroes don't wear costumes in order to fight crime; they fight crime in order to wear the costumes.* See Bukatman, "The Boys in the Hoods."

79. Freedberg, *The Power of Images,* 307.

1. DRAWN AND DISORDERLY

1. *Little Nemo in Slumberland* appeared weekly in the *New York Herald* from 1905 until 1911, before moving to Hearst's *New York American.* There it continued until 1914 under the title *In the Land of Wonderful Dreams.* It was briefly, and unconvincingly, revived under its original title from 1924 to 1927.

2. In conversation Tom Gunning has observed that the images also strongly suggest the undulating, whimsical animals on a fairground carousel.

3. Quoted in Braun, *Picturing Time,* 30.

4. Ibid., xviii.

5. "Muybridge's concern [was] with narration, not with movement" (ibid., 249).

6. Ibid., 251.

7. See Gunning, "Never Seen This Picture Before."

8. Crary, *Suspensions of Perception,* 147.

9. Muybridge's sequences "at least suggest the possibility of novel social/historical intuitions, 'flashing up' amid their disruptions of presumed continuities or their shattering of the self-sufficiency of an autonomous image" (ibid.). Crary emphasizes that he is only concerned with the motion studies of 1878–79, "not [Muybridge's] subsequent work at the University of Pennsylvania in the mid-1880s that produced *Animal Locomotion,*" thus disqualifying my personal favorite motion study, the one with the nude blacksmiths (Crary, *Suspensions of Perception,* 140n112).

10. McCloud, *Understanding Comics,* 67.

11. Fell, *Film and the Narrative Tradition,* 91. Fell emphasizes the strong connection between the media, with particular emphasis on Winsor McCay. He notes the profound spatiotemporal malleability of the world McCay creates on the comics page, notes Rodolphe Töpffer's treatment of the page as both sequence and graphic whole, and even praises more recent superhero comics for the "dynamic framing" that Eisenstein had once called for (his—uncredited—examples are by Gene Colan, Don Heck, and Gil Kane).

12. Prodger, "Make It Stop," 218.

13. McCloud, *Reinventing Comics,* 207.

14. John Fell writes that comic strip artists and filmmakers were "confronting common problems of space and time within the conventions of narrative exposition" (Fell, *Film and the Narrative Tradition,* 89).

15. See Kunzle, *The History of the Comic Strip,* 2:348–375.

16. "Caricature and comic strip were always in the vanguard of a kind of graphic speed-up, of which Rodolphe Töpffer is the recognized pioneer" (Kunzle, "The Voices of Silence," 4).

17. Kunzle, *The History of the Comic Strip,* 2:349.

18. Ibid.

19. Kunzle calls this a "crystalline isolation of climactic physical moments" (Kunzle, "The Voices of Silence," 5).

20. Kunzle, *The History of the Comic Strip*, 2:349.

21. Ibid., 2:203–12.

22. Kunzle sees the mute menagerie of cats and dogs (and their sibling species) that continue to populate comics and cartoons as "natural mimes," like Chaplin's Little Tramp of a short while later, perpetuating a darkly entertaining cycle of violence that seems to be their sole lot; "social victims expressing themselves in a wordless language of movements and attitudes which may not succeed in communicating at all. Mute by nature, further muted by human cruelty and ignorance, animals fit into the wordless comic strip as if the medium were created for them" (Kunzle, "The Voices of Silence," 18). Kunzle's gorgeous phrasing also suggests that perhaps the sinuous movement of the cat demands the development of more supple and flowing techniques for rendering time's small movements, making animal locomotion just as natural and necessary a subject for comics as it was for Muybridge and Marey.

23. Rabinbach, *The Human Motor*, 44.

24. Braun, *Picturing Time*, 320 (emphasis mine).

25. Ibid., 321.

26. Quoted in Rabinbach, *The Human Motor*, 91.

27. Ibid., 97.

28. Kunzle, *The History of the Comic Strip*, 2:357.

29. Gunning, "Never Seen This Picture Before," 225.

30. Thanks to Richard Vinograd for this extremely valuable observation.

31. I would like to note that I am, myself, quite fond of cats.

32. *New York Herald,* Oct. 9, 1904.

33. Ibid., Sept. 24, 1905.

34. See Williams, *Hard Core*, 51–53.

35. *New York Herald,* Feb. 5, 1905.

36. Ibid., May 7, 1905.

37. Spiegelman, "Polyphonic Polly: Hot and Sweet," 6.

38. Ware, *Quimby the Mouse, or, Comic Strips, 1990–1991 (with a Small Number from 1992–93) as Mostly Originally Collected in the Pages of the Acme Novelty Library, and Released during the Years 1993 and 1994,* 14. The images can indeed be cut out and filmed, as a visit to flickr will confirm: www.flickr.com/photos/vindog/3332909819/.

39. Ford and Thompson. "Interview with Chuck Jones," 28.

40. Deleuze, *Cinema 1, 2,* 5.

41. Grant Morrison's *Animal Man* story "The Coyote Gospel" proposes that the Coyote has struck a deal with the god of the cartoons and must suffer this eternal cycle of destruction and regeneration so that other cartoon characters can be free. See Morrison, Truog, and Hazlewood, "The Coyote Gospel."

42. In conversation.

43. Originally published in the June 1980 issue of *Esquire,* the essay was widely circulated by the Institute of Electrical and Electronics Engineers. It is available online under the title "The Cartoon Laws of Physics" at http://remarque.org/~doug/cartoon-physics.html.

44. "Uncle Josh" was the rube character featured in early narrative films from the Edison Manufacturing Company.

45. See Singer, *Melodrama and Modernity.*

46. Shaya, "Mayhem for Moderns," 55, 50.

47. Ibid., 27, 50.

48. See, e.g., Baker and Brentano, *The World on Sunday.*

49. Canemaker, *Winsor McCay,* 79.

50. *Peanuts* was another strip that spoke to the anxieties of modern life. In one episode, from June 4, 1961, Lucy, in her role as psychiatrist, tries to help her brother. She runs down a list of phobias, none of which seem quite right. "Are you afraid of responsibility? If you are, then you have hypengyophobia . . . How about cats? If you're afraid of cats, you have ailurophasia . . . Are you afraid of staircases? If you are, then you have climacaphobia. Maybe you have thalassophobia. This is fear of the ocean, or gephyrobia, which is the fear of crossing bridges. Or maybe you have pantophobia. Do you think you have pantophobia?" Linus reasonably asks, "What's pantophobia?" "The fear of everything," Lucy replies, to which Linus yells "THAT'S IT!" [Note: I am well aware that in the television production *A Charlie Brown Christmas,* it is Charlie Brown, not Linus, who is so self-diagnosed. Please do not send me letters.]

51. Lutz, *American Nervousness, 1903,* 4, 27.

52. Beard, *American Nervousness, Its Causes and Consequences,* vi.

53. Quoted in ibid., 39.

54. Silverman, *Art Nouveau in fin-de-siècle France,* 10.

55. *New York Evening Telegram,* circa 1911–12 (exact date unknown).

56. Ibid., March 18, 1905.

57. Ibid., April 19, 1905.

58. Ibid., August 21, 1911.

59. *New York Herald,* Feb. 9, 1913.

60. *New York Evening Telegram,* Jan. 3, 1905.

61. Quoted in Schivelbusch, *The Railway Journey,* 159.

62. Singer, *Melodrama and Modernity,* 119, 121.

63. This "modernity thesis" has been the subject of extended debate in the field of film studies. David Bordwell has long held that the notion of a sudden change in the human apperceptive apparatus is so much hogwash. Ben Singer's *Modernity and Melodrama* does a fine job of elaborating the terms of that debate. For my purposes it doesn't matter one bit whether or not there was an actual change in the human sensorium under the pressures of modernity and rapid technological intensification—it's enough that there was a pervasive rhetoric at the time and that writers on both sides of the Atlantic were clearly worried about the impact of modernity on the human subject.

64. *New York Evening Telegram,* April 22, 1905.

65. Ibid., Nov. 11, 1905.

66. Ibid., Dec. 2, 1905.

67. Ibid., June 4, 1911, and May 19, 1906, respectively.

68. Ibid., April 26, 1905.

69. O'Sullivan, "The Art of Winsor Z. McCay," 79.

70. *New York Evening Telegram,* Feb. 4, 1905.

71. Ibid., March 29, 1905.

72. Ibid., May 6, 1909.

73. Ibid.

74. Ibid., March 8, 1905.

75. Ibid., Feb. 18, 1905.

76. Ibid., June 11, 1908.

77. Ibid., Nov. 14, 1904.

78. Ibid., Dec. 13, 1904.

79. Ibid., Feb. 1, 1905, and Jan. 10, 1905, respectively.

80. Max Nordau, for example, writes that the symptoms of neurasthenia "are the consequences of states of fatigue and exhaustion, and these, again, are the effect of contemporary civilization, of the vertigo and whirl of our frenzied life, the vastly increased number of sense impressions and organic reactions" (Nordau, *Degeneration,* 42). He continues, noting that while nervous disorders were always with us, "it was only the vast fatigue which was experienced by the generation on which the multitude of discoveries and innovations burst abruptly, imposing upon it organic exigencies greatly surpassing its strength, which created favourable conditions under which these maladies could gain ground enormously, and become a danger to civilization."

81. Beard, *American Nervousness, Its Causes and Consequences,* 104 (emphasis mine).

82. Ibid., viii.

83. Nordau, *Degeneration,* 34.

84. O'Sullivan, "The Art of Winsor Z. McCay," 78.

85. *New York Herald,* April 26, 1906.

86. De Quincey, *The Confessions of an English Opium Eater,* 233.

87. Ibid., 234.

88. Nordau, *Degeneration,* 20.

89. Ibid., 21.

90. Crary, *Suspensions of Perception,* 3.

91. It's unclear whether this is something more than wishful thinking on Crary's part. By the book's restlessly repetitive conclusion, euphoria and pessimism chase one another like cartoon cats and mice.

92. Crary, *Suspensions of Perception,* 63.

93. Bergson, *Laughter,* 18, 19, 29.

94. This pairs very well with Ngai's writings on the dialectical tension she finds in animatedness—see chap. 3, "Labor and Anima" for discussion of elasticity and the cartoon character.

95. Rabinbach, *The Human Motor,* 6. Crary finds something similarly radical: nervous disorders "disclosed a subject incapable of conforming to such disciplinary imperatives" (*Suspensions of Perception,* 14). But although Crary agrees with Simmel and company that distraction has its virtues, he argues that the rhetoric of these key theorists of twentieth-century modernism betrays a nostalgia for the coherence of a lost classicism that nineteenth-century perceptual models had already rendered untenable. Throughout fin de siècle Europe an "unbinding of vision" occurred on numerous levels, as "new knowledge about the behavior and makeup of a human subject coincided with social and economic shifts, with new representational practices, and [not coincidentally] with a sweeping reorganization of visual/auditory culture" (149, 2). Instead of regarding distraction as the sign of a disrupted, ahistorical mode of perception, then, Crary argues that "attention and distraction cannot be thought

outside of a continuum in which the two ceaselessly flow into one another, as part of a so-cial field in which the same imperatives and forces incite one and the other" (51).

96. Crary, *Suspensions of Perception,* 77.

97. Bachelard, *The Poetics of Reverie,* 14, 5. To return to the issue of *play,* Thomas Hen-ricks has written that, "Disorderly play celebrates—and develops—impish, creative qualities in people. . . . Such rebellions against good form—represented by the class clown, *the goof-off, the daydreamer,* the doodler, the hacker, and the bathroom poet—also have their func-tions" (Henricks, "Orderly and Disorderly Play," 35 [emphasis mine]).

98. Crary, *Suspensions of Perception,* 47.

99. Many *Little Nemo* episodes did employ a fixed perspective but less frequently than *Rarebit Fiend.* See chapter 2 for an extended analysis of *Little Nemo in Slumberland.*

100. *New York Evening Telegram,* May 24, 1906.

101. Ibid., April 12, 1905; May 18, 1907; and Dec. 6, 1906, respectively.

102. Ibid., April 17, 1909.

103. Crary, *Suspensions of Perception,* 47.

104. Huizinga, *Homo Ludens,* 136, 140.

105. Merkl, *The Complete "Dream of the Rarebit Fiend" (1904–1913).* My categories are taken from Stam, *Reflexivity in Film and Culture.*

106. *New York Evening Telegram,* Nov. 22, 1906.

107. Ibid., Dec. 6, 1906.

108. Ibid., March 14, 1908.

109. Ibid., March 30, 1907.

110. Ibid., August 6, 1908.

111. Ibid., Nov. 9, 1907.

112. Ibid., Sept. 9, 1909.

113. Ibid., August 30, 1906. John Fell, writing of the "environmental transience" of Mc-Cay's *Little Nemo in Slumberland*—but it applies to *Rarebit Fiend* as well—argues that a "sim-ilar freedom of movement through space does not appear in the film until Buster Keaton's dream sequence as a projectionist in the 1924 *Sherlock Jr.,* to be followed by Buñuel's *Un Chien Andalou* in 1928, and Maya Deren's experimental *Meshes of the Afternoon* [1943]" (Fell, *Film and the Narrative Tradition,* 109).

114. *New York Evening Telegram,* May 28, 1908. In a much more recent comic strip, Richard Thompson's *Cul de Sac,* the little girl, Alice, was unable to grasp that the sequential pictures of a cat in a comic strip were *all the same cat.*

115. See Wells, *Understanding Animation,* 24–28; and Ngai, *Ugly Feelings,* 100–101.

116. *New York Evening Telegram,* July 31, 1909.

117. In considering the presence of McCay as a kind of performance, in which the nor-mally hidden artist makes his control felt, it's worth noting that Steven Millhauser's stories also make the "dreamer," the creator of fabulous worlds, visible, staging the act of dreaming as well as the realization of the dream. In this sense the Millhauser stories are little biopics, presenting the artist as a "crazy dreamer" who is shunned by mainstream culture for his or her dedication to dreams. In *The Benny Goodman Story* Benny is constantly told, "Benny, don't be that way!" until he finally turns the phrase into a song title. For more on the biopic and the performance of image-making see chapter 5 on *Lust for Life.*

118. Stam, *Reflexivity in Film and Culture*, 129.

119. *New York Evening Telegram*, Feb. 25, 1905.

120. Millhauser, "The Little Kingdom of J. Franklin Payne," 38.

121. Nordau, *Degeneration*, vii–viii.

122. Millhauser, "The Little Kingdom of J. Franklin Payne," 26.

123. Ibid., 17.

124. Huysmans, *Against Nature (À rebours)*, 39.

125. Ibid., 35–36.

126. Millhauser, "The Little Kingdom of J. Franklin Payne," 39.

127. Millhauser, *Martin Dressler*, 129, 181, 194.

128. Millhauser, "The Little Kingdom of J. Franklin Payne," 107.

129. Huysmans, *Against Nature (À rebours)*, 36. My edition of the book uses the word *vision*, whereas an online translation uses the word *dream* (http://books.google.com/books?id=gNE-m3mAOGoC&printsec=frontcover#v=onepage&q&f=false). I've opted for the latter.

130. Millhauser, "The Little Kingdom of J. Franklin Payne," 107.

131. Huysmans, *Against Nature (À rebours)*, 84.

132. Nordau, *Degeneration*, 541.

133. As we will see in chapter 5, the tension between American and European creators also plays out in Minnelli's *Lust for Life*.

2. THE MOTIONLESS VOYAGE OF LITTLE NEMO

1. Benjamin, "A Glimpse into the World of Children's Books," 435.

2. Benjamin, "Old Forgotten Children's Books," 410.

3. *New York Herald*, July 19, 1908.

4. Nemerov, *The Body of Raphaelle Peale*, 15.

5. See Abrams, *The Mirror and the Lamp*, 66–67 (quoted in Nemerov, *The Body of Raphaelle Peale*, 21).

6. Quoted in Nemerov, *The Body of Raphaelle Peale*, 21.

7. Ibid., 23.

8. Ibid., 26.

9. Wolf, *Romantic Re-vision*, 26.

10. Nemerov, *The Body of Raphaelle Peale*, 26.

11. The animating sensibility of the artist is also privileged in the artist's films that will be discussed in later chapters, beginning, of course, with McCay's own appearance in the *Little Nemo* film.

12. Ngai, *Ugly Feelings*, 94.

13. Nemerov, *The Body of Raphaelle Peale*, 31.

14. See Maresca, *Little Nemo in Slumberland: Splendid Sundays 1905–1910;* and Maresca, *Little Nemo in Slumberland: Splendid Sundays 1906–1926*.

15. See Smolderen, preface to *Stuff and Nonsense*, 13.

16. See Burch, *Life to Those Shadows*, esp. "The Motionless Voyage: Constitution of the Ubiquitous Subject," 202–33.

17. This is what Burch refers to, not entirely accurately, as the "haptical space" of the cinema (much more on this below).

18. Ibid., 163–64.

19. Ibid., 173.

20. Willems, " 'This Strangest of Narrative Forms,' " 133.

21. Kunzle, "The Voices of Silence," 4. Willems points out that Eckermann and Soret do not compare Töpffer's work "with any third-person storytelling form, be that sequences of prints, the broadsheet, the illustrated tale, the novel, oral storytelling, satirical prose, or with any visual art" (" 'This Strangest of Narrative Forms,' " 133); there is, however, an evocation of the more performative art of the theater.

22. Lanier, "Review of Rodolphe Töpffer," 116.

23. *New York Herald,* Oct. 22, 1905, and Oct. 28, 1905, respectively.

24. Ibid., Nov. 26, 1905, and Dec. 3, 1905, respectively.

25. Looking at the complete run of McCay's *Little Nemo* strips is rather like watching D. W. Griffith's learning curve on the hundreds of short films he produced nearly contemporaneously for Biograph.

26. *New York Herald,* Sept. 23, 1906.

27. Ibid., July 10, 1906.

28. Ibid., Jan. 27, 1907.

29. Ibid., June 20, 1909.

30. Ibid., Nov. 8, 1908.

31. Ibid., Nov. 15, 1908.

32. Ibid., May 2, 1909.

33. Ibid., Aug. 7, 1910.

34. Ibid., Dec. 1, 1907.

35. My thanks to Graham Larkin for pointing this out.

36. Hildebrand, *The Problem of Form in Painting and Sculpture,* 125 (quoted in Lant, "Haptical Cinema," 55).

37. *New York Herald,* Nov. 15, 1908.

38. Lant, "Haptical Cinema," 63.

39. Ibid., 45.

40. See Gorky, "The Kingdom of Shadows."

41. Hildebrand, *The Problem of Form in Painting and Sculpture,* 23–24 (quoted in Lant, "Haptical Cinema," 55).

42. Yi-Fu Tuan similarly writes that "touching and manipulating things with the hand yields a world of objects—objects that retain their constancy of shape and size. Reaching for things and playing with them disclose their separateness and relative spacing. Purposive movement and perception, both visual and haptic, give human beings their familiar world of disparate objects in space" (Tuan, *Space and Place,* 12).

43. See Riegl, *Late Roman Art Industry,* 23–27.

44. Deleuze, *Cinema 2,* 59.

45. Ibid., 61.

46. *New York Herald,* July 26, 1908.

47. Ibid., Oct. 4, 1908.

48. Ibid., Oct. 25, 1908. The film version from 1939 makes movement of world quite explicit: as her house sails off toward the land of Oz, the unconscious Dorothy lies quite motionless as the vertiginous view outside her window—a view of the storm's center (and a kind of dream screen)—offers up increasingly absurd kinetic characters.

49. *New York Herald,* Feb. 2, Jan. 26, Feb. 16, and March 1, 1907, respectively.

50. This is a variation of an episode of *Dream of the Rarebit Fiend* from the *New York Evening Telegram,* Sept. 21, 1907.

51. Deleuze, *Cinema 2,* 63.

52. Bazin, "Theater and Cinema," 97.

53. The relation of Art Nouveau to the art of Winsor McCay is often mentioned but seldom explored. Surely the best discussion belongs to Judith O'Sullivan, who simply claims him as an artist working within the Nouveau tradition. Noting that in the early years of the twentieth century, American interest in the European movement was at its peak, O'Sullivan observes in McCay's work Nouveau's sinuous line, especially in McCay's heavy outlines, and the flat patterning associated with such poster artists as Mucha. She also notes that the confluence moves beyond the formal and thematic concerns with natural, organic forms and metamorphosis. She points out that McCay's status as a practitioner of applied, rather than fine, arts further links him to the "culminating achievements" of Art Nouveau in poster art, book illustration, interior decoration, and architecture. See O'Sullivan, "The Art of Winsor Z. McCay," esp. 55.

54. Watterson, "An 'Incredible Ride' to the End," 195.

55. Greenhalgh, "The Cult of Nature," 61.

56. Silverman, *Art Nouveau in Fin-de-Siècle France,* 1.

57. Greenhalgh, "The Style and the Age," 26.

58. Sembach, *Art Nouveau Utopia,* 11.

59. O'Sullivan, "The Art of Winsor Z. McCay," 2.

60. Klee, *Pedagogical Notebook,* 16.

61. Clifford and Turner, "Modern Metal," 232.

62. Bachelard, *The Poetics of Space,* 4, 15.

63. Ibid., 31.

64. Ibid., 5.

65. Langeveld, "The 'Secret Place' in the Life of the Child," 181.

66. Ibid., 183; Langeveld, "The Stillness of the Secret Place," 11–17. Langeveld also emphasizes the "creative simplicity" of the secret place. In this, perhaps, Slumberland represents something else: it is surely a more elaborate fantasy in which effortless daydream morphs into an immersive alternate reality. It is somewhat less tranquil and more systematic than the more casual reverie that Langeveld describes. However, since we are here describing the experiences of a fictive, rather than an actual, child, and an adult version of the childhood world of the secret place, these differences do not strike me as overly significant to this study.

67. "The child sees himself already formed in comparison to things outside himself; these things ground his existence, but his 'I' has distanced very little from his world" (Langeveld, "The Stillness of the Secret Place" 16.). This also connects to Freud's sense that the uncanny returns us to a moment in our psychic growth when our ego boundaries were not yet fully formed, when the "self" was a fragile enterprise, very much under construction. Yi-Fu Tuan

adds that "place is a special kind of object. . . . It is an object in which one can dwell" (Tuan, *Space and Place,* 12).

68. Bachelard, *The Poetics of Space,* 149, 155. Noting how frequently the miniature world is the world of the garden or the plant, Bachelard writes that such gazes "demand participation in a really intimate vegetism" (162), a phrase that inevitably here summons up images of immense berries possessed of a mysterious animism.

69. Stewart, *On Longing,* 46–47.

70. *New York Herald,* Sept. 22, 1907.

71. Tuan, *Space and Place,* 27.

72. Stewart, *On Longing,* 56.

73. Langeveld, "The 'Secret Place' in the Life of the Child," 190.

74. Heather Ann Crow has written about the repeated iterations of *Alice in Wonderland* in the history of film and animated film: "Though she was created by Lewis Carroll more than thirty years before the invention of cinema (a creation which problematizes any notion of original, in light of the 'real' girl Alice Liddell, Carroll's inspiration for the character), Alice emerges as a pivotal figure and driving force in the history of animated film. Alice is encountered in this history as successive reverberations of an already unstable body, a body that questions the boundaries and self-identity of the subject" ("Possessions," 101).

75. Langeveld, "How Does the Child Experience the World of Things?" 215. Langeveld begins this essay by stating that he would have no qualms about retitling it "The Child in the World of the Things," a phrase that cannot help but echo "*Little Nemo in Slumberland.*" The rather more sardonic Seth Lerer reminds us that more is going on in the child's experience: "Childhood is many things: it is a time of exploration, an arena of adventure. Every shipping box becomes a canoe or a spaceship. Every backyard is an island empire. But childhood is, as well, a prison. How many of us sought to run away, to escape those confederacies of parents who made us toil at chores, who limited our freedom, who took us far away from friendships? Our fantasies balloon into strange skies, and they may take us to new island ports or over rainbows" (Lerer, *Children's Literature,* 150).

76. From the first sentence of Brakhage's *Metaphors on Vision.*

77. Lerer, *Children's Literature,* 106–7.

78. Bachelard, *The Poetics of Space,* 33.

79. Ibid., xvi, xxii–xxiii.

80. Ibid., 16.

81. Ibid.

82. Ibid., 183.

83. Ibid., 191.

84. Baudelaire, "Richard Wagner and Tannhäuser in Paris," 117, 116.

85. Bachelard, *The Poetics of Space,* 195.

86. Stewart, *On Longing,* 67.

87. Ibid., 69.

88. Nemerov, "The Boy in Bed," 7, 14.

89. Ibid., 24.

90. Ibid., 19.

91. Ibid., 21.

92. Proust, *Swann's Way*, 9.

93. Ibid., 1.

94. Bachelard, *The Poetics of Space*, xxiii, xxii.

95. Langeveld, "The Stillness of the Secret Place," 12.

96. Nemerov, "The Boy in Bed," 15–16.

97. Ibid., 16.

98. Thanks to Elizabeth A. Kessler for this.

99. Looking at some of Wilcox's work, especially her *Waterbabies* series, it seems plausible that she was somewhat influenced by *Little Nemo*.

100. Benjamin, "One-Way Street," 463.

3. LABOR AND ANIMA

1. Eisenstein, *Eisenstein on Disney*, 2, 31, 10.

2. Ibid., 54–55. Eisenstein distinguishes here between two kinds of knowledge, even giving sensual knowledge a kind of priority. But he also describes a pleasurable confusion in the viewing subject. Animation represents a categorical mistake in the sense that Mary Douglas described it (see Douglas, *Purity and Danger*, 49); what we know to be inanimate takes on a simulacrum of life, blurring the boundaries between living and dead, organic and inorganic. More on the categorical mistake at the end of this essay.

3. Ibid., 21.

4. Ibid., 8.

5. Kunzle, *The History of the Comic Strip*, 2:357.

6. Wells, *Understanding Animation*, 22.

7. See Crafton, *Before Mickey*, 162.

8. Crafton remarks that "the animation industry . . . could have served as an admirable model for the enthusiasts of 'scientific management' " (*Before Mickey*, 163).

9. The relation between labor and anima can also be understood as part of a far longer debate between animists, for whom the world was suffused with spirit or material substance, and mechanists, for whom the universe, and everything in it, could be explained through straightforward physical laws. Alan Cholodenko, referring to this debate, notes that cartoons are complex forms that finally complicate "any simple distinction between animism and mechanism" (Cholodenko, introduction to *The Illusion of Life*, 16).

10. Ngai, *Ugly Feelings*, 91. See also Donna Haraway's "A Cyborg Manifesto," where Haraway observes, "Our machines are disturbingly lively, and we ourselves frighteningly inert" (152).

11. Ngai, *Ugly Feelings*, 91.

12. Mention should also be made of the episode of *Beavis and Butthead* in which their teacher extols the unfettered wonders of animation while the camera holds, seemingly endlessly, on the absolutely motionless forms of the titular heroes (thanks to Carlton Evans for showing this to me).

13. Veblen, *The Theory of Business Enterprise*, 8.

14. Shapiro, "Machine Crafted," 4.

15. Ibid., 42.

16. Ibid., 153.

17. Ibid., 54.

18. Shapiro notes that early artistic experiments with photography "downplayed the mechanical and reproductive nature of their medium" in favor of the "possibilities for chemical and physical manipulation offered by the printing process" (7).

19. See Crafton, *Before Mickey,* 138, 55–57.

20. Solomon, " 'Twenty-Five Heads under One Hat,' " 5.

21. See Harris, *Humbug,* 59–90.

22. Crafton, *Before Mickey,* 129.

23. It's actually kind of a Sammy Sneeze gag!

24. "The temporality of Western representational painting is rarely the deictic time of the painting as process; that time is usurped and cancelled by the aoristic time of the [viewing] event" (Bryson, *Vision and Painting,* 92).

25. Rabinbach, *The Human Motor,* 2. See also the discussion of chronophotography, reverie, and fatigue in my first chapter.

26. Eisenstein, *Eisenstein on Disney,* 21.

27. Ibid., 22.

28. Ibid., 41, 33.

29. Crafton notes of Otto Messmer's Felix the Cat cartoons that "the independent, detachable nature of his limbs acknowledges that these parts actually exist separately as sheets, cels, and cutouts" (Crafton, *Before Mickey,* 343).

30. Vidler, *The Architectural Uncanny,* 11.

31. Mulvey, *Death 24x a Second,* 43.

32. Paul Wells has written that "animation intrinsically provides the opportunity to express the life within drawing/sculpting etc., on its own terms, before expressing the obligation to narrate or make representational associations" (Wells, *Understanding Animation,* 32).

33. Klee, *Pedagogical Notebook,* 16. Klee's comment always makes me think of Crockett Johnson's brilliant *Harold and the Purple Crayon.*

34. The images are constructed in a slightly different order—the seemingly self-generating image of Flip appears in the following order: facial profile, cigar, hair, collar, hair color, and body outline. The image that McCay is seen to draw outlines the collar before the hair; the hair is colored immediately, and Flip's costume is given more detail. The resulting drawings, however, are confoundingly similar—it is difficult to say with assurance that they are, in fact, different pictures.

35. It's interesting that the earliest films featuring animated drawings appeared in 1908 (Cohl) and 1911 (McCay), just as the cinema of attractions yielded to a system dominated by transparent codes of narrative, a "narrator-system" in which the story seemed to tell itself. It could be argued that animation, as a novel form, recapitulated, with a delay of only a few years, the trajectory of live-action cinema. Early animation was performative, exhibitionistic, and explicitly a "trick." As the form became less novel, and as it moved into mass, assembly-line production, it was easily assimilated into structures of narration and diegetic homogeneity.

36. He has become what Norman Klein refers to as the *controller* figure (more below).

37. This is very different from the slow-motion footage in *Henri Matisse,* a 1946 film by

François Campaux and Jean Cassou, in which one sees the act of decision, and about which Yves-Alain Bois writes: "Each one of his strokes and lines is like the end of a dance in which his hand has surveyed the space" (Bois, *Painting as Model,* 46). Matisse himself found the footage a revelation that left him "feeling naked."

38. In the lightning-sketch film, as Crafton describes it, "the artist makes his drawings and they become endowed with the magic ability to move, spontaneously change their shape, or become 'real' (three-dimensional). They may attempt to assert their independence from the artist by teasing him or by refusing to be eradicated" (Crafton, *Before Mickey,* 48–50).

39. Gorky, "The Kingdom of Shadows," 10.

40. Carroll, *Theorizing the Moving Image,* 64.

41. Picasso will continue to add figures and layers until the first trio is almost entirely obscured, while McCay will simply begin another picture once his three figures are complete.

42. See Bazin, "A Bergsonian Film: *The Picasso Mystery.*"

43. The promotional material for *Le mystère Picasso* states: "Clouzot wished that the viewer would come to believe that the real world is in black and white, while painting opens us to a wealth of color" ("Henri-Georges Clouzot's *The Mystery of Picasso,*" 5). This is a strategy similar to the one employed by Michael Powell and Emeric Pressburger in their earlier film, *A Matter of Life and Death* (1946), in which the afterlife is presented in gray tones while the earth below is rendered in the most saturated of Technicolor palates.

44. Bazin, "A Bergsonian Film," 215.

45. Ibid., 211.

46. Ibid., 212, 214.

47. Picasso, belching smoke, is something of a "painting locomotive." See chapter 5 for more on this phrase of Van Gogh's.

48. In the later Out of the Inkwell cartoons, Max Fleischer interacts only with Ko-Ko, and any picture he produces comes immediately to life, eliding entirely the laborious process of producing animation.

49. This "cheating director" anticipates the gamesmanship of Orson Welles's *F for Fake,* which concluded with a tale of Pablo Picasso!

50. Or does it? it looks very much like the beginning of the next image is produced with the same real-time technique used in the preceding sequences, but then slabs of color appear—not the oils, though, that we were expecting but watercolors. Over this base, finally, do dabs and strokes of oil paint appear.

51. "Henri-Georges Clouzot's *The Mystery of Picasso,*" 4.

52. Klein, *Seven Minutes,* 37.

53. A few Warner Bros. cartoons ended with Bugs Bunny, rather than Porky, bursting through the drum and saying, "And that's the end!"

54. Ngai, *Ugly Feelings,* 100–101.

55. Bazin, "A Bergsonian Film," 213.

56. Ibid.

57. Bergson, *An Introduction to Metaphysics,* 11.

58. This sense of the animated image as radically unstable and destabilizing informs writ-

ings by such theorists of animation as Alan Cholodenko, Broadfoot and Butler, Kristen Thompson, and Vivian Sobchack. It should be said, however, that *Little Nemo* is less a suspense film than is *Le mystère Picasso*. Because McCay is drawing familiar characters, the audience is in less doubt as to when the picture will be finished. Picasso is more unpredictable.

59. Crowther, "Artist at Work."

60. I would also put *Gertie* in this camp, mostly because of the vivacity of its vibrating lines.

61. Crafton, *Before Mickey*, 120.

62. Deleuze, *Cinema 2*, xi.

63. Although Picasso seems to defer to Clouzot ("if you want"), he clearly, and often capriciously, sets the parameters for his work, whereas McCay is operating in a more Taylorist mode, tied to the production of a quantifiable number of images. Thanks to Annie Ronan for this observation.

64. "Henri-Georges Clouzot's *The Mystery of Picasso*," 6 (emphasis mine).

65. Clarke, *Profiles of the Future*, 21.

66. Crafton writes, "The 'hand of the artist' disappears, its place now occupied by characters who become agents of his will and ideas and through which his presence is known. They are his amanuensis" (Crafton, *Before Mickey*, 298).

67. Ibid.

68. Ibid., 57.

69. Ngai, *Ugly Feelings*, 113.

70. Stewart, *On Longing*, 60.

71. George Herriman once stated that his creation, Krazy Kat, was "a spirit—a pixie—free to butt into anything" (quoted in McDonnell, O'Connell, and de Havenon, *Krazy Kat*, 54).

72. Krauss, "'The Rock,'" 16.

73. Castle, *The Female Thermometer*, 80.

74. Krauss, "'The Rock,'" 16.

75. My own feeling is that Krauss puts too much weight on the word *revolt*. From Eisenstein's overheated pen, the word doesn't bother me very much, but in the context of twenty-first-century scholarship it becomes more problematic—too reminiscent, perhaps, of *subversion*, a word overused within the academy (along with another favorite: *crisis*). If we soften Eisenstein's rhetoric, and are willing to place Disney's animation in a more dialogic relation to other aspects of culture, then the films do become easier to understand as playfully toxic side effects or little pockets of resistance. After all, Eisenstein writes, in anticipation of Bachelard: "But the revolt is lyrical. The revolt is a daydream" (Eisenstein, *Eisenstein on Disney*, 3–4).

76. Spiegelman, "Forms Stretched to Their Limits," 80.

77. Schaffer, "Animation 1," 462.

78. Broadfoot and Butler, "The Illusion of Illusion," 277.

79. Ibid., 287.

80. Ngai, *Ugly Feelings*, 117.

81. This idea is explored by Kenneth Gross in *The Dream of the Moving Statue*.

4. DISOBEDIENT MACHINES

1. Klein, *Seven Minutes*, 6, 75, 37.

2. Or, as Leonard Cohen put it, with unintentional applicability to the American short cartoon, "to determine who will serve and who will eat" ("Democracy").

3. Schaffer, "Animation 1," 463.

4. Curiously, with the addition of the live-action sequences to the animation, there was no longer a need for the "live" McCay—he was superseded once again.

5. Bloom, "Pygmalionesque Delusions and Illusions of Movement," 292.

6. Vidler, *The Architectural Uncanny*, 3.

7. Todorov, *The Fantastic*, 46.

8. For more on the representations of scientists, mad and otherwise, see Haynes, *From Faust to Strangelove*.

9. And, of course, Shelley is played by Elsa Lanchester, who will also appear as the monster's bride. The creator becomes the creation. Also, note the metonymic shift in the name *Frankenstein*: what was once the creator's name has, over the years, become the name of the creation.

10. Čapek, "R. U. R. (Rossum's Universal Robots)," 99.

11. Quoted in Freud, "The 'Uncanny,' " 202.

12. Stewart, *On Longing*, 70, 73.

13. Ibid., 74, 70.

14. Vidler, *The Architectural Uncanny*, 11.

15. Mulvey, *Death 24x a Second*, 46.

16. Wood, *Edison's Eve*, 183.

17. Manovich, *The Language of New Media*, 298.

18. Mulvey, *Death 24x a Second*, 52.

19. At first glance Disney's *Pinocchio* would seem to belong to the realm of the playful and the uncanny rather than the sublime and terrifying—Pinocchio is no monster. But when one considers the dark consequences of the little wooden boy's behavior, it becomes arguably the most traumatic tale of all.

20. See Douglas, *Purity and Danger*; and Carroll, *The Philosophy of Horror, or, Paradoxes of the Heart*.

21. There is an admixture of live action and animation at the end of *Gertie the Dinosaur*, but in this instance it is the real person (McCay) who crosses over *into* the animated realm—this clearly does not pose the same threat as Kong's unboundaried rampage.

22. Perhaps Pinocchio's real character flaw is that he's too trusting rather than that he's dishonest or disobedient.

23. Thanks to David Fresko for this suggestion.

24. See Nesbet, "Inanimations." Esther Leslie has linked Walter Benjamin's concept, introduced in his essay "Karl Krauss," of the *unmensch*—a barbarian, an un-person—to his take on Mickey Mouse, and we can find hints of this surviving in *Pinocchio* but now wedded to a narrative that chronicles Pinocchio's attempt to move beyond that status. See Leslie, *Hollywood Flatlands*, 81. Thanks to Jim Thomas for this observation.

25. Riskin, "Introduction," 1. It can also be understood as an image of the transfer of energy from animator to animated . . .

26. Mention should be made of an intermediate text here, the 1938 film adaptation of *Pygmalion,* directed by Anthony Asquith and Leslie Howard, and featuring two superb performances from Howard as Higgins and Wendy Hiller as Eliza. Shaw wrote a major new scene, the ball that is the scene of the mutual triumph of Eliza and Higgins (over the oily linguistic challenger, Karpathy), and this scene is transposed, quite faithfully, into *My Fair Lady.*

27. Goldstone, preface to *Pygmalion and My Fair Lady,* ix (emphasis mine).

28. Brooks, *Flesh and Machines,* 173, 174.

29. Ibid., 174–75.

30. Provocatively, near the book's conclusion, Hadaly says to Lord Ewald, Edison's friend on whose behalf she has been created, "Attribute a being to me, affirm that I am! Reinforce me with your self. And then suddenly I will come to life in your eyes, to precisely the extent that your creative Good Will has penetrated me" (Villiers de l'Isle-Adam, *The Future Eve,* 726). This seems to anticipate Rodney Brooks and Eliza Doolittle, but here Hadaly's being is largely a function of a man's projected desire, not the recognition of a shared humanity. In this, Hadaly is something like Olympia, the mechanical doll at the center of Hoffmann's "The Sandman."

31. For the story of Edison's talking doll see the third chapter of Gaby Wood's *Edison's Eve.*

32. This paragraph is entirely indebted to my colleague Henry Lowood, with whom I've been teaching a course on "Humans and Machines" at Stanford University for the past few years.

33. See Cavell, *Pursuits of Happiness.* The 1938 film adaptation introduced the ending in which Eliza returns to Higgins, repeating her line about having washed her face and hands, so it can be fairly said that this is the version that introduces the possibility of romance. However, this version also retains far more of Shaw's original dialogue in which that possibility is precluded; its inclusion thus feels a bit arbitrary. Further, Higgins dominates this production as he did the stage play; Eliza's experience is not as central as it will be in *My Fair Lady.*

34. Any simple assumptions about the work's gender politics are further complicated by the reoccurring queerness in the odd and hilarious homoerotic bachelor life of Higgins and Pickering, much more emphatic in *My Fair Lady* than in *Pygmalion.* My favorite moment:

> *Higgins:* Where does one go to buy a lady's gown?
>
> *Pickering:* Whiteley's of course.
>
> *Higgins:* How do you know that?
>
> *Pickering:* Common knowledge.

Common for whom? is the question that always comes to mind. The film, of course, is directed by George Cukor, a tightly closeted gay director (one biography is subtitled, provocatively for our purposes, *A Double Life*).

35. Koestenbaum, *The Queen's Throat,* 11.

36. Quoted in Bukatman, "Paralysis in Motion," 190.

37. For an analogous history see Jenkins, " 'Shall We Make It for New York or for Distribution?' "

38. Ngai, *Ugly Feelings,* 91.

39. The echo of live-action comedy isn't unique to Tashlin's work, of course—much the same thing could be said of the teaming of Bugs and Daffy in such films as *Ali Baba Bunny,*

directed by Chuck Jones. But with Tashlin it does seem to portend his later work with figures like Bob Hope or Jerry Lewis.

40. What Henry Jenkins has called the "vaudeville aesthetic" of early sound cinema allowed for breaking out of character, addressing the audience, bringing the narrative to a halt, and some of this survives in the Martin-and-Lewis films. See Jenkins, " 'Shall We Make It for New York or for Distribution?' "

41. See Lewis, *The Total Film-Maker.*

42. See Bukatman, "Paralysis in Motion."

43. See Deleuze, *Cinema 2,* 61–63.

44. McLuhan, *Understanding Media,* xi.

45. See Bukatman, *Terminal Identity.* As I used it, *terminal identity,* a phrase borrowed from William Burroughs (McLuhan's evil twin), referred to both the demise of traditional notions of the subject and the rise of new subjectivities around the pervasion of electronic technology. While many of the examples that I used in the first chapter of that book dated from the mid-1960s, Lewis had temporarily fallen off my radar.

46. Krutnik, *Inventing Jerry Lewis,* 39.

47. McLuhan, *Understanding Media,* 241. The phrase "the national chest" fairly begs for some Tashlinesque response.

48. Ibid. This is, we must understand, written *avant la karaoke.*

49. In an email Greg Smith pointed out to me an amusing superhero connection here, in the form of Andy Kaufman's own "dummy act," in which he lip-synched the chorus of the theme song from *Mighty Mouse.*

50. Krutnik, *Inventing Jerry Lewis,* 159.

51. Levy, *Rat Pack Confidential,* 42.

52. McLuhan, *Understanding Media,* 243, 373.

53. *Who's Minding the Store?* introduced a celebrated routine in which Jerry types on an invisible machine to the tune of Leroy Anderson's sprightly piece from 1950, "The Typewriter." At one point Jerry misses the cue for a carriage return, snaps his fingers with a "darn it" expression, and goes back into the bit. An accident? (Once again, one wonders what it would take to do a retake.) But the routine became a perennial of Lewis's stage act, and he "flubs" the cue every time. Scenes of breakdown or staged breakdowns?

54. McLuhan, *Understanding Media,* 81–82.

55. Ibid., 253.

56. Ibid.

57. Comedy teams were always another story.

58. See Carroll, "Keaton: Film Acting as Action." For more on the representation of craft in the age of industrialization see the previous chapter.

59. See my essay "Paralysis in Motion." Any comments about Jerry's lack of physical control must always except the moment of dance when a glorious, temporary reconciliation between body and stimulus is effected.

60. McLuhan, *Understanding Media,* 253.

61. To paraphrase Martin Short's brilliant late-Jerry parody on SCTV: even if it was the same it would be entirely different because of the earlier thing . . .

62. Thanks to Daniel Hoffman-Schwartz for this suggestion.

63. Deleuze, *Cinema 2*, 63.

64. Mention should be made of that other comedian of the electronic medium, Jim Carrey, about whom Vivian Sobchack has written very effectively in "Thinking through Jim Carrey." Carrey, in such films as *The Cable Guy*, seems to channel the full range of popular culture through his own bodily performance. But Carrey is a self-professed control freak of a different order: one gets the sense that if Carrey did five takes, he'd hit every mark precisely every time, a level of precision that Lewis could not (and perhaps might not want to) attain. Lewis seems to create in the moment, while Carrey provides a more carefully mapped performance.

5. LABOR AND ANIMATEDNESS

1. Ngai, *Ugly Feelings*, 93.

2. Nemerov, *The Body of Raphaelle Peale*, 26, 22. Recall the statement by Charles Brockden Brown: "To his strong and vivid fancy, there is scarcely a piece of mere unanimated matter existing in the universe" (ibid., 22).

3. Ngai, *Ugly Feelings*, 96.

4. Van Gogh, *The Letters of Vincent van Gogh*, 174.

5. Pollock's first solo show was in 1943, and in 1947 he developed his large-scale drip paintings. His fatal car crash occurred in 1956—the same year that *Lust for Life* was released, and one year after James Dean's similar demise.

6. See Guilbaut, "Post-War Painting Games." These ideas are elaborated in his *How New York Stole the Idea of Modern Art*.

7. Rosenberg, "The American Action Painters," 25.

8. See Belton, *Widescreen Cinema*.

9. Rosenberg, "The American Action Painters," 28.

10. Leja, *Reframing Abstract Expressionism*, 4, 7.

11. Clark, "In Defense of Abstract Expressionism," 382. Clark revives Clement Greenberg's sense of the word *kitsch* to describe Abstract Expressionist production: "Kitsch is manic. Above all, it is rigid with the exaltation of art. It believes in art the way artists are supposed to—to the point of absurdity, to the point where the cult of art becomes a new philistinism" (396). *Lust for Life* gives us Van Gogh as the avatar of this cult, this exaltation. And if, in the terms of Hollywood melodrama, it goes "too far" and reaches into the realm of impassioned caricature, this, too, can be seen as analogous to the "new philistinism" of Abstract Expressionism.

12. Ibid., 387, 397.

13. Leja, *Reframing Abstract Expressionism*, 9.

14. Leja notes of the abstract expressionists that "the subject of the artists was the artist as subject" (ibid., 7).

15. See Sobchack, " 'Surge and Splendor.' "

16. Ibid., 24.

17. See Berger, *Ways of Seeing*, 80.

18. Naremore, "Vincente Meets Vincent," 151.

19. Sobchack, " 'Surge and Splendor,' " 28.

20. See Elsaesser, "Tales of Sound and Fury."

21. Leja, *Reframing Abstract Expressionism,* 109.

22. Leja links Pollock's terse language to noir, but his "spare use of adjectives, tough guy idiom ('I've knocked around some in California') and reticence" are at least as typical of westerns—Pollock did, after all, hail from Cody, Wyoming.

23. Van Gogh, *The Letters of Vincent van Gogh,* 144.

24. Stone, *Lust for Life,* 156. One thinks of Jonathan Shields's confrontation with Georgia Lorrison in *The Bad and the Beautiful,* in which a flood of words pours forth until the male character breaks down into an inarticulate rage of self-loathing.

25. Van Gogh, *The Letters of Vincent van Gogh,* 306–7.

26. Elsaesser, "Tales of Sound and Fury," 52.

27. Some examples: Vincent's earnest but inept sermon on humility, the God of the clergy "dead as a doornail" to him, and his own analysis of one of his final paintings ("But there is no sadness in this death, this one takes place in a broad daylight with a sun flooding everything with a light of pure gold" [Van Gogh, *The Letters of Vincent van Gogh,* 124, 452]).

28. For more on the long-take aesthetics of Minnelli see McElhaney, "Medium Shot Gestures."

29. As Naremore notes, "In place of Parisian nightlife, *Lust for Life* offers the visual spectacle of Van Gogh's own work" (Naremore, "Vincente Meets Vincent," 139).

30. Van Gogh, *The Letters of Vincent van Gogh,* 399.

31. Quoted in Clark, "In Defense of Abstract Expressionism," 385.

32. Pollock, "Crows, Blossoms and Lust for Death," 232.

33. Ibid., 230.

34. Ibid., 231.

35. Ibid., 231–32.

36. I am of course invoking Thomas Elsaesser's central dictum that Minnelli's melodramas represent the tragic flip side of his utopic musicals. See Elsaesser, "Vincente Minnelli."

37. Guilbaut, *How New York Stole the Idea of Modern Art,* 47–48, 31.

38. In 1980 Art Spiegelman did a comic for *RAW* titled "Two-Fisted Painters Action Adventures."

39. See Krauss, *The Optical Unconscious,* 244; Bataille, "Sacrificial Mutilation and the Severed Ear of Vincent van Gogh," 61–72; and Landau, "The Wild One."

40. Hoberman, "Action Figures," www.villagevoice.com/film/0107,hoberman,22216,20.html. Hoberman adds that Ed Harris, director and star of *Pollock,* is, of course, "a product of the same Actors Studio epitomized by Brando; there are multiple Marlons in his inarticulate, tormented, highly physical, man's-man performance."

41. Van Gogh, *The Letters of Vincent van Gogh,* 178.

42. Ibid., 73.

43. This is another reason why I cannot accept Griselda Pollock's argument that, in the Arles montage, "pure perception slides effortlessly into art."

44. Naremore, "Vincente Meets Vincent," 144. It's worth noting that Douglas here and in *The Bad and the Beautiful* (in which he plays a driven movie producer) gives us two men obsessed with *making pictures.*

45. Cited in Krohn, "Specters at the Feast," 58.

46. Van Gogh, *The Letters of Vincent van Gogh,* 347.

47. They are also reminiscent of Roy Lichtenstein's large-scale renderings of brushstrokes produced a few years later.

48. It is no secret that the Abstract Expressionists were fascinated by Van Gogh: the drama of his life, his commitment to the purity of his aesthetic and ethos, the complete merging of self with art. In a lecture at Stanford University in 1996, for example, T. J. Clark pointed out that Willem de Kooning's 1958–59 canvas *Suburb in Havana,* with its dark slashes against a yellow background, is a direct quotation of Van Gogh's final painting, *Crows in a Wheatfield.* And the Falkenberg-Namuth film practically begins with an homage to Van Gogh, via a shot of Pollock's paint-spattered shoes that clearly evokes Van Gogh's *Peasant Shoes.* Fredric Jameson has traced the trajectory from modernism to postmodernism in the distance between *Peasant Shoes* and Warhol's *Diamond Dust Shoes* (1980); Pollock's shoes fit neatly between these. Van Gogh depicts worker's shoes, worn and lived, while Warhol creates abstracted, ornamental, objects—artist's shoes. But, I would argue, with Pollock's shoes, the worker's shoes and the artist's shoes are one; art and labor belong to the same realm of materiality and production. See Jameson, *Postmodernism, or, The Cultural Logic of Late Capitalism,* chap. 1.

49. Frank, *Jackson Pollock,* 79.

50. Krauss, *The Optical Unconscious,* 302.

51. Mattis, "Morton Feldman," www.cnvill.net/mfmattis.htm. I would add that in certain shots Pollock resembles Bob Fosse a bit.

52. Rosenberg, "The American Action Painters," 27–28.

53. Broadfoot and Butler, "The Illusion of Illusion," 288.

54. This is preceded by a shot of Pollock's shadow looming on a wall, suggesting both Murnau's *Nosferatu* and Astaire's "Bojangles of Harlem" dance from *Swing Time.*

55. Greenberg had noted in 1939 that the avant-garde was not immune to the blandishments of kitsch, a profitable mode: "Ambitious writers and artists will modify their work under the pressure of kitsch" (Greenberg, "Avant-Garde and Kitsch," 11). On some level Namuth's film of Pollock is kitsch to the core: Pollock the iconoclast painting for the camera and, through glass, even painting *to* the camera. Pollock here is perhaps kitsch in Greenberg's sense, whereas Minnelli's work stands closer to the petty-bourgeois populism of Clark's "vulgarity."

56. Rosenberg, "The American Action Painters," 28.

57. Van Gogh, *The Letters of Vincent van Gogh,* 178. Pollock: "I want to express my feelings rather than just illustrate them."

58. Naremore, "Vincente Meets Vincent," 147.

59. Rosenberg, "The American Action Painters," 27.

6. PLAYING SUPERHEROES

1. Morrison and Quitely, *All-Star Superman.*

2. Like Harold's purple crayon, the wand is another nascent power ring and another overlap between superheroes and children's stories.

3. Heiler, "Red Kryptonite's 9 Dumbest Effects on Superman," www.toplessrobot.com/2009/04/red_kryptonites_9_dumbest_effects_on_superman.php.

4. *New York Herald,* March 4, 1906.

5. Mxyzptlk actually dates from quite a bit earlier in Superman's history but became a mainstay of Silver Age stories.

6. Morrison, *Supergods,* 70, 71. Morrison's often intriguing memoir-meditation appeared as I was completing the writing of this book and so receives less attention than it deserves. *Superman* scribe Mark Waid has written that Weisinger solicited story ideas from the children in his Long Island suburban neighborhood, which led to stories of Superman as a fireman, or a millionaire, or anything else the kids wanted to see. Recall that McCay, too, solicited reader ideas for *Dream of the Rarebit Fiend.* Waid is cited in de Haven, *Our Hero,* 117. De Haven also points out that these are some of the more emotionally resonant stories in the Superman corpus; these characters now had memories and histories, and subtler motivations guided the stories, often toward an understated pathos (116–17).

7. Ibid., 70, 69.

8. Eco, "The Myth of Superman," 153.

9. For more on this see my "The Boys in the Hoods."

10. See Caillois, *Man, Play, and Games,* chap. 2, "The Classification of Games."

11. Huizinga, *Homo Ludens,* 13.

12. Caillois, *Man, Play, and Games,* 23, 19.

13. Ibid., 20.

14. Ibid., 23.

15. Morrison et al., "Secret Origins," 97. In an earlier essay I considered the "reality-morphing" that occurs in Alan Moore's own Silver Age homage, *Supreme. Animal Man* predates Moore's book. See Bukatman, "Taking Shape." Moore imagined what the endless process of revision and rebooting must feel like to the inhabitants of those shifting diegeses.

16. Morrison et al., "Spooks," 130–31.

17. Morrison et al., "Fox on the Run," 34.

18. Morrison et al., "Purification Day," 157.

19. Morrison et al., "Deus Ex Machina."

20. In *Flex Mentallo* Morrison makes a similar statement about the grim 'n' gritty superhero fad: "Only a bitter little adolescent boy could confuse realism with pessimism" (Morrison and Quitely, *Flex Mentallo,* no. 4, 17).

21. Morrison et al., "A New Science of Life," 41.

22. Morrison and Weston, *The Filth,* 58–61.

23. Much of this metatextuality was also being played through, and much more playfully, in John Byrne's nearly contemporaneous *She-Hulk.* Late for an appointment, the title character simply stepped from a panel set in her apartment to a panel set in her office—a real time-saver! Another shortcut involved burrowing through one of the advertising pages in order to jump ahead in the story.

24. Morrison and Mahnke, *Final Crisis,* n.p.

25. This is a variation of Michael Moorcock's "roads between the worlds."

26. Morrison and Murphy, *Joe the Barbarian.*

27. Iser, *The Act of Reading,* 296.

28. Ibid., 280, 285, 279 (my emphases).

29. Ibid., 295. Christopher Sorrentino refers to the task of filling in his Marvel collec-

tion as "a scholarly experience. To work my way back through Marvel was to grab hold of, understand, and form opinions about a literary canon. It was to intuit something about the nature of literary history, to see, literally graphically, the tumultuous effects of innovation on an art form" (Sorrentino, "The Ger Sheker," 62).

30. Barry, *What It Is,* 51.

31. O'Brien, "Nick Fury's Dream," 128.

32. Iser, *The Act of Reading,* 287.

33. Frere-Jones, "Drablands," 10.

34. O'Brien, "Nick Fury's Dream," 120.

35. Lee and Kirby, "This Man . . . This Monster," *Fantastic Four* 51 (1966), 13.

36. O'Brien, "The Return of Burt Bacharach," 17.

37. O'Brien, "The Lonely Sea," 232.

38. O'Brien, "Nick Fury's Dream," 124.

39. O'Brien, "The Return of Burt Bacharach," 17.

40. Ibid., 17–18.

41. O'Brien, "Nick Fury's Dream," 122–23.

42. O'Brien, "The Lonely Sea," 202.

43. Sorrentino, "The Ger Sheker," 69.

44. Updike, "Mixed Messages," 138.

45. Hodgman, "Righteousness in Tights."

46. Ibid. Hodgman is clearly a member of the superhero-reading tribe, which, for me, tempers his sarcasm.

47. See Lethem, "Who's Afraid of Doctor Strange?"

48. Carrier, *The Aesthetics of Comics;* Brooker, *Batman Unmasked;* Jenkins, "Death-Defying Superheroes." For my own gestures in my own direction see Bukatman, "X-Bodies."

49. For the tip of that iceberg see works by R. Crumb, Harvey Pekar, Art Spiegelman, Julie Doucet, Joe Matt, or Jeffrey Brown. I am using the term *autobiography* loosely to incorporate naturalist comics sagas about people much like the authors themselves—low-rent twenty-somethings struggling to survive within a mundane world of first loves and dead-end day jobs.

50. O'Brien, "Nick Fury's Dream," 123. O'Brien's language evokes that of Wallace Stevens: "The exquisite truth is to know that it is a fiction and that you believe in it willingly" (Stevens, *Opus Posthumous,* 163). Thanks to Joe Abbott for spotting the similarity.

51. O'Brien, "Nick Fury's Dream," 124.

52. See Jenkins, " 'Shall We Make It for New York or for Distribution?' "

53. Dyer, "Judy Garland and Gay Men," 154.

54. See Michelson, "Bodies in Space."

55. Ebert, "Spider-Man," 568. Thanks to Joe Abbott for steering me to this.

56. Furthermore, Greg Smith points out (in an email) that the mask covers his face—a major locus of identification and performance in the cinema, further driving a wedge between performer and audience.

57. Please note that I am not making the argument that film's essence can be found in the indexical imprint of reality that it provides; rather, I am arguing that this genre, which can speak so eloquently to bodily possibility, loses something when the body is no longer real.

58. See Bukatman, "Taking Shape."

59. Chung, "The Worlding of Affect."

60. A digital body in a virtual world: in both respects the superhero film inherits from cyberpunk—but represents a rather recuperative mainstreaming of cyberpunk's salient concerns about cyberspaces and postmodern fragmentation—new ways of being and of seeing.

61. In the words of Yunior, the narrator of Junot Diaz's novel *The Brief, Wondrous Life of Oscar Wao:* "With great power comes great responsibility—*bullshit*" (94).

62. On the other hand, the narrative structures of such films as *The Dark Knight* and *Spider-Man 3* are so uncontrolled as make the term oxymoronic. Overloaded with multiple villains and deprived of any sense of a narrative arc, these are very messy films. But mess is not necessarily chaos. Sometimes a mess is just a mess.

63. Millhauser, "The Little Kingdom of J. Franklin Payne," 107.

64. Sean Collins made this observation on The Savage Critics blog. See Collins, "Favorites: *All-Star Superman.*"

65. Quoted at "All-Star Superman," Wikipedia, http://en.wikipedia.org/wiki/All_Star_ Superman.

66. See Bukatman, "The Boys in the Hoods"; and Bukatman, "X-Bodies."

67. Morrison and Quitely, *All-Star Superman.*

68. Smith, "All Star Memories: Grant Morrison on All Star Superman, 1."

69. Smith, "All Star Memories: Grant Morrison on All Star Superman, 6."

70. In an ode to Red Kryptonite, Flex encounters a mysterious substance that affects him in different ways. He wonders which it will be: "Shocking Pink Mentallium, under the influence of which I was invariably invited to explore complex issues of gender and sexuality? Silver Mentallium, which robbed me of my sense of humor?" (Morrison and Quitely, *Flex Mentallo,* no. 2, 6).

71. Morrison and Quitely, *Flex Mentallo,* no. 4, 11. Long tied up in legal limbo (Flex was something of a parody of Charles Atlas and his famous "The Insult That Made a Man Out of Mac" comics advertisement), *Flex Mentallo* finally appeared in a collected edition in 2011.

72. Morrison and Quitely, *Flex Mentallo,* no. 4, 14.

73. Ibid., 22.

74. Morrison, *All-Star Superman.*

75. On further reflection one realizes that Superman has created *them.*

76. The two greatest creations of midwestern Jewry: Superman and Bob Dylan.

BIBLIOGRAPHY

Abrams, M. H. *The Mirror and the Lamp: Romantic Theory and the Critical Tradition.* London: Oxford University Press, 1953.

Bachelard, Gaston. *The Poetics of Reverie: Childhood, Language, and the Cosmos.* Boston: Beacon, 1971.

———. *The Poetics of Space.* Translated by Maria Jolas. Boston: Beacon, 1964.

———. *The Right to Dream.* Translated by J. A. Underwood. Edited by Joanne H. Stroud. Dallas, TX: Dallas Institute of Humanities and Culture, 1971.

Baker, Nicholson, and Margaret Brentano. *The World on Sunday: Graphic Art in Joseph Pulitzer's Newspaper (1898–1911).* New York: Bulfinch, 2005.

Barry, Lynda. *What It Is.* Montreal: Drawn and Quarterly, 2008.

Bataille, Georges. "Sacrificial Mutilation and the Severed Ear of Vincent Van Gogh." In *Visions of Excess: Selected Writings,* edited by Allan Stoekl, 61–72. Minneapolis: University of Minnesota Press, 1985.

Baudelaire, Charles. "Richard Wagner and Tannhäuser in Paris." In *The Painter of Modern Life and Other Essays,* edited by Jonathan Mayne, 111–46. New York: Da Capo Press, 1964.

Bazin, André. "A Bergsonian Film: *The Picasso Mystery.*" In *Bazin at Work: Major Essays and Reviews from the Forties and Fifties,* edited by Burt Cardullo, 211–20. London: Routledge, 1997.

———. "Theater and Cinema." In *What Is Cinema?* Edited by Hugh Gray. Vol. 1, 76–124. Berkeley: University of California Press, 1967.

Beard, George M. *American Nervousness, Its Causes and Consequences.* New York: G. P. Putnam's Sons, 1881.

Belting, Hans. *Likeness and Presence: A History of the Image before the Era of Art.* Translated by Edmund Jephcott. Chicago: University of Chicago Press, 1994.

Belton, John. *Widescreen Cinema.* Cambridge, MA: Harvard University Press, 1992.

Benjamin, Walter. "A Glimpse into the World of Children's Books." In *Selected Writings,* Vol. 1,

1913–1926, edited by Marcus Bullock and Michael W. Jennings, 414–43. Cambridge, MA: Harvard University Press, 1996.

———. "Old Forgotten Children's Books." In *Selected Writings,* Vol. 1, *1913–1926,* edited by Marcus Bullock and Michael W. Jennings, 406–13. Cambridge, MA: Harvard University Press, 1996.

———. "One-Way Street." In *Selected Writings,* Vol. 1, *1913–1926,* edited by Marcus Bullock and Michael W. Jennings, 444–88. Cambridge, MA: Harvard University Press, 1996.

Berger, John. *Ways of Seeing.* Middlesex: Penguin, 1972.

Bergson, Henri. *An Introduction to Metaphysics.* Translated by T. E. Hulme. New York: G. P. Putnam's Sons, 1912.

———. *Laughter: An Essay on the Meaning of the Comic.* Translated by Cloudesley Brereton and Fred Rothwell. New York: Macmillan, 1914.

Bettelheim, Bruno. *The Uses of Enchantment: The Meaning and Importance of Fairy Tales.* New York: Vintage, 1977.

Blackbeard, Bill, ed. *R. F. Outcault's "The Yellow Kid": A Centennial Celebration of the Kid Who Started the Comics.* Northampton, MA: Kitchen Sink, 1995.

———. "The Yellow Kid, the Yellow Decade." In *R. F. Outcault's "The Yellow Kid": A Centennial Celebration of the Kid Who Started the Comics,* 17–136. Northampton, MA: Kitchen Sink, 1995.

Blackmore, Tim. "McCay's Mechanical Muse: Engineering Comic-Strip Dreams." *Journal of Popular Culture* 32, no. 1 (1998): 15–38.

Bloom, Michelle E. "Pygmalionesque Delusions and Illusions of Movement: Animation from Hoffmann to Truffaut." *Comparative Literature* 52, no. 4 (2000): 291–320.

Bois, Yves-Alain. *Painting as Model.* Cambridge, MA: MIT Press, 1990.

Bouldin, Joanna. "The Body, Animation and the Real: Race, Reality and the Rotoscope in Betty Boop." Paper presented at the "Affective Encounters: Rethinking Embodiment in Feminist Media Studies" conference, Turku, 2001.

Brakhage, Stan. *Metaphors on Vision.* New York: Film Culture, 1976.

Braun, Marta. *Picturing Time: The Work of Etienne-Jules Marey (1830–1904).* Chicago: University of Chicago Press, 1992.

Broadfoot, Keith, and Rex Butler. "The Illusion of Illusion." In *The Illusion of Life: Essays on Animation,* edited by Alan Cholodenko, 263–98. Sydney: Power Publications, 1991.

Brooker, Will. *Batman Unmasked: Analyzing a Cultural Icon.* New York: Continuum, 2001.

Brooks, Rodney. *Flesh and Machines: How Robots Will Change Us.* New York: Vintage, 2002.

Bryson, Norman. *Vision and Painting: The Logic of the Gaze.* New Haven, CT: Yale University Press, 1983.

Bukatman, Scott. "The Boys in the Hoods: A Song of the Urban Superhero." In *Matters of Gravity: Special Effects and Supermen in the 20th Century,* 184–223. Durham, NC: Duke University Press, 2003.

———. "Paralysis in Motion: Jerry Lewis's Life as a Man." In *Comedy/Cinema/Theory,* edited by Andrew S. Horton, 188–205. Berkeley: University of California Press, 1991.

———. "Taking Shape: Morphing and the Performance of Self." In *Matters of Gravity: Special Effects and Supermen in the 20th Century,* 133–56. Durham, NC: Duke University Press, 2003.

————. *Terminal Identity: The Virtual Subject in Postmodern Science Fiction.* Durham, NC: Duke University Press, 1993.

————. "X-Bodies: The Torment of the Mutant Superhero." In *Matters of Gravity: Special Effects and Supermen in the 20th Century,* 48–78. Durham, NC: Duke University Press, 2003.

Burch, Noël. *Life to Those Shadows.* Berkeley: University of California Press, 1990.

Busiek, Kurt, Brent Anderson, and Alex Ross. *Astro City: Life in the Big City.* La Jolla, CA: Homage Comics, 1996.

Caillois, Roger. *Man, Play, and Games.* Translated by Meyer Barash. Champaign: University of Illinois Press, 2001.

Campbell, W. Joseph. *The Year That Defined American Journalism: 1897 and the Clash of Paradigms.* New York: Routledge, 2006.

Canemaker, John. *Winsor McCay: His Life and Art.* New York: Abbeville Press, 1987.

Čapek, Karel. "R. U. R. (Rossum's Universal Robots)." In *Toward the Radical Center: A Karel Čapek Reader,* edited by Peter Kussi, 34–109. North Haven, CT: Catbird, 1990.

Carrier, David. *The Aesthetics of Comics.* University Park: Pennsylvania State University Press, 2000.

Carroll, Noël. "Keaton: Film Acting as Action." In *Interpreting the Moving Image,* 44–63. Cambridge, UK: Cambridge University Press, 1998.

————. *The Philosophy of Horror, or, Paradoxes of the Heart.* New York: Routledge, 1990.

————. *Theorizing the Moving Image.* Cambridge, UK: Cambridge University Press, 1996.

Castle, Terry. *The Female Thermometer: 18th-Century Culture and the Invention of the Uncanny.* New York: Oxford University Press, 1995.

Cavell, Stanley. *Pursuits of Happiness: The Hollywood Comedy of Remarriage.* Cambridge, MA: Harvard University Press, 1981.

Chabon, Michael. *The Amazing Adventures of Kavalier & Clay.* New York: Random House, 2000.

Cholodenko, Alan. "Introduction." In *The Illusion of Life: Essays on Animation,* edited by Alan Cholodenko, 9–36. Sydney: Power Publications, 1991.

————. "Speculations on the Animatic Automaton." In *The Illusion of Life II: More Essays on Animation,* edited by Alan Cholodenko, 486–528. Sydney: Power Publications, 2007.

Chung, Una. "The Worlding of Affect: James Cameron's *Avatar* in Imax 3D." Unpublished essay.

Clark, T. J. "In Defense of Abstract Expressionism." In *Farewell to an Idea: Episodes from a History of Modernism,* 371–403. New Haven, CT: Yale University Press, 1999.

Clarke, Arthur C. *Profiles of the Future: An Inquiry into the Limits of the Possible.* New York: Harper and Row, 1958.

Clifford, Helen, and Eric Turner. "Modern Metal." In *Art Nouveau, 1890–1914,* edited by Paul Greenhalgh, 220–35. London: V and A Publications, 2000.

Cohen, Leonard. "Democracy." *The Future.* Columbia CK 53226, 1992. Compact disc.

Collins, Sean. "Favorites: *All-Star Superman.*" The Savage Critics. March 11, 2010. www.savage critic.com/superman/favorites-all-star-superman/.

Couperie, Pierre. *A History of the Comic Strip.* New York: Crown, 1968.

Crafton, Donald. *Before Mickey: The Animated Film, 1898–1928.* Chicago: University of Chicago Press, 1993.

———. *Emile Cohl, Caricature, and Film.* Princeton, NJ: Princeton University Press, 1990.

Crary, Jonathan. *Suspensions of Perception: Attention, Spectacle, and Modern Culture.* Boston: MIT Press, 2000.

———. *Techniques of the Observer: On Vision and Modernity in the Nineteenth Century.* Cambridge, MA: MIT Press, 1990.

Crow, Heather Ann. "Possessions: Animated Bodies in Mediated Performance." PhD diss. University of California, Berkeley, 2006.

Crowther, Bosley. "Artist at Work; 'The Mystery of Picasso' by Clouzot Arrives at Fine Arts Theatre." *New York Times,* Oct. 8, 1957.

Debord, Guy. *Society of the Spectacle.* Detroit: Black and Red, 1983.

de Haven, Tom. *Our Hero: Superman on Earth.* New Haven, CT: Yale University Press, 2010.

Deleuze, Gilles. *Bergsonism.* New York: Zone, 1991.

———. *Cinema 1: The Movement-Image.* Translated by Hugh Tomlinson and Barbara Habberjam. Minneapolis: University of Minnesota Press, 1986.

———. *Cinema 2: The Time-Image.* Translated by Hugh Tomlinson and Robert Galeta. Minneapolis: University of Minnesota Press, 1989.

Della Vacche, Angela. "Vincente Minnelli's *An American in Paris:* Painting as Psychic Upheaval." In *Cinema and Painting: How Art Is Used in Film,* 13–42. Austin: University of Texas Press, 1996.

De Quincey, Thomas. *The Confessions of an English Opium Eater.* London: J. M. Dent and Sons, 1907.

Diaz, Junot. *The Brief, Wondrous Life of Oscar Wao.* New York: Penguin, 2007.

Douglas, Mary. *Purity and Danger: An Analysis of the Concepts of Pollution and Taboo.* London: Routledge, 1984.

Dyer, Richard. "Judy Garland and Gay Men." In *Heavenly Bodies: Film Stars and Society,* 141–94. Houndmills, Basingstoke: Macmillan, 1986.

Ebert, Roger. "Spider-Man." Review of *Spider-Man.* In *Roger Ebert's Movie Yearbook 2003,* 568–69. Kansas City, MO: Andrews McMeel, 2002.

Eco, Umberto. "The Myth of Superman." In *Arguing Comics: Literary Masters on a Popular Medium,* edited by Jeet Heer and Kent Worcester, 146–64. Jackson: University Press of Mississippi, 2004.

Eisenstein, Sergei. *Eisenstein on Disney.* Translated by Alan Upchurch. Edited by Jay Leyda. Calcutta: Seagull, 1986.

Elsaesser, Thomas. "Tales of Sound and Fury: Observations on the Family Melodrama." In *Home Is Where the Heart Is: Studies in Melodrama and the Woman's Film,* edited by Christine Gledhill, 43–69. London: British Film Institute, 1987.

———. "Vincente Minnelli." In *Vincente Minnelli: The Art of Entertainment,* edited by Joe McElhaney, 79–96. Detroit: Wayne State University Press, 2009.

Epstein, Jean. "Bonjour Cinéma and Other Writings." *Afterimage* 10 (1981): 8–39.

———. "Magnification and Other Writings." *October* 3 (spring 1977): 9–25.

Feiffer, Jules. *The Great Comic Book Heroes.* New York: Dial, 1965.

Fell, John. *Film and the Narrative Tradition.* Berkeley: University of California Press, 1974.

Frank, Elizabeth. *Jackson Pollock.* New York: Abbeville Press, 2001.

Franzen, Jonathan. "The Comfort Zone: Growing Up with Charlie Brown." *New Yorker,* Nov. 29, 2004.

Freedberg, David. *The Power of Images: Studies in the History and Theory of Response.* Chicago: University of Chicago Press, 1991.

Frere-Jones, Sasha. "Drablands." *New Yorker,* May 9, 2005.

Freud, Sigmund. "The 'Uncanny.'" In *Writings on Art and Literature,* 193–233. Stanford, CA: Stanford University Press, 1997.

Goldstone, Richard. Preface to *Pygmalion and My Fair Lady,* vii–ix. New York: Signet Classics, 1975.

Gorky, Maxim. "The Kingdom of Shadows." In *Movies,* edited by Gilbert Adair, 10–13. London: Penguin, 1999.

Greenberg, Clement. "Avant-Garde and Kitsch." In *Art and Culture: Critical Essays,* 3–21. Boston: Beacon, 1961.

Greenhalgh, Paul. "The Cult of Nature." In *Art Nouveau, 1890–1914,* edited by Paul Greenhalgh, 54–71. London: V and A Publications, 2000.

———. "The Style and the Age." In *Art Nouveau, 1890–1914,* edited by Paul Greenhalgh, 14–33. London: V and A Publications, 2000.

Gross, Kenneth. *The Dream of the Moving Statue.* Ithaca, NY: Cornell University Press, 1993.

Guilbaut, Serge. *How New York Stole the Idea of Modern Art: Abstract Expressionism, Freedom, and the Cold War.* Chicago: University of Chicago Press, 1985.

———. "Post-War Painting Games: The Rough and the Slick." In *Reconstructing Modernism: Art in New York, Paris, and Montreal, 1945–1964,* edited by Serge Guilbaut, 30–85. Cambridge, MA: MIT Press, 1990.

Gunning, Tom. "Never Seen This Picture Before: Muybridge and Multiplicity." In *Time Stands Still: Muybridge and the Instantaneous Photography Movement,* edited by Phillip Prodger, 222–72. New York: Oxford University Press, 2003.

Hammond, Paul. *Marvellous Méliès.* New York: St. Martin's, 1975.

Haraway, Donna. "A Cyborg Manifesto: Science, Technology and Socialist-Feminism in the 1980s." In *Simians, Cyborgs, and Women: The Reinvention of Nature,* 149–81. New York: Routledge, 1991.

Harris, Neil. *Humbug: The Art of P. T. Barnum.* Chicago: University of Chicago Press, 1981.

Harvey, Stephen. *Directed By Vincente Minnelli.* New York: HarperCollins, 1990.

Haynes, Roslynn D. *From Faust to Strangelove: Representations of the Scientist in Western Literature.* Baltimore: Johns Hopkins University Press, 1994.

Heiler, Brian. "Red Kryptonite's 9 Dumbest Effects on Superman." ToplessRobot.com. www.toplessrobot.com/2009/04/red_kryptonites_9_dumbest_effects_on_superman .php.

Henricks, Thomas. "The Nature of Play: An Overview." *American Journal of Play* 1, no. 2 (2008): 157–80.

———. "Orderly and Disorderly Play: A Comparison." *American Journal of Play* 2, no. 1 (2009): 12–40.

"Henri-Georges Clouzot's *The Mystery of Picasso.*" Press kit. www.milestonefilms.com/pdf/ mysteryofpicassoPK.pdf.

Hildebrand, Adolf von. *The Problem of Form in Painting and Sculpture.* Translated by Max Meyer and Robert Morris Ogden. New York: G. E. Stechert, 1907.

Hoberman, J. "Action Figures." *Village Voice,* Feb. 13, 2001.

Hodgman, John. "Righteousness in Tights." *New York Times,* April 24, 2005.

Huizinga, Johan. *Homo Ludens.* 2002 ed. London: Routledge, 1949.

Huysmans, Joris-Karl. *Against Nature (À rebours).* Translated by Robert Baldick. London: Penguin, 1959.

Iser, Wolfgang. *The Act of Reading: A Theory of Aesthetic Response.* Baltimore: Johns Hopkins University Press, 1978.

Jacobs, Fredrika H. *The Living Image in Renaissance Art.* Cambridge, UK: Cambridge University Press, 2005.

Jameson, Fredric. *Postmodernism, or, The Cultural Logic of Late Capitalism.* Durham, NC: Duke University Press, 1991.

Jenkins, Henry. "Death-Defying Superheroes." In *Evocative Objects: Things We Think With,* edited by Sherry Turkle, 194–207. Cambridge, MA: MIT Press, 2007.

———. "'Shall We Make It for New York or for Distribution?' Eddie Cantor, *Whoopee,* and Regional Resistance to the Talkies." In *What Made Pistachio Nuts? Early Sound Comedy and the Vaudeville Aesthetic,* 153–84. New York: Columbia University Press, 1992.

Johnson, Crockett. *Harold and the Purple Crayon.* New York: Harper and Brothers, 1955.

Jones, Chuck. *Chuck Amuck: The Life and Times of an Animated Cartoonist.* New York: Farrar, Straus and Giroux, 1999.

Klee, Paul. *Pedagogical Notebook.* Translated by Sibyl Moholy-Nagy. London: Faber and Faber, 1968.

Klein, Norman. *Seven Minutes: The Life and Death of the American Animated Cartoon.* London: Verso, 1993.

Koestenbaum, Wayne. *The Queen's Throat: Opera, Homosexuality, and the Mystery of Desire.* New York: Poseidon Press, 1993.

Koolhaas, Rem. *Delirious New York.* New York: Monacelli Press, 1994.

Kracauer, Siegfried. "The Cult of Distraction: On Berlin's Picture Palaces." In *The Mass Ornament: Weimar Essays,* translated and edited by Thomas Y. Levin, 323–28. Cambridge, MA: Harvard University Press, 1995.

Krauss, Rosalind. *The Optical Unconscious.* Cambridge, MA: MIT Press, 1993.

———. "'The Rock': William Kentridge's Drawings for Projection." *October* 92 (spring 2000): 3–35.

Krohn, Bill. "Specters at the Feast: French Viewpoints on Minnelli's Comedies." In *Vincente Minnelli: The Art of Entertainment,* edited by Joe McElhaney, 52–63. Detroit: Wayne State University Press, 2009.

Krutnik, Frank. *Inventing Jerry Lewis.* Washington: Smithsonian Institution Press, 2000.

Kunzle, David. *[The] History of the Comic Strip.* Vol. 1, *The Early Comic Strip: Narrative Strips and Picture Stories in the European Broadsheet from c. 1450 to 1825.* Berkeley: University of California Press, 1973.

———. *The History of the Comic Strip.* Vol. 2, *The Nineteenth Century.* Berkeley: University of California Press, 1990.

———. "The Voices of Silence: Willette, Steinlen and the Introduction of the Silent Strip in the *Chat Noir,* with a German Coda." In *The Language of Comics: Word and Image,* edited by Robin Varnum and Christina T. Gibbons, 3–18. Jackson: University Press of Mississippi, 2001.

Landau, Ellen G. "The Wild One." In *Jackson Pollock,* 11–21. New York: Harry N. Abrams, 1989.

Langeveld, M. J. "How Does the Child Experience the World of Things?" *Phenomenology + Pedagogy* 2, no. 3 (1984): 215–23.

———. "The 'Secret Place' in the Life of the Child." *Phenomenology + Pedagogy* 1, no. 2 (1983): 181–89.

———. "The Stillness of the Secret Place." *Phenomenology + Pedagogy* 1, no. 1 (1983): 11–17.

Lanier, Chris. "Review of *Rodolphe Töpffer: The Complete Comic Strips* and *Father of the Comic Strip: Rodolphe Töpffer.*" *Comics Journal,* no. 294 (2008): 116–23.

Lant, Antonia. "Haptical Cinema." *October* 74 (autumn 1995): 45–73.

Lears, Jackson. *Fables of Abundance: A Cultural History of Advertising in America.* New York: Basic Books, 1994.

———. *No Place of Grace: Antimodernism and the Transformation of American Culture, 1880–1920.* Chicago: University of Chicago Press, 1994.

———. *Rebirth of a Nation: The Making of Modern America, 1877–1920.* New York: HarperCollins, 2010.

Lee, Stan, and Jack Kirby. "This Man . . . This Monster." *Fantastic Four,* no. 51, June 1966.

Leja, Michael. *Reframing Abstract Expressionism: Subjectivity and Painting in the 1940s.* New Haven, CT: Yale University Press, 1993.

Lerer, Seth. *Children's Literature: A Reader's History from Aesop to Harry Potter.* Chicago: University of Chicago Press, 2009.

Leslie, Esther. *Hollywood Flatlands: Animation, Critical Theory and the Avant-Garde.* London: Verso, 2002.

Lethem, Jonathan. *The Fortress of Solitude: A Novel.* New York: Doubleday, 2006.

———. Who's Afraid of Doctor Strange? www.randomhouse.com/features/fortress/essay2.html.

Levy, Shawn. *Rat Pack Confidential: Frank, Dean, Sammy, Peter, Joey, and the Last Great Showbiz Party.* New York: Doubleday, 1998.

Lewis, Jerry. *The Total Film-Maker.* New York: Random House, 1971.

Lutz, Tom. *American Nervousness, 1903: An Anecdotal History.* Ithaca, NY: Cornell University Press, 1991.

Manovich, Lev. *The Language of New Media.* Cambridge, MA: MIT Press, 2001.

Maresca, Peter, ed. *"Little Nemo in Slumberland": Splendid Sundays! 1905–1910.* Palo Alto, CA: Sunday Press Books, 2005.

———, ed. *"Little Nemo in Slumberland": Splendid Sundays, 1906–1926.* Palo Alto, CA: Sunday Press Books, 2009.

Marschall, Richard. *America's Great Comic Strip Artists.* New York: Abbeville Press, 1989.

Marx, Leo. *The Machine in the Garden: Technology and the Pastoral Ideal in America.* New York: Oxford University Press, 1964.

Mast, Gerald. *Can't Help Singin': The American Musical on Stage and Screen.* New York: Overlook Press, 1987.

Mattis, Olivia. "Morton Feldman: Music for the Film *Jackson Pollock* (1951)." In *Settling New Scores: Music Manuscripts from the Paul Sacher Foundation*, edited by Felix Meyer, 165–67. Mainz: Schott, 1998.

McCloud, Scott. *Reinventing Comics*. New York: Paradox Press, 2000.

———. *Understanding Comics: The Invisible Art*. Northampton, MA: Kitchen Sink, 1993.

McDonnell, Patrick, Karen O'Connell, and Georgia Riley de Havenon. *Krazy Kat: The Comic Art of George Herriman*. New York: H. N. Abrams, 1986.

McElhaney, Joe. "Medium Shot Gestures: Vincente Minnelli and *Some Came Running*." In *Vincente Minnelli: The Art of Entertainment*, edited by Joe McElhaney, 322–35. Detroit: Wayne State University Press, 2009.

McLuhan, Marshall. *Understanding Media: The Extensions of Man*. New York: New American Library, 1964.

Merkl, Ulrich. *The Complete "Dream of the Rarebit Fiend" (1904–1913)*. Germany: Ulrich Merkl, 2007.

Michelson, Annette. "Bodies in Space: Film as 'Carnal Knowledge.'" *Artforum* 7, no. 6 (1969): 54–63.

Miller, Frank. *The Dark Knight Returns*. New York: DC Comics, 1987.

Millhauser, Steven. *Edwin Mullhouse: The Life and Death of an American Writer, 1943–1954, by Jeffrey Cartwright; a Novel*. New York: Vintage Books, 1972.

———. "The Little Kingdom of J. Franklin Payne." In *Little Kingdoms*, 11–115. New York: Vintage Books, 1993.

———. *Martin Dressler: The Tale of an American Dreamer*. New York: Vintage, 1997.

Modleski, Tania. "The Woman Who Was Known Too Much: *Notorious*." In *The Women Who Knew Too Much: Hitchcock and Feminist Theory*, 57–72. London: Routledge, 1989.

Morgenstern, John. "The Children's Novel as a Gateway to Play: An Interview with John Morgenstern." *American Journal of Play* 2, no. 4 (2010): 391–400.

Morrison, Grant. *Supergods: What Masked Vigilantes, Miraculous Mutants, and a Sun God from Smallville Can Teach Us about Being Human*. New York: Spiegel and Grau, 2011.

Morrison, Grant, and Doug Mahnke. *Final Crisis*. Edited by Eddie Berganza. New York: Vertigo / DC Comics, 2009.

Morrison, Grant, and Sean Murphy. *Joe the Barbarian*, no. 1, Jan. 2010.

Morrison, Grant, and Frank Quitely. *All-Star Superman*. Absolute edition. New York: DC Comics, 2010.

———. *Flex Mentallo*, no. 2, July 1996.

———. *Flex Mentallo*, no. 4, Sept. 1996.

———. *Flex Mentallo: Man of Muscle Mystery*. New York: Vertigo / DC Comics, 2011.

Morrison, Grant, Chas Truog, and Doug Hazlewood. "The Coyote Gospel." In *Animal Man*, 30–54. New York: Vertigo / DC Comics, 1991.

———. "Deus Ex Machina." In *Animal Man: Deus Ex Machina*, 205–29. New York: Vertigo / DC Comics, 2003.

———. "A New Science of Life." In *Animal Man: Deus Ex Machina*, 30–54. New York: Vertigo / DC Comics, 2003.

———. "Purification Day." In *Animal Man: Deus Ex Machina*, 155–79. New York: Vertigo / DC Comics, 2003.

————."Secret Origins." In *Animal Man: Origin of the Species,* 74–98. New York: Vertigo / DC Comics, 2002.

————. "Spooks." In *Animal Man: Origin of the Species,* 124–48. New York: Vertigo / DC Comics, 2002.

Morrison, Grant, Chas Truog, and Mark McKenna. "Fox on the Run." In *Animal Man: Origin of the Species,* 25–48. New York: Vertigo / DC Comics, 2002.

Morrison, Grant, and Chris Weston. *The Filth.* New York: Vertigo, 2004.

Mulvey, Laura. *Death 24x a Second: Stillness and the Moving Image.* London: Reaktion Books, 2006.

Munitic, Ranko. *Alisa Na Putu Kroz Podzemlje I Kroz Svemir.* Beograd: Decje novine, 1986.

Naremore, James. *The Films of Vincente Minnelli.* Cambridge, UK: Cambridge University Press, 1993.

————. "Vincente Meets Vincent: Lust for Life." In *The Films of Vincente Minnelli,* 135–53. Cambridge, UK: Cambridge University Press, 1993.

Nemerov, Alexander. *The Body of Raphaelle Peale: Still Life and Selfhood, 1812–1824.* Berkeley: University of California Press, 2001.

————. "The Boy in Bed: The Scene of Reading in N. C. Wyeth's *Wreck of the 'Covenant.'*" *Art Bulletin* 88 (2006): 7–27.

Nesbet, Anne. "Inanimations: *Snow White* and *Ivan the Terrible.*" *Film Quarterly* 50, no. 4 (1997): 20–31.

Nestrick, William. "Coming to Life: Frankenstein and the Nature of Film Narrative." In *The Endurance of Frankenstein: Essays on Mary Shelley's Novel,* edited by George Levine, and U. C. Knoepflmacher, 290–315. Berkeley: University of California Press, 1979.

Ngai, Sianne. *Ugly Feelings.* Cambridge, MA: Harvard University Press, 2005.

Nordau, Max. *Degeneration.* New York: D. Appleton, 1895.

O'Brien, Geoffrey. "Central Park West (Side B)." In *Sonata for Jukebox: Pop Music, Memory, and the Imagined Life,* 201–28. New York: Counterpoint, 2004.

————. "The Lonely Sea." In *Sonata for Jukebox: Pop Music, Memory, and the Imagined Life,* 231–54. New York: Counterpoint, 2004.

————. "Nick Fury's Dream." In *Give Our Regards to the Atomsmashers! Writers on Comics,* edited by Sean Howe, 118–32. New York: Pantheon, 2004.

————. "The Return of Burt Bacharach." In *Sonata for Jukebox: Pop Music, Memory, and the Imagined Life,* 5–28. New York: Counterpoint, 2004.

O'Sullivan, Judith. "The Art of Winsor Z. McCay." PhD diss., University of Maryland, 1976.

Pentcheva, Bissera. "The Performative Icon." *Art Bulletin* 88, no. 4 (2006): 631–55.

Pinxtere, Kees. "Van Gogh in Eighty-Seven Films and Videos." In *The Mythology of Vincent Van Gogh,* edited by Kodera Tsukasa and Yvette Rosenberg, 197–215. Tokyo: Asahi National Broadcasting, 1993.

Pollock, Griselda. "Crows, Blossoms and Lust for Death—Cinema and the Myth of Van Gogh the Modern Artist." In *The Mythology of Vincent Van Gogh,* edited by Kodera Tsukasa and Yvette Rosenberg, 217–39. Tokyo: Asahi National Broadcasting, 1993.

Preziosi, Donald. "A Crisis in, or of, Art History?" In *Rethinking Art History: Meditations on a Coy Science,* 1–20. New Haven, CT: Yale University Press, 1989.

Prodger, Phillip. "Make It Stop: Muybridge and the New Frontier in Instantaneous Photography." In *Time Stands Still: Muybridge and the Instantaneous Photography Movement*, edited by Phillip Prodger, 112–211. New York: Oxford University Press, 2003.

Proust, Marcel. *Swann's Way*. Translated by C. K. Scott Montcrieff. New York: Random House, 1981.

Rabinbach, Anson. *The Human Motor: Energy, Fatigue, and the Origins of Modernity*. Berkeley: University of California Press, 1990.

Riegl, Alois. *Late Roman Art Industry*. Translated by Rolf Winkes. Rome: Giorgio Bretschneider Editore, 1985.

Riskin, Jessica. "Introduction: The Sistine Gap." In *Genesis Redux: Essays in the History and Philosophy of Artificial Life*, edited by Jessica Riskin, 1–32. Chicago: University of Chicago Press, 2007.

Ronan, Annie. "Shoot at Any Ole Ting: Decoding the Out of Control Pleasures of *Hogan's Alley*." Paper presented at the Stanford Art History Graduate Student Symposium, Stanford, CA, 2009.

Rosenberg, Harold. "The American Action Painters." In *The Tradition of the New*, 23–39. New York: Horizon, 1960.

Schaffer, William. "Animation 1: The Control-Image." In *The Illusion of Life II: More Essays on Animation*, edited by Alan Cholodenko, 456–85. Sydney: Power Books, 2007.

Schivelbusch, Wolfgang. *The Railway Journey: The Industrialization of Time and Space in the 19th Century*. Berkeley: University of California Press, 1986.

Schudson, Michael. *Discovering the News: A Social History of American Newspapers*. New York: Basic Books, 1978.

Seagle, Steven T., and Teddy Christiansen. *It's a Bird*. New York: Vertigo, 2005.

Sembach, Klaus-Jürgen. *Art Nouveau Utopia: Reconciling the Irreconcilable*. Köln: Taschen, 1996.

Shapiro, Emily. "Machine Crafted: The Image of the Artisan in American Genre Painting, 1877–1908." PhD diss., Stanford University, 2003.

Shaw, George Barnard, and Alan Jay Lerner. *Pygmalion and My Fair Lady*. New York: Signet Classics, 1975.

Shaya, Gregory. "Mayhem for Moderns: The Culture of Sensationalism in France." PhD diss., University of Michigan, 2000.

Silverman, Debora L. *Art Nouveau in Fin-de-Siècle France: Politics, Psychology, and Style*. Berkeley: University of California Press, 1989.

Singer, Ben. *Melodrama and Modernity: Early Sensational Cinema and Its Contexts*. New York: Columbia University Press, 2001.

Smith, Zack. "All Star Memories: Grant Morrison on *All Star Superman*, 1." Newsarama.com. Oct. 21, 2008. www.newsarama.com/comics/100821-All-Star-Morrison-01.html.

———. "All Star Memories: Grant Morrison on *All Star Superman*, 6." Newsarama.com. Oct. 28, 2008. www.newsarama.com/comics/100828-Morrison-Superman6.html.

Smolderen, Thierry. Preface to *Stuff and Nonsense (A. B. Frost: An Anthology)*. Seattle: Fantagraphics Books, 2003.

———. Why the Brownies Are Important. www.old-coconino.com/s_classics/pop_classic/brownies/brow_eng.htm.

Sobchack, Vivian. "The Line and the Animorph, or, 'Travel Is More Than Just A to B.'" *Animation: An Interdisciplinary Journal* 3, no. 3 (2008): 251–65.

———. "'Surge and Splendor': A Phenomenology of the Hollywood Historical Epic." *Representations* 29 (1990): 24–49.

———. "Thinking through Jim Carrey." In *More Than a Method: Trends and Traditions in Contemporary Film Performance,* edited by Cynthia A. Baron, Diane Carson, and Frank P. Tomasulo, 275–96. Detroit: Wayne State University Press, 2004.

Solomon, Matthew. "'Twenty-Five Heads under One Hat': Quick-Change in the 1890s." In *Meta-Morphing: Visual Transformation and the Culture of Quick Change,* edited by Vivian Sobchack, 3–20. Minneapolis: University of Minnesota Press, 2000.

Sorrentino, Christopher. "The Ger Sheker." In *Give Our Regards to the Atomsmashers! Writers on Comics,* edited by Sean Howe, 52–69. New York: Pantheon, 2004.

Spiegelman, Art. "Forms Stretched to Their Limits." *New Yorker,* April 19, 1999.

———. "Polyphonic Polly: Hot and Sweet." In *The Complete Color "Polly and Her Pals."* Vol. 1, *1926–1927,* edited by Richard Marschall, 5–6. Princeton, WI: Kitchen Sink, 1990.

———. "Two-Fisted Painters Action Adventures." *RAW* 1, no. 1 (July 1980): insert.

Stam, Robert. *Reflexivity in Film and Culture: From Don Quixote to Jean-Luc Godard.* New York: Columbia University Press, 1992.

Stevens, Wallace. *Opus Posthumous.* New York: Alfred A. Knopf, 1957.

Stewart, Susan. *On Longing: Narratives of the Miniature, the Gigantic, the Souvenir, the Collection.* Durham, NC: Duke University Press, 1993.

Stone, Irving. *Lust for Life.* London: Penguin, 1984.

Sutton-Smith, Brian. *The Ambiguity of Play.* Cambridge, MA: Harvard University Press, 1997.

Thompson, Kristen. "Implications of the Cel Animation Technique." In *The Cinematic Apparatus,* edited by Teresa de Lauretis and Stephen Heath, 106–20. London: Macmillan, 1980.

Todorov, Tzvetan. *The Fantastic: A Structural Approach to a Literary Genre.* Translated by Richard Howard. Ithaca, NY: Cornell University Press, 1975.

Tuan, Yi-Fu. *Space and Place: The Perspective of Experience.* Minneapolis: University of Minnesota Press, 1977.

Updike, John. "Mixed Messages." *New Yorker,* March 14, 2005.

———. "The Mystery of Mickey Mouse." In *The Best American Essays College Edition,* edited by Robert Atwan, 385–92. Boston: Houghton Mifflin, 1995.

Van Gogh, Vincent. *The Letters of Vincent van Gogh.* Edited by Ronald de Leeu. Translated by Arnold Pomerans. New York: Penguin, 1996.

Veblen, Thorstein. *The Theory of Business Enterprise.* New York: Scribner's, 1904.

Vidler, Anthony. *The Architectural Uncanny: Essays in the Modern Unhomely.* Cambridge, MA: MIT Press, 1992.

Villiers de l'Isle-Adam, Auguste. *The Future Eve.* In *The Decadent Reader: Fiction, Fantasy, and Perversion from Fin-de-Siècle France.* Edited by Asti Hustvedt. New York: Zone, 1998.

Ware, Chris. *Quimby the Mouse, or, Comic Strips, 1990–1991 (with a Small Number from 1992–93) as Mostly Originally Collected in the Pages of the Acme Novelty Library, and Released during the Years 1993 and 1994.* Seattle: Fantagraphics, 2003.

Watterson, Bill. "An 'Incredible Ride' to the End." In *The Best of "Little Nemo in Slumberland,"* edited by Richard Marschall, 195. New York: Stewart, Tabori and Chang, 1997.

Waugh, Carlton. *The Comics.* Jackson: University Press of Mississippi, 1947.

Wells, Paul. *Understanding Animation.* London: Routledge, 1998.

Wertham, Fredric. *Seduction of the Innocent.* New York: Rinehart, 1954.

Willems, Philippe. "'This Strangest of Narrative Forms': Rodolphe Töpffer's Sequential Art." *Mosaic: A Journal for the Interdisciplinary Study of Literature* 41, no. 2 (2008): 127–48.

Williams, Linda. *Hard Core: Power, Pleasure, and the "Frenzy of the Visible."* Berkeley: University of California Press, 1989.

Wolf, Bryan Jay. *Romantic Re-vision: Culture and Consciousness in Nineteenth-Century American Painting and Literature.* Chicago: University of Chicago Press, 1982.

Wood, Gaby. *Edison's Eve: A Magical History of the Quest for Mechanical Life.* New York: Anchor, 2003.

Abrams, M. H., 78–79

Abstract Expressionism, 44, 165–69, 175, 233nn11,14, 235n48

Acme Corporation, 46

Action Comics, 185*fig*, 195

"action painting," 24, 165–68, 175, 178–80, 195

Adams, Neal, 189–90

Adorno, Theodor, 159

advertising, 14, 214n19

aesthetic, 83, 92; Art Nouveau, 94; Eisenstein and, 107; of hand and machine, 112; *Little Nemo in Slumberland*, 1–2, 23, 113; Millhauser stories, 15, 74, 75; Minnelli films and, 177, 180; Muybridge's, 29–31; "operational aesthetic," 70, 108, 113; popular music, 196, 197; *Rarebit Fiend*, 70; Road Runner cartoons, 46; sublime, 137; uncanny, 114–15, 137, 140–41; "vaudeville aesthetic," 232n40

Aesthetics of Comics (Carrier), 199

African Americans, popular images of, 21

A la recherche du temps perdu (Proust), 103

Ali Baba Bunny (Jones), 231–32n39

Alice comedies, Disney, 130–31

Alice in Wonderland, 20, 98, 131, 216n68, 225n74. *See also* Carroll, Lewis

All-Star Superman (Morrison and Quitely), 25, 182, 205–11, 208*fig*, 210*fig*

Alton, John, 122

America: Abstract Expressionism, 44, 165–69, 175; African American images, 21; character

animation, 5; dreamers, 72–76; machine and human, 161; modern art, 7, 165–67; painting, 165–66; progress, 73; self-identified clichés, 174–75; tension between American and European creators, 76, 165, 167, 175, 177, 222n133; urban, 7, 48, 51–53, 94; and Van Gogh, 174–75, 177. *See also* cartoons; comics

American Nervousness (Beard), 48, 50, 51, 57, 72–73

Andersen, Hans Christian, 77

Anderson, Leroy, 232n53

Andrews, Julie, 154

anima, 13, 106; compromised, 134; Eisenstein and, 13–14, 106–7, 114, 115, 126, 128, 132, 136, 146; labor and, 23–24, 106–34, 226n9; performance of, 136; and *spirito*, 23. *See also* animatedness; animism

Animal Man (Morrison et al.), 188, 190–95, 191*fig*, 192*fig*, 205, 218n41, 236n15

animals: characters taking on attributes of, 188, 189, 190; in Frost's picture stories, 34, 37; locomotion, 28, 32, 37, 43, 217n9, 218n22; in McCay comics, 14, 28, 32, 34, 217n2; mimicry, 189; muteness, 218n22; Muybridge and, 28, 29, 43; superhero genre and, 19, 188

animated disobedience, 135–63

animated film, 4, 5, 109–34, 213n8; Alice and, 225n74; disobedient machines, 135–63; Kentridge, 19; Pollock film and, 179; "secret

My Fair Lady, 150, 153–55; Pollock, 234n22; Pygmalion, 154. See also speech

Lanier, Chris, 83

Lant, Antonia, 88, 89

"Laugh-o-gram" (Disney), 130–31

laughter, 59

law and order, superhero genre and, 188–89

Lears, Jackson, 3–4, 14, 214n19

Lee, Stan, 19, 198

Leja, Michael, 166–67, 169, 233n14, 234n22

Lerer, Seth, 98–99, 225n75

Lerner, Alan Jay, 148, 152

Leslie, Esther, 230n24

Lethem, Jonathan, 198, 199, 201

Levi, Pavle, 47, 216n55

Lewis, Jerry, 22–23, 24, 155–63, 164; Artists and Models, 156–57, 157fig, 160, 161, 162; jerking, 155, 162; and Martin, 22–23, 155–60, 232n40; parody on SCTV, 232n61; Tashlin and, 69, 156–57, 160, 163, 232n39; and technologies, 155, 157–58, 161–63, 232n45; "total film-maker," 157; twitching, 161, 162; Who's Minding the Store?, 161, 162, 232n53

Life, 175

lightning sketch artist, 228n38; McCay, 15, 70, 112–13, 118; Picasso, 128

"The Little Kingdom of J. Franklin Payne"/ fictional version of McCay (Millhauser), 15, 18, 72, 73–76

Little Nemo film (1911), 5, 43–44, 109–30, 120fig, 134, 227n35; Art Nouveau, 95; creation-of-life film, 139; credits, 109–10; drawing quality, 116–17; ending, 117; introducing artist, 122–23; labor, 24, 109–30; McCay in group photo, 111fig, 122–23; McCay at work, 15, 22, 70, 110–30, 110fig, 178, 227n34, 228n41, 229nn58,63; oscillation between flat and volumetric image, 88–89; vanishing animator, 125, 134, 178, 179

Little Nemo in Slumberland (McCay), 1–2, 14–15, 23, 77–105; architectural detail, 87; berries, 78–81, 93–94, 183, 225n68; child-subject, 95–105; disorderliness, 99; dreams, 2, 8, 27–28, 92, 96, 188, 213n5; ending, 117; "environmental transience," 221n113; ethnically stereotyped characters, 21, 134; first episode, 27–29, 84–85, 86; fixed perspective, 85, 221n99; Freud and, 2, 213n5; immersion, 23, 85–87, 90, 95, 100, 105, 224n66; In the Land of Wonderful Dreams, 96, 213n1, 217n1; intimate immensity, 100–101; meta-

morphosing, 1, 5, 14–15, 28, 50, 78, 85, 91–97, 100, 105; movement, 28–29, 31, 34, 91–92; New York Herald, 27–29, 217n1; "optical" and "haptical," 90; plasmatic and animistic, 1, 23, 134, 204; play with panels, 50; publication history of, 1, 217n1; Rarebit Fiend and, 60, 79–80, 87; "secret places," 97, 103, 224n66; size, 80; spatiality, 1–2, 88, 90, 95–105; The Story of Hungry Henrietta and, 43; Sunday newspaper, 27, 78, 84, 94, 100, 104, 112, 116, 182; superhero genre and, 182–88, 195; suspense film, 229n58; "tactile vision," 90, 95–96; "thereness," 90. See also Little Nemo film (1911)

Little Orphan Annie (Gray), 12

Little Sammy Sneeze (McCay), 14, 23, 41fig, 44; bodily control, 60; chronophotographic influence, 38–43, 50; Millhauser version, 73; "wallpaper comics," 81

live-action films, 109, 139, 227n35, 230nn4,21; Alice in Wonderland, 20, 98, 131, 216n68, 225n74; film noir, 169, 234n22; Little Nemo, 119; My Fair Lady, 147; Le mystère Picasso, 119–20; superhero films and, 203, 205; Tashlin and, 156, 231n39; uncanny, 141, 143. See also biopics; epic; film noir; musicals

liveliness, 89, 214n19. See also animatedness; vitality

living images, 5, 13

Locke, John, 98–99

Loewe, Frederick, 152

London, Mme. Tussaud's, 142

Lorrison, Georgia, 169

Lucas, George, 128–29

Lumière Brothers, 31, 81–82, 118, 139, 141

Lusitania, McCay's The Sinking of the Lusitania, 17–18, 95, 129–30

Lust for Life (Minnelli), 6–7, 22, 24, 164–81, 165fig, 233n5, 235n55; Abstract Expressionism, 165–69, 175, 233n11; "all-overness," 173–74; Douglas, 7, 167, 169, 175, 177, 234n44; Paris, 170, 171, 173, 234n29; Rozsa score, 168, 170, 178, 181; Stone's novel, 165, 167, 169, 170; tension between American and European creators, 222n133

Lutz, Tom, 50, 58

Lye, Len, 119–21

machine: artist as, 117, 128–29, 132, 134, 176; body as, 18–19, 36–37, 46–47, 51, 59, 107, 112, 150–51; disobedient, 6, 7, 25, 135–63;

machine *(continued)*
  malfunctioning, 24, 155–63; Man of Steel,
  205; worker as, 113. *See also* automaton;
  industrialism; railway
MacLaine, Shirley, 160
mad scientists, 138–39, 140, 149
Maguire, Tobey, 203
maladjustment, 159
malfunction, 2, 24, 155–63
Mann, Anthony, 122, 201–2
Manovich, Lev, 141
Mansfield, Jayne, 156
mapping, temporal, 31–32, 34, 114
Marey, Etienne Jules, 28–32, 36, 44, 45, 114
Martin, Dean, 22–23, 155–60, 232n40
Martin Dressler (Millhauser), 73, 74–75
Marvel comics, 196, 198, 201, 206, 236–37n29
Marx Brothers, 159
Mast, Gerald, 203
Matisse, Henri, 227–28n37
A Matter of Life and Death (Powell and Press-
  burger), 228n43
Matters of Gravity (Bukatman), 203
Max and Moritz, 32
McCay, Winsor, 14–18, 23–24, 217n11, 223n25,
  230n4; Alice comedies and, 131; and Art
  Nouveau, 88, 93–95, 111, 224n53; clown, 72,
  194; creation-of-life films, 139; "The Curse of
  Civilization," 17*fig*; editorial cartoonist, 53;
  "The Famous Cartoonist of the *New York
  Herald*," 109; hand, 110–17, 110*fig*, 128, 190;
  imperative of creation, 174; *In a Cartoon
  Studio* (Van Buren) and, 131; lightning
  sketch artist, 15, 70, 112–13, 118; as machine,
  134; Millhauser story of, 3, 15, 18, 72, 73–
  76, 221n117; Morrison and, 190; movement,
  28–29, 31, 34, 37; *A Pilgrim's Progress by
  Mister Bunion*, 14; plasmatic and animistic,
  1, 3, 14–15, 18, 23, 134, 182–83, 204; *The
  Sinking of the Lusitania*, 17–18, 95, 129–30;
  The Story of Hungry Henrietta, 14, 40–43,
  42*fig*, 60; superhero genre and, 186; "sympathetic ink," 57; "temporal map," 31–32, 34,
  114; whiplash curve, 94–95; at work, 3, 14–
  15, 22, 110–30, 110*fig*, 178, 227n34, 228n41,
  229nn58,63. See also *Dream of the Rarebit
  Fiend; Gertie the Dinosaur; Little Nemo in
  Slumberland; Little Sammy Sneeze; Little
  Nemo* film
McCloud, Scott, 30, 34
McFadden's Row of Flats (Outcault), 8, 9, 215n28

McLaren, Norman, 119–21
McLuhan, Marshall, 157–61, 232n45
mechanists, 226n9. *See also* machine
media: Lewis and, 157–62; McLuhan and, 157–
  61; unruly, 4. *See also* cartoons; cinema;
  comics; newspapers; phonograph; photography; television
Meet Me in St. Louis (Minnelli), 174
melancholy, 18, 205, 216n57
Méliès, Georges, 5, 82, 88, 141
melodrama, 167, 168–71, 175, 176, 234n36
Merkl, Ulrich, 63
Merleau-Ponty, Maurice, 80
Messmer, Otto, 227n29
metamorphosis, 13, 19–20, 69, 127, 199;
  advertising, 14; Alice, 20, 98; Art Nouveau,
  93–94; Disney cartoon, 106; *Dream of the
  Rarebit Fiend*, 14–15, 50, 53–54, 60, 62, 72;
  Eisenstein's ecstatic freedom, 14, 19, 20, 114,
  116; *Fantasmagorie*, 5, 109; lightning sketch
  artist, 112; *Little Nemo* film, 109, 112, 116,
  118, 121, 126; *Little Nemo in Slumberland*,
  1, 5, 14–15, 28, 50, 78, 85, 91–97, 100, 105;
  Little Sammy Sneeze, 50; *Le mystère Picasso*,
  121, 125, 126; origin story, 188, 203–5. *See
  also* morph; plasmaticness
Metropolis (Lang), 137–40, 138*fig*, 142, 148,
  149*fig*
MGM, 165, 168, 173
Michelangelo, 146
Michelson, Annette, 202
Mickey Mouse, 114, 146–47, 230n24
Middle Ages: Bibles, 12; Christian art, 25–26
Miller, Frank, 187, 206
Millhauser, Steven, 3, 23, 73, 198, 199; "The
  Little Kingdom of J. Franklin Payne"/
  fictional version of McCay, 3, 15, 18, 72,
  73–76, 221n117; *Martin Dressler*, 73, 74–
  75; "secret melancholy," 18, 205
mimicry, 12, 189–90
miniature, 97–98, 101, 225n68
Minnelli, Vincente, 75, 91, 92; emotionalism,
  177; melodramas, 167, 171, 234n36; narrative compression, 170; and nature, 173;
  "problem of the artist," 177. *See also individual titles of Minnelli films*
Miracles de Notre Dame, 26
The Mirror and the Lamp (Abrams), 78–79
misbehavior, 142, 143–47. *See also* disobedience
misperception, 142–43
modernism: Art Nouveau and, 93–94; Lewis,

TEXT
10/12.5 Minion Pro

DISPLAY
Gotham

COMPOSITOR
Integrated Composition Systems

INDEXER
Barbara Roos

PRINTER AND BINDER
Sheridan Books, Inc.